American Architects and Texts

Juan Pablo Bonta

American Architects and Texts

A Computer-Aided Analysis of the Literature

The MIT Press
Cambridge, Massachusetts
London, England

This book was set in Times Roman by Asco Trade Typesetting Ltd., Hong Kong and was printed and bound in the United States of America.

Library of Congress Cataloging-in-Publication Data
Bonta, Juan Pablo.
  American architects and texts : a computer-aided analysis of the literature / Juan
Pablo Bonta.
    p.   cm.
  Includes bibliographical references and index.
  ISBN 0-262-02400-4 (hc : alk. paper)
  1. Architectural writing—United States. 2. Discourse analysis.
I. Title.
NA2540.B58   1996
720'.973—dc20   95-380
                                                                         CIP

In memoriam *Julio Caillet-Bois, 1910–1988*

Contents

Foreword

William J. Mitchell

The following tale may be found in a dusty, rarely visited corner of the Library of Babel. Borges did not write it, but he might have.

Long ago, in a land far away, marauding barbarians destroyed the nation's great architectural library. But a librarian had made a meticulous index for each volume, and by some miracle the collection of indices was saved. Later, a scholar from the south came upon this collection, and realized that he could unlock its secrets by counting and analyzing citations. He began by ranking the names of architects according to the numbers of texts in which they were cited; in this way he identified the most famous. Encouraged by this success, he refined his procedures and conducted further investigations. Soon he was able to chart the growth and decay of reputations, to trace lines of influence, and to sort architects into schools. Without reading a single text or looking at any buildings he finally constructed a fascinating overview of an architectural discourse that had evolved over more than a century and a half.

That scholar, of course, is Juan Pablo Bonta. The nation is the United States. And the results of his analysis are presented and discussed in the pages that follow. Not that any library was actually destroyed, though; instead, Bonta simply recognized that the indexes of architectural books were wonderfully convenient, computer-processable abstractions of the corresponding texts. By focusing rigorously on these highly condensed representations, rather than on the endless details of narratives, lives, and works, he could effectively summarize a vast and otherwise unmanageable corpus of information.

The results of this meticulous labor are valuable both in substance and for their methodological suggestiveness. For architectural scholars and students of the mechanics of fame and influence, the highlight is a ranked list of the 100 most famous architects, headed, not surprisingly, by Frank Lloyd Wright. Further analyses pull apart the data in different ways, and provide finer-grained views of evolving architectural careers and the responses to them by critics and historians. The results are imaginatively displayed in computer-generated graphs and charts. Best of all, the author has made available (in machine-readable form) the complete data base and the analysis software. Thus interested readers can test the consequences of varying the assumptions under which the analyses were conducted, and can embark on statistical investigations of their own.

We can all play the irresistible game of looking for our mentors and heroes, and we can compare our own judgments, rankings, and groupings with the tale told by the computer. But beyond this, the panoramic view that Bonta constructs provides a rewarding new way to contextualize both architects and texts, to locate and assess them in relation to general evolutions and transformations of the architectural community's values, tastes, and interests.

Methodologically, this work also provides us with a glimpse of what scholarship will be like in the coming world of digital libraries. Until now, computer explorations and analyses of texts have been limited by scarcity of the necessary text data bases. (Pioneering scholars like Bonta have often faced the daunting task of creating their own data bases from scratch.) But those days will soon be over. From the desktop computer on which I am writing this paragraph, I can instantly access on-line versions of the *Oxford English Dictionary* and the *Encyclopaedia Britannica*. By way of the Internet, I can connect to the Project Gutenberg server and download numerous out-of-copyright novels and other literary works. And I can quickly mount disks containing the complete works of Shakespeare and the entire corpus of surviving ancient Greek text. Even more ambitious plans are under way; the National Science Foundation, Advanced Research Projects Agency, and National Aeronautic and Space Administration have jointly launched a $24.4-million Digital Library Initiative,[1] and humanities scholars have called for a 10-million-volume, digital, on-line, humanities research library.[2] As a result, it is becoming an increasingly realistic scholarly ambition to make analyses not just of individual works or of a small sample of works, but of a complete corpus.

As on-line text grows in volume and importance, our reading practices and scholarly tools will change too. Increasingly, we will find ourselves following hyperlinks among servers instead of flipping the pages of codex books. Footnotes will point to complete, on-line source documents rather than to titles and page numbers of printed texts. Sophisticated directories and search engines will help us navigate through large text data bases as tables of contents and indices keyed to page numbers have traditionally guided us through collections of bound pages. Autonomous software agents will be delegated tasks of searching out, filtering, organizing, and presenting information according to our particular needs and interests. As the World Wide Web (WWW) already vividly demonstrates, print's privileging of textual autonomy, closure, and stability will give way to a condition under which an on-line text is just a local, easily alterable fragment of a vast, constantly growing, densely cross-linked hypertext. And interest in a subject may be measured by the number of hyperlinks pointing to WWW pages with information about it and the frequency with which those pages are accessed. The more sophisticated tools and techniques for navigating and managing large on-line data collections will depend—like those developed and demonstrated by Bonta—on some form of machine analysis and interpretation of content.

So Bonta's learned and provocative study, part book, part electronic data base, and analysis software, may be read both as a celebration of the 150-year era in which printed books have been primary vehicles of architectural discourse and as an intimation of that era's passing. It appears at a moment when new electronic media are increasingly challenging books, and when it seems more and more likely that new editions of Banister Fletchers and *Space, Time, and Architectures* will be CD-ROMs or web sites. Perhaps some future scholar will survey the architectural discourse of the twenty-first century by sending out software agents to surf through cyberspace.

Notes

1. For details see "Digital Libraries," special issue of *Communications of the ACM*, April 1995, vol. 38, no. 4.

2. See *Technology, Scholarship, and the Humanities: The Implications of Electronic Information* (Santa Monica: The Getty Art History Information Program, 1993), p. 23. For a general discussion of the move toward on-line libraries, see John Browning, Libraries Without Walls for Books Without Pages, *Wired*, 1993, vol. 1, no. 1, pp. 62–110.

Preface

No architect is discussed, no text is analyzed, no building is portrayed, no writer is evaluated, and yet the book is called *American Architects and Texts*. This calls for an explanation.

Readers interested in architecture will find in the book a dynamic picture of the architects populating the professional literature, with their changing numbers and chronological distribution. They will be faced with a new way of assessing the importance of architects, based not on individual dicta but on collective judgment as distilled from a large mass of written material. They will follow the ups and downs of the architects' changing literary fortunes, and correlate them with events in their lives, their professional careers, or the larger historical picture. Readers will be able to assess the normalcy or unusualness of the architects' evolutionary curve, measuring it against standards derived from the literature itself. They will recognize two specific classes of architects, the alphas and the omegas, who are often found at the beginning and end of narrative lines. They will also inspect similarities or contrasts between the evolutionary lines of various architects, and estimate their distance in the literature. The imaginary readers will recognize whether an architect has enjoyed a wider currency in a national or an international frame of reference, or among male and female writers.

Those who are interested in texts more than in architects should also get some benefit from the book. They will learn to assess the chronological coverage of texts, which may not coincide with the promise of the title. They will detect multinuclear texts, and question the appropriateness of that structure to the subject matter of the work. They will look at gamma values, and recognize the level of comprehensiveness of the text. They will learn to measure its foresight, and will be able to spot unexpected as well as potentially missing names in the index. Readers will have a tool to distinguish influential texts, and recognize the ones influenced. They will be able to follow a text's evolution through a cloud of culturally active texts, moving toward the center of the configuration as the text more closely corresponds with current interests and preoccupations, and drifting toward the peripheries of the system as it ceases to do so; and they will date each station in the text's journey. The work's standing in relation to national or international frames of reference and its position in the gender war will also be accessible.

Still a third type of reader may be interested in the larger historical and cultural picture rather than individual architects or texts. These individuals will cluster cotextual architects in a variety of ways, exploring classification systems beyond the customary ones based on style or chronology, and will identify the texts in which each group of architects is typically cited. They will see how these groupings change with time, with new associations continually established and older ones broken up. They will recognize isonomic texts and classify them into families, tribes, nations, and will find blocks of related architects and texts.

None of this brings the pleasure of visiting an outstanding building, talking to a sensitive architect or critic, or reading a fine book on architecture; but it may help to locate those persons, buildings, and readings, and to enjoy them better when interacting with them, because of having added new dimensions to their comprehension. Broadening the scope of knowledge, of course, is also a source of joy.

I struggled in vain for a better title. *Names in American Architecture* was a working title for a while; although perhaps more accurate, it was equally ineffectual at conveying the real nature of the project, and it was flat. I refer to what I do as *index analysis*; but using these words in the title, I was warned, was nearly suicidal.

Latin Americans and Canadians receive an apology for my using the name of the continent for only one country. *U.S. Architects and Texts* would have been more precise, although it would have suggested (erroneously) that the study is restricted to post-Colonial times. But this is an investigation of prevalent attitudes as reflected in discourse; it favors description over prescription. In keeping with this approach, I chose a title that follows common parlance rather than one that would have attempted to change it.

Except where noted otherwise, the computer software was especially written for this project (more than 100,000 lines of code). It could easily be used to analyze other bodies of data, such as the architecture of a particular state or region of the country, a certain building type, or the architecture of other countries or areas of the world. It is also applicable to other disciplines: fine arts, poetry, music, philosophy, economy, law, science—any field that has a corpus of literature (especially a historical corpus) is amenable to computer-aided index analysis.

As I release this study, I inevitably wonder whether a major mistake may have escaped my attention and come back to haunt me and invalidate some of the findings. It is a measure of my temerity that I do not really envision this as a possibility. I base my confidence, perhaps foolhardily, on the fact that many results of the analysis of indexes are compatible with previous knowledge, and as far as I can see none conflicts with common sense. The prospect of failing to provoke any interest, even negative, gives me, on the other hand, more pause. After years of work on indexes I developed more tolerance for criticism than silence. The time may come, I sometimes speculate, when I must taste my own medicine. The concern is not entirely frivolous.

Whether index analysis will develop beyond the stage at which I am leaving it, it is too soon to tell. But this much I know: if it flourishes it will not be because of my pleas. As a student of fame, I am aware of the inscrutable ways of societal moods. If no amount of reasoning or logic can stop wars or alleviate famine, index analysis will not succeed because of arguments for its timeliness. I also recognize that the technique will not remain under this guise if it is to have a future. Every procedure I devised was selected from among a number of alternatives, many equally attractive, and some more promising but more difficult to implement. Persons with a greater command of programming or statistics or more familiar with American architecture will have more and better choices.

As I write these lines, the twenty-fifth anniversary of the first human lunar landing is being commemorated. My generation was awed beyond belief by that implausible event. I remember a peasant in the Western mountains of my Argentina laughing it off as a prank, an idea that could not be entertained seriously. How things have changed! Today technology (especially information-processing technology) seems suspect in its goals, limitless in its power. This reflects in young persons' reactions before index analysis. They wonder what it is for, or question specific issues—how to measure this factor, how to generate that curve—but are generally unperturbed by the unusualness, not to say freakishness, of the enterprise. They perceive it as consistent with the information-intensive society in which they are growing up. Perhaps there is only a limited window of opportunity to initiate this course of studies, in the intersection between my generation and theirs, when we can still bring together the wonder of the middleaged with the confidence of the young.

No new field can develop without involving a collective effort. Even if the necessary expertise could be gathered under a person assisted by consultants, no individual can provide the many and sometimes divergent personal qualities and insights needed—analytic strength along with synthetic vision, descriptive detachment and prescriptive rigor, risk taking and prudence, wisdom and poetry. Cultural creation and assimilation in architecture as in other fields is contingent on other people's willingness to partake in public discourse. Myriad messages must flash back and forth through societal communication channels for collective dialogue to function effectively and the social engine to do its work. Collective mood can be monitored through the analysis of discourse precisely because of these exchanges.

I envision ways to process the data base for additional information, beyond what I could develop. I am releasing the project at this time not because it is complete, or because I have nearly exhausted the patience of my university and my publisher, but because the idea is sufficiently formalized to be exposed to commentary. A field bereft of public discussion cannot survive. Some of the communications will hit the sensors of an index analyst. Index analysis is especially qualified among all disciplines to monitor its own future; there will be none unless it succeeds in detecting itself.

The field as I see it does not support or undermine any architectural style or ideology. This is puzzling, but it may be a consequence of my personal makeup, not a necessary feature of the technique. Other contributors will bring their own inclinations and impel the discipline in other directions; here is another reason to invite their participation at this time. In concluding, I would like to reveal my own motivation. I admit to be more intrigued with the inner logic of index analysis than with its practical implications. My fascination with the field arises from the discovery of order and regularity, and therefore meaning, in an area where none was seen to exist before.

Acknowledgments

This study was initially supported by a grant from the Graham Foundation for Advanced Studies in the Fine Arts: It was continued with the support of the Department of Housing and Design, the Computer Science Center, the Division of Human and Community Resources, the College of Arts and Humanities, and the School of Architecture, all of the University of Maryland at College Park.

Architects Pablo Meninato, Roberto Szemzo, Mariano Goñi, Verónica Azcona and Julieta Rodríguez Pujol were research interns for periods ranging from a few months to several years. My research assistants were Gretchen Mahoney, Julie Whethereau, Sofía Veniard, and Raquel Schwald.

A team of architects directed by María Zulema Amadei from *Taller de Arte y Arquitectura* in Rosario, Argentina, compiled a substantial collection of indexes from the Argentine architectural literature to test my system on an alternative body of data. The results of this endeavor have not been published. Roxanne Kuter Williamson allowed me to use for a preliminary version of this study the citation data collected for her book *American Architecture and the Mechanics of Fame* (1991).

Paul Smith and Adam Kleppner of the Department of Mathematics, C. Mitchell Dayton and Doug Coulson of the Department of Measurement and Statistics, Chip Denman of the Computer Science Center, and Ralph Bunker of the Department of Statistics at the George Washington University helped me with several matters in mathematics, statistics, and computer science. None of them bears any responsibility for misconceptions or mistakes. Richard J. Atlee, Lu Hoai Nguyen, and William Kupersanin excelled for their helpfulness among a larger staff of dedicated consultants at the Computer Science Center. Guido Francescato, Remi Clignet, Richard J. Atlee, Diego Bonta, Neil Baljon, and Chip Denman read the manuscript at various stages and suggested many improvements. Ben Shneiderman and Catherine Plaisant, of the Human Computer Interaction Laboratory, helped me make the electronic companion more user-friendly. William Jordy, Henry Millon, Stanford Anderson, Eugene Garfield, Marilyn Schmitt, Alan Gowans, Glenn Ricart, David Johnson,

Eleanor Johnson, and Vicky Porter attended demonstrations or used my software at different stages and identified areas for further development.

Estudio Bonta—Arquitectura Digital, Buenos Aires, plotted the three-dimensional models used in chapter 5. Anna Bonta encouraged me to write the chapter on gender issues.

Steven W. Hurtt, Dean of the School of Architecture, and Robert W. Griffith, formerly Dean of the College of Arts and Humanities, took extraordinary steps to preserve my ability to complete this book during the academic reorganization of the university in 1992. My greatest appreciation is for Guido Francescato, who as chair of the Department of Housing and Design secured my appointment to the university in 1980 with a major research assignment, encouraged me to develop this project, and over years of close association gradually turned from a respected administrator into a trusted friend.

J.P.B.

School of Architecture, University of Maryland at College Park, February 1996

When a book about the literature of the eighteen-nineties was given by Mr. Holbrook Jackson to the world, I looked eagerly in the index for SOAMES, ENOCH. I had feared he would not be there. He was not there. But everybody else was. Many writers whom I had quite forgotten, or remembered but faintly, lived again for me, in Mr. Holbrook Jackson's pages. The book was as thorough as it was brilliantly written. And thus the omission found by me was an all the deadlier record of poor Soames' failure to impress himself on his decade.

I daresay I am the only person who noticed the omission. Soames had failed so piteously as all that!
—Max Beerbohm, *Seven Men*, 1919

Books are not made to be believed, but to be subjected to inquiry.
—Umberto Eco, *The Name of the Rose*, 1984

1   Text Analysis and Index Analysis

Some time ago, the school of architecture where I was working hired a new slide curator. At a faculty meeting early during his tenure the young man told us that our slide collection had been growing over the years in a haphazard manner, which resulted in the existence of gaps in certain sections of the collection and excessive coverage in others. He intended to correct this state of affairs with a carefully planned acquisitions program, and enlisted our help to identify the wanting areas.

Some faculty made an honest effort to name the gaps, others submitted lists of their pet buildings and favored architects, whereas still others consulted catalogues and brochures but ultimately failed to act because of other demands on their time. As it turned out, we were behaving the way we always had, which was only likely to accentuate, rather than ameliorate, whatever imbalances there were in the collection. Suspecting that the assignment was not as simple as it had seemed at first, some of us met again to discuss what it was that we were trying to accomplish and how to do it cleverly.

It was quickly acknowledged that the collection could not possibly include every building raised on the face of the earth; selectivity was of the essence. We also agreed that different styles, periods, regions, and building types had to be represented, with a full visual documentation for important examples and fewer slides for lesser works. It was easy to concur on the list of masterpieces, such as the Parthenon, the cathedral at Chartres, St. Peter's Basilica, and Falling Water. But this was not particularly helpful since this was not the problem area of the collection; these buildings were adequately covered. The difficulties appeared when dealing with works in the fourth or fifth rank of importance.

Consider, say, Gothic architecture in northern Spain: should the cathedrals in Burgos and León both be granted full documentation, or would one be enough, with just a slide or two of the other? If so, which one? And why one rather than the other? Matters became even murkier when we recognized that there was disagreement in the literature, as well as among us, not only about the lesser examples of the styles but also about stylistic or period subdivisions, and occasionally even about the major stylistic units themselves.

We then tried a different approach. Rather than searching for lists of buildings, architects, or styles, we attempted to spell out the criteria whereby an excellent slide collection could be distinguished from a merely good one. Although he never formulated it that way, we hypothesized that the curator would be content if the number of times he could not fulfill a customer's request could be minimized. A well-balanced collection is one that contains what users are looking for. Here we had, at last, an operational criterion to begin identifying the gaps.

Which architects and buildings attract the interest of library users? The ones that are being talked about. And which buildings pop up in conversation among faculty and students? Implanting listening devices in classrooms and hallways to find out would be intrusive and costly; it is easier to scan current books and periodicals, because people talk about what they read, and write about what they talk. If the library were regularly to procure slides of the sites featured in journals and books as they are published, the number of unfulfilled requests would gradually diminish. We advised to institute such a policy.

As it turns out, the idea was far from unprecedented. In the good old times when matters were simpler, curators ordered slides based on a limited selection of leading text books, such as the successive editions of Sir Banister Fletcher's *History of Architecture on the Comparative Method*. Some librarians may have honestly believed they were pursuing complete coverage of the Great Architectural Works of All Times; others, intellectually less pompous or epistemologically more sophisticated, knew that they were merely following the lead of the Great Books. Be that as it may, architectural discourse as reflected in the literature was indeed controlling their choices. With the diversification of literature and the interests it reflected, the system in its intuitive directness eventually broke down, making it necessary to recreate it, so to speak, on a more self-conscious level.

My theme, however, is not slide collection management. I wish to introduce two ideas. The first is that architectural writings provide tell-tale indications of people's values and interests. By examining systematically large masses of texts, including not only leading scholarly sources but everything that achieves social currency, one can identify societal architectural preferences that are hard to capture by other means. The reach of the technique extends to the past when one analyzes a body of historical writing. But the systematic study of large corpora is difficult and time consuming; unless the material is encoded into an alternative, more manageable format, the complexity of the task daunts even the most valiant researcher.

This leads to the second idea, which sounds utterly silly at first but provides the kernel of this project: rather than the books, one may study merely their indexes of names cited. I started looking at indexes as a shortcut to identify the books worth examining; eventually, I became convinced that with electronic data-processing techniques, index analysis could grow into a discipline worth pursuing in its own right. Text analysis and index analysis are discussed separately below.

Text Analysis

The literature provides indications of changing societal values more effectively than people's conversations. This occurs because the written word is easier to retrieve, process, and store, and because publishing is restrictive and selective, just like building. The erection of the Pyramids or the medieval cathedrals demanded huge resources. For that fact alone they bear witness to the belief systems of the peoples who built them and their power structures, even in the case of artistically less distinguished buildings. Because of the expenditures involved, only certain utterances ever make their way into print. Publication, like construction, signals a certain level of social approval, even in the case of texts with limited intrinsic value.

The built record of architecture has been thoroughly analyzed by generations of scholars. The published record, although rich and significant, has rarely been subjected to systematic study. With the advent of electronic text-processing techniques the imbalance can be redressed; perhaps for the first time ever, the study of the published record may prove to be as fruitful for historical and theoretical purposes as the analysis of architecture itself.

Analyzing the published record is different from reading it; the latter is of secondary importance to the discourse analyst, and it may be bypassed altogether in certain cases. When reading, the information acquired is spelled out plainly. Not so when analyzing discourse: the insights obtained, although derived from the written material, are not explicitly stated. Stevens[1] plotted the productive lives of the architects cited in the *Macmillan Encyclopedia of Architects* (Placzek, ed., 1982) and the *Penguin Dictionary of Architecture* (Fleming et al., 1980); he also examined the dates of commencement of their buildings. He noted that the chronological growth of the numbers of architects and buildings important enough to deserve a place in those reference works was approximately exponential. Next, he focused on the deviations between exponential growth, and growth as exhibited in those books. He defined two major peaks with more architects and buildings than expected—one from 1455 to 1565, associated with the Renaissance and Mannerism, and the other from 1915 to 1925, associated with the Modern Movement. Had the writers stated that the recognized architectural production during these periods exceeded in volume the average, the information would have reached us through reading. But they did not; it was unearthed through text analysis.

Many words used in architectural discourse, such as column, entablature, and balcony, have unequivocal formal referents. An architectural historian interested in the use of any of these elements would examine a body of built work to trace their emergence, frequency of employment, and (if applicable) demise. Alternatively, a discourse analyst could scan a corpus of architectural writings looking for occurrences of the associated words. People interested in columns will talk and write about them in addition to building them, and when the allure wanes, columns will gradually vanish from their discourse as well as their buildings. It is therefore reasonable to expect that results obtained from discourse analysis will be congruent with the teachings of traditional architectural history. In one sense, however, discourse analysis reaches farther. Many terms often used by architects, such as logic, truth, justice, and *Zeitgeist*, have no formal equivalents; they can be searched in discourse, but not in the actual fabric of buildings. Even formal or visual concepts such as beauty, or architectural ideas such as function, offer a dimension for textual inquiry that is hardly accessible to conventional, building-oriented research. Discourse analysts may investigate when these terms were first used, how often, and for how long, and thus acquire information about the currency of the associated ideas. It is more difficult, in comparison, to visualize effective means for determining if and when buildings started or stopped being beautiful or functional.

Discourse analysis is limited only by the ingenuity and imagination of the researcher, and by the limitations of the technology at the individual's command. One can look at the frequencies of citations of given architects, buildings, or events, or the rate of usage of certain key words. It is possible to determine, for example, when environmental control, or the conservation of energy and natural resources, the preservation of historical monuments and areas, and sustainable development, became issues in the literature. One's grasp expands considerably if one looks for close occurrences of pairs of words; one can often surmise, even without reading the text, not only what is being talked about but also what is being said. By counting electronically how often the associated words appear in the same sentence the researcher is able to determine, for instance, when Sullivan started to be called a master, or Wright a genius, or his architecture organic, and for how long.

The analysis of discourse is also geared to its limitations; if every topic or every building were equally likely to appear in conversation, the study of linguistic behavior would be of less consequence. Discourse, like architecture itself, is free only in the most abstract sense; utterances and buildings are constrained by a matrix of individual and collective restrictions, explicit as well as implicit. The most consequential restrictions are those embedded in the fabric of social convention, invisible to the naked eye. Seen from the inside, discourse appears deceivingly boundless, seamless, and without gaps; the boundaries are visible only from the outside. A list of notable buildings or architects, a checklist of important topics, a book, a bibliography, an exhibition of current architectural work, or a slide collection, looks comprehensive if molded on current architectural parlance; but gaps and redundancies surface when approached from the angle of another discourse. Rather than substituting one for another, the analyst's goal is to build a frame of reference from which alternative discourses can be distinguished and described.

Literature's cycle of response to cultural change is exceedingly shorter than architecture's: publications change faster than buildings, and are almost invariably precisely dated. Researchers can trace the prevalence of ideas in architectural discourse with a finer grain than would be possible by searching an actual body of built work. The technique holds great promise for historical studies.

Text analysis is particularly effective at measuring repetitiveness. Repetition is pointless in scientific discourse; a scientific proposition is worth publishing only if it differs from previously stated assertions. Not so in the architectural literature, which resembles from this perspective narrative practices prevalent in folktale and myth; in family, ethnic, and national traditions; in advertising and political speech, and in religious ritual. Here, repetition is the very vehicle by which content becomes socially established. Scientific knowledge is legitimized by argumentation and proof; narrative knowledge is legitimized by its transmission and consumption.

Text analysis demands the examination of large masses of publications, and this can be done effectively only if the materials are available in machine-readable form. Texts can be converted into electronic files by optical scanning, but the process is laborious, error prone, or expensive, depending on the technology used. Some texts are already available electronically, and more are likely to appear in the near future, perhaps starting with newly published books and following with the classics. The Bibliothèque de France is in the process of producing electronic versions of 100,000 canonical works of the twentieth century.[2] But this, alas, is not nearly enough. Participants at a recent conference on electronic information in the humanities recommended the creation, as a national priority, of a 10 million-volume digital library encompassing the full spectrum of the humanities.[3] Although such a library would be an extraordinary asset, many texts important for this project would probably remain outside of its scope.

To grasp architectural thinking and its historical evolution, all library holdings (the entire collective memory of society) should be accessible to automatic searching and processing; fulfillment of this goal still exceeds by much current technical possibilities. One of the obstacles is lack of universal agreement on a formatting language. The Bibliothèque de France is using memory-intensive bit-mapped images of pages that yield extraordinarily voluminous files of several gigabytes per book, and that could not be searched comprehensively and systematically for the word "column" (or any other word) with current technology. Machine-readability's promise of an environment for text analysis will remain unfulfilled for the foreseeable future.

Index Analysis

Index analysis can reap some of the fruits of text analysis at a much lower cost. It requires neither reading nor electronic access to the texts; only the indexes are studied. I collected the names of architects cited in nearly 400 books about American architecture published since 1815 (see the list at the end of the volume). There are, altogether, more than 7,000 architects. The number of times an architect is cited, the length of these citations, and their content are not taken into consideration: commendatory passages count for as much as acerbic criticisms, and brief references in passing are granted the same weight as detailed analysis extending over several pages, or even entire chapters. This imposes a considerable burden on the credulity of persons approaching index analysis for the first time. How can anything worth while be learned from such flimsy data? The approach seems flippant, if not outright inimical to attentive scholarship.

Let us look at an example. In *The Architecture of America* (1961), Burchard and Bush-Brown dismissed Frank Furness as an "eccentric," whose buildings are "large, dark affairs ... dressed in Gothic." Compare this assessment with that of Alan Gowans, who writing about "the ponderous massiveness and play of textures of Richardsonian Romanesque" cited the very same Furness buildings as "the best examples" (*Images of American Living*, 1964). Such divergent interpretations are invisible in the indexes. Gowans's appreciation for Victorian eclecticism, however, led him to discuss many of Furness's contemporaries of similar orientation and standing, whereas Burchard and Bush-Brown, contemptuous of the entire style, ignored most of the persons associated with it. A perceptive index analyst would not miss the clue.

Once the foundations of the discipline have been laid out, such seemingly flimsy starting points can lead to fresh insights about architecture and its literature. No attack on scholarship is involved; far from hastening the forsaking of libraries, index analysts are responsible for continual additions to the shelves. Rather than undermining the reading of texts, their work provides glimpses on still unexplored perspectives and contributes to defining new research goals and strategies.

In the case of architecture, the analysis could be centered on the names of the architects, the buildings, or both. In this particular project attention is paid to citations of architects alone.

The study of names is justified on pragmatic as well as conceptual reasons. Practically, it is faster and less resource intensive than other types of text analyses in three critical areas: data gathering, data processing, and sharing and storing the results. Indexing is often cheap and fast; texts that could not possibly be read or scanned electronically in full may be granted a reading or scanning of the index only. Even when slow and tedious, as indexing sometimes is, once the names of the architects or buildings have been entered into the data base, indexes are easily encoded into strings of yes and nos—this one is cited, that one is not. Such strings can then be subjected to a variety of arithmetic and logical operations that could not be executed on full-fledged books. Unlike texts, indexes can be analyzed on personal computers in use today. Finally, everyone must read for himself, but citation frequencies, once obtained and processed, can be stored and shared.

Cognitively, the names of architects and buildings being discussed are of the very essence in architectural discourse. Opinions are volatile; the list of buildings and architects deserving of an opinion is more stable. Outcasts often become prophets, and heroes turn into villains as new philosophies emerge; the roles are reassigned, but the actors often remain the same. Important as they are in the short run, such changes are inessential from a larger perspective. They would be of only limited concern to the slide curator: as long as Mies van der Rohe remains a participant in the plot, either as a hero or a villain, slides of his work are likely to remain in demand.

The richest and most perceptive interpretations of architecture usually come from sensitive individuals. They progressively degrade in definition and focus as they are absorbed by wider social circles, like waves in the water when a stone is thrown in a quiet pond. At the outer edge of the ripple effect, the content of discourse becomes almost shapeless. The only datum that remains is who or what is being talked about; literally, the names. A considerable social capital is spent to ensure that they remain solidly anchored in the collective memory. The effort is conducted not only by the obvious beneficiaries, the architects and the institutions for whom they work, but by society at large; persons at the receiving end of the information distribution system are as eager to learn the significant names as distributors are to broadcast them. The distribution channels include universities, professional institutions, and the media. When students come to academia or people attend to communications, the first and foremost thing they learn is not what to say, but what to talk about; the persons, projects, and ideas dominating current interests and the words required to handle them: their names.

Despite efforts for permanence, however, nothing is cast in concrete, not even at this basic level. Slow changes take place all the time. Some names and issues gradually fade away, and those riding the next wave gradually enter discourse. This generates repercussions in the nomenclature that are detected by analysts, who can then chart the fortunes and fluctuations of individual terms and their associated entities.

Indexes as Clues

To determine whether a book was worth reading, he [Marshall McLuhan] usually looked at page 69 of the work, plus the adjacent page and the table of contents. If the author gave no promise of insight or worthwhile information on page 69, McLuhan reasoned, the book was probably not worth reading. If he decided the book did merit his attention, he started by reading only the left hand pages.[4]

The analysis of indexes yields information not only about architects or buildings, but also about the texts themselves. As experienced library and bookstore browsers know well, one learns a great deal about scholarly books merely by looking at their index, especially if one is familiar with the subject matter. Suppose that someone is examining a new survey of American architecture. It contains the names of persons who are likely to appear in every survey, such as Henry H. Richardson, Louis H. Sullivan, and Frank Lloyd Wright. It also includes names of minor figures, perhaps unknown to the researcher, associated with events of passing or merely local interest. Neither universally recognized names nor totally obscure ones are useful in establishing a preliminary categorization of the book; categorization occurs on the basis of the broad range of names in between.

The interested person might inquire about a reference to Bernard Maybeck. If it is there, the architecture of the San Francisco Bay area is likely to be within the scope of the book, and perhaps also a more general discussion of regionalism. Is William Lescaze listed? If he is, the prospective reader can surmise that the book will include an analysis of the beginnings of modernism in America. Minoru Yamasaki?: corporate architecture. Robert Venturi?: Postmodernism. Frank Gehry?: Deconstructivism, and so on.

The reader's initial hunches may be confirmed by other names in the index. The Greene brothers, if listed, validate the inferences originated by the citation of Maybeck, and so do Irving Gill and William W. Wurster; Raymond Hood and Eliel Saarinen lend force to the expectations created by the mention of Lescaze; I. M. Pei and Gordon Bunshaft reinforce the presence of Yamasaki in the text; Charles Moore, Stanley Tigerman, and Robert A. M. Stern, if included, augment the importance of Venturi's presence. Eisenman and Tschumi do the same for Gehry. Once one such chain of associated names has been identified, the observer anticipates other names likely to follow; noting whether or not they are listed, the initial impressions of the scope of the book is focused.

Machines furnished with the indexes of large numbers of books perform this type of analysis more systematically and much faster, obtaining results far beyond the reach of casual browsers. To be able to categorize effectively, such persons must know from experience which architects are usually discussed together. An index analyst is free from such preoccupations; the clusters of architects conducive to a consistent categorization of surveys is derived automatically from the investigation itself. Because of our limited ability to process information, browsing through indexes leads only to blurry impressions. Computerized techniques, in contrast, yield distinct taxonomies of architects and texts.

Let us consider the following list of famous American architects and architectural firms, presented in order according to their birth dates:

Thomas Jefferson

Charles Bulfinch

Benjamin Latrobe

Richard Morris Hunt

William Le Baron Jenney

Henry Hobson Richardson

Daniel H. Burnham

Louis Sullivan

Frank Lloyd Wright

Eliel Saarinen

Walter Gropius

Ludwig Mies van der Rohe

Skidmore, Owings, & Merrill

Louis I. Kahn

Eero Saarinen

I. M. Pei

Charles Moore

Robert Venturi

Faced with such a list, readers knowledgeable of American architectural history could surmise a continuous developmental line linking all the names into a historical narrative; in other words, they would conceive an ideal text whose index would match the list, except that it would be in alphabetical rather than chronological order.

Conceiving the narrative line is not unlike drawing a figure by linking numbered points, or creating a melody following a sequence of preselected notes. The musical analogy is better because a composer who chooses to follow such creative device enjoys a degree of freedom denied to children working on numbered points. The names of the list may be arranged into a narrative more than one way; in fact, given the same list, different historians are likely to propose slightly divergent narratives. Furthermore, the linkage need not be historical. Other texts could conceivably be generated by arranging the architects' work geographically, as in a guidebook, or alphabetically, as in a dictionary. By fleshing out the skeleton of names in a variety of ways, a series of possible texts are seen where before there was only an index.

Not any text, however, could be built on a given index, and if the index is changed it alters the gamut of possible texts. Imagine, for instance, that Bulfinch, Latrobe, Hunt, and Burnham are removed from the list, but Philip Johnson, Richard Meier, and Peter Eisenman are added; or, alternatively, that Moore and Venturi are deleted, but Robert Mills, John Russell Pope, McKim Mead & White, and Thomas Gordon Smith are inserted. The texts that could be paired to these indexes would be substantially different. All the disparate books, real or imaginary, that share the same index have a common thread—not what is being said, but what is being talked about.

The index is not the only clue available about the scope and nature of a text, but in many senses it is the best. Genette[5] coined the term *paratext* to refer to everything that broadcasts information about a book other than the text itself: the title, cover, dust jacket, illustrations, format, typography, price, quality of paper, list of chapters, even the number and arrangement of footnotes.

However, perhaps because he was uninterested in technical books, he completely neglected the index of names cited. Although of less visual impact than the cover, the index is more firmly anchored in the real nature of the work. Accomplished book designers may propose alternative, equally satisfying covers, jackets, or formats. Reliable indexers, in contrast, are expected to produce invariably the same index. The appearance of a book may change substantially with new editions or translations into other languages; the index will change only to the extent of text revisions. Jackets, illustrations, and lists of chapters are probably more revealing than indexes when taken one at a time, and are likely to attract the attention of casual browsers. For someone dealing with a large number of texts, however, indexes offer a special advantage: they are amenable to computerized analysis in a way that large numbers of jackets or chapter listings are not.

A sequence of names of famous architects stands as an abstract characterization of a historical narrative, it was said before. Similarly, a series of indexes of strategically selected architectural books is a representation of the entire literature. To use the metaphor of the numbered points again, by connecting the names of an index one can draw the face of a text; and by relating with appropriate techniques the indexes of many texts it is possible to build a model of the evolution of the entire architectural literature and, by extension, of architectural thinking itself. The operations are facilitated if the elements of the sequences are arranged chronologically: the names in an index by order of birth of the architects, and the indexes of a literary corpus by the publication dates of the texts. Architectural index analysis is thrice removed from architecture: first, because it deals with writings, not buildings; second, because it focuses on indexes, not texts; and third, because it looks at the literature as a sequence of indexes, not a sequence of texts.

Architects may approach index analysis looking for ways to promote their own presence in the literature, to become the heroes of new, still untold narratives. Writers may be motivated by a desire to augment their impact over their readers and other writers. The public may be searching for clues about the architects to pay attention to and the books to be read. Librarians and merchants may seek to learn about books or slides to meet the needs of their customers. Scholars may be attracted by new research paradigms. The analysis of discourse "determines in a single stroke what one must say in order to be heard, what one must listen to in order to speak. and what role one must play ... to be the object of a narrative."[6]

Examples of Applications

Reviewing a new guidebook to the architecture of the District of Columbia,[7] Forgey recently wrote[8]:

The architecture of the last decade or so gets short shrift. This is true even in sections devoted to residential areas such as Capitol Hill, where none of Amy Weinstein's fine additions of the late '80s or early '90s was noticed. Omissions are more serious and harder to comprehend in downtown districts that have been largely rebuilt over two decades. Unmentioned in the Foggy Bottom section is Vincent Kling's International Monetary Fund, which, with its towering modern atrium, set a pattern for all of commercial Washington. In the old downtown district, east of 15th Street, the list of omissions—including major buildings by Philip Johnson and Hartman-Cox on Franklin Square, among many others— is long enough to constitute a serious distortion of history . . .

The reviewer noted later that quarreling with inclusions and omissions in such books may be pointless, because they are highly selective by nature. But quarrel he did, and so do others when reviewing architectural texts, not only guidebooks but also history works and other types of literature. Indeed, listing the omissions or inclusions that depart from standard expectations is an effective means to capture the particular slant or flavor of a text.

Without the new technology, knowledgeable reviewers are needed to identify oversights or questionable inclusions. With the computer-aided analysis of indexes, the list could be derived automatically by scanning the names cited and comparing them against information stored in a data base of citations of Washington architecture. Tasks that used to call for human intervention now can be performed electronically. Scarce resources such as expert reviewers are freed for other, higher-level undertakings, and lower-level expertise is made readily available at a lower cost in a wider array of circumstances. Certain slants of a text, if any, can be detected much earlier during the writing and editing processes; if desired, they could be corrected before reaching publication.

A book published half a century ago may have featured a peculiar selection of architects, but the norms and expectations prevalent at the time have long been forgotten: what might then have been a novel or unexpected choice of names is lost for modern readers. With access to average citation frequencies from the past, index analysts can reconstruct hypothetical reactions of reviewers contemporary to the writer.

Information about specific architects is also effectively uncovered by index analysis. By examining their citation records one can learn a great deal about their fortunes in the literature and by extension about their life and career. Bruce Goff's first two citations in publications of national scope—the only ones considered in the project[9]—occurred simultaneously in 1930, when he was barely twenty-six years old. The publications are *The New World Architecture* by Sheldon Cheney, and *Modern Architecture*, an issue in the series University Prints edited by Kenneth L. Conant. A full twelve years elapsed before Goff made another appearance in the literature, in 1942.[10] His citation record started to grow only in 1950, slowly at first, gaining momentum later: he was cited in seven texts of the corpus during the 1950s, ten during the 1960s, fifteen during the 1970s, and thirty-five during the 1980s.

Even a cursory examination of the record reveals an oddity. Were Cheney and Conant endowed with an exceptionally perceptive eye, capable of detecting still unrecognized talent? Or were they being too generous to Goff, perhaps because he was their friend, or (conceivably) in return for past or future favors? At first, these questions seem to hold only local interest, limited to those who are concerned with Cheney, Conant, or Goff. They become more provocative on learning that once an analyst has developed an electronic technique to investigate this particular instance, the procedure can be used at no extra cost to look into other cases as well. In fact, the system will even tell us automatically which are the cases worth looking into! It will do it by searching for occurrences that depart from norms derived from the data themselves—but let us not rush ahead of ourselves.

Suppose we approach the experts for more information about these early citations of Goff. An index analyst would give us a different type of information than an architectural historian. Using a computer, the analyst would look into the age of every architect on record at the time of his or her first citation and would discover that only four among the thousands of architects referenced were published at an even earlier age than Goff: Michael Rotondi was twenty-five, Henry Ives Cobb was twenty-four, and Frederick Law Olmsted, Jr. and Maya Ying Lin were first published in a text of national scope at the age of twenty-three.[11] Henry Hobson Richardson was twenty-six, like Goff. The analyst would confirm Goff's case as unusual, but not extreme. A historian, on the other hand, would look into the early stages of Goff's architectural career. As one of his biographers put it,

[*Goff*] ... *began working for an architect in 1916, when he was twelve years old. Within two years one of his designs had been published and within three another was under construction. By 1925, when he turned twenty-one, he had some twenty-five designs to his credit, of which twelve were built.*[12]

By 1930, when *The New World Architecture* and *Modern Architecture* were published, Goff had already designed eighty-three projects, thirty of which had been built, and his work had been featured in numerous local and regional publications, including a book. Cheney's early citations were not an anomaly within his career; rather, the career itself was atypical. The intriguing fact, it turns out, is that Goff was overlooked in texts of national or international scope for the next two decades. This would not have become apparent without cooperation between an analyst and a historian.

How many years must elapse between an architect's early citations and his becoming an expected feature in the literature for the fact to be noteworthy? Twenty, as in Goff's case? Would twelve years have been remarkable? Eight? Five? Henry Niccolls Wright was cited in the corpus for the first time in 1952, in *Forms and Functions of Twentieth-Century Architecture* by Talbot Hamlin. He was ignored for the next two decades, like Goff. After a citation in 1972 there were only two more, one in 1980 and one in 1985. Nobody would claim that Hamlin demonstrated special foresight for citing H. N. Wright twenty years before anybody else, because the architect never achieved national prominence. Goff's case is noteworthy not because of a particular interval between his early citations, but because the entire pattern departs from normal expectations. Index analysts can devise a working definition of normalcy to confirm that Goff's citation record is indeed unusual, but not Wright's. Armed with such a definition, they may identify the architects with the most unusual citation patterns. Historians, if interested, may then look into the specifics of each case. Index analysis can help set such research agendas.

Analysts are concerned with writers as much as with architects. They are after the unusual in Cheney and Conant as much as in Goff; and finding interconnections between architects and texts is one of their goals. What, then, about *The New Architecture of the World*? Is Goff's early citation an isolated episode, or is the book filled with instances of comparable foresight? How many times, as an average, do authors succeed in uncovering still relatively obscure architects with brilliant careers in the profession and in the literature ahead of them? (In examining the record, analysts may be looking for departures from the norm, or they may be interested in the norms themselves, which are also worthy of intellectual curiosity.) And is *Modern Architecture* equally foresighted as *The New Architecture*? More so? Less so?

Although the questions make some intuitive sense, before computer-aided index analysis there was no way to consider them rigorously. By scanning the data it is possible to confirm the sagacity in the choice of names of Cheney's book, which is ranked in the ninety-second percentile, meaning that it is more foresighted than 92 percent of the texts of the corpus. In contrast, Conant's work commands a respectable but less astonishing foresight in the sixtieth percentile. Goff's citation pattern, in turn, is more unusual than that of 98 percent of the architects in the roster.

Cheney's and Conant's works were published almost simultaneously, and although the latter covers a wider time period, their subject matter overlaps to a degree. Indeed, many architects are featured in both publications. Conant's collection of prints lacks an introductory or critical text; his selection of examples is therefore the main, if not the only, criterion by which his work can be judged. Comparing his choice of names with those of Cheney or other authors is therefore particularly relevant. An index analyst may report that the association between the indexes of Conant and Cheney equals 0.38, which places the works somewhat close to each other but not in the immediate vicinity. Furthermore, the analyst will point out that Cheney's work is closer to Suzanne LaFollette's *Art in America* of 1929 (association 0.47) and to Henry-Russell Hitchcock's *Modern Architecture: Romanticism and Reintegration*, also of 1929 (association 0.45). Conant, in turn, is more closely associated with Talbot Hamlin's *Architecture Through the Ages* (1940; 0.45).

Explaining the generation and meaning of these figures takes the best part of the coming chapters; at this stage it should suffice to say that index analysts can draw a variety of comparisons and establish connections between texts, between architects, and between architects and texts.

Computers

"That day [when the *Nautilus* plunged for the first time beneath the waters] I bought my last volumes, my last pamphlets, my last newspapers, and from that time I wish to think that men no longer think or write," declared Captain Nemo, the commander of the submarine in Jules Verne's novel, to Professor Aronnax, his captive guest. Although Verne anticipated the possibility of undersea travel, he did not foresee wireless communications. The *Nautilus* had to be self-sufficient not only in energy and food, but also in information. No exchange with the rest of the world was possible. The scientific results the good captain expected to achieve in his lengthy reconnaissance had to be rooted in the body of knowledge he took with him at the time of his departure.

Captain Nemo's exploration makes a terrible model for the analysis of discourse. Buildings, like the world inspected by the *Nautilus*, are stationary entities; what is true about them at one time is likely to remain true later. But continual updating is essential in the case of research on discourse, when the very subject matter under scrutiny is information. It becomes critical when studying current thinking, reflected in recent communications such as those Captain Nemo could no longer obtain.

More than one-third of the texts referenced were published after I started working on the project in 1980. Ignoring this material would have been inexcusable; the results would have been outdated before they reached publication. It was imperative to employ a system capable of providing continual, automated updating of all files, with instantaneous recalculation of all values and tables, and self-controlled redrawing of the charts and diagrams. Only computers can provide an environment in which this is feasible.

Digital technology must play a role in the distribution of the results as well. About 100 architect histograms are presented throughout the book, but more than 7,000 have been generated and are available to potential users. Similar numbers hold for many other items of information. Print is bulky, unwieldy, and hard to update; diskettes are an effective means to distribute citation tallies, histograms, and other index analytical results. Readers are referred to the electronic companion of this book.

Notes

1. Stevens, Garry: *Quantitative Studies in Art and Science. A Case Study from Architecture.* Master's degree thesis. Sydney: University of New South Wales, 1988.

2. Browning, John: Libraries Without Walls for Books Without Pages. What Is the Role of Libraries in the Information Economy? *Wired,* 1993, vol. 1, no. 1.

3. *Technology, Scholarship, and the Humanities: The Implications of Electronic Information. Summary of Proceedings.* American Council of Learned Societies and the J. Paul Getty Trust, 1993.

4. Marchand, Philip: *Marshall McLuhan: The Medium and the Messenger*. New York: Ticknor & Fields, 1989 (p. 129).

5. Genette, Gerard: *Seuils*. Paris: Editions du Seuil, 1987.

6. Lyotard, Jean Francois: *The Postmodern Condition: A Report on Knowledge*. Minneapolis: University of Minnesota Press, 1984 (pp. 21, 27). (Original French: 1979.)

7. Scott, Pamela, and Antoinette J. Lee: *Buildings of the District of Columbia*. New York: Oxford University Press. 1993.

8. Forgery, Benjamin: Cityscape. Let Your Fingers Do the Walking. *Washington Post*, 16 October 1993, pp. D1, D9.

9. The texts referenced are listed at the end of volume, and their selection is explained in chapter 2.

10. The text was *History of Modern Architecture*, by Rexford Newcomb.

11. Ages at publication are computed as the difference between publication date and year of birth, without taking months into account.

12. De Long, David G.: *Bruce Goff. Toward Absolute Architecture*. New York: Architectural History Foundation; Cambridge, London: MIT Press, 1988.

2   The Data

The data for this project are composed of the architects cited in 380 texts about American architecture published since 1815 (see the list at the end of the volume). Text publication dates and the years of birth of the more than 7,000 architects (estimated to the nearest decade when unknown) are also part of the data; and so is the gender of writers, editors, and architects, if known. Everything to be presented from chapter 3 onward derives directly and explicitly from this point of departure.

This chapter, devoted to the guidelines followed in selecting texts and architects, is not necessary to understand the remainder of the book and may be skipped. The guidelines, however, affect the results; to assess the significance of the latter, it is helpful to be familiar with the former.

Selection of Texts

The texts of the corpus are listed by publication date at the end of the volume. The items are very diverse: they include history books, textbooks, guidebooks, picture books, exhibition catalogs, interviews, book reviews, architectural dictionaries and encyclopedias, and general encyclopedias. There are articles from magazines, journals, and dictionaries. Collections of articles anthologized as books are included, and so are collections not anthologized. There are special issues of journals and groupings of journal issues. They vary in size from mere pamphlets to aggregates of several volumes. Some are the work of a single author, others are the product of collaborative efforts. Texts were published as a unit, or they appeared in installments over a period of time.

Several texts are devoted exclusively to architecture; others face the topic from a wider perspective, including the arts, furniture, urbanism, industrial design, taste, and even the entire framework of civilization. Some writers look at architecture in terms of style, others are interested in building or in social and political matters.

Many works deal only with the United States; many others refer to the entire world. A few titles are devoted to the present, or at what was the present at the time of writing; some focus on a past period or style, whereas still others encompass the entire duration of history.

Some follow a chronological sequence, as in a historical narrative. Others are composed of a series of relatively independent parts, which may be arranged alphabetically as a dictionary, geographically as in a guidebook, or by order of publication as in a collection of essays, or lack any particular order at all.

Despite such variations, the items of the corpus are linked by a common thread: they all deal with American architecture.

How were the texts selected?

Initially I tried to duck responsibility for the choices by using an independent authoritative source. My first attempt was to follow the category "American architecture" from the subject card catalog of the Library of Congress; but the catalog, which has grown in a process of accretion without explicit rules, is marred with inconsistencies and irregularities.[1] Bibliographies became my next target; several have been published, and any one could have served my purposes, or so I believed at the outset. But bibliographies are selective, and selectivity defeats one of the goals of the study. I am interested in distinguishing, on the basis of index analysis alone, trend-setting texts from others that are mere followers. To be able to do this, unoriginal works have to be in the corpus together with the classics. Also, new, relevant texts are inserted as they are published, and this is inconsistent with using a bibliography.

What is a text? Literary theorists disagree. Crystal[2] maintains that "text" is a pretheoretical term. Van Dijk,[3] De Beaugrande,[4] and De Beaugrande and Dressler,[5] on the contrary, propose that texts, as opposed to sentences, be considered the basic entities for linguistic analysis. The units purported in their definitions, however, range from a single word to an entire literary oeuvre, and even language in its totality. I found little guidance in discourse or textual theory about how to choose the items, how to select their scale (from small to large), or how to distinguish related texts from one another.

Works of architecture are also difficult to define, yet this does not preclude us from referring to them effectively. Thinking of texts as buildings, I transferred insights from one field into the other. Buildings are often contiguous physical units sitting on separate city lots, distinguishable from other such units. Like the typical suburban house, the typical text occupies one volume. But this is not absolutely necessary: works of architecture may be attached to other buildings, or comprise separate wings, or be intertwined with other works. Similarly, texts may occupy less or more than one volume.

Sometimes the boundaries of an architectural project are denoted by common materials, shapes, or style. The individuality of a text, in turn, may rest on common stylistic features, either in its literary content or in its physical, printed form. But such commonalities are not essential to the singularity of the building or the writing.

Single authorship is often a useful criterion in setting the boundaries of a work of architecture or literature, and so is single construction or publication time. Joint authorship is also possible, however, and so is sequential design and construction of a building, or writing and publishing a text over an extended period.

Ultimately, projects are held together by an inner consistency that is easier to perceive than to define. Coherence is more important than physical contiguity, visual unity, and single authorship or production time. The same is true for texts. A string of discourse qualifies as a text if it possesses a certain unity in terms of content, argument, or intention. To use terms of Ducrot and Todorov,[6] texts are characterized by autonomy and closure.

The following rules were observed in collecting the corpus:

1. Texts must be national in scope, to the exclusion of the regional and local. "Nation," used broadly, includes the colonies.

2. Texts must deal with the whole gamut of architecture; studies limited to only one or a few building types are not acceptable.

3. The intrinsic worth of a text is irrelevant. The silly appears together with the masterpiece.

4. Texts must be printed. No manuscripts, movies, television programs, videodisks, or exhibitions, unless they occur in conjunction with a publication.

5. The text must be or have been an active component of architectural culture in America. This is presumed to be the case if it was prepared, edited, translated, or published in this country. Significant foreign publications with wide circulation in the United States are also included.

6. Revised editions of works, when sufficiently different from the previous one, are regarded as new, independent texts. This is justified in chapter 7.

7. In the case of certain encyclopedias two separate entries are granted, one with the names given individual articles only, and the other for all names cited. The rationale is given in chapter 8.

8. To comply with rules 1 and 2, related publications are sometimes consolidated into a single text, as in the case of item #23 in the list of texts. (The sign # is used through the work to refer to texts in the corpus as numbered in the list.)

9. When a text covers an area larger than the United States (e.g., the Western hemisphere, the entire world), only American architecture is indexed. Let us call this a geographical focalization. Similarly, only architects are referenced when texts deal with arts other than architecture or with other aspects of civilization, a disciplinary focalization in this case. Except for dictionaries and encyclopedias, these focalizations are mutually exclusive; texts calling for both, such as general histories of art, are left out.

10. Texts must cover the entire history of American architecture or a chronologically identifiable segment of it. The segmentation can be stylistic, especially if the style is used to name a period, as in *American Colonial Architecture*.

11. The latter part of the preceding rule is sometimes difficult to apply. For example: Is *Architecture in Transition* (#351) a review of "architecture today ... [which] is providing a possible start for a new and visionary architectural language," as claimed in the introductory essay? Or is it merely a selective presentation of a small, unrepresentative group of architects—Coop Himmelblau, Hadid, Liebeskind, and a few others—who do not deserve a place in the corpus? The same issue could have been raised in 1932 against *The International Style: Architecture Since 1922* (#63) or other publications that trumpeted the work of architects who were a minority at the time and became mainstream only several decades later. Postmodernism, Deconstructivism, and Classicism did not originate as chronological labels, but may end up designating periods nevertheless, such as Modern and Art Deco; their literature is included in the corpus. The consequences of mistaking stylistic for chronological segmentations are discussed in chapter 7.

12. Names of architects must actually be reported. Books dealing with architecture but no architects have no place in this project. This precludes consideration of Native American and vernacular architecture. It also poses some problems with early Colonial buildings, when architects were often not involved or not known, and with early architectural publications that often omitted the names of the architects. In the case of very early publications I worked out the names of architects from the list of buildings.[7]

13. Texts must not be restricted to architects who are members of minorities or religious, national, ethnic, or gender groups.

14. On the other hand, they must be selective: reference works in which every architect is expected to be included have been avoided also.

15. Texts must have a credible index, or one should be attainable at a moderate cost. Indexers are notoriously undependable.[8] Faced with a bad index, one must choose between redoing the list of architects or disregarding the text altogether.

Some of the rules are essential, others are merely convenient. All architects must be citable in all texts, except when they do not belong there chronologically; in other words, if an architect is not featured in a text, it must be because the writer saw fit not to include that person. This is the reason for rules 1, 2, 8, 10, and 13.

Architects are distinguished in this study on the basis of their citation patterns. Texts in which everybody is cited are ineffectual; when numerical methods are used, they tend to blur the distinctions. This accounts for rule 14.

Taken collectively, the corpus is expected to reflect societal rather than individual preferences. Cultures are multifaceted, including the valuable and the banal; this is the rationale for rule 3.

Rules 6 and 7 are intended to allow for finer discriminations than would otherwise be possible. They can be rationalized as giving double weight to main citations in encyclopedias, and multiple weight to citations in texts that have achieved numerous editions.

Rules 4, 5, and 15, and the end of rule 9 are necessary to keep the task at manageable proportions. The policy described at the end of rule 12 is designed to expand the reach of the method.

The corpus includes every major scholarly work on American architecture published in this country and many lesser ones, and some that originated abroad. Despite the rules, the choices were inevitably judgmental, but so is any writer's selection of architects or works considered worthy of mention in a book on American architecture. Index analysts must not be subjected to higher standards of objectivity than those in other areas of the humanities.

Some of the results of the study are closely dependent on my specific choices, but most are likely to remain unchanged even if other texts had been selected. The problem is examined in more depth in the appendix.

Selection of Architects

Listing the American architects included in an index seems a reasonably straightforward operation. In fact, it is not that simple: many problems arise during the process. To curtail inconsistencies to the extent possible, I observed the following criteria.

The word "architect" is used in the widest sense to encompass professionals from allied disciplines and even laypersons who contribute to shape the physical environment. Americans living abroad are included. So are foreigners who did work for America, even if unbuilt, but only if their American work is explicitly cited.

The roster includes planners, urban designers, bridge and highway engineers, landscape architects, industrial designers, and interior designers. Furniture designers and cabinetmakers are covered when their work is discussed with architecture, but ignored if dealt with in separate sections of a text. Structural engineers are entered in the data base if their work is recognized as influencing the form of buildings, but not if merely listed among other technical credits. The same is true for contractors, developers, and preservation and restoration experts.

Homeowners are treated on the same footing as architects when they are responsible for shaping their houses. The extent of their participation on the design process, however, is seldom stated explicitly. In the early stages of the project I presumed that owners of smaller seventeenth-century houses had helped shaping them, but that the larger eighteenth-century homes had been designed professionally. The distinction worked well with the original colonies, but it was less useful in the Midwest, where the situation during the nineteenth century was comparable to that in the East 150 years earlier, or in the mountain and western states where the layering was complicated with successive waves of European settlement—Spanish, French, and Easterners. Ultimately, I adopted a merely textual criterion. If the text read "X built his house in 1800," X was included as an architect, but not if the text read "X's house was built in 1800." This places much weight on the writer's wording, which may not always be deliberate; but it allows for unequivocal decisions in every case, regardless of who is doing the data entry. The practical consequences of this policy are limited anyhow, because most homeowners are not mentioned in the literature often enough to influence the results.

Carpenters, masons, and persons who supervised building tasks are entered when it is implied in the text that they helped shape the project. The founders of the early missions in the Southwest are credited as designers of their churches, and the founders of cities are presumed to have laid them out, unless stated otherwise.

In the outer edges of the design professions the distinctions sometimes become a bit tenuous. Military personnel are included when credited with building forts or comparable structures. Being responsible for the shape of space and materials, ship designers are included, but not the inventor of the steamboat. The inventor of the elevator, however, is listed because of his frequent citation in the literature as a formative influence on the shape of the American city. Sculptors, painters, and craftsmen are generally excluded, but with exceptions. Sculptors are listed if their work has an urban dimension, as in the case of a monument; and painters are included if their work is essentially architectural in content (case in point, Thomas Cole's *Architect's Dream*).

A quotation from a personality known primarily as a practicing architect counts as a citation; a citation of a writer does not. Architectural writers are not included unless they are significant architects in their own right, as in the case of Robert Venturi. Personalities better known as writers but also credited occasionally as architects, such as A. D. F. Hamlin, Peter Blake, Vincent Scully, and Charles Jencks, are tallied only if specifically featured as designers. Authors of books that are essentially design work, as the early American pattern books, are counted as architects. Architectural educators are included.

Anybody credited with architectural work directly or by implication is entered into the roster. It does not matter whether the person was an architect or even did architectural work; only how the individual is featured counts. Charles Louis Clerisseau is credited by Scully (#176) as coauthor of a model of the Virginia state capitol; consequently, he is listed among the architects cited in this text. Hitchcock (#116), in contrast, merely states that Jefferson was influenced by Clerisseau when he (Jefferson) designed the Virginia state capitol. The latter is not included as an architect in this case.

The content of the citation is irrelevant. Intimating his misgivings about "what passed for taste in the 1920s," Andrews declared in *Architecture in America* (#125) that "there will be no illustrations ... of the work of Ralph Adams Cram, then so highly regarded," and did not even list Cram in his index. Yet despite the writer's effort to exclude him, Cram crept into the discourse: he is listed in my indexing of the text.

In *The Story of Architecture in America* (#49), Tallmadge recognizes Christopher Wren as the designer of the Wren building at William and Mary College, Williamsburg, Virginia. It is doubtful that Wren had anything to do with the building, but he is included in the list. Norman (#171) brands Wren's authorship a legend; but Wren is included in the list of citations of this case too: his name still appears in the discussion of Williamsburg.

Wren receives a citation for not having designed the building in Williamsburg, but Clerisseau does not get one for influencing Jefferson. Where is the consistency? Designing is an architectural operation, exerting influence is not, according to my usage. The criterion is predicated on practical reasons: if influences were to be counted, scores of European architects, from Vitruvius to Aldo Rossi, would become part of the discourse on American architecture, complicating the data entry enormously.

The list of architects includes individuals, firms, and even government agencies and commercial institutions if they are credited with architectural work. Persons working both individually and in firms, or with more than one firm affiliation, are listed in the way most often followed in the corpus itself. When the format is a firm, a citation of any member is recorded as for the entire firm. When the members are referenced individually, firm citations are counted as being for each individual.

Architects' dates of birth are part of the record. When a date is unknown, it is estimated to the nearest decade. Firms are assigned the birth date of their leading partner. Government offices and other such groups are assigned fictitious birth dates reflecting the probable age of their members at the time of their first commission.

Only architects cited in at least two texts of the corpus, not counting different editions of the same work, are taken into consideration; lesser names appearing in only one text are ignored. This rule, too, rests on practical reasons. It cuts in half the total number of architects to reference. Uncertainties about identity, achievements, and birth date can be postponed until the name surfaces for a second time.

The listing of architects involves a higher component of personal judgment than the selection of texts. The issues at stake, however, are less critical. Every significant American architect is included in the roster, regardless of the selection criteria. The rules affect only the outer edges of the population of architects, whose names bear little weight on most of the results generated in this study in any case.

Notes

1. Chan, Lois Mai: *Library of Congress Subject Headings. Principles and Application.* Littleton, CO.: Libraries Unlimited, 1978.

2. Crystal, David: *A Dictionary of Linguistics and Phonetics*, 3rd ed. Oxford, Cambridge, MA: B. Blackwell, 1991.

3. Van Dijk, Teun S.: *Text and Context. Explorations in the Semantics and Pragmatics of Discourse.* London, New York: Longman, 1977.

4. de Beaugrande, Robert-Alain: *Text, Discourse, and Process: Toward a Multidisciplinary Science of Texts.* Norwood, NJ: Ablex, 1980.

5. de Beaugrande, Robert-Alain and Wolfgang Dressler: *Introduction to Text Linguistics.* London, New York: Longman, 1981.

6. Ducrot, O., and T. Todorov: *Dictionnaire encyclopédique des sciences du langage.* Paris: Editions du Seuil, 1972. (*Encyclopedic Dictionary of the Sciences of Language.* Baltimore: Johns Hopkins University Press, 1979.)

7. I did not perform this operation for more recent texts because modern authors presumably follow their own logic in deciding when or whom to cite. Their logic, however, is not always easy to grasp: in volume I of *The Smithsonian Guide to Historic America* (#333) Henry Bacon is recognized as the architect of the Lincoln Memorial in Washington, but Paul Cret is not acknowledged for the Folger Shakespeare Library, although allocated the same number of pages and more illustrations. Similarly, Maya Ying Lin is given credit for her Vietnam Memorial, but I. M. Pei is not mentioned in connection with the East Building of the National Gallery of Art.

8. Names are often misspelled, and variations of the same name may go undetected, but the most vexing problem is the existence of scores of names featured in a text but omitted from the index out of sheer carelessness. Two extreme cases are Patricia Bayer's *Art Deco Architecture* (#359) and *The Smithsonian Guide to Historic America series* (#333). The index of the former misses 127 of the 240 American architects or firms cited, which amounts to a failure rate of 53 percent. One thousand one hundred thirty-three of the 1,948 names cited in the twelve volumes of the Smithsonian series are missed in the indexes; with an average failure rate of 58 percent, it is the worst index in the entire corpus. (The index of volume 11, *Texas and the Arkansas River Valley*, ignores 94 percent of the pertinent names.)

3   The Universe

The universe[1] is composed of the architects[2] cited in the literature often enough to be considered established in the picture of American architecture, at least as seen by learned observers.

How often is often enough? Twice, if we are to follow the rule set in chapter 2; to be in the roster, an architect must have been cited in two texts of the corpus as a minimum. (Two is an arbitrary threshold. Most of the conclusions of this and following chapters hold true regardless of the value. See the appendix for a discussion.) The roster and the universe, however, are not the same thing. The roster is a list of names in a data base. The universe represents the cumulative memory of society as reflected in all library holdings. An architect enters the universe on receiving a second citation, and joins the roster when an index analyst references the publication. The roster contains the information necessary to build a model of the universe.

The universe comprises all architects in the country who did significant work. Again, a distinction is in order. Important architects are an ill-defined class; most people would agree on its core components, but class boundaries are hazy and subject to individual judgment. The universe, in contrast, has a finite number of enumerable members, and can be subjected to logical and arithmetic operations that would be impracticable on loose listings of famous architects. The universe is based on all relevant texts, past and present; unlike a list of luminaries, it reflects collective, socially shared judgment rather than individual choice.

The universe is a necessary building block for the following chapters. Without it, the coverage of texts could not be calculated (chapter 4); without coverage there would be no adjusted citations or histograms (chapter 5), which in turn are required to assess the foresight of writers (chapter 6), and so on. But the universe also deserves to be studied in its own right as a resource for historical analysis.

Architects have always had a date of birth, dates for their main contributions, and (if applicable) a date of death; now they are assigned, in addition, a date of entry into the universe, that is, the date of their second citation. As younger people join the ranks of the profession and are recognized in publications, the universe is in a state of continual expansion. Fresh studies of the past often spotlight earlier individuals previously neglected, enlarging the universe with older architects as well. The universe is layered chronologically, like a rich archeological site; its composition and evolution reveal many aspects of architectural history in America. Until very recently there were no practical means conducive to its study; consequently, it has not yet been recognized as a legitimate area of scholarly research.

Growth of the Universe

The universe had 33 architects in 1880; by 1994 the number had swelled to 2,807. Figure 3.1 (heavy line) shows the evolution year by year. The light dotted line presents a hypothetical exponential growth[3] with the same starting and ending points. Exponential growth is characteristic of natural or social populations in the absence of external forces accelerating or impeding change; deviations between real and exponential growth are indicative of disturbances. Although the cause of the deviations can only be surmised, their date and intensity can be plotted precisely.

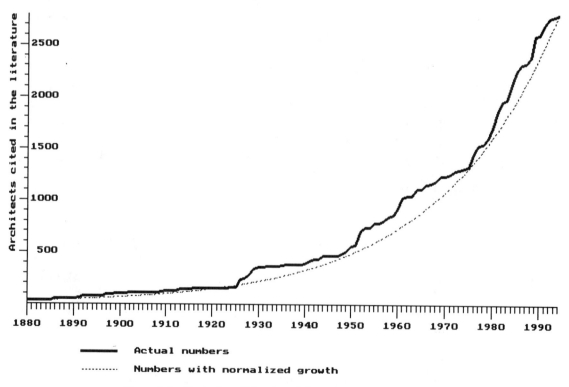

Figure 3.1   Evolution of the size of the universe

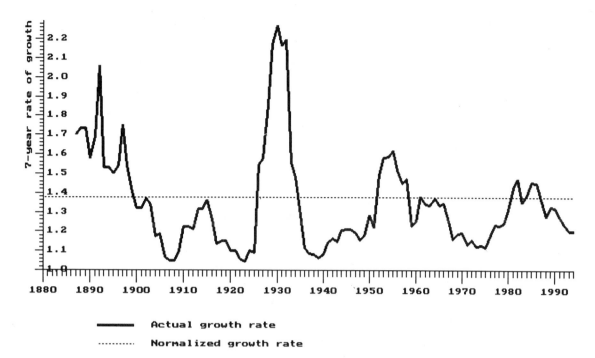

7-year rate of growth

Actual growth rate

·········· Normalized growth rate

Figure 3.2   Rate of growth of the universe

The heavy line in figure 3.2 shows the evolution of the growth rate of the universe for seven-year periods.[4] The dotted horizontal line marks the growth rate that, if sustained between 1880 and 1994, would have led to equivalent overall growth. When the curve is above the line, the universe is growing faster than average; it grows more slowly otherwise.

The growth of the universe depends on writing and publishing, rather than design and construction. Provocative new buildings, however, are likely to be recognized in the literature, impelling their architects into the universe if they were not already there. Texts that merely rehash known territory and unremarkable buildings leave the universe unchanged. For the universe to grow, significant numbers of texts must be published bringing forward the work of architects previously unnoticed, either from the past or the present. This typically happens with rich contemporary production, a renewed interest in bygone times, or a shift of attention to new areas of the architectural experience. In 1993 an American Institute of Architects (AIA) task force recommended that its annual design awards be granted taking into account, in addition to design excellence, a number of other categories such as technical, environmental, or societal advancement, and preservation-restoration, presumably overlooked previously. If juries were to sustain emphasis on such new categories, practitioners, educators, and writers would presumably follow suit, and neglected architects excelling in those areas would be recognized in the literature. The universe expands whenever building and writing are blooming and architectural interests widen.

Figure 3.2 shows three peaks of intense growth, from 1887 to 1903, 1926 to 1934, and 1951 to 1958, the last not as pronounced as the other two. They correspond to pinnacles in American architectural culture—the Chicago School and Columbian Exposition at the turn of the century, the first machine age after World War I, and the post-World War II era when America achieved worldwide architectural leadership. Growth slowed during the early years of this century, around the two world wars, during the late 1960s and early 1970s, and again since the mid-1980s. There may be a certain parallelism with economic cycles; be that as it may, systolic and diastolic periods in the accession of names to the literature follow each other, with consolidation coming after expansion.

Montgomery Schuyler, A. D. F. Hamlin, Russell Sturgis, Henry Van Brunt, William Ware, and Claude Bragdon were the most conspicuous writers during the first outburst. Lewis Mumford, Joseph Jackson, Talbot Hamlin, Thomas Tallmadge, George Edgell, Fiske Kimball, Henry-Russell Hitchcock, and Sheldon Cheney led the way during the second pinnacle. The third wave came with the writings of Sigfried Giedion, Talbot Hamlin, Henry-Russell Hitchcock, Wayne Andrews, and Vincent Scully (see the list of texts). The names of the architects associated with each of the peaks are disclosed later.

The population of the universe doubled approximately every twenty years throughout the last century. As it cannot exceed the population of architects, such explosive growth cannot be sustained indefinitely. Still, if the trend were to continue, every architect in practice could expect to be cited (twice?) in the national professional press before too long. Everything built or merely designed may at some point become available for retrieval, possibly by electronic means. But this is not to imply that everything will be under the limelight permanently: with so many architects and publications, the weight of any one citation must necessarily dwindle. Rather than moving toward equal exposure, the gap between coverage-rich and coverage-poor architects is continually growing. Figure 3.3 shows the evolution of the number of citations accumulated by the most frequently cited architects; as the least-cited have been cited only twice, the curve also represents the widening gap between the exposure-rich and the exposure-poor. The gap would be even greater if the frequency of citations within the same text or citation lengths were factored into the equation.

Leading Architects

A roll of prominent American architects is obtained by ranking the names in the roster according to the number of texts in which they are cited; figure 3.4 shows the list up to the one-hundredth rank, indicating each architect's rank,

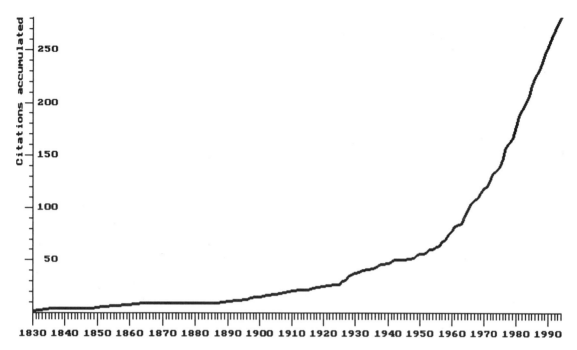

Figure 3.3   Citations accumulated by the most famous architects

number of texts in which he is cited, and year of birth. The procedure is simple and the results are easy to understand, but they are also open to facile criticism.

Some objections can be addressed by using more ingenious data-processing techniques; others are more general, and are likely to affect not only this ranking but other results of index analysis as well. The broadest objection is that the stature of an architect in the literature (let alone position on the architectural scene) can hardly be derived merely from citation counts that are impervious to content, citation frequency within the text, and length. The critique calls for a weighing mechanism to account for such differences. The issue will be considered in chapter 5, where some of these shortcomings are corrected by using a more sophisticated data-processing technique.

Citation counts, it could also be argued, reveal precious little that is not already known. Anyone could have predicted that Frank Lloyd Wright, the most conspicuous American architect, would head the ranking of figure 3.4. Knowledgeable readers could also have foreseen that Mies van der Rohe and Gropius would rank higher than Wallace Harrison or Edward Stone, or that the latter would surpass Henry Van Brunt or Alfred B. Mullett. Why should one engage in laborious indexing and tallying if the outcome can be anticipated by people familiar with the field?

The two criticisms are incompatible. Content-free citation tallies may be meaningless, a set of random variables with no connections to the real world; alternatively, their relation may be so obvious that the value of the variables

Figure 3.4   The 100 most famous architects (raw ranking)

Column headings:
[1]   Rank
[2]   Number of texts in which architect is cited
[3]   Birth date
[4]   Architect or firm name

[1]	[2]	[3]	[4]
1	281	1867	Frank Lloyd Wright
2	256	1856	Louis Sullivan
3	232	1886	Ludwig Mies van der Rohe
4	230	1838	Henry Hobson Richardson
5	221	1847	McKim, Mead, & White
6	208	1883	Walter Gropius
6	208	1910	Eero Saarinen
8	207	1906	Philip Johnson
9	206	1846	Daniel Hudson Burnham
10	198	1743	Thomas Jefferson
11	197	1897	Skidmore, Owings, & Merrill
12	177	1764	Benjamin Henry Latrobe
13	174	1902	Marcel Breuer
14	170	1881	Raymond Mathewson Hood
14	170	1892	Richard J. Neutra
16	167	1763	Charles Bulfinch
17	165	1827	Richard Morris Hunt
18	164	1850	John Wellborn Root
19	162	1873	Eliel Saarinen
19	162	1901	Louis I. Kahn
21	151	1832	William Le Baron Jenney
22	150	1895	Wallace K. Harrison
23	147	1844	Dankmar Adler
23	147	1918	Paul Rudolph
25	145	1917	I. M. Pei
26	144	1859	Cass Gilbert
26	144	1895	Buckminster Fuller
28	143	1781	Robert Mills
29	139	1912	Minoru Yamasaki
30	136	1804	Thomas Ustick Walter
31	135	1818	James Renwick, Jr.
31	135	1925	Robert Venturi
33	134	1788	William Strickland
33	134	1896	William Lescaze
35	133	1802	Richard Upjohn
36	130	1869	Bertram Grosvenor Goodhue
37	129	1759	Dr. William Thornton
38	127	1869	Albert Kahn
39	125	1754	Pierre Charles L'Enfant
39	125	1854	Holabird & Roche
41	123	1803	Alexander Jackson Davis
42	122	1886	George Howe
43	120	1862	Bernard Maybeck

Figure 3.4   (continued)

[1]	[2]	[3]	[4]
43	120	1902	Edward Durrell Stone
45	116	1858	Carrère & Hastings
46	114	1868	Greene & Greene
47	112	1922	Roche & Dinkeloo
47	112	1925	Charles W. Moore
49	110	1822	Frederick Law Olmsted
50	107	1762c	James Hoban
51	106	1899	Pietro Belluschi
51	106	1908	Max Abramovitz
53	105	1863	Cram, Goodhue, & Ferguson
53	105	1887	Rudolph Schindler
55	104	1815	Andrew Jackson Downing
56	102	1784	Ithiel Town
56	102	1898	Alvar Aalto
58	100	1837	George Browne Post
58	100	1839	Frank Furness
60	98	1716	Peter Harrison
60	98	1757	Samuel McIntire
60	98	1934	Richard Meier
63	96	1909	Gordon Bunshaft
63	96	1934	Michael Graves
65	95	1866	Henry Bacon
66	94	1895	Wurster, Bernardi, & Emmons
67	92	1800	James Bogardus
67	92	1907	Charles Osmand Eames
69	91	1874	John Russell Pope
69	91	1877	Shreve, Lamb, & Harmon
71	90	1868	John Mead Howells
72	89	1904	Bruce Alonzo Goff
73	85	1806	John Augustus Roebling
73	85	1824	Calvert Vaux
75	84	1887	Eric Mendelsohn
76	83	1887	Le Corbusier (Charles Eduard Jeanneret)
77	82	1761?	Mangin & McComb
77	82	1873	Harvey Wiley Corbett
79	80	1870	Irving John Gill
80	78	1771	Asher Benjamin
80	78	1800	Isaiah Rogers
80	78	1876	Paul Philippe Cret
83	76	1864	Warren & Wetmore
83	76	1915	Kallmann, McKinnell, & Knowles
85	74	1926	Cesar Pelli
85	74	1939	Robert A. M. Stern
87	73	1760c	Étienne Sulpice Hallet
87	73	1880	Purcell & Elmslie
87	73	1883	The Architects' Collaborative
87	73	1931	Denise Scott Brown
91	71	1792	John Haviland
91	71	1932	Peter D. Eisenman

Figure 3.4   (continued)

[1]	[2]	[3]	[4]
93	69	1883	William Van Alen
94	68	1890	C. F. Murphy Associates
94	68	1902	Josep Lluis Sert
96	66	1915	Edward Larrabee Barnes
96	66	1930	John Rauch
96	66	1938	Charles Gwathmey
100	65	1780	Alexander Parris
100	65	1848	Charles B. Atwood
100	65	1916	John Maclane Johansen

can be predicted from the outset. One or the other of the objections may be endorsed, but not both.

Indeed, certain results of citation rankings may be predicted in broad terms by competent scholars. Coincidence between expectations and results does little to extend the scope of knowledge, but sometimes it is a welcome confirmation of the soundness of the approach, especially when more complex data-processing operations are involved. It is also true that minor numerical differences in ranking are neither significant nor relevant. The benefits reaped by index analysis lie in the broad territory bracketed between the obvious and the inconsequential. When used properly, it pushes back the limits of ignorance; quickly and inexpensively, it brings to nonspecialists insights normally restricted to dedicated architectural scholars.

Had the ranking of figure 3.4 been compiled around the midcentury, the distinction of heading it would have fallen on Henry Hobson Richardson, not Wright; even earlier, the front-runners were William Thornton, Charles Bulfinch, and Benjamin Latrobe. Figure 3.5 shows the three architects (or more, in case of ties) with the highest accumulation of citations year by year since 1830. (The bars reflect dominance in discourse, not life and work or influence. Sullivan and Wright were long deceased by the time they first appeared in the chart.)

Figure 3.6 shows once again the bars of the architects with the highest numbers of citations, this time introducing an additional dimension. As in figure 3.5, the bars reflect publication dates along the horizontal axis. They also align with a vertical time scale to show the year of birth of the architects. A train of shaded and unshaded diagonal bands connects the two time scales. Each band corresponds to a particular number of years elapsed since the date of birth, as annotated in the middle of the diagram. By following the bars as they traverse the bands one can see the evolution of the architects' age during their literary dominance. (Age equals years elapsed since birth, regardless of months or of the architect's death.)

Most architects were past their eighties when they achieved fame. Strickland was the only one to reach a position of leadership during his forties; his fol-

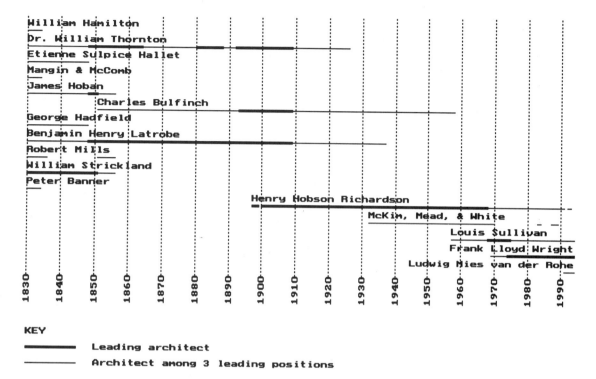

KEY

━━━━━━━━━━   Leading architect

──────────   Architect among 3 leading positions

Figure 3.5   The three most famous architects from 1830 to 1994

lowers (writers and readers) were his contemporaries. When he faded from attention in the last third of the century to the benefit of Thornton, Hoban, Latrobe, and Bulfinch, all of them his predecessors, the change affected not only the cast of characters but also the literary temporal horizon. The time lag between building and writing burst from nothing to as much as two generations, seventy or eighty years apart. Perhaps for the first time in America a historical perspective arose in the literature. Contemporary concerns returned to the forefront at the end of the century with Richardson, the only architect other than Strickland who would have reached dominance within his lifetime had he not died prematurely in 1886. The gap between building and literary dominance gradually increased again with his successors, Sullivan and Wright.

The universe is conservative and expansive; once admitted, no architect leaves it, causing the universe to grow in size permanently. For its size to remain stable, old names would have to be knocked out to make room for new ones. Figure 3.5 describes one group constructed that way, limited to the first three positions within the citation ranking. Figure 3.7 shows the architects in the twelve and the fifty top positions, year by year. It depicts the evolution of architectural fame in America in a way not hitherto attempted.

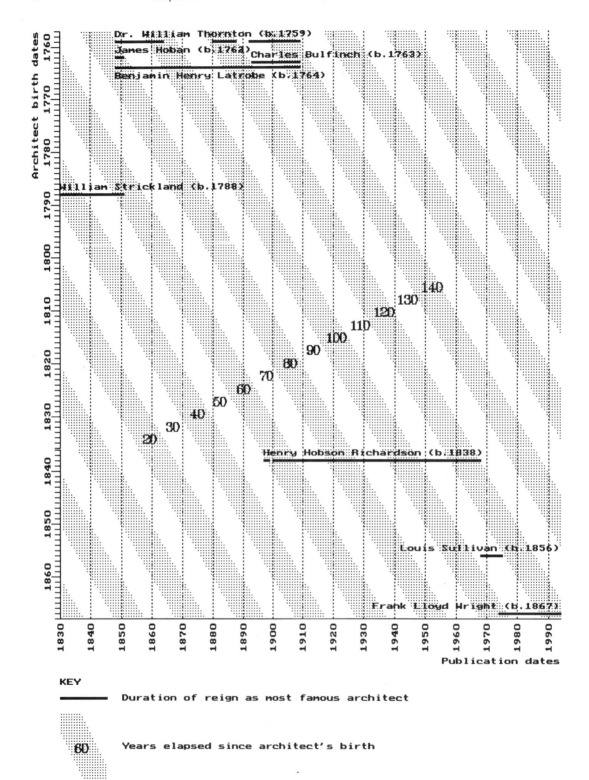

Figure 3.6   Ages of the most famous architects

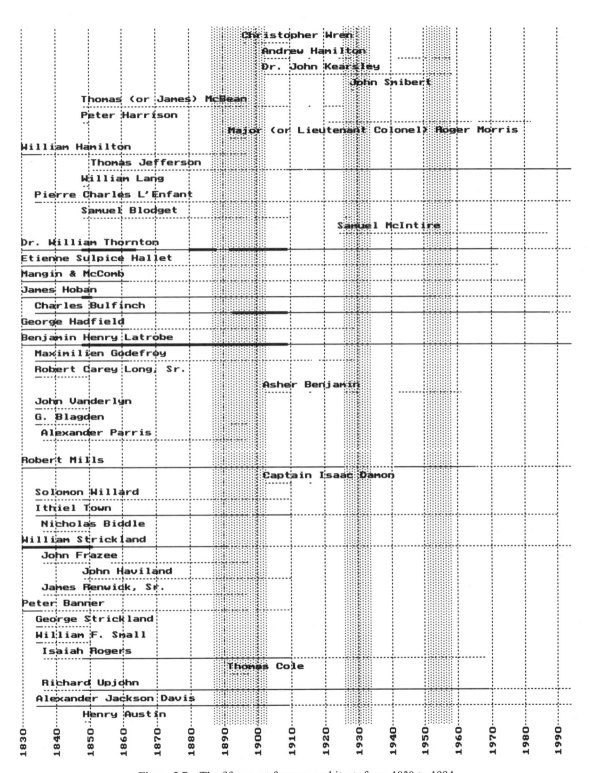

Figure 3.7 The fifty most famous architects from 1830 to 1994

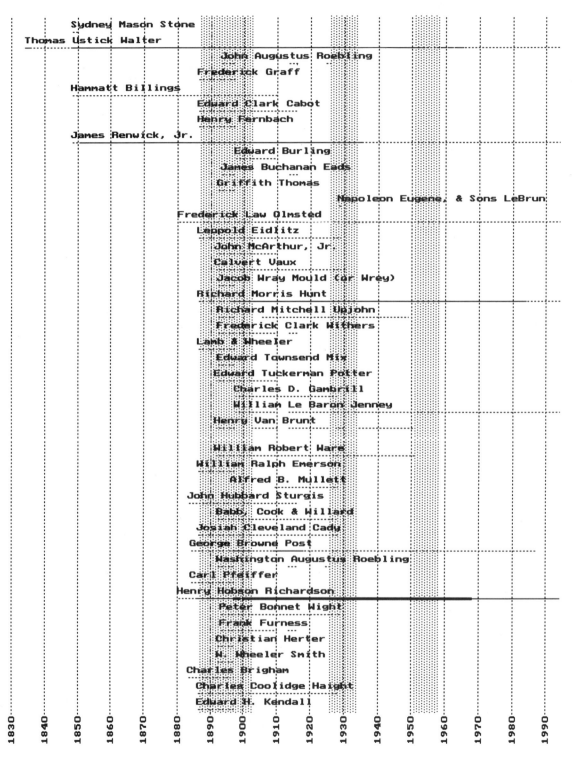

Figure 3.7   (continued)

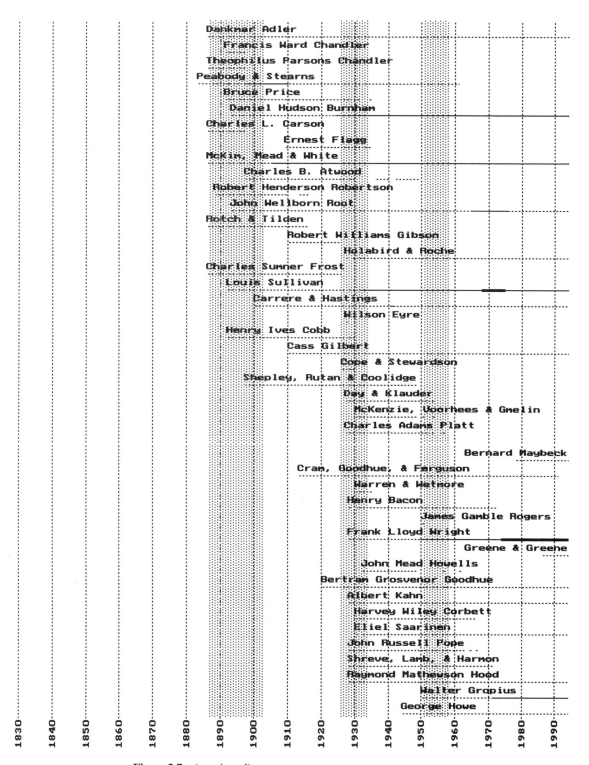

Figure 3.7   (continued)

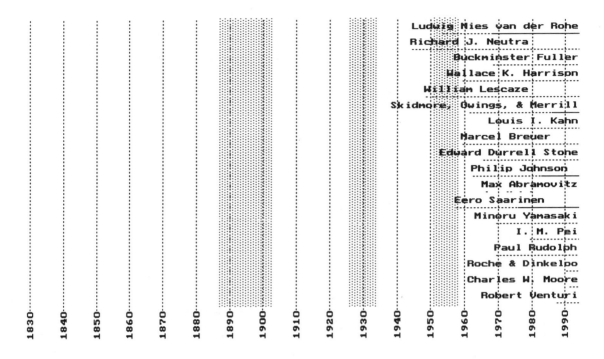

KEY

━━━━━━━━   Leading architect

──────────   Architect among 12 leading positions

··············   Architect among the 50 leading positions

Figure 3.7   (continued)

It seems reasonable to hypothesize that with developing architectural education, a person becomes familiar with an increasing number of famous architects. Let us suppose that people invariably first become conversant with work of those who are most frequently cited. The groupings of one, three, twelve, and fifty architects could embody the changing outlooks of increasingly more sophisticated readerships. The diagrams suggest the dates at which important architects are presumably recognized by different segments of the population, from the least informed, who may have heard of only one or two, to the most discriminating, who may be aware of as many of fifty names. Every architect in figure 3.5 is also in figure 3.7; the better-educated learn of them earlier and remember them longer.

The periods of intense growth identified in figure 3.2 are shaded in figure 3.7. Growth is coupled with change: many of the bars begin, vary in line style, or end during these periods, because it is during times of architectural and historiographical effervescence that reputations are made and broken.[5] Some of the changes are captured in lists of "ins" and "outs" (figure 3.8).

Figure 3.8   Realignments during periods of intense growth

First realignment, 1887–1903

In:	**Out:**
Charles B. Atwood	Charles Brigham
Babb, Cook, & Willard	Charles L. Carson
Asher Benjamin	Theophilus Parsons Chandler
Edward Burling	William Ralph Emerson
Daniel Hudson Burnham	Henry Fernbach
Carrère & Hastings	John Frazee
Henry Ives Cobb	Frederick Graff
Captain Isaac Damon	William Hamilton
Frank Furness	Edward H. Kendall
Charles D. Gambrill	Lamb & Wheeler
Andrew Hamilton	Alexander Parris
Richard Morris Hunt	Carl Pfeiffer
William Le Baron Jenney	James Renwick, Sr.
Dr. John Kearsley	William Strickland
John McArthur, Jr.	
McKim, Mead, & White	
Peabody & Stearns	
Edward Tuckerman Potter	
Bruce Price	
Henry Hobson Richardson	
Robert Henderson Robertson	
John Wellborn Root	
Shepley, Rutan, & Coolidge	
Louis Sullivan	
Richard Mitchell Upjohn	
Henry Van Brunt	
Calvert Vaux	
William Robert Ware	
Peter Bonnet Wight	
Frederick Clark Withers	
Christopher Wren	

Second realignment, 1926–1934

In:	**Out:**
Henry Bacon	Charles B. Atwood
Harvey Wiley Corbett	Babb, Cook, & Willard
Day & Klauder	Asher Benjamin
Holabird & Roche	Samuel Blodget
Raymond Mathewson Hood	Josiah Cleveland Cady
John Mead Howells	Henry Ives Cobb
Albert Kahn	Cope & Stewardson
McKenzie, Voorhees, & Gmelin	Leopold Eidlitz
McKim, Mead, & White	Charles D. Gambrill
Charles Adams Platt	Maximilien Godefroy
John Russell Pope	George Hadfield
Eliel Saarinen	Charles Coolidge Haight
Shreve, Lamb, & Harmon	Andrew Hamilton
Louis Sullivan	Alfred B. Mullett
Henry Van Brunt	Calvert Vaux
Warren & Wetmore	Peter Bonnet Wight
Frank Lloyd Wright	

Figure 3.8   (continued)

Third realignment, 1951–1958	
In:	**Out:**
Ludwig Mies van der Rohe	Charles Bulfinch
Eero Saarinen	Day & Klauder
Louis Sullivan	James Hoban
Charles Adams Platt	
Thomas Ustick Walter	

To be listed, an architect must cross one of the "gates" arbitrarily set at the third, twelfth, and fiftieth positions in the ranking, upward or downward as the case might be. No particular style, orientation, or epoch dominates among the winners or losers during the first two realignments. The incoming names for 1887–1903, for example, include members of the Chicago School (Sullivan, Root, Jenney) as well as individuals and firms of an opposite orientation (Burnham, Carrère & Hastings, McKim, Mead, & White). Colonial architects Andrew Hamilton and John Kearsley make their late appearance in the picture, even as their contemporary William Hamilton is already retreating from the public eye. During the second realignment, members of the first modern generation (Wright, Eliel Saarinen, Albert Kahn, Raymond Hood) share the limelight with traditionally minded Bacon, Pope, and McKim, Mead, & White. The third realignment, although less numerous, presents a more unified ideological profile: it marks the triumph of the Modern Movement. More about this later.

Architects' careers in the literature can be portrayed metaphorically as underwater vessels sailing the oceans. Precious few break the surface, only to plunge as others come out. Most boats lurk in dark waters at various depths all the time, struggling to come closer to the light. The surface is populated by indifferent creatures that pay scant notice to the ships, and then only to those that occasionally emerge from the waters. A few onlookers, however, busy themselves with various types of underwater viewing and listening gear, trying to enlarge the scope of their perceptions; some of them (the best critics and historians) succeed remarkably. Architects, unlike submariners who embark and land at the pier, start their journey from the darkest depths of the sea and return there on completing their voyage. Whereas seamen face certain death at one time or another, the literary odyssey often endures forever.

The Young Turks

Let us examine the distribution of birth dates of the architects populating the literary universe. Their numbers born within twenty-year periods are graphed in figure 3.9 (dotted lines). The majority were born between 1860 and 1940.

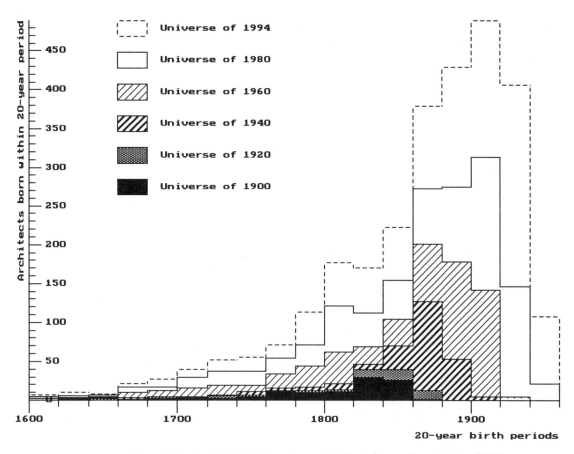

Figure 3.9   Architects in the universe distributed according to date of birth

Assuming their productive years to have started at age thirty, it follows that the bulk of the architectural literature in America is devoted to the 1890s and the twentieth century. This is not necessarily related to emerging importance of American architecture during that period. The diagram shows in various types of shading the birth distribution for various cutoff dates of the literature. All areas have approximately the same shape as the overall outline, and they peak about sixty or eighty years prior to the cutoff date. Focusing on the recent past has always been a feature of architectural discourse in this country, and perhaps in other countries as well.

Colonial and early Federal architects were almost completely ignored in the corpus until 1940, as shown by the flatness of the three lowest layers in the left side of figure 3.9; the number of architects in the universe born before 1820 has rapidly increased since. They were ignored not only by the modernist writers but also by their enemies, the classicists. The revaluation of the earliest past only came during the midtwentieth century. Before index analysis, this could be surmised impressionistically; now it is supported by figures.

Figure 3.10 Architects entering the universe classified according to age at entry and date of entry

Age at entry	Date of entry								
	1900s	1910s	1920s	1930s	1940s	1950s	1960s	1970s	1980s
40 or less	0	0	9	10	17	24	26	30	40
	0%	0%	5%	22%	13%	7%	7%	8%	4%
41–50	4	3	42	6	13	69	53	37	115
	24%	9%	22%	13%	10%	20%	14%	10%	12%
51–60	4	6	73	7	10	52	58	43	138
	24%	18%	39%	15%	8%	15%	15%	12%	14%
61–75	3	5	31	8	16	60	58	36	163
	18%	15%	16%	17%	13%	17%	15%	10%	16%
76–100	4	6	16	8	8	52	42	48	158
	24%	18%	9%	17%	6%	15%	11%	13%	16%
101–150	0	4	5	5	33	35	58	85	161
	0%	12%	3%	11%	26%	10%	15%	23%	16%
151 and up	2	9	12	2	30	54	81	84	216
	12%	27%	6%	4%	24%	16%	22%	23%	22%
Totals	17	33	188	46	127	346	376	363	991
	100%	100%	100%	100%	100%	100%	100%	100%	100%

A significant number of young architects entered the universe during the 1930s and 1940s; many were 50 years old or younger, and some were under 40 (figures 3.10 and 3.11). Never before were so many young men among the new arrivals, and their percentage, if not their numbers, steadily dwindled since. Concomitantly, old, long-dead architects reached an all-time low among the newcomers during the 1920s and the 1930s, but became an increasingly more important segment of the incoming population since.

Richard Neutra, Wallace Harrison, Marcel Breuer, Eero Saarinen, Edward Stone, and Harwell Hamilton Harris were the most conspicuous, entering the literature between 1931 and 1950 before their fortieth birthday; other young individuals or firms entering at the time were Perkins & Will, Vernon DeMars, Raphael Soriano, Carl Koch, Frederick Kiesler, Lloyd Wright, Norman Bel Geddes, Oscar Stonorov, Hugh Stubbins Jr., and John B. Yeon. Younger than fifty years of age at entry were Rudolph Schindler, Reinhard and Hofmeister, Gardner A. Daily, Buckminster Fuller, George Keck, Paul Nelson, William Wurster, and the firm of Skidmore, Owings Merrill, Pietro Belluschi, Alden Dow, and Philip Johnson, among others. The group came to dominance after the generation of Gropius and Mies. They not only altered the physical and educational landscape of America, they burst into the literature with a power that no other generation has been able to muster before or thereafter.

This could not have happened without the participation of writers. The authors associated with their emergence were Henry-Russell Hitchcock, Jr., Random Williams Sexton, Sheldon Cheney, Alfred H. Barr, Jr., Philip Johnson,

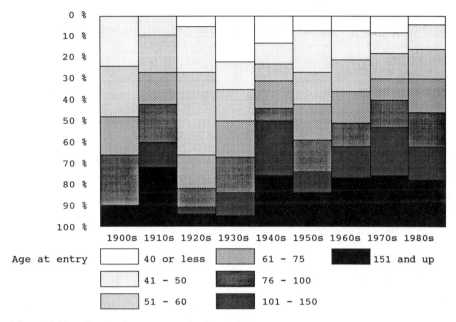

Figure 3.11   Graph of percentages in figure 3.10.

Lewis Mumford, Alfred Roth, Elizabeth Mock, and James Marston Fitch. Their works, published between 1929 and 1948, are listed at the end of this book.

Groups of architects and writers often appear involved in a complex symbiotic relationship in which some function as originators of new ideas, others as followers or reactors; they behave as an interdependent system and must be regarded as a single event in the history of architectural culture. One such group has just been mentioned; others were identified earlier in connection with the three reaccommodations. Architects and writers may participate in more than one group. A technique to search systematically for such clusters is presented in chapter 9.

Notes

1. My usage is patterned on what logicians call the *universe of discourse*, defined in *Webster's Third New International Dictionary* (1976) as an inclusive class explicitly containing all the entities to be discussed in a given discourse or investigation.

2. If the study were conducted at the scale of buildings, the universe would be composed of all the buildings cited in the literature. Only architects, however, are considered in this project.

3. Exponential growth occurs when the growth rate remains constant.

4. The seven-year rate of growth is the ratio between the size of the universe in a given year and its size seven years earlier. Seven-year periods are used to circumvent unimportant short-term fluctuations.

5. Line quality shifts are almost twice as likely to occur on a shaded area as in an unshaded one. The shaded periods last for thirty-four years, which is only 20 percent of the time represented; yet 36 percent of the bar shifts in figure 3.7 occurred during a shaded period.

4   Text Coverage

Concept and Computation Process

Certain texts of the corpus cover the entire history of architecture of the nation or the world; others are targeted to a briefer period, perhaps a century or just a few decades. One way or the other, the narrative unfolds along a delimited chronological period, which I will call the coverage span of the text. Knowing the span is a way of knowing something about the text; this is always welcome, especially if the knowledge is generated automatically by the system, using the information already collected.

Reference works such as dictionaries and guidebooks lack a plot in the conventional sense. Still, they stake out, implicitly if not explicitly, a certain temporal environment; like surveys or history books, they cover the entire span of architectural development or they focus on a shorter period. The temporal environment depends on the author's conception of history, even if it is not articulated explicitly. The coverage span of reference works is reflected in the selection of entries or examples. I doubt that texts exist that do not lend themselves to a temporal categorization, but if they do, they do not belong in the corpus: they are excluded by rule 10 set for the selection of texts in chapter 2.

Seldom do writers set clear delimiting points; more often their story has a temporal focus, with the narrative blending gradually from the preceding and into the following eras. The span can sometimes be estimated from the title, the date of publication,[1] the preface, or the chapter names. Such approximations, however, are not enough; index analysts require precise opening and closing delimiters for the coverage span. Although unusual in this context, discrete representations of continuous phenomena are routine in the sciences.

To attribute coverage spans judgmentally, one text at a time, is prohibitively taxing. It would be nearly impossible to maintain consistency, even if one were to follow rules. Fortunately, there is a better way: tentative coverage spans can be assigned automatically to every text in the corpus solely on the basis of the the lists of names cited.

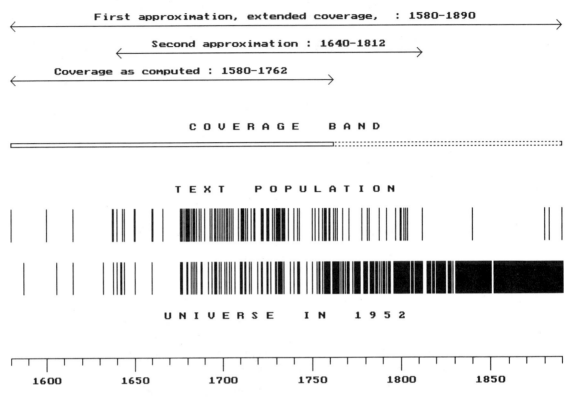

Figure 4.1   Coverage for *Early American Architecture*, by Morrison (1952)

The logic of the computation process is easy to follow. As a first approximation, the system picks the dates of birth of the earliest and latest architects cited. For example, the earliest architect cited in *Early American Architecture* by H. S. Morrison (1952) is Kryn Fredericks, born in 1580; the latest one is Harvey Partrige Smith, born around 1890. The coverage of the book is bracketed, as an outer limit, by the work of these two architects. If developments beyond this span had been featured, earlier or later names would appear in the index. Real coverage, however, may be shorter, because the outermost names could have been mentioned in passing without being significantly treated in the narrative.

This indeed is what transpires from the distribution of birth dates among the population of the text (figure 4.1). Each line in the band "text population" represents the birth date of a cited architect, aligned with the time scale at the bottom of the graph. Few, loosely scattered lines appear before 1640 or after 1812; in contrast, they are densely packed between those dates.

The second approximation to the solution of the puzzle is 1640–1812; it is more discriminating than the first, but the system can do even better. Rather than absolute density, it looks for density as it relates to the universe. As defined in chapter 3, the universe is composed of the architects cited in the literature often enough to be established in the field as seen by learned observers. The authors of the texts themselves are presumed to have been familiar with the universe as it was at the time of their writing. The universe of 1952, when *Early American Architecture* was published, is graphed in the lower band of the diagram; it is sparser during early times (left) and it becomes denser at more recent times (right).

Some names in the universe are cited in the book, others are not. Conversely, some of the names in the text are not in the universe because they have not yet obtained their second citation. Comparing the two bands it becomes apparent that Morrison picked a higher proportion of available names from the left side of the universe than from the right side; one may presume, consequently, that the book treats more thoroughly the early stages of American architecture than the later ones.

The span with the most thorough coverage is invisible to the naked eye, but it can be tentatively determined by computation, following a procedure discussed in the technical appendix. The interval obtained for Morrison is 1580–1756. Although the text population is arranged symmetrically in relation to the middle of the diagram, the period of most intense coverage is strongly tilted to the left. This is consistent with the title and content of the book. I will sometimes use *extended coverage* to refer to the entire duration between the outer limits of the text population (1580–1890). Coverage and extended coverage are represented in ensuing graphs using the notation presented as "coverage band" in figure 4.1.

Compared with the burden of case-by-case examination, the automatic procedure is very expedient. For the operation to be possible, however, it is necessary to have access to a large body of data portraying the yearly evolution of the universe. And the convenience comes at a price: the format of the results is governed by the way information is stored in the data base. If citations were arranged by building, spans could be expressed in a familiar format, by construction date of the buildings involved; but no such data base is available. The citations are organized by architect, and architects are dated by their birth; coverage spans come expressed in terms of birth dates. Actual production years can be estimated by adding approximately thirty years to the beginning and sixty or seventy years to the end of the span, to account for the time elapsed between the architects' birth and the beginning and end of their productive career. I generally refrain, however, from performing the addition, to avoid tainting observations and conclusions with an unknown quantity; readers interested in converting birth dates into project execution dates should make their own allowances.

My usage departs from the normal in other ways as well. Intensity of coverage is normally associated not only, and certainly not primarily, with the number of architects cited, but with the level of detail of the treatment, the accuracy of the statements, and the depth of the approach. Obviously none of these more substantial issues can be tested by analyzing indexes alone. Still, the number and distribution of names tells us something worth knowing about the level of detail of the discussion. This is especially true for span comparisons in a single text, as the ones made in the procedure to identify the coverage span. Coverage intensity values (as opposed to coverage spans) must not be used for comparisons between different texts, one of which might be superficial but contain many names, while the other is profound but sparse in examples.

Coverage spans must not be accepted blindly. An operator (myself in this case) must check for consistency the span returned by the system with the title and thrust of the work. If the dates obtained are at variance with the expectations, the operator must look into specifics. In most cases, the discrepancy will signal a divergence between what a book promises and what it delivers.

The U.S. Information Agency's *Architecture USA*, published in 1957, was found by the system to focus on the work of architects born between 1905 and 1924, suggesting that it represented only recent work. In a later edition (1975), the title was changed to *Modern Architecture America*, implicitly recognizing that the earlier version had been misnamed.

Rarely are computational results incongruous with actual coverage, and there is always an explanation for the discrepancy: the author may have failed to name the architects of the work discussed, the text may include background material exceeding the real thrust of the book, or the index may be defective. In such cases analysts may enter the missing names, override the results of the computation, or eliminate the text from the corpus altogether.

Coverage depends on the distribution of birth dates in the text population and in the universe, not the absolute numbers. If one of every two names in the universe (figure 4.1, lower band) were to be removed, or if a name were to be inserted in between any two, the span as computed would remain the same. This has an important practical consequence: coverage results are largely independent of the minimum number of citations stipulated for an architect to be counted in the universe. The use of two citations here is arbitrary, but it is not critical; the choice has little bearing on the computation of text coverages, which is what the universe is primarily used for in this study.

Testing the Results

Sometimes, the beginning and end of coverage are revealed or implied in the title or subtitle of a text; when that is the case, it is possible to compare system performance against authorial claims. Such texts are tabulated in figure 4.2, with the coverage as declared (in construction dates) and as computed (in architect birth dates). To facilitate the comparison, lag differentials are reported in the far right column of the table. Lags are the differences between declared and computed coverage—one for the beginning and one for the end of the period. The expected lags are forty years at the beginning of the span and seventy years at the end, reflecting the ages that bracket the most productive

Figure 4.2   Comparison of text coverages as declared in title and computed with formula

Date	Title	Coverage as Declared	Computed	Differential Begin	End
1916	Hamlin, A.D.F.: 25 Years of American Architecture	1891–1916	1832–1869	19	23
1926	Jackson: Development of American Architecture 1783–1830	1783–1830	1748–1804	5	44
1932	Hitchcock & Johnson: The International Style	1922–1932	1895–1906	13	44
1941	Architectural Record: American Architecture 1891–1941	1891–1941	1883–1905	32	34
1944	Mock: Built in America 1932–1944	1932–1944	1896–1916	4	42
1950	AIA: Contemporary Architecture in the US 1947–1949	1947–1949	1896–1926	11	47
1950	P/A: US Architecture 1900–1950	1900–1950	1858–1918	2	38
1952	Hitchcock & Drexler: Built in USA	1945–1952	1896–1923	9	41
1956	Architectural Record: 100 Years of Significant Building	1856–1956	1846–1918	30	32
1957	Gutheim: 1857–1957. One Hundred Years of Architecture in America	1857–1957	1802–1917	15	30
1959	Bode: The Anatomy of American Popular Culture 1840–61	1840–1861	1764–1818	36	27
1965	Collins: Changing Ideals in Modern Architecture	1750–1950	1839–1918	129	38
1966	Jacobus: 20th C Architecture. The Middle Years 1940–66	1940–1966	1867–1926	33	30
1969	Joedicke: Architecture Since 1945	1945–1969	1883–1923	22	24
1969	Whiffen: American Architecture Since 1780	1780–1969	1757–1887	17	12
1974	Kidney: Architecture of Choice: Eclecticism in America 1880–1930	1880–1930	1822–1883	18	23
1976	Hammett: Architecture in the United States	1776–1976	1743–1934	7	28
1976	Panek: American Architectural Styles 1600–1940	1600–1940	1716–1883	156	13
1979	The American Renaissance 1876–1917 (without Catalogue)	1876–1919	1811–1874	25	25
1979	The American Renaissance 1876–1917 (Catalogue only)	1876–1919	1818–1874	18	25
1980	Davern: Architecture 1970–1980	1970–1980	1917–1942	13	32
1980	GA Document Special Issue 1970–1980	1970–1980	1915–1949	15	39
1981	Whiffen & Koepper: American Architecture 1607–1976	1607–1976	1615–1938	48	32
1982	Curtis: Modern Architecture Since 1900	1900–1982	1846–1942	14	30
1982	McCoy & Goldstein: Guide to US Architecture 1940–80	1940–1980	1901–1946	1	36
1982	Wright: Highlights to Recent American Architecture 1945–1978	1945–1978	1895–1938	10	30
1983	Frampton (w. Futagawa): Modern Architecture 1851–1945	1851–1945	1832–1902	21	27
1986	Wilson et al: The Machine Age in America 1918–1941	1918–1941	1875–1903	3	32
1987	Oppenheimer Dean: 75 Turbulent Years of American Architecture	1912–1987	1846–1949	26	32
1988	Pulos: The American Design Adventure. 1940–1975	1940–1975	1895–1919	5	14
1989	Russell: Architecture and Design 1970–1990	1970–1990	1938–1959	8	39
1990	AIA: American Architecture of the 1980s.	1980–1989	1936–1959	4	40
1992	Whiffen: American Architecture Since 1780, rev. ed.	1780–1992	1757–1886	17	36

Note: Shaded background flags large differentials.

years in the lives of most architects. The lag differentials are the differences in absolute value between the lags as expected and as found.

Ideally, all lags should equal zero, but this is unrealistic for several reasons. First, not every architect starts work at age forty or retires at seventy. Second, buildings are not necessarily published immediately on completion. Third, many birth dates of architects cited in the texts are unknown, and were estimated to the nearest decade. Fourth, not every writer necessarily delivers to the mark what he or she promises. And last but not least, estimating coverage on the basis of indexes alone cannot possibly duplicate titles exactly.

What is an admissible error? This is a matter of judgment. A system that pinpoints coverages with an approximation of one generation (32 years) seems acceptable to me. In the case of the five texts marked with half-tone background in figure 4.2, the divergence between spans as declared and as computed is clearly excessive. Let us examine them one by one.

To commemorate its first half-century, *Architectural Record* published a special issue in January 1941 entitled "American Architecture: 1891–1941." The architects featured in the journal, either on the illustrated pages or in an introductory symposium, are listed in figure 4.3, sorted by birth date. The span as computed is 1883–1905, represented by the clear area. If the span is correct, the title is wrong: rather than half a century, the work seemingly covers only two decades. A more appropriate pair of dates for the title would have been 1921–1941.

One may wonder whether the earlier names, printed in the figure in half-tone, are sufficiently significant to justify the coverage as claimed. The list includes architects of limited importance and it misses Eliel Saarinen and Frank Lloyd Wright. This casts a shadow over the judgment of the editors, but that is not what is at stake here. The declared coverage is called into question not because of the choice of names (the subject matter of chapter 7), but because of the distribution of birth dates. Too few architects of the list were born before 1883, compared with the large numbers found in the universe. A twenty-year hiatus is seen from 1862 to 1882, yet more than 350 architects in the roster were born during those two decades. Almost an entire generation of architects has been ignored! Coverage as computed reflects the real contents of the text more accurately than coverage as declared.

The next case is different. Peter Collins appended the dates 1750–1950 to the title of his book *Changing Ideals in Modern Architecture* (1965); the formula yields 1839–1918, or 1870–1950 if expressed as work years. No contradiction exists this time. As indicated in chapter 2, only American architects are referenced in this project. Collins deals with two centuries, but the American contribution to the events described, which is what the formula measures, is concentrated in the last eight decades.

In his monograph *American Architectural Styles 1600–1940* (1976), R. T. Panek chose to identify by name only professional architects or builders; the work of persons designing or building their own houses and the contributions

Figure 4.3 Architects cited in *Architectural Record: American Architecture 1891–1941* sorted by birth date

Date	Name
1832	William Le Baron Jenney
1838	Clinton & Russell
1847	Henry Janeway Hardenbergh
1849	Robert Henderson Robertson
1850?	Classic Design & Detail Co.
1850?	Joseph K. Frietag
1853	Bradford Lee Gilbert
1856	Louis Sullivan
1859	James Brown Lord
1861	John and Donald B. Parkinson
1883	Walter Dorwin Teague, Sr.
1886	Holabird & Root
1888	Gordon B. Kaufman
1889	Julius R. Davidson
1890?	Donald Dwight Williams
1890?	Emmons H. Woolwin
1890?	Morris Sanders
1890?	Sebastian J. Tauriello
1892	Richard J. Neutra
1892	Thimothy L. Pflueger
1893	Raymond Loewy
1894	Gilbert Rohde
1895	Wurster, Bernardi, & Emmons
1895	Gardner A. Dailey
1895	George Fred Keck
1895	William Henley Dietrick
1897	Skidmore, Owings, & Merrill
1897	Albert Mayer
1900	Miller, Martin, & Lewis
1900	Arthur T. Brown
1900?	George B. Brigham
1900?	J. H. Christie, H. L. Gilman, R. J. Wirth
1900?	Aaron Colish
1900?	Oscar Fisher
1900?	William E. Foster
1900?	H. L. Gogerty
1900?	Harold Spitznagel
1900?	John Harwood
1900?	Huntington, Jones, & Hunter
1900?	Bernard A. Morse
1900?	Edouard J. Mutrux and William A. Bernoudy
1900?	Paul Bry
1900	Richard Sundeleaf
1900	Sewall Smith
1900?	C. B. Troedsson
1900?	D. O. Whilldin

Figure 4.3   (continued)

Date	Name
1900?	Williams & Grimes
1901	Mario F. Corbett
1902	Morris Lapidus
1903	Harwell Hamilton Harris
1904	Alden B. Dow
1905?	Clarence W. W. Mayhew
1912	Wilson, Morris, Crain, & Anderson

of early Spanish missionaries is discussed, but the builders themselves remain nameless. If one were to include them in the index, the real range of the monograph would come through when processed. The same applies to *American Architecture 1607–1976*, by Whiffen and Koepper (1981). The title opening date was elected because of the founding of Jamestown, Virginia, the first permanent British settlement in America.[2] The beginning as detected by the formula is around 1615, the birth date of Arthur Allen, the earliest architect cited in the work. The discrepancy is due to the scarcity of names of architects in the earliest Colonial times; under the circumstances, the system cannot perform any better.

When Whiffen first published *American Architecture Since 1780* in 1969, the title implied that coverage was extended to publication time, and the implication was born out by index analysis. The revised edition of 1992 included twenty-five young new architects; still, the universe had grown faster in the intervening years, and the system assigned the new version almost the same coverage as the old one. The text is flagged in figure 4.2 because, despite the additions, not enough younger architects are featured to warrant extension of the coverage up to 1992.

Divergence between authorial declarations and system estimates has been, I believe, rationalized. The operator may adjust the coverage of certain texts to make allowances for special circumstances. As far as I can tell, however, the formula need not be changed: it works better than any of the alternatives considered.

Coverage Spans

The coverage span of every text in the corpus as appraised by the system and accepted or modified by an operator is now included in the data base. The values are accessible through the electronic companion to this book.

Looking at the information collected, it becomes clear that not every period in American architectural history is granted the same attention in the literature; some have been examined in more texts of the corpus than others. Aggregate yearly text coverage is graphed in figure 4.4. Birth dates are represented along

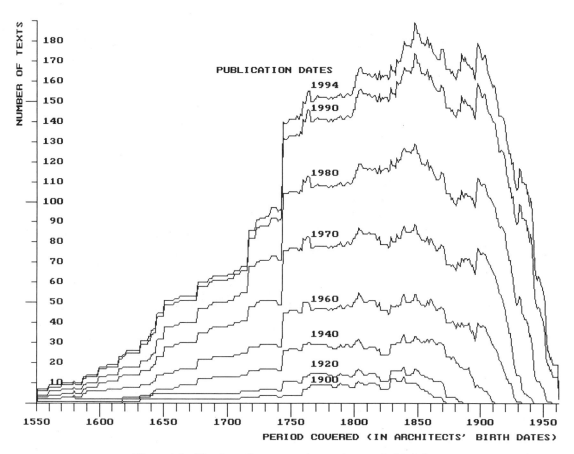

Figure 4.4   Number of texts covering various periods of the past

a horizontal axis; numbers of texts are displayed vertically. Several curves are drawn, each for a specific cut-off publication date. As time passes, more texts are published, raising the height of the curves. The graph complements figure 3.9. That figure portrays the number of architects in the literary universe born within various date intervals; this one represents the number of texts in the corpus dealing with their work. Both reveal a heavy tilt in favor of architects born around the midnineteenth century: not only do the texts include more architects of that period, but more texts are devoted to their work than to any other group.

A notorious discontinuity occurs for 1743, the date of birth of Thomas Jefferson. Fully forty-three texts in the corpus start their coverage of American architecture precisely at this point. Significantly, the dislocation begins to be noticeable only in the years after 1940. Viewing Jefferson as the dawn of American architecture implies disregard of the Colonial tradition, and this started to materialize coincidentally with the rise of the Modern Movement. The demise of Modernism, in turn, is congruent with the revaluation of the earliest past; the breakpoint in the curves for 1743 is not likely to continue growing.

The curves of figure 4.4 also represent the number of texts covering each architect's lifetime as a function of birth date. The number defines their potential citations; the citations would be actual if the individual had been cited in every text that included the birth date in its coverage span. This rarely happens, and most architects have far fewer citations. An exceptional case is an architect who may be cited more often than his potential if he is featured in texts not specifically devoted to his times. This is often true of Frank Lloyd Wright. Potential citations are very consequential pieces of information; much of the material in the following chapters is built around them.

The coverage of the 1910 edition of *The Encyclopaedia Britannica* spans from 1519 to 1870. In addition, 1519 is the birth date of the earliest architect documented in the entire data base; 1870 was the birth of the very youngest architect in the universe of 1910: the text's coverage coincides with the range of the entire universe! The case is extraordinary; it happens with only four other items in the corpus.[3] It does not mean that the *Encyclopaedia* features everybody in the universe, which would be neither possible nor desirable; but it shows that the weight given to the various historical periods in these five texts (as reflected in their distribution of names) coincides with a norm collectively developed over the years and represented by the entire corpus. The *Encyclopaedia Britannica* maintained its normative character through subsequent editions, despite continual enlargements in the range of the universe. It was still true for the 1964 edition, but the work started to loose ground in 1972. In terms of the relation between text and universe, the fifteenth edition of 1981 was unremarkable.

Such fluctuations are reflected in the evolution of *gamma*, one more variable computed automatically by the system. Gamma is the ratio between a text's span and the range of the universe at publication time. It varies between zero and one. When most of the range of the universe as known at publication time is covered, gamma is high; otherwise it is low. The decline of gamma through successive editions of the *Encyclopaedia Britannica* is shown in figure 4.5. Pe-

Figure 4.5 Gamma values for select editions of the *Encyclopaedia Britannica* (by publication date)

Gamma	Date	Title	Low coverage periods
1.00	1910	*The Encyclopaedia Britannica*, 11th ed.	None
1.00	1964	*Encyclopaedia Britannica*, 14th ed. (1964)	None
0.96	1972	*Encyclopaedia Britannica*, 14th ed. (1972)	1920s–1930s
0.60	1981	*The New Encyclopaedia Britannica*, 15th ed.	1600s–1720s 1930s–1950s

Note: periods are expressed in terms of architects' birth dates

riods of low coverage are reported in the right-hand column. The relatively low gamma of the 1981 edition, for example, results from too few architects featured in the work at both ends of the spectrum. More Colonial architects, cabinetmakers, and builders, and more architects of the younger generation should have been included to keep up with the tradition of comprehensiveness established in earlier editions, and to remain responsive to evolving societal interests.

High gamma values are neither necessary nor appropriate for every type of text. Gamma is always small in works devoted to shorter periods; but a low value in a general reference work or a comprehensive history flags the possibility of a deficient coverage for certain epochs. Gammas and periods of low coverage for selected texts[4] in the corpus are shown in figure 4.6.

Coverage Profiles

The coverage profile is another useful text descriptor generated by the system.

The coverage span described and used in the preceding sections is the interval that maximizes an intensity value returned by a formula, presented in the technical appendix; to find the value, the system must test every relevant interval. Figure 4.7 displays some of the results[5] obtained for *Early American Architecture*, the example used for figure 4.1. The highest value, noted in the table with clear background, occurs in row 1580, column 1762, which mark the beginning and end of the coverage of the text. It is assigned conventionally the value 100. Coverage intensity, expressed as a percentage of the maximum, decreases as one moves away from the peak. Shading is used in the figure to help visualize the pattern, with darker gray for higher percentages. The distribution of these values holds the key to the coverage profile.

Examination of the matrix is cumbersome, even with the help of shading. Profiles are easier to visualize if the information is displayed in a three-dimensional graph, with horizontal coordinates used for the beginning and ending dates of the spans, and coverage intensities displayed in the third dimension. By linking contiguous points in the matrix with segments, one generates a lattice, like a fisherman's net, rising and plunging through crests and valleys. This surface is the coverage profile. The peak is at the highest value in the matrix; its horizontal coordinates represent the coverage span.

As shown in figure 4.8, these same profiles can be represented as flat diagrams. A time scale runs along the base from the birth of the earliest to the latest architect cited in the text. Every point in the triangle corresponds to an interval defined by two coordinates (dates)—beginning and end. The closer a point to the apex of the triangle, the longer the span; the closer to the base, the shorter. Points toward the left correspond to earlier spans; toward the right, to more recent ones. Coverage intensity (in the third dimension) is read with the help of appropriately spaced level curves, as in a topographic map. Stars are

Figure 4.6   Gamma values for select texts (by decreasing gamma values)

Gamma	Date	Title	Low coverage periods
1.00	1960	Pierson & Davidson: *Arts in the United States*	None
1.00	1964	Tschacbasov: *Teachers Manual for the Study of Art History*	None
1.00	1992	Gowans: *Styles and Types of North American Architecture*	None
0.99	1976	Smith, K.: *A Pictorial History of Architecture in America*	1930s–1940s
0.96	1968	Norman: *Traveler's Guide to American Art*	1920s–1930s
0.95	1928	Kimball: *American Architecture*	1630s–1640s
0.92	1981	Whiffen & Koepper: *American Architecture 1607–1976*	1600s–1610s 1930–1950s
0.91	1994	Packard (ed.): *Encyclopedia of American Architecture* (main entries only)	1600s–1630s
0.91	1984	Hunt: *American Architecture: A Field Guide*	1600s–1610s 1930s–1950s
0.89	1985	Klein & Fogle: *Clues to American Architecture*	1600s–1620s 1940s–1950s
0.85	1966	Green: *American Art: A Historical Survey*	1600s–1640s
0.85	1902	Schuyler: "United States Architecture"	1630s–1630s 1810s–1840s
0.85	1979	Roth: *A Concise History of American Architecture*	1600s–1640s 1940s–1950s
0.83	1966	Fitch: *American Building: The Historical Forces that Shaped It*	1600s–1640s 1920s–1930s
0.82	1988	Norberg–Schulz: *New World Architecture*	1600s–1640s 1940s–1950s
0.81	1981	Rugoff: *Encyclopedia of American Art*	1600s–1630s 1920s–1950s
0.81	1949	Larkin: *Art and Life in America*	1850s–1910s
0.81	1929	LaFollette: *Art in America*	1630s–1670s
0.80	1970	Mendelowitz: *A History of American Art*	1600s–1640s 1920s–1930s
0.79	1928	Jackman: *American Arts*	1630s–1680s
0.78	1985	Handlin: *American Architecture*	1600s–1630s 1910s–1950s
0.75	1979	Brown et al.: *American Art*	1600s–1630s 1900s–1930s
0.74	1971	Cohen: *History of American Art*	1600s–1640s
0.69	1935	Cahill & Barr: *Art in America*	1630s–1710s
0.69	1964	Gowans: *Images of American Living*	1820s–1930s
0.69	1986	Stern: *Pride of Place: Building the American Dream*	1600s–1630s 1880s–1950s
0.68	1955	Andrews: *Architecture, Ambition, and Americans*	1600s–1640s 1860s–1910s
0.67	1980	Hunt: *Encyclopedia of American Architecture*	1600s–1700s
0.66	1969	Scully: *American Architecture and Urbanism*	1600s–1710s
0.64	1970	Osborne: *The Oxford Companion to Art*	1600s–1610s 1830s–1930s

Figure 4.6   (continued)

Gamma	Date	Title	Low coverage periods
0.64	1981	Thorndike: *Three Centuries of Notable American Architects*	1600s–1710s 1940s–1950s
0.64	1972	Bacon: *Architecture and Townscape*	1600s–1640s 1860s–1930s
0.61	1976	*The World Almanac and Book of Facts 1977*	1600s–1710s 1920s–1940s
0.57	1927	Tallmadge: *The Story of Architecture in America*	1630s–1740s
0.56	1976	Hammett: *Architecture in the United States*	1600s–1740s 1930s–1940s
0.56	1961	Burchard & Bush-Brown: *The Architecture of America*	1600s–1740s
0.56	1968	McLanathan: *The American Tradition in the Arts*	1600s–1640s 1830s–1930s
0.55	1948	Fitch: *American Building: The Forces that Shape It*	1600s–1740s
0.51	1960	Andrews: *Architecture in America*	1600s–1710s 1840s–1870s 1910s–1920s
0.49	1968	Condit: *American Building . . . from beginning to the Present*	1600s–1750s 1920s–1930s
0.48	1983	Pulos: *American Design Ethic: A History of Industrial Design to 1940*	1600s–1740s 1910s–1950s
0.48	1971	*The World Almanac and Book of Facts 1972*	1600s–1760s 1920s–1930s
0.46	1981	*The World Almanac and Book of Facts 1982*	1600s–1760s 1920s–1950s
0.45	1982	Condit: *American Building: Materials and Techniques*	1600s–1750s 1910s–1950s
0.45	1990	*The World Almanac and Book of Facts 1991*	1600s–1760s 1920s–1950s
0.44	1955	Tunnard & Reed: *American Skyline*	1600s–1740s 1880s–1910s
0.43	1985	Maddex: *Built in the USA: American Buildings from A to Z*	1600s–1740s 1890s–1950s
0.38	1966	*The World Almanac and Book of Facts 1967*	1600s–1760s 1870s–1890s 1910s–1930s
0.38	1969	Whiffen: *American Architecture Since 1780*	1600s–1750s 1880s–1930s
0.38	1893	Baedecker: *The United States*	1710s–1800s
0.37	1949	Bannister: *From Colony to Nation*	1600s–1640s 1760s–1910s
0.36	1980	Rifkind: *A Field Guide to American Architecture*	1600s–1740s 1870s–1950s
0.33	1987	Kostof: *America by Design*	1600s–1730s 1860s–1950s
0.33	1962	*The World Almanac and Book of Facts 1962*	1600s–1760s 1870s–1920s

Figure 4.6   (continued)

Gamma	Date	Title	Low coverage periods
0.26	1984	Poppeliers et al.: *What Style Is It?*	1600s–1790s 1890s–1950s
0.18	1880	Benjamin: *Art in America*	1710s–1820s
0.17	1851	Greenough: "American Architecture" and "Aesthetics at Washington"	1710s–1790s
0.16	1909	Bragdon: "Architecture in The United States"	1630s–1740s 1750s–1840s
0.14	1926	Hamlin, T.: *The American Spirit in Architecture*	1630s–1850s
0.11	1932	*The World Almanac and Book of Facts 1932*	1630s–1830s 1860s–1900s
0.10	1964	Creighton: *American Architecture*	1600s–1890s
0.09	1925	Kimball: *Three Centuries of American Architecture*	1630s–1740s 1760s–1870s
0.08	1937	*The World Almanac and Book of Facts 1937*	1600s–1830s 1860s–1900s
0.07	1957	USIA: *Architecture USA* (ed.: Blake?)	1600s–1900s

Note: periods are expressed in terms of architects' birth dates

used to mark the peak, which may or may not coincide with the apex of the triangle. Coverage profiles of selected texts (figures 4.9–4.35) are scaled so that the extended coverage always coincides with the width of the diagram. The coverage band is shown at the bottom, between the surface and the time scale. Three-dimensional views are provided for figures 4.9, 4.14, and 4.27. They are helpful at first, but once users are familiarized with flat projections they will find them more informative.

The profile of *Early American Architecture* (figure 4.9) shows a plateau of considerable size around the peak, delimited (say) by the highest-level curve. Intervals within this area are covered in the book with acceptable detail. The profile drops toward the right-hand corner of the triangle, signaling scant coverage for late nineteenth- and early twentieth-century architecture. It looses height toward the left corner almost as precipitously as toward the right, showing that *Early American Architecture* is not a good source for architects born between 1580 and 1650. This could not have been deduced from the title of the book or even its span. Although the terrain is not as low near the apex of the triangle as it is near the other two corners, it is considerably lower than near the peak, indicating that the text does not provide good coverage of the entire period between the earliest and latest architects cited.

Profiles come in a limited number of typical patterns, some of which are more adequate than others for certain types of texts: a pattern admissible in a collection of essays may prove dubious in a history book or a reference work.

Development of American Architecture 1783–1830, by Joseph Francis Ambrose Jackson (1926, figure 4.10) displays the same pattern, even if the dates

Figure 4.7 Morrison: *Early American Architecture* (1952). Coverage profile in matrix form

	1600	1637	1650	1666	1680	1688	1697	1705	1713	1722	1730	1740	1754	1762	1771	1782	1792	1802	1840	1890
1580	20	20	31	39	52	61	67	74	79	85	91	98	100	100	96	92	87	83	68	45
1615		14	28	36	50	60	65	73	78	84	90	98	99	99	95	91	86	82	67	44
1643			28	40	53	61	66	73	78	84	90	98	98	99	94	90	84	81	65	43
1660				30	45	54	60	68	74	80	86	94	95	95	91	86	81	78	63	41
1676					36	48	55	63	69	76	82	91	92	92	88	84	79	75	61	40
1684						25	36	49	56	64	71	81	82	83	79	75	71	68	55	36
1693							25	41	50	58	66	77	78	79	75	71	66	64	51	33
1701								25	38	49	58	69	71	72	69	65	60	58	46	30
1709									27	41	51	64	66	67	64	60	56	54	43	28
1718										29	42	57	59	60	57	53	49	48	38	24
1726											23	45	48	51	48	45	42	41	33	21
1734												29	33	38	36	35	32	32	26	17
1750													15	26	26	25	24	25	20	13
1758														14	17	18	17	19	16	11
1767															8	11	11	14	12	8
1778																11	10	13	11	7
1788																	8	11	9	6
1797																		9	8	5
1812																			2	3
1880																				3

Maximum coverage
75–99% of maximum coverage
50–74% of maximum coverage
25–49% of maximum coverage
0–24% of maximum coverage

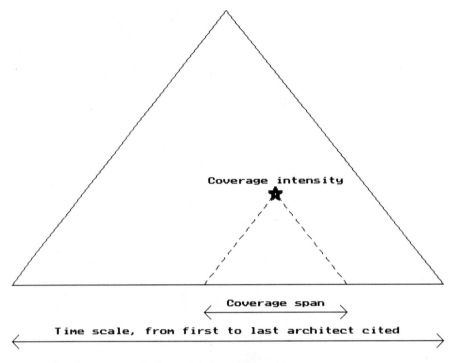

Figure 4.8   Coverage profile in graphic form (diagram)

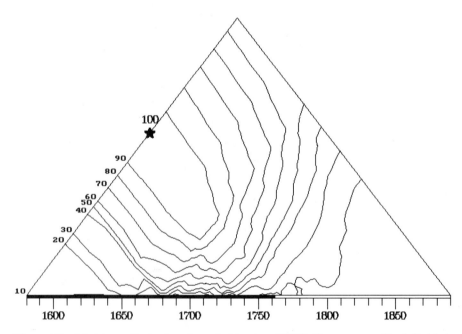

Figure 4.9   Morrison: *Early American Architecture* (1952). Coverage profile: left-sided half-hill

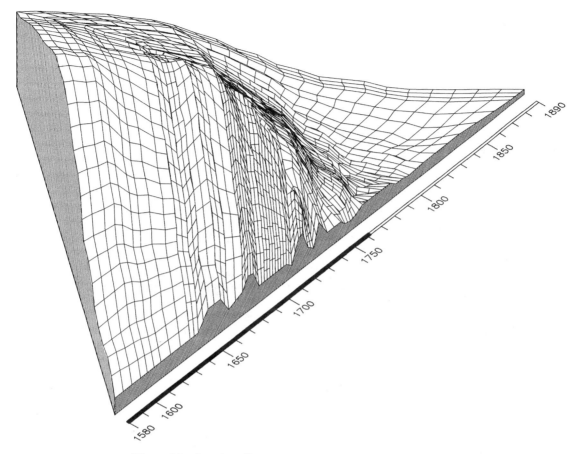

Figure 4.9   (continued)

and the position of the peak vary. Let us call it a left-sided half-hill because it resembles a hill sliced in two at the left edge of the diagram. The peak and the surrounding plateau on the left show that the text focuses on the distant past.

The pattern also occurs in texts covering the present. *Images of American Living* by Gowans (1964) is a general historical survey reaching the twentieth century, including a section on the last fifteen years. But Gowans paid more attention to the seventeenth and eighteenth centuries than was customary in the literature at the time of his writing, and that triggered the pattern (figure 4.11). The same is true of *Architecture Nineteenth and Twentieth Centuries* (1958) by Henry-Russell Hitchcock (figure 4.12), a book that underscores American contributions to the architecture of the world during the nineteenth century more forcefully than was (and is) usual.

Right-sided half-hills (figures 4.13–4.20) reveal a concentration on the present and immediate past. The present varies from case to case; Sylvia Hart Wright's *Sourcebook of Contemporary North American Architecture from Postwar to Postmodern*, published in 1989 (figure 4.20), does not cover the same

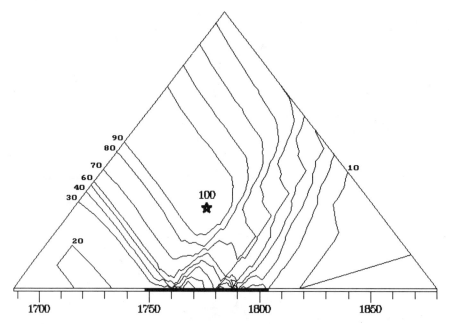

Figure 4.10   Jackson: *Development of American Architecture 1783–1830* (1926). Coverage profile: left-sided half hill

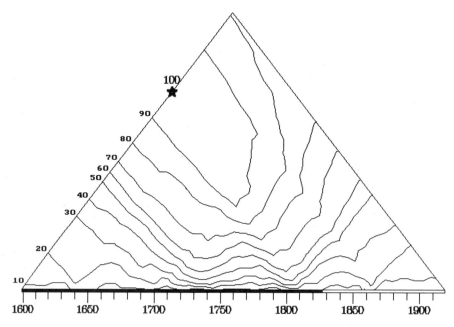

Figure 4.11   Gowens: *Images of American Living* (1964). Coverage profile: left-sided half-hill

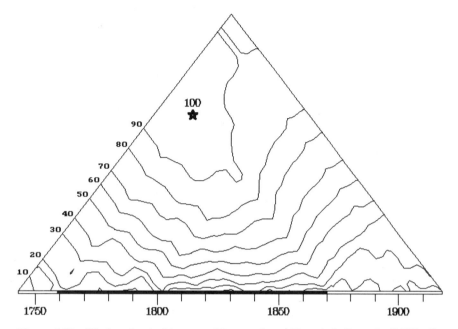

Figure 4.12 Hitchcock: *Architecture: Nineteenth and Twentieth Centuries* (1958). Coverage profile: left-sided half-hill

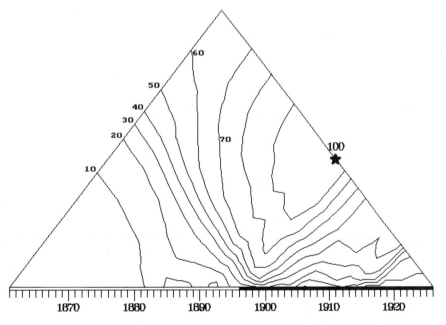

Figure 4.13 AIA: *Contemporary Architecture in the United States 1947–1949* (1950). Coverage profile: right-sided half-hill

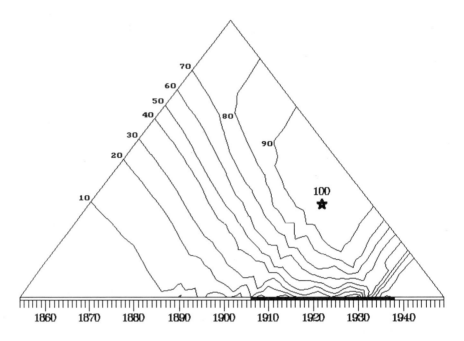

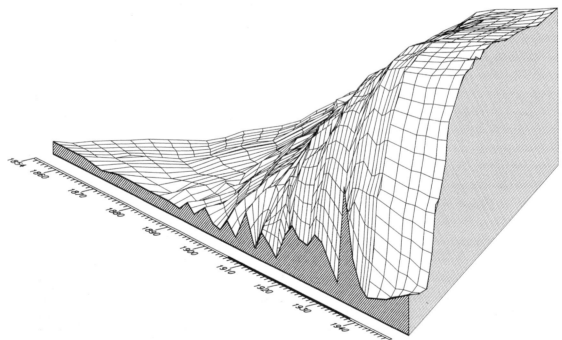

Figure 4.14   Drexler: *Transformations in Modern Architecture* (1979). Coverage profile: right-sided half-hill

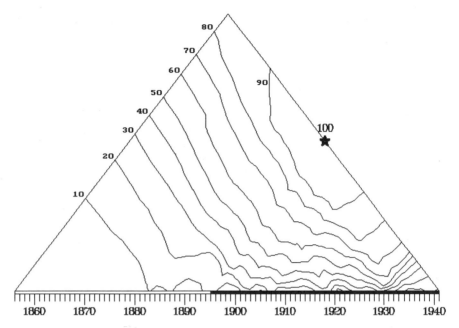

Figure 4.15   Emanuel (ed.): *Contemporary Architects* (1980). Coverage profile: right-sided half-hill

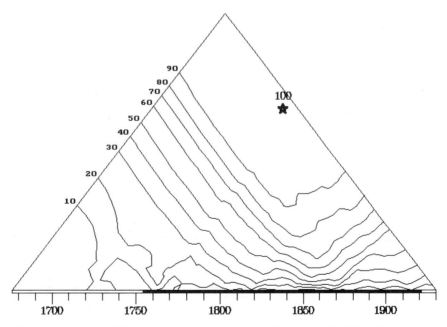

Figure 4.16   *Macmillan Encyclopedia of Architects* (Placzek, ed.) (1982). Coverage profile: right-sided half-hill

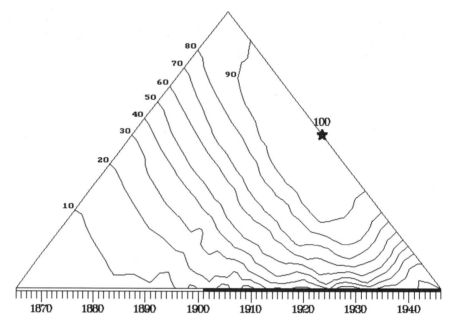

Figure 4.17 McCoy & Goldstein: *Guide to United States Architecture 1940–1980* (1982). Coverage profile: right-sided half-hill

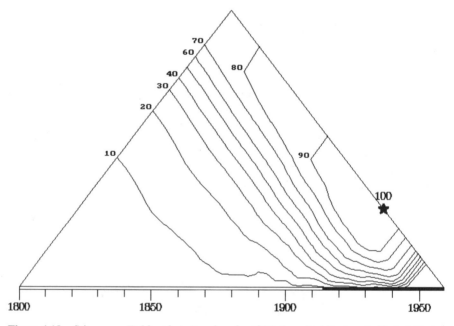

Figure 4.18 Stimpson: *Fieldguide to Landmarks of Modern Architecture in United States* (1985). Coverage profile: right-sided half-hill

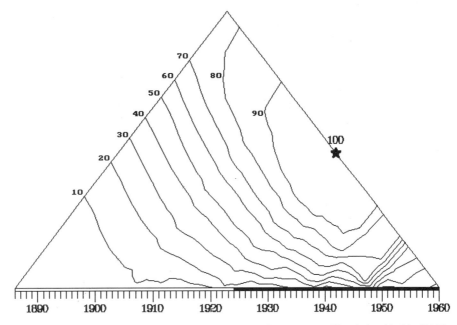

Figure 4.19   Krantz: *American Architects* (1989). Coverage profile: right-sided half-hill

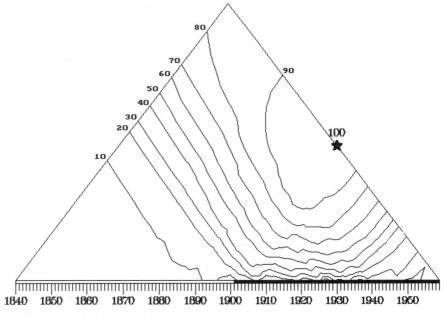

Figure 4.20   Wright: *Sourcebook of Contemporary North American Architecture* (1989). Coverage profile: right-sided half-hill

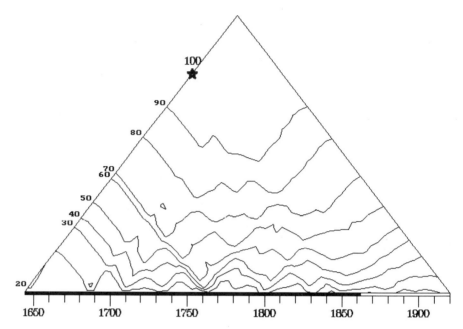

Figure 4.21   Andrews: *Architecture, Ambition, and Americans* (1955). Coverage profile: wedge

ground as, say, AIA's *Contemporary Architecture in the United States* (1950, figure 4.13). They are connected by coverage pattern, not by subject matter. Interestingly, most reference works have this kind of profile. This type of equivalence has not yet been explored because until very recently we lacked the necessary conceptual constructs.

Still another pattern found in the corpus is the wedge or quarter hill. The peak is on or near the apex, and the surface is bilaterally symmetrical, with no preference shown for the past or the present; because of its ecumenicity, it is desirable for general histories, text books, and reference works (figures 4.21–4.29).

One of the most interesting patterns, and one of the rarest, is the multinuclear, which features not one peak, but two or more. Newcomb's *Spanish-Colonial Architecture in the United States* (1937) displays two crests, one for 1519–1580 and the other for 1876–1900 (figure 4.30). The two areas of concentration are congruent with the subject matter: one is for the original Colonial builders of the sixteenth and early seventeenth centuries, and the other is for the late nineteenth- and early twentieth-century Neocolonial architects.

Macrae-Gibson's *The Secret Life of Buildings* (1985) is also multinuclear (figure 4.31). It features a series of essays on works by seven contemporary architects, Gehry, Eisenman, Pelli, Graves, Stern, Greenberg, and Venturi Rauch & Scott Brown, all born between 1923 and 1939. These names trigger one of the peaks of the profile. But the author uncovers "figures in the shadows" behind their work, a "secret life" populated by the ghosts of Richardson,

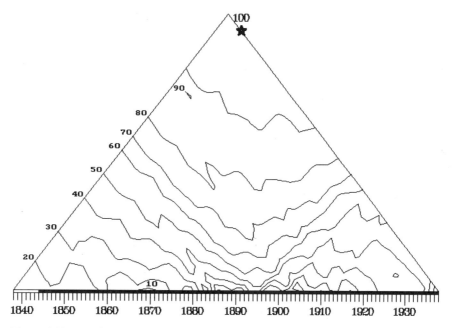

Figure 4.22   Jacobus: *American Art of the 20th Century* (1973). Coverage profile: wedge

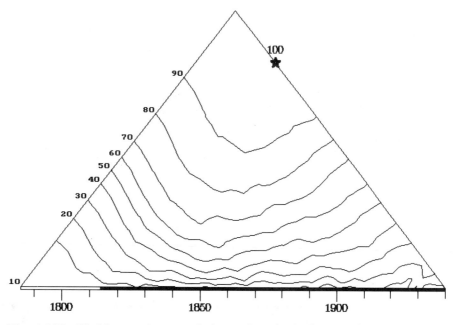

Figure 4.23   Wodehouse: *American Architects from the Civil War to the Present* (1976). Coverage profile: wedge

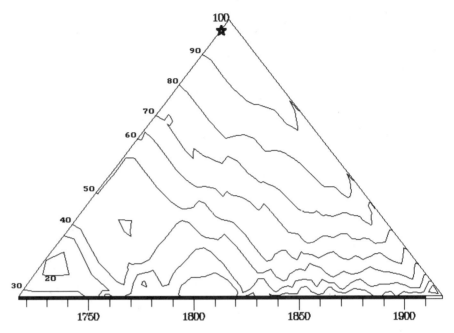

Figure 4.24   Richards: *Who's is Who in Architecture* (1977) (main entries only). Coverage profile: wedge

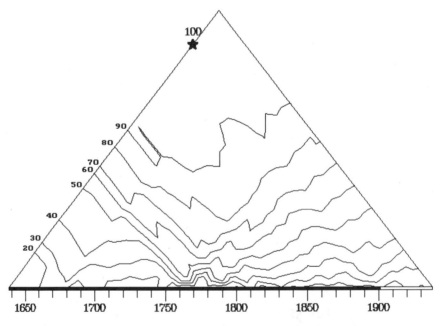

Figure 4.25   Brown et al.: *American Art* (1979). Coverage profile: wedge

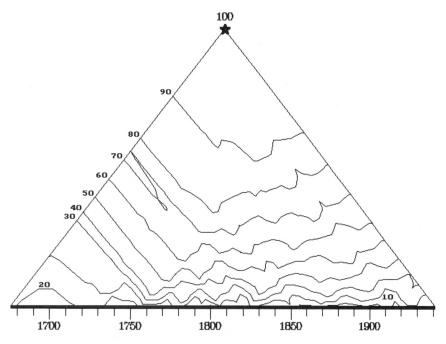

Figure 4.26   Reid: *The Book of Buildings* (1980). Coverage profile: wedge

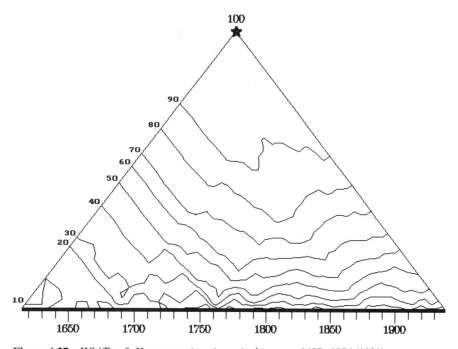

Figure 4.27   Whiffen & Koepper: *American Architecture 1607–1976* (1981)

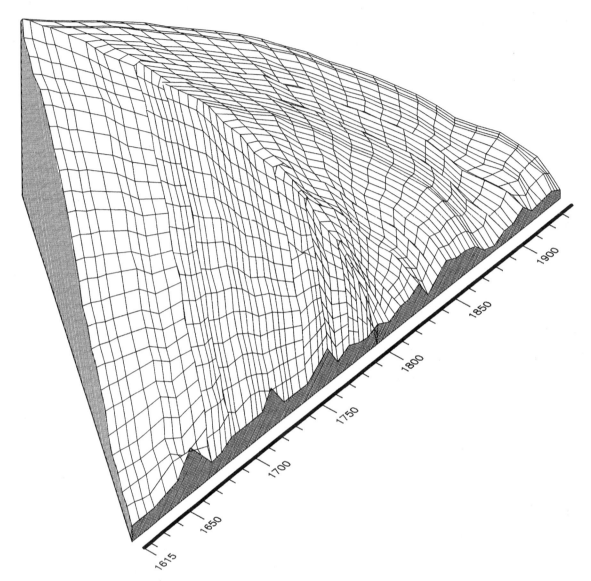

Figure 4.27   (continued)

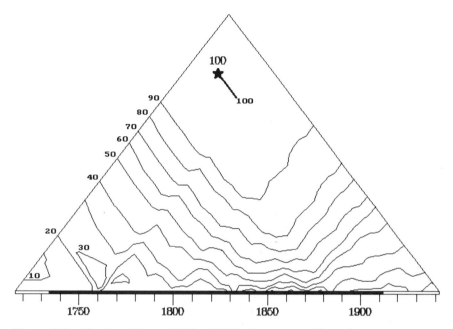

Figure 4.28   Maddex: *Master Builders* (1985) Coverage profile: wedge

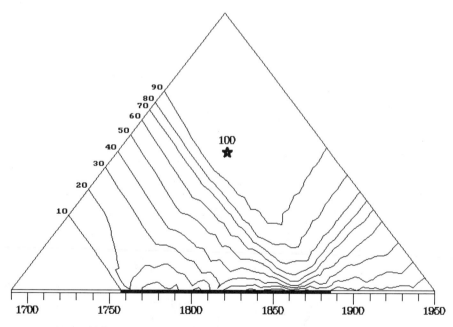

Figure 4.29   Whiffen: *American Architecture Since 1780* (1992). Coverage profile: wedge

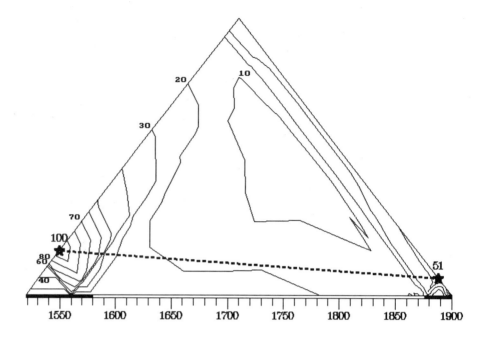

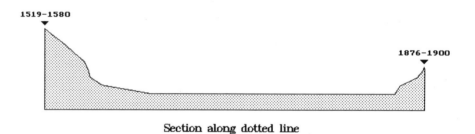

Section along dotted line

Figure 4.30 Newcomb: *Spanish-Colonial Architecture in the United States* (1937). Coverage profile: multinuclear

Sullivan, Cram, Wright, Mies, and the firm of McKim, Mead, & White. This older group of architects configures the other focus in the author's discourse.

Key Monuments in the History of Architecture, edited by Millon, (1965, figure 4.32) has not two but three peaks. Conceived as a companion to Janson's *Key Monuments of the History of Art*, which in turn was intended to provide historically significant examples compatible with any interpretation of art history, the work deliberately lacks a narrative line; in an aggregate of semiindependent chapters, polinuclearity is almost to be expected. (Another cause for multiple peaks in *Key Monuments* is discussed in chapter 10.)

The plurality of peaks in these examples is consistent with the goals and program of the writers. This, however, is not necessarily always true; when the

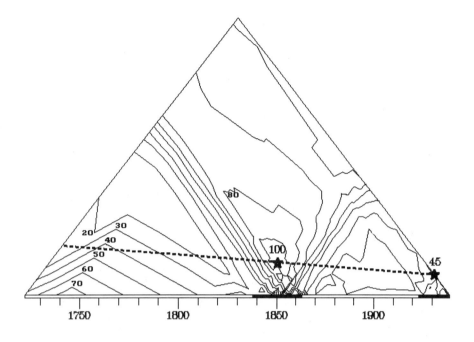

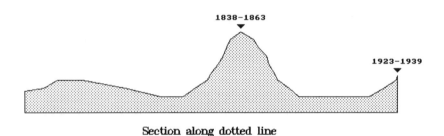

Section along dotted line

Figure 4.31 Macrae-Gibson: *The Secret Life of Buildings* (1985). Coverage profile: multinuclear

profile is inconsistent with the nature of the work, as in the case of comprehensive surveys and guidebooks, multinuclearity is often a sign of insufficient coverage between the peaks. Montgomery Schuyler's article on United States architecture (1902, figure 4.33) features only one name (Richardson) born between 1815 and 1846. Claude Bragdon's "Architecture in the United States" (1909, figure 4.34) has few names between 1754 and 1844; and *The American Artist and His Times* (Saint-Gaudens, 1941, figure 4.35) cites fewer architects than expected between 1764 and 1834. These oddities are flagged by the multiplicity of peaks in the profiles of those texts.

Who should be interested in this kind of information? The analysis of coverage has something to offer at every stage in the production and consumption of texts. Interested parties include authors together with their editors

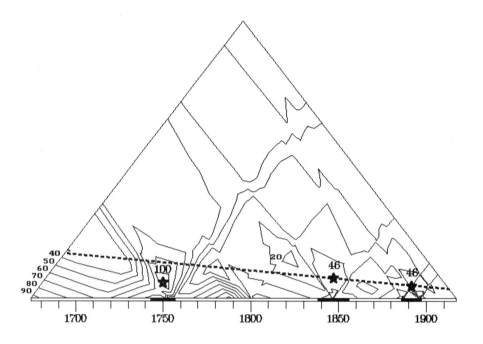

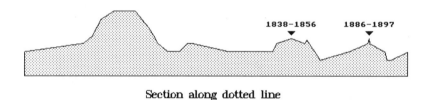

Section along dotted line

Figure 4.32 Millon (ed.): *Key-Monuments in the History of Architecture* (1965). Coverage profile: multinuclear

and publishers; book reviewers, merchants. library personnel, and the general public; as well as cultural historians, political activists, and index analysts. Each of them has a stake in the results.

Authors may consider checking the profile of their texts before releasing them, preferably while the projects are still malleable. They require only the list of names cited in the manuscript and electronic access to the data base. They may reconsider the list if the values returned do not match their intended coverage, if the system detects more than one focus and this is incongruent with their program, or if the gamma value is suspiciously low for a comprehensive work. The system will specify the dates with seemingly insufficient coverage. (If prompted, it could also generate a list of architects to be considered for inclusion. The issue at stake, however, is not the particular names chosen but only

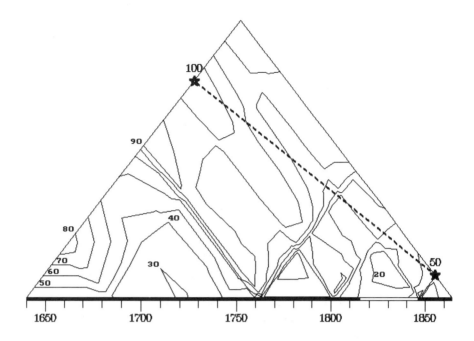

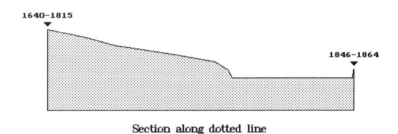

Section along dotted line

Figure 4.33 Schuyler: "United States Architecture" (1902). Coverage profile: multinuclear

normalcy in the distribution of dates; as with affirmative action programs, it is the relative representation of different groups that matters, not the presence of specific individuals.) Unusual profiles are flagged on the basis of statistical averages alone. Valid reasons may exist to depart from precedent in many cases. The decision to do so or to take corrective action belongs to the writers and their advisors.

Editors and publishers may ask a question or two if confronted with a manuscript with architects clustered for no apparent reason in several disconnected temporal lumps. If the gap between what the title promises and what the text delivers is excessive, a publisher may opt to rename the piece altogether. (This is what the USIA did with *Architecture USA* of 1957, which became *Modern Architecture America* in 1975, as already reported.) Examination of

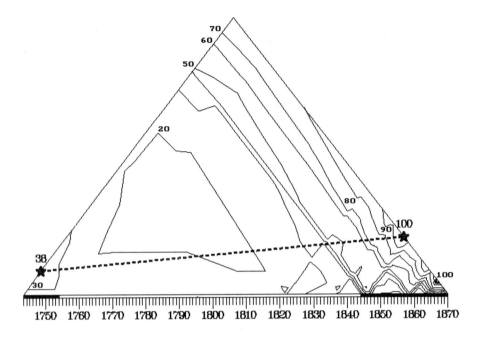

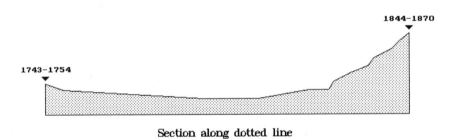

Section along dotted line

Figure 4.34   Bragdon: "Architecture in The United States" (1909). Coverage profile: multinuclear

profiles may be particularly helpful in revising or updating an earlier work; making sure that the pattern remains similar will go a long way in keeping the character and flavor of the new version in line with the older one.

Coverage profiles remain useful after publication. Reviewers can glance at aspects of a work that are not visible to the naked eye; the periods with the greatest concentration of names as well as the ones skimmed over hint at the writer's slants and preferences. When the reviewer leaves the computer desk for the easychair he has a program staked out for him—a series of assumptions to be confirmed or discarded with a targeted reading of certain sections of the book.

Older texts are amenable to coverage and profile analysis no less than recent ones. The larger the information pool, the richer the comparisons and possible inferences.

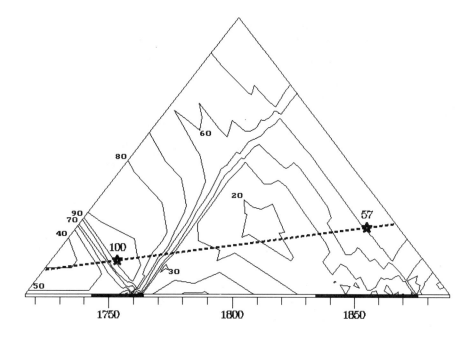

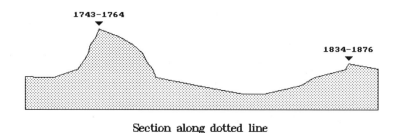

Section along dotted line

Figure 4.35 Saint-Gaudens: *The American Artist and his Times* (1941). Coverage profile: multinuclear

When I was growing up there were a few small bookstores in Buenos Aires whose owners handled their books with love and could comprehend them on the basis of a few clues. They talked with customers, and perhaps passed on to one patron what they had heard from another. Be that as it may, if asked about a particular subject, more often than not they would recommend an appropriate source. Such stores and their owners are long gone. Across the street from my campus is the largest bookstore in town. The staff at the information desk can locate on a computer screen any book in print, from coast to coast and often from overseas, provided they are given at least a few words from the title, an incomplete reference to the author, or the subject matter. But in most cases they have never seen the book, and probably will not, even if it is ordered; offering advice is not in their job description. With frequent career changes and increasing numbers of titles, the staff at superstores and libraries are forced to rely on electronic technology.

Computerized searches of books in print and in stock are only a modest beginning; index analysis opens the door for more penetrating approaches. For example, the system may be queried for texts with the highest number of names of architects born prior to 1700. Although its treatment of architectural matters is uneven, with more than 100 early architects and builders *The Smithsonian Guide to Historic America* series of 1989–1990 is clearly the front runner. Morrison's *Early American Architecture* (1952, 33 names), Gowans's *Images of American Living* (1964, 24 names), and Smith's *A Pictorial History of Architecture in America* (1976, 23 architects) are distant seconds. These are the titles that a knowledgeable bookstore owner may have offered, if available, to customers interested in seventeenth-century American architecture; a store clerk with access to the data base of this project could locate the same information.

Cultural historians, another group of potential users, may be interested in shifts in public interest for certain periods, or in texts that impelled change one way or another. Their goal would be served by examining the ratio between the architects from a period in a text and in the universe at the time of publication. From this perspective, *A Text-Book of the History of Architecture* by A. D. F. Hamlin (1896) and *The Georgian Period* by William Ware (1899), with twice as many early architects in the text as in the universe, outrank the three books listed in the preceding paragraph. The bookstore owner of yesteryear would not have been able to produce this information; neither would the professor emeritus with the longest memory on campus, or the brightest academic librarian, unless they used the new technology.

Historians are seldom interested in promoting specific courses of action; their approach is descriptive, not prescriptive. It is often the case, however, that when a tool becomes available to determine how things are, an incentive is created for someone to start pondering about how they ought to be. Coverage has a social and a political dimension. Issues of gender equity among writers and architects are examined in chapter 11; if the relevant information were to be collected, racial and ethnic equity could also be examined on the basis of indexes. It seems implausible, however, that chronological coverage—the subject of this chapter— would ever become a politically charged issue in this country, like gender or race.

Who would ever fight for (or against) granting wider coverage to a certain stylistic or historical period? But the architecture of Hitler, Stalin, Mussolini, or Perón was expunged for decades from orthodox architectural history, at least while the associated political movements were in power; concomitantly, scholars under the control of those regimes were compelled to deal with their accomplishments with more zest than otherwise warranted. Even in this country architectural choices occasionally acquired a political dimension: Grecian architecture was preferred at one point because its republican connotations were considered more appropriate for the new nation than the medieval, monarchic associations of Gothic.

Cultural politics are unpredictable; activists may some day find it convenient to promote or to repudiate the architecture of, say, the New Deal or the Reagan-Bush years. As the productive life of an architect runs through several decades, architect citation analysis is too coarse a tool to deal with such short periods; but citations of buildings could be used to detect certain forms of discrimination or to control progress toward the implementation of social and political goals.

Index analysts have reasons of their own to examine the coverage of texts. They must ensure that spans as returned by the system are consistent with the texts' perceived nature and content; if they aren't, they may occasionally override a result or strive for better, more reliable computation procedures. Last but not least, index analysts have to know the coverage of texts as a basis for what comes in the next chapters.

Alpha and Omega

Fairy tales typically start with the phrase "Once upon a time . . ." and end with ". . . and they lived happily ever after." The plot is presented, unfolded, and resolved between those magic words; nothing significant is supposed to occur before the beginning of the story or after closure. The opening carries the seeds for all subsequent dramatic action—finding the treasure, recovering the kingdom, curing the ailment of the princess. The closing, in turn, includes appropriate rewards for the hero and heroine and just punishment for the evildoers to settle moral or pecuniary imbalances and justify the expectation of steady, uneventful, and everlasting happiness. The same basic narrative structure is also present in many novels, plays, and motion pictures, and although few people notice it, in art and architectural history.

Discourse unfolds in a hierarchically structured temporal environment, punctuated by beginnings and ends at various levels. The text is organized into chapters, with an opening and a closing chapter; each chapter, in turn, has its own opening and closing markers. The story is arranged into relatively independent segments grouped into larger sequences, like stones in an arch.

Temporal arches have distinct beginnings and ends. Unlike spatial arches, the abutments of temporal arches are not interchangeable. Certain architects or artists become more effective building blocks for the beginning of the arch, others provide better support when placed at the end. With his introduction of a new formal vocabulary and a new conception of the architect's profession, Filippo Brunelleschi originated a program that was developed by ensuing generations of practitioners; consequently, his work is a fitting starting point for a narrative that covers the fifteenth century onward. By the same token, he would make for a rather unwieldy ending point of a narration spanning the Middle Ages.

John Balthazar Von Neumann, on the other hand, pushed the spatial complexity and formal intricacies of the Late Baroque to a level that could hardly be surpassed. As further advancement on the same lines became problematic, architectural development was impelled to move in new directions, and the old narrative was brought to an anticipated end. A chapter in architectural history was closed figuratively in the real word and literally in the texts; often the entire book, not only a chapter, was brought to a conclusion.

The same is true about the music of Johann Sebastian Bach, the painting of Jackson Pollock, the poetry of Luis de Gongora. Art and architectural history narratives have alphas and omegas. Personalities who break with the past and propose new programs of action are typically story openers; those who push previous work to a culmination tend to become closers. Artists such as Bramante who build on precedent and in turn provide a basis for further development are characteristically placed in the middle of the narrative arch. Certain architects show a propensity to appear at the beginning, the middle, or the end of story lines.

Whether this tendency is governed by intrinsic attributes of the person's work, or is itself a product of narrative convention and repetition, is open to question. The idea that Brunelleschi initiated a line of exploration leading from Renaissance to Mannerism and Baroque may have emerged from story-telling practices as much as from reality itself; if historians of European art had articulated their views around issues other than the ones they selected, the roles of story opener and closer (and all the other roles in their narratives) may have fallen on other persons.

Propp maintains that the plots and roles of wonder tales are limited in number[6]; some of them recur under a plurality of guises. The same could be true of art historical discourse: in a provocative study of the historiography of the Modern Movement,[7] Scalvini and Sandri show the existence of an underlying dramatic structure common to all major histories; the names and dates associated with the various nodes of the narrative change from text to text, but the nodes themselves remain recognizably the same.

Two obvious nodes in any narration—the person with whom the story starts and the one with whom it concludes—are amenable to detection by analyzing indexes. Tales unfold in a temporal continuum bracketed between starting and closing dates. Architects born on or shortly after the beginning operate as curtain raisers; the ones placed on or shortly before the closing date mark the end of the story. Sorting by birth date the architects cited in *The Dictionary of Architecture* of 1892, for example, one obtains the listing of figure 4.36. Jefferson opens the arch; Downing closes it.

Finding the names at the beginning and end of a span is easy; but before accepting them as legitimate openers and closers, some sort of validation is in order. One could check the texts themselves to see whether the architects at the beginning or end of their coverage are actually identified, in so many words, as the origin or the conclusion of an evolving line. No such assurances will be

Figure 4.36   *The Dictionary of Architecture* (1892): architects sorted by birth date

Date	Name
1743	Thomas Jefferson
1754	Andrew and Joseph Ellicott
1754	Pierre Charles L'Enfant
1759	Dr. William Thornton
1762	James Hoban
1763	Charles Bulfinch
1763	George Hadfield
1764	Benjamin Henry Latrobe
1765	Maximilien Godefroy
1780	G. Blagden
1780	Lewis Wernag
1781	Robert Mills
1800	Henry Sellon Boneval Latrobe
1802	Richard Upjohn
1803	John Hazelhurst Boneval Latrobe
1804	Thomas Ustick Walter
1815	Andrew Jackson Downing

found in the *Dictionary*; but in any case, the search would entail a misinterpretation of the point. The notion of a tale unfolding along the coverage of the text is an abstract one. The actual story being told need not coincide with it, nor does it have to start with the story opener or end with the concluder. In fact, a story is not necessary at all; as indicated earlier, an encyclopedia organized alphabetically and a guidebook arranged geographically do not tell a story as history books do, yet they occupy a circumscribed temporal environment delimited by an opening and an end.

The findings can be verified in another way. Although not much can be derived from the coverage of one text alone, patterns may emerge when faced with large numbers of cases. If a name appears at the beginning or end of a span just once or twice in the corpus, it may well be coincidental. It is more meaningful if it is found in that position many times, and the presumption of significance increases if an architect were consistently at the beginning of story lines but not at the end, or vice versa. Architects that are most often at the beginning or end of coverage are listed in figure 4.37. The tally was done observing the following rules:

1. To be counted, an architect need not be born exactly at the beginning or end of a span; it is enough if the birth date is within an approximation set at 20 percent of the span duration or 18 years, whichever is less. In the case of *The Dictionary of Architecture* (figure 4.35), Ellicott and L'Enfant open the narrative line together with Jefferson; Upjohn, Latrobe, and Walter close it together with Downing. This softens the starkness of punctual beginnings and ends, acknowledges the approximate nature of spans, and recognizes the ambiguities due to using birth dates in lieu of construction dates.

Figure 4.37 Architects most often found at the beginning or the end of text coverage spans

Column headings
[1]   Number of times at the beginning of coverage
[2]   Number of times at the end of coverage
[3]   Birth date
[4]   Name

[1]	[2]	[3]	[4]
Openers			
50	1	1743	Thomas Jefferson
33	5	1759	Dr. William Thornton
30	6	1754	Pierre Charles L'Enfant
21	0	1716	Peter Harrison
21	6	1760	Étienne Sulpice Hallet
21	8	1764	Benjamin Henry Latrobe
20	13	1846	Daniel Hudson Burnham
19	8	1763	Charles Bulfinch
18	5	1757	Samuel McIntire
18	10	1838	Henry Hobson Richardson
16	12	1883	Walter Gropius
16	15	1886	Ludwig Mies van der Rohe
16	17	1897	Skidmore, Owings, & Merrill
16	20	1931	Denise Scott Brown
16	23	1856	Louis Sullivan
15	14	1859	Cass Gilbert
15	14	1895	Buckminster Fuller
15	23	1932	Peter D. Eisenman
14	4	1761	Mangin & McComb
14	4	1832	William Le Baron Jenney
14	14	1847	McKim, Mead, & White
14	24	1896	William Lescaze
13	0	1722	Charles Louis Clérisseau
13	12	1850	John Wellborn Root
13	7	1929	John Hejduk
13	10	1930	Stanley Tigerman
13	21	1895	Wallace K. Harrison
13	15	1926	Cesar Pelli
Closers			
8	49	1918	Paul Rudolph
7	45	1910	Eero Saarinen
6	42	1922	Roche & Dinkeloo
5	41	1934	Richard Meier
11	38	1925	Robert Venturi
3	35	1912	Minoru Yamasaki
8	35	1917	I. M. Pei
6	33	1906	Philip Johnson
6	33	1934	Michael Graves
8	33	1939	Robert A. M. Stern

Figure 4.37   (continued)

[1]	[2]	[3]	[4]
2	32	1938	Charles Gwathmey
11	32	1925	Charles W. Moore
9	29	1902	Marcel Breuer
2	27	1935	William Turnbull, Jr.
5	26	1933	John H. Burgee
8	26	1924	John Calvin Portman, Jr.
1	25	1936	Donlyn Lyndon
1	25	1949	Arquitectonica (or DPZ)
14	24	1896	William Lescaze
4	23	1908	Max Abramovitz
16	23	1856	Louis Sullivan
15	23	1932	Peter D. Eisenman
13	21	1895	Wallace K. Harrison
3	21	1909	Gordon Bunshaft
2	21	1923	Victor Alfred Lundy
16	20	1931	Denise Scott Brown
8	19	1924	Mitchell Giurgola Associates
11	19	1892	Richard J. Neutra
11	19	1930	John Rauch
9	18	1902	Edward Durrell Stone
16	17	1897	Skidmore, Owings, & Merrill
0	17	1948	Thomas Gordon Smith
8	17	1881	Raymond Mathewson Hood

2. Names outside of the span are ignored. For example, all names printed on gray in figure 4.3 are disregarded, even if they are within the permissible approximation to the limits of the span.

3. Each span of a multinuclear text has its own beginning and end.

The top of figure 4.37 lists the most frequent opening architects; the most recurrent closers are at the bottom. Certain architects are in both lists.

Jefferson is often recognized as the initiator of American architecture: in *American Architects and the Mechanics of Fame* (1991), Williamson, for example, places him at the root of a "career connections" tree from which all other American architects branch out. Analysis of indexes abundantly confirms this assessment: appearing at or near the span beginning in fifty texts of the corpus, Jefferson leads the list of coverage openers, well ahead of the closest followers. The significance of this fact has already been discussed.

Sullivan opens the narrative line in several texts and closes it in others. Let us examine one of the latter. He is at the end of the narrative in *L'Architecture Americaine*, published in 1886. At thirty years of age, Sullivan was a promising young architect, like Goff when he was detected in 1930, Maya Ying Lin more recently, and many other young architects before and thereafter. Wright, like Sullivan, started his citation history as a text closer; in his case it was with

American Architects and Other Writings, by Montgomery Schuyler (1913), his first citation in the corpus.

In the latter part of their literary careers, many years after their death, Sullivan and Wright appear again at the end of the narrative line of texts, as they did during their youth. But the texts are of a different kind (they tend to be recent works looking at a far more distant past), and the masters are used as watersheds that separate recent from not-so-recent history. Sullivan plays this role in *The Smithsonian Guide to Historic America* series (1989) and in *Nineteenth Century Architecture* by Reynolds (1992), whereas Wright does the same in *A Field Guide to American Architecture* by Rifkind (1980) and in Scully's *Architecture. The Natural and the Manmade* (1991).

Generalizing from these observations, a four-step process can be seen in the data. First, important architects often make their initial appearance in the literature as end points in the chronicling of current events, as the brightest stars of the younger generation. Eero Saarinen, one of the most frequent closers, started this way during the 1940s; Paul Rudolph, Minoru Yamasaki, and I. M. Pei did the same during the 1950s; closer to us Robert Stern, and later Thomas Gordon Smith, Arquitectonica, and Maya Ying Lin went through the same process. The pattern was also there with Bertram Goodhue, who closed the coverage span for the 1909 edition of Hamlin's *A Text-Book of the History of Architecture* when he was barely 40 years old.

Second, as time passes, these architects are superseded by ensuing, newer waves of *Wunderkinds*; they remain in the literature, but no longer at the end of the narrative. Third, many years later, in the case of exceptional leadership and influence over ensuing developments, they turn into starting points for new histories.

Finally, equally important, although perhaps not as obviously significant, is the ability to appear again at the end of a new cycle of narrations, when the next generation of architects is already established. The first time around, the person makes it to the end of the list because he is brilliant, or perhaps merely promising, and because of his age: literally, there is nobody younger with whom to continue the story. During the second cycle the writers close the texts on his work by choice, not necessity: something special in the person's contribution must justify this decision. The crowning achievement in this morphology of literary dominance, one that presumably eluded Brunelleschi, but graced Richardson, Burnham, Sullivan, and Wright, is the ability to be perceived simultaneously as beginning and end, as alpha and omega.

Figures 4.38 through 4.41 highlight aspects of the citation histories of these four giants. Dotted lines mark their birth dates as they intersect the coverage of selected texts in which they are cited. Most of the early citations are graphed; to reduce clutter, only texts in which the architect appears at the beginning or end of the coverage (or extended coverage) are included in the figure once the personality is established.

Text coverage (opening and closing periods in black)
Text extended coverage
o   Text publication date
Architect birth date

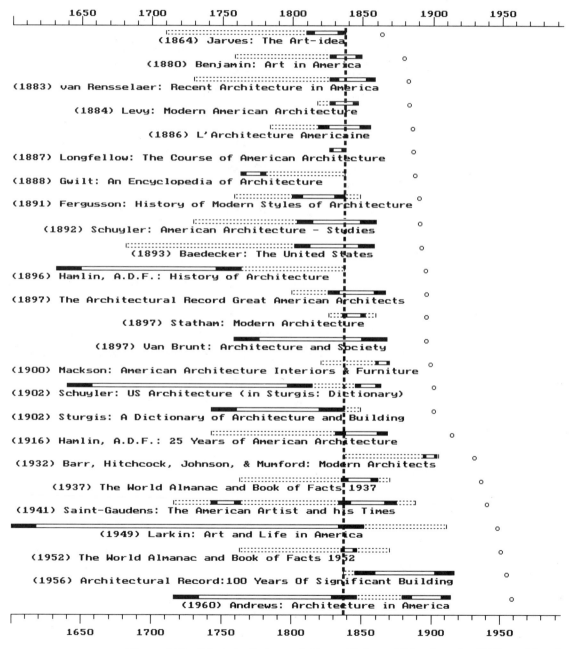

Figure 4.38 Selected citations of Henry Hobson Richardson (b. 1838) positioned within text coverage

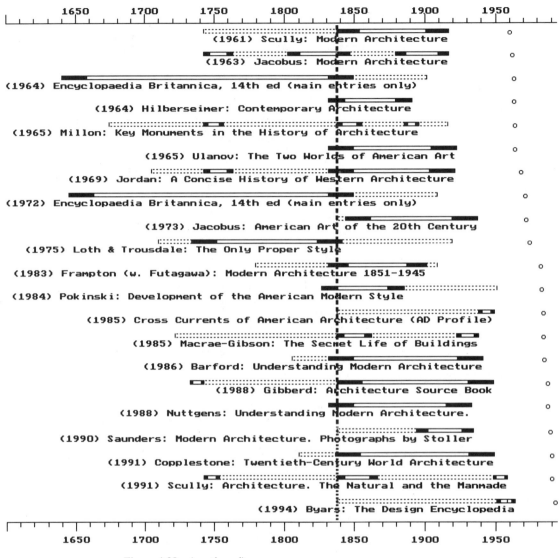

Figure 4.38   (continued)

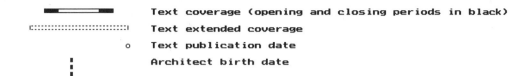

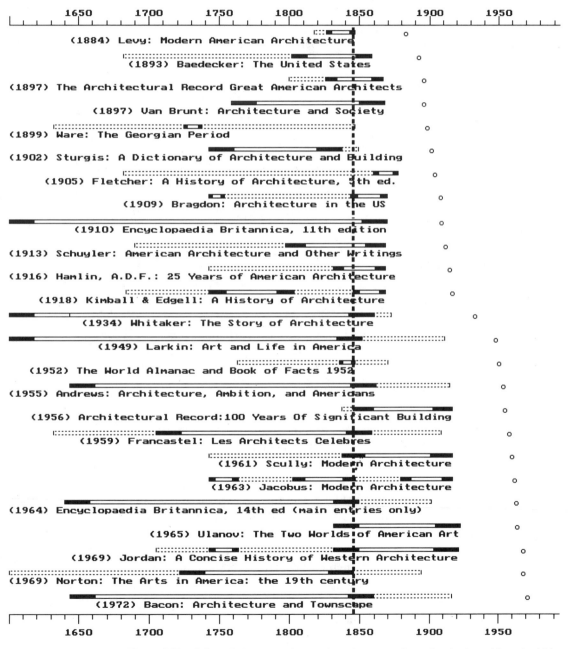

Figure 4.39 Selected citations of Daniel Hudson Burnham (b. 1846) positioned within text coverage

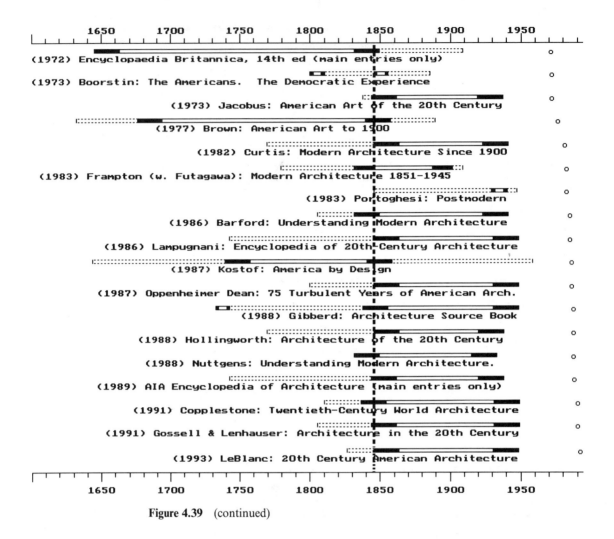

Figure 4.39   (continued)

The four are not alone; the citation histories of earlier personalities Alexander Jackson Davis and Walter Thomas Ustick display a similar pattern, and the same is true to varying degrees of Raymond Hood, Wallace Harrison, William Lescaze, Louis Kahn, Marcel Breuer, Philip Johnson, I. M. Pei, Paul Rudolph, and the firm of Skidmore, Owings, & Merrill. Because of their late arrival in this country, Gropius and van der Rohe missed out, so to speak, on the first step of the valse. As for the current generation of architects, it is too soon to tell.

To use computers effectively in the humanities one must devise procedures that are as meaningful to scholars as they are practical to machines. The examination of the beginning and end of text coverage passes the test because it is simple, readily understandable, and easily used as a criterion in electronic searches of the data base.

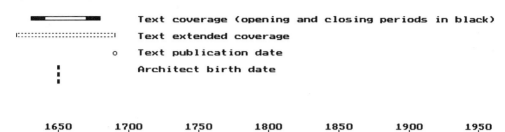

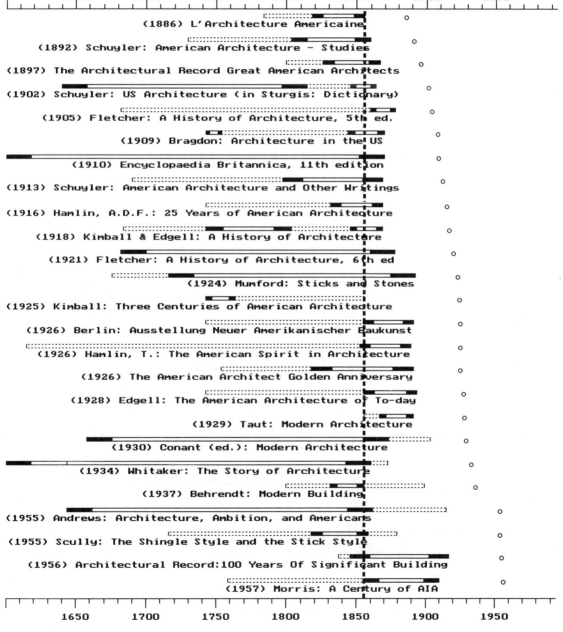

Figure 4.40 Selected citations of Louis Sullivan (b. 1856) positioned within text coverage

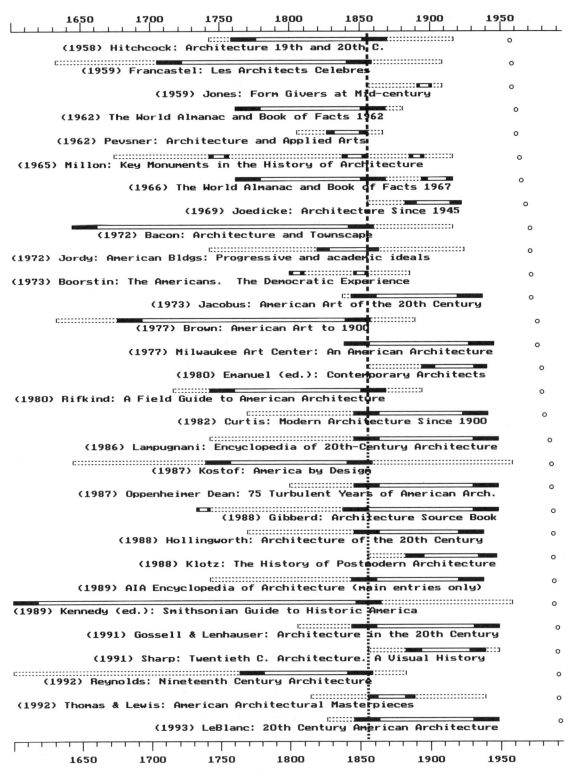

Figure 4.40   (continued)

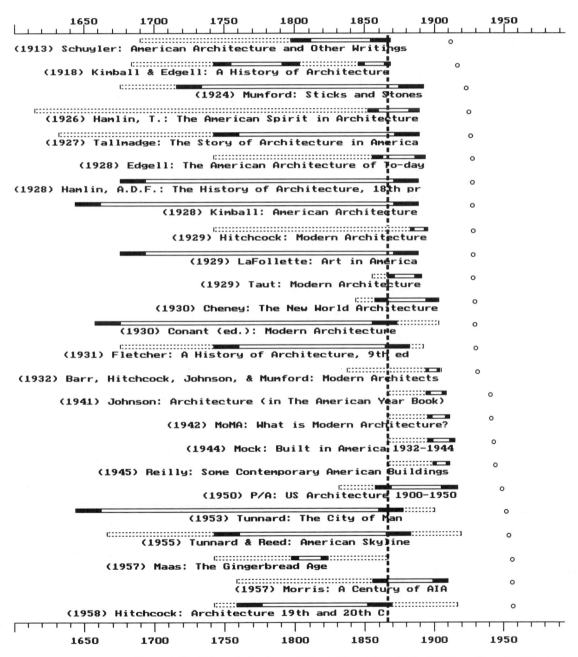

Figure 4.41   Selected citations of Frank Lloyd Wright (b. 1867) positioned within text coverage

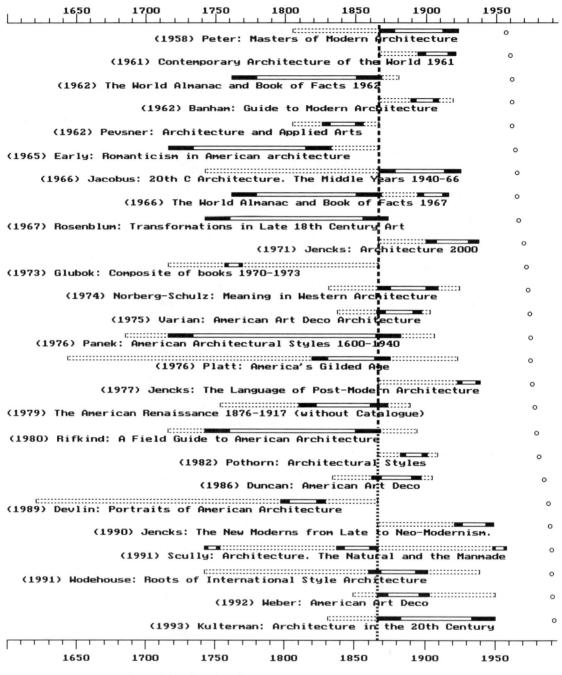

Figure 4.41   (continued)

Notes

1. Despite their similar titles, *American Architecture of the Twentieth Century* (#48) and *Architecture of the 20th Century* (#320) cover different material, as one was published in 1927 and the other in 1988.

2. Marcus Whiffen, personal communication, September 10, 1991.

3. The texts are Pierson, W. H., and M. Davidson (eds.): *The Arts in the United States* (1960); *Styles and Types of North American Architecture* by Alan Gowans (1992); *Teachers Manual for the Study of Art History and Related Courses* (Tschacbasov, compiler, 1964); and the 1964 edition of the *Encyclopaedia Britannica*.

4. With few exceptions, three groups of texts have been excluded from figure 4.4: (a), Those with a limited coverage. such as a period or a style, because their gammas are consistently and predictably low. (b), Texts that address the architecture of the entire world, rather than the United States; gamma values in this case also tend to be low, because America started to play a major international role in architecture rather late, thus making the *Encyclopaedia Britannica*'s case even more remarkable, (c), Texts published before 1850. With few earlier publications in the corpus, these works tend to define the universe and their gammas are predictably close to 1.

5. Only selected dates are reported in figure 4.7 to reduce clutter. The system examines larger arrays of numbers.

6. Propp, Vladimir: Morphology of the Folktale. *International Journal of American Linguistics* 1958, 24(4). Original Russian: 1928. See also Vladimir Propp: *Theory and History of Folktale*. Minneapolis: University of Minnesota Press, 1984.

7. Scalvini, Maria Luisa, and Maria Grazia Sandri: *L'immagine storiografica dell' architettura contemporanea da Platz a Giedion*. Roma: Officina Edizioni, 1984.

5 Histograms: From Commencement to Retirement and Beyond

Adjusted Citations

We are now ready to correct certain shortcomings in the raw ranking of famous architects of figure 3.4. Thomas Jefferson, Benjamin Latrobe, and Charles Bulfinch, inescapable references for American architecture of the early Republican times, place somewhat poorly in that ranking. This is due, at least in part, to the fact that fewer texts in the corpus deal with the early periods of American architecture than, say, with the late nineteenth and twentieth centuries. Rather than reflecting their standing in the literature, their relatively low ranking signals an unevenness in the literary coverage itself. The luminaries of today are also relegated to modest places, if not left out altogether. Some among the younger architects may be capable of as strong an impact as their most illustrious predecessors, but their bibliographies, if not their oeuvres, are still in progress. They cannot possibly approximate the number of citations of successful earlier architects. The standing of very early or very recent architects is also depressed in figures 3.5, 3.6, and 3.7.

A corrective mechanism for more meaningful comparisons is easily devised. The number of texts in the corpus addressing each architect's life and work is known (figure 4.4). A new, adjusted ranking is based on the quotient between the number of citations (from column [2], figure 3.4) and the number of texts in which he or she could foreseeably have been featured (from figure 4.4). Comparisons are made after all architects have been granted, so to speak, the same opportunity to be cited. But before implementing the new ranking we must consider one more factor.

Juan de Panonia and Aureliano were the two most eminent theologians of their time. Juan was quick and witty; he enjoyed disentangling the most vexing problems intuitively, with brief and elegant axioms. Aureliano was a profound but slow syllogist. Although they were fighting the same heresies, Aureliano developed a silent hatred for his comrade, sustained in jealousy. Juan had a real weakness: he was not a penman. The written legacy of his entire lifetime was a meager twenty words. Aureliano, in turn, possessed a weapon that he used mercilessly. He wrote indefatigably: in 6,000 pages of tightly knit argument he examined the contributions, as well as the fallacies, of every writer, Christian and non-Christian, living or dead. Not once, however, did he mention Juan's name. Generation after generation of students read his tracts. Finally, when the two men were aging, Aureliano made his move. He falsely accused his rival of heresy. Juan's defense was impeccable, the most brilliant argued before the tribunal in a generation; but his standing had been so hopelessly debilitated by the stratagem that the judges did not trust him and sent him to the stake.

Politicians and public relation directors, familiar with the importance of name exposure, will grasp the point of the story as told by Jorge Luis Borges.[1] Oscar Wilde would have understood it too, for he intimated that there was only one thing in the world worse than being talked about—not being talked about. But even shrewd media manipulators may miss an aspect of Borges's plot: for Aureliano's trick to work, it was not enough for him to remain silent about Juan; he also had to write 6,000 pages. *Soft* absences—lack of citation when no citation is expected—are harmless; but to be left out when the flow of discourse calls for one's name—to be hit with a *hard* absence—is devastating.

Adjusted rankings take into account the distinction between hard and soft absences. Lack of citation is counted only if the architect was born within the text's coverage span, and he had entered the universe by the time of publication of the text. The first condition indicates that the architect is pertinent to the subject matter. The second signals that the person was already discovered and the author of the text was presumably cognizant of his or her work. (Publication date is used as an approximation writing date, which is generally unavailable.) Both conditions are easily tested by the system.

The criteria for text selection (chapter 2) are now easier to justify. Only comprehensive texts are included in the corpus to ensure that meaningful citation omissions may be inferred from content spans and architect birth dates alone. In books restricted to specific regions, building types, or ethnic groups, many chronologically pertinent architects are absent not because of authorial judgment but because of the subject matter itself.[2] Precise cut-off dates for text coverage spans were sought in chapter 4 to allow for unambiguous distinctions between soft and hard citation absences.

Adjusted citations are obtained by dividing the number of an architect's citations by the sum of that number and the hard omissions. Soft absences have no effect on the value.[3] Adjusted rankings (figure 5.1) are based on adjusted citations. They are shielded from the effect of the uneven bibliographical coverage, and they take into account whether writers could have known the work of the architect at the time of writing.

It is not surprising that eighteenth-century architects improved their standing in relation to raw rankings. Jefferson advanced from the tenth position to the first, displacing Wright as the brightest star. Latrobe moved to the second position from the twelfth, and Bulfinch advanced from sixteenth to seventh place. Earlier builders made even more impressive gains: John Smibert, John

Figure 5.1 The 100 most famous architects (adjusted from raw rankings in figure 3.4)

Column headings:
[1]   Rank
[2]   Percentage of pertinent texts in which architect is cited
[3]   Birth date
[4]   Architect or firm name
[5]   Raw ranking

[1]	[2]	[3]	[4]	[5]
1	0.98	1743	Thomas Jefferson	10
2	0.96	1764	Benjamin Henry Latrobe	12
3	0.96	1856	Louis Sullivan	2
4	0.95	1867	Frank Lloyd Wright	1
5	0.95	1910	Eero Saarinen	6
6	0.94	1838	Henry Hobson Richardson	4
7	0.92	1763	Charles Bulfinch	16
8	0.90	1847	McKim, Mead, & White	5
9	0.90	1886	Ludwig Mies van der Rohe	3
10	0.89	1846	Daniel Hudson Burnham	9
11	0.87	1906	Philip Johnson	8
12	0.86	1827	Richard Morris Hunt	17
13	0.85	1918	Paul Rudolph	23
14	0.84	1883	Walter Gropius	6
15	0.83	1897	Skidmore, Owings, & Merrill	11
16	0.83	1881	Raymond Mathewson Hood	14
17	0.83	1781	Robert Mills	28
18	0.82	1716	Peter Harrison	60
19	0.82	1925	Robert Venturi	31
20	0.80	1902	Marcel Breuer	13
21	0.79	1892	Richard J. Neutra	14
22	0.78	1788	William Strickland	33
23	0.78	1934	Richard Meier	60
24	0.77	1917	I. M. Pei	25
25	0.77	1850	John Wellborn Root	18
26	0.76	1759	Dr. William Thornton	37
27	0.76	1818	James Renwick, Jr.	31
28	0.76	1754	Pierre Charles L'Enfant	39
29	0.75	1925	Charles W. Moore	47
30	0.74	1912	Minoru Yamasaki	29
31	0.74	1804	Thomas Ustick Walter	30
32	0.74	1832	William Le Baron Jenney	21
33	0.73	1873	Eliel Saarinen	19
33	0.73	1901	Louis I. Kahn	19
35	0.73	1934	Michael Graves	63
36	0.73	1939	Robert A. M. Stern	85
37	0.72	1922	Roche & Dinkeloo	47
38	0.72	1895	Wallace K. Harrison	22
39	0.71	1802	Richard Upjohn	35
40	0.71	1844	Dankmar Adler	23
41	0.70	1859	Cass Gilbert	26

Figure 5.1   (continued)

[1]	[2]	[3]	[4]	[5]
42	0.69	1803	Alexander Jackson Davis	41
43	0.69	1949	Arquitectonica (or DPZ)	185
44	0.69	1895	Buckminster Fuller	26
45	0.67	1896	William Lescaze	33
46	0.65	1762c	James Hoban	50
47	0.64	1784	Ithiel Town	56
48	0.64	1869	Bertram Grosvenor Goodhue	36
49	0.64	1757	Samuel McIntire	60
50	0.63	1869	Albert Kahn	38
51	0.63	1854	Holabird & Roche	39
52	0.62	1822	Frederick Law Olmsted	49
53	0.62	1886	George Howe	42
54	0.61	1908	Max Abramovitz	51
55	0.61	1902	Edward Durrell Stone	43
56	0.61	1938	Charles Gwathmey	96
57	0.59	1858	Carrère & Hastings	45
58	0.59	1815	Andrew Jackson Downing	55
59	0.59	1931	Denise Scott Brown	87
60	0.58	1932	Peter D. Eisenman	91
61	0.57	1862	Bernard Maybeck	43
62	0.57	1676c	Andrew Hamilton	171
63	0.57	1926	Cesar Pelli	85
64	0.56	1868	Greene & Greene	46
65	0.56	1863	Cram, Goodhue, & Ferguson	53
66	0.56	1935	William Turnbull, Jr.	116
67	0.55	1887	Rudolph Schindler	53
68	0.55	1899	Pietro Belluschi	51
69	0.55	1685c	Richard Munday	185
70	0.54	1684c	Dr. John Kearsley	194
71	0.53	1898	Alvar Aalto	56
72	0.53	1837	George Browne Post	58
73	0.53	1839	Frank Furness	58
74	0.52	1909	Gordon Bunshaft	63
75	0.52	1877	Shreve, Lamb, & Harmon	69
76	0.52	1800	James Bogardus	67
77	0.52	1930	John Rauch	96
78	0.51	1907	Charles Osmand Eames	67
79	0.51	1866	Henry Bacon	65
80	0.51	1824	Calvert Vaux	73
81	0.50	1761?	Mangin & McComb	77
82	0.50	1688	John Smibert	211
82	0.50	1874	John Russell Pope	69
84	0.50	1933	John H. Burgee	116
85	0.49	1940	Helmut Jahn	153
86	0.49	1771	Asher Benjamin	80
87	0.49	1941	Thomas Hall Beeby	211
88	0.48	1868	John Mead Howells	71
89	0.48	1924	John Calvin Portman, Jr.	106

Figure 5.1   (continued)

[1]	[2]	[3]	[4]	[5]
90	0.48	1930	Stanley Tigerman	112
91	0.48	1959	Maya Ying Lin	353
92	0.47	1806	John Augustus Roebling	73
93	0.47	1904	Bruce Alonzo Goff	72
94	0.47	1895	Wurster, Bernardi, & Emmons	66
95	0.47	1915	Kallmann, McKinnell, & Knowles	83
96	0.47	1710?	Thomas (or James) McBean	211
97	0.46	1760c	Étienne Sulpice Hallet	87
98	0.46	1800	Isaiah Rogers	80
99	0.46	1924	Mitchell Giurgola Associates	106
100	0.46	1722	Charles Louis Clérisseau	147

Kearsley, Richard Munday, Thomas McBean, and Andrew Hamilton were catapulted more than 100 positions in the ranking.

Twentieth-century architects made advances too: Eero Saarinen moved from the sixth to the fifth rank, and Rudolph from the twenty-third to the thirteenth. Venturi and Moore advanced twelve and eighteen points, respectively; Tigerman, Pelli, Scott-Brown, and Graves advanced twenty or more; Burgee, Eisenman, Meier, Gwathmey, and Stern gained at least thirty points; William Turnbull and Helmut Jahn moved forward in the ranking fifty points or more, and the firm Arquitectonica, Thomas Beeby, and Maya Ying Lin were propelled more than 100 places.

Some of the most conspicuous names in American architectural history—Wright, Mies, Gropius, Johnson, and Eliel Saarinen, and the firm of Skidmore, Owings, & Merrill—appear demoted in the new ranking. The biggest losers were born between 1800 and 1915, and lived in the period addressed in the greatest number of texts in the literature; the correction places them on equal footing with everybody else. Raw rankings are tilted in favor of only three or four generations; adjusted rankings yield a more balanced cross section of architects, including the most eminent names of every period.

Other Adjustments

Several alternative adjustment techniques were considered. They are described in the appendix; together with the reasons for not having used them.

Tallies, Fame, and Excellence

Citation counts capture some aspects of fame or eminence only indirectly, if at all: academic distinctions, professional awards, recognition in the nonprofessional press, volume of work, financial accomplishment. Citation tallies measure only an architect's presence in the literature. Writers do not necessarily share the outlook of users, clients, or bankers; nor can they be expected to speak for society at large. Still, their assessments are intertwined. Writers mold the opinions of their readership and are themselves subject to societal checks and balances. Citations correlate to fame, even to eminence; common sense suggests that this is the case, and the rankings obtained offer ample supporting evidence.

The connection between tallies and excellence is more questionable. In a society used to ranking athletes, books, corporations, and even universities, it is easy to jump to the conclusion that the most frequently cited architects are the best. Nothing in index analysis supports such a leap. A scholar with a more guarded view of consensual judgments may see the rise in the reputation of a second-rate architect, or the decline in the fortunes of a truly exceptional one, as an indication of corruption in the public taste. Assessment of artistic excellence is beyond the boundaries of this project; but social and architectural historians can learn a great deal about the development of architectural ideas, including those concerning excellence, by studying the evolution of the literary standing of architects.

The tallies and rankings developed thus far, based on an architect's entire record, are of limited value in detecting social change; a look at the dynamic evolution of the person's fame would be more valuable. Indeed, the travails of an architect's lifetime are collapsed in the preceding rankings into a single measurement of success. Careers, however, are not punctual; they are like continuous lines rising or plunging over an extended period of time, from commencement to retirement, reflecting the effect of successive victories and defeats. The same is true for an architect's place in the literature, but in this case the line continues to unfold well beyond retirement and even death. From an index analytical perspective, each citation is an achievement and each hard absence a setback. Let us chart the evolution of an architect's fortunes—the *histogram*[5]—as reflected in the changing pattern and frequency of citations, and look at the histograms of selected architects.

Short-Term Memory

To obtain a histogram, one must observe the dates when citations (and lack thereof) actually occurred. The simplest way would be to tally citations year by year, but the corpus does not contain enough items for meaningful yearly results, especially in the early times when publications were few and sparse. Histograms based on yearly data would be subject to inconsequential short-term trends; longer periods must be considered to unveil the patterns in the evolution of an architect's literary fortunes.

The rankings presented earlier do not contain any allowance for the age of texts; old works count the same as recent ones, implying that, once published, texts remain culturally active forever. At the opposite end of a spectrum of possible assumptions is the proposition that texts are effectual only the year they are published. But texts are neither ephemeral nor eternal; they have a lifetime with a beginning and an end.

What is a current publication, and how can it be distinguished from an outdated one? Duncan[6] pointed out that the endurance of books depends not on their materiality—paper, ink, cloth, and the like—but on the presence of readers as active participants in the communication process. The massive damage to books after the fall of the Roman Empire came neither from wear and tear nor from bonfires lit by barbarian hordes or fanatical censors: the culprit was neglect. Texts perished not because authors or libraries were under attack but because no one was interested in reading them. Current publications are the ones that command the attention of readers in schools, offices, libraries, and homes.

The life cycle of a text can be charted just like the career of an architect. Its arrival on the scene is always noticeable in the public as well as the private domain: announcements appear in the media, autographing sessions are held in bookstores, packages are unwrapped at home. The impact often peaks shortly after publication, with frequent reviews and brisk sales. If it is successful, the text is cited in the secondary literature. When demand declines and inventories are bulging, the publisher places the title on sale. Eventually, the book will be out of print; reprints or updated editions may follow. Sooner or later, however, most texts will complete their useful life and be buried in library shelves, to collect dust if not to become it.

It is more difficult to pinpoint the fading away of a text than its emergence. Perec[7] fantasized about limiting his personal library to 361 volumes; once the limit had been reached, a book already owned would have to be discarded before a new one could be acquired. The hardest part of the project was to choose the titles to be dumped, not the ones to be purchased. The difficulty was the same, Perec observed, regardless of the size of the library—361, 1,000, or 3,000. But whether their demise is noticed or not, texts do exit the scene at the individual as well as the collective level. As second-hand book merchants would attest, once popular books often end up without any repurchase value. Like other products and institutions, most texts cease to reflect societal norms gradually but inexorably.

Only a limited number of texts is culturally active at any particular time, embodying a collective, short-term societal memory. Like biological or social populations, their scores are continually depleted and replenished. Change occurs, with consistent arrivals and departures; but a certain level of continuity also exists, because books remain in the short-term memory for more than just one year. Architects' histograms are to be charted according to their citation tallies in these shifting sets of texts.

The cumulative collective societal memory is composed of everything that was ever central to architectural interests. Such memory does not exist in any tangible way. Metaphorically, it is embodied in all the books of the library, or better, of all the libraries. Short-term memory is also an abstract construct, but it is more difficult to model.

Several ways to test empirically the currency of a text are described in the next section, but each one has drawbacks. Finally, I was compelled to resort to a hypothesis. As new books are published, older ones fade away in the order of their arrival; but rather than assigning an arbitrary limit to the size of the memory expressed in numbers of texts, as in Perec's fantasy, I elected to give it a fixed duration; for example, five, ten, or twenty years. Publications younger than the threshold are presumed to be active; as they reach the age limit they exit from short-term memory.

Books had longer life cycles in the past; nowadays, as time passes, they seem to remain in public memory for shorter and shorter spans. This may be due to the increased rate of production of new texts, as reflected in the corpus: one-fourth of the items were published during the last decade. With the explosion of new bibliographical resources and the limits to our ability to receive and process information, older books become more cumbersome to summon. Accelerated technical and social change, in turn, reduces their validity and the incentive to recall them.

A sliding scale seems appropriate, with text durability set as a function of publication date. A lengthy memory duration is assigned for the older books, and gradually diminishing values for more recent ones. Readers in 1880 had in mind, according to the hypothesis, every text published during the preceding eighty years. Today's typical readership, in contrast, does not care much for texts older than five years, at least according to the assumption hereby set.[8] Memory spans for intermediate dates are supposed to follow a continuous parabolic curve, tending toward a horizontal asymptote (see figure 5.2). Although unsupported by empirical evidence, the values are not entirely arbitrary; they were selected to ensure the presence of enough texts to allow for meaningful histograms for most architects (see the appendix for details).

The jagged line of figure 5.2 portrays the number of texts in short-term memory, year by year, according to the hypothesis.[9] Unlike the years in memory line, which results from convention, this one conveys some factual information. It plunges for the early 1940s, reflecting the decline in architectural scholarship due to the war. The mid-1960s and the early 1980s, in contrast, were particularly productive in architectural writing, at least judging by the corpus.

Other Tests

Several means to assess empirically the life span of a text were considered and abandoned. One was to look for its citations in still other texts: frequent cita-

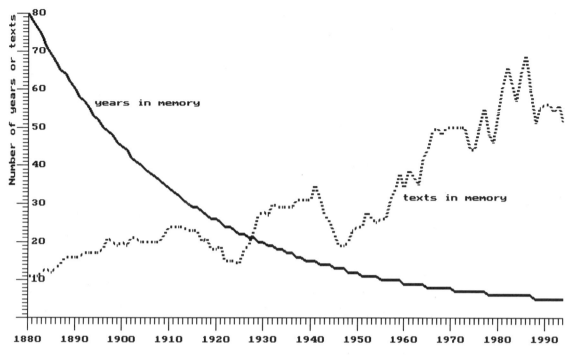

Figure 5.2   Evolution of short-term memory

tions reveal vitality, lack of citations signals death. Although consistent with the
evaluation of architects by their citation pattern, the mechanism is impractical.
Several citation indexes cover the literatures of science, the social sciences, and
the arts and humanities,[10] but most of the texts of the corpus, alas, are not
referenced in them.

Books could be presumed alive for as long as they are in print. Failure to
reissue an unavailable text suggests that it has lost commercial and presumably
cultural appeal; reprints, on the other hand, signal continued or renewed interest. Culturally active books are those that can be purchased in bookstores.
Their evolution can be charted from back issues of the *Cumulative Book Index*
and the *Books in Print* series. If there ever was a living example of a dead text,
it would be an outdated, out-of-print set of these collections. I found them in
the remotest, dustiest chamber of the university library; nobody had been there,
I was told, for a quarter of a century. Although I used the method for an early
version of this project, I ultimately abandoned it, not because it is slow, un-
describably tedious, and insalubrious, but because of misgivings about its validity: as noted by Wellish,[11] books with little demand stay in print for long years.
Besides, the procedure is not applicable to periodicals.

Library circulation data could provide another clue. But reference works do
not circulate, reading room usage is not recorded, and in the case of periodicals,
the available data refer to journals, not articles.

Histograms

Histograms display the ratio, year by year, between an architect's citations in texts in short-term memory, and the number of pertinent texts in memory[12]; in other words, they show the relationship between citations received and the ones expected if the person were cited in every pertinent text. Histograms portray the ups and down of an architect's presence in the literature. The fluctuations often parallel significant career developments, such as the completion of major commissions, the receipt of awards, the formation or dissolution of partnerships, retirement, and death. The curves are not limited to the person's lifetime; his or her standing in the literature continues to evolve after death, impelled perhaps by the publication of monographs, by homages, or by shifts in historical trends and societal stylistic preferences. Because of their dynamic, temporal dimension. they are more informative than rankings based cumulatively on the entire corpus.

To publish a text on American architecture dealing with the times of Frank Lloyd Wright without acknowledging him would be unthinkable today; but this has not always been the case. Wright's histogram (figure 5.3) shows that he reached this position of dominance, reflected in the long stretch of citations at 100 percent, only in the 1940s. It took him nearly thirty years to get there after his earliest citation in the corpus in 1913.

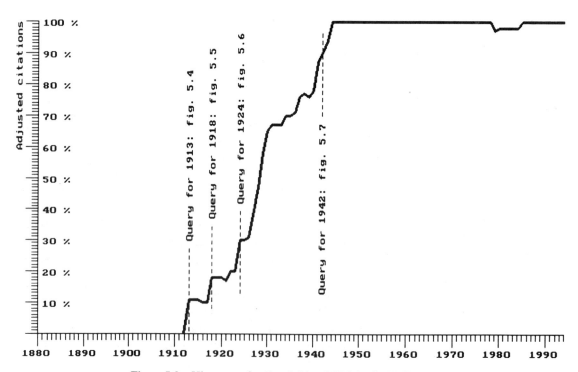

Figure 5.3   Histogram for Frank Lloyd Wright (b. 1867)

The meaning of the histogram is best grasped by following it through a series of points. Let us look at 1913 (figure 5.4). According to our assumptions, only texts published since 1883 were in short-term memory that year; nine of them are pertinent to Wright. He is mentioned in only one, by Montgomery Schuyler,[13] his first appearance in the corpus. The adjusted citations for 1913 are 1/9. The second citation came in 1918, by Fiske Kimball and George H. Edgell. A query for that year (figure 5.5) shows that in the interim there was another omission (A. D. F. Hamlin, 1916), bringing the value of the curve to 0.18. The third citation came in 1924 (figure 5.6).

Wright became strongly established in current literature by 1942 (figure 5.7). He suffered no omissions since 1930. Most of the texts that omitted him earlier already vanished from shore-term memory; the remaining ones would do so shortly, ceasing to influence the histogram.

A small notch appears in the curve around 1979, detracting somewhat from Wright's otherwise impressive performance. The dent is due to the guide and

Figure 5.4 Frank Lloyd Wright: Query for 1913 (pertinent texts from 1883 to 1913)

Citations: 1

#35	1913	Schuyler: American Architecture and Other Writings

Omissions: 8

#23	1897	*The Architectural Record Great American Architects Series*
#25	1897	Van Brunt: *Architecture and Society*
#27	1900	Mackson: *American Architecture Interiors & Furniture*
#30	1905	Fletcher: *A History of Architecture*, 5th ed.
#31	1909	Bragdon: "Architecture in The United States"
#32	1909	Hamlin, A.D.F.: *A Text-Book of the History of Architecture*, 8th ed.
#33	1910	*Men and Women of America. A Biographical Dictionary*
#34	1910	*The Encyclopaedia Britannica*, 11th ed.

Adjusted citations: 0.11

Figure 5.5 Frank Lloyd Wright: Query for 1918 (pertinent texts from 1892 to 1918)

Citations: 2

#35	1913	Schuyler: *American Architecture and Other Writings*
#38	1918	Kimball & Edgell: *A History of Architecture*

Omissions: 9

#23	1897	*The Architectural Record Great American Architects Series*
#25	1897	Van Brunt: *Architecture and Society*
#27	1900	Mackson: *American Architecture Interiors & Furniture*
#30	1905	Fletcher: *A History of Architecture*, 5th ed.
#31	1909	Bragdon: "Architecture in The United States"
#32	1909	Hamlin, A.D.F.: *A Text-Book of the History of Architecture*, 8th ed.
#33	1910	*Men and Women of America. A Biographical Dictionary*
#34	1910	*The Encyclopaedia Britannica*, 11th ed.
#37	1916	Hamlin, A.D.F.: "25 Years of American Architecture"

Adjusted citations: 0.18

Figure 5.6   Frank Lloyd Wright: Query for 1924 (pertinent texts from 1902 to 1924)

Citations: 3

#35	1913	Schuyler: *American Architecture and Other Writings*
#38	1918	Kimball & Edgell: *A History of Architecture*
#42	1924	Mumford: *Sticks and Stones*

Omissions: 7

#30	1905	Fletcher: *A History of Architecture, 5th ed.*
#31	1909	Bragdon: "Architecture in The United States"
#32	1909	Hamlin, A.D.F.: *A Text-Book of the History of Architecture*, 8th ed.
#33	1910	*Men and Women of America. A Biographical Dictionary*
#34	1910	*The Encyclopaedia Britannica*, 11th ed.
#37	1916	Hamlin, A.D.F.: "25 Years of American Architecture"
#40	1921	Fletcher: *A History of Architecture*, 6th ed.

Adjusted citations: 0.30

Figure 5.7   Frank Lloyd Wright: Query for 1942 (pertinent texts from 1929 to 1942)

Citations: 18

#54	1929	Hitchcock: *Modern Architecture*
#55	1929	LaFollette: *Art in America*
#57	1929	Taut: *Modern Architecture*
#58	1930	Cheney: *The New World Architecture*
#59	1930	Conant (ed.): *Modern Architecture*
#61	1931	Fletcher: *A History of Architecture*, 9th ed.
#62	1932	Barr, Hitchcock, Johnson, & Mumford: *Modern Architects*
#66	1935	Cahill & Barr: *Art in America*
#67	1936	Tallmadge: *The Story of Architecture in America*, rev. ed.
#68	1937	Behrendt: *Modern Building*
#71	1938	Richardson & Corfiato: *The Art of Architecture*
#72	1940	Hamlin, T.: *Architecture Through the Ages*
#73	1940	Roth: *The New Architecture*
#76	1941	Giedion: *Space, Time, and Architecture*
#77	1941	Johnson: "Architecture" (in *The American Year Book*)
#78	1941	Saint-Gaudens: *The American Artist and His Times*
#79	1942	Museum of Modern Art: *What is Modern Architecture?*
#80	1942	Newcomb: *History of Modern Architecture*

Omissions: 2

#56	1929	Sexton: *Composite of books published in 1928–31*
#60	1930	Hoak & Church: *Masterpieces of Architecture in the United States*

Adjusted citations: 0.90

illustrated catalogue for the Exhibition *The American Renaissance 1876–1917*, organized by the Brooklyn Museum in 1979,[14] in which he was ignored. The episode is more telling about the publication than about the architect, and it is in this capacity that the mark on the curve is useful; it pinpoints something about the Brooklyn Museum exhibit that might have been overlooked otherwise. A procedure to search systematically for this sort of event is presented in chapter 7.

Locating on the histogram important dates in the architect's life and career, such as the completion of major projects and the acceptance of awards, is often helpful to understand the connections between built and published records. Reading the texts, I might add, is also important, not only the ones citing the architect but also those ignoring him. Such work, however, exceeds the limits of this project.

Citations in journals and periodicals are often more strongly intertwined with the professional career than citations in books. Kanter and Herbert[15] counted the articles on Louis Kahn in professional and popular journals from 1950 to 1984, finding a series of peak years in correspondence with the termination of Kahn's major projects, his death, and the tenth anniversary of his death. The decisive factors behind book citations are often other citations rather than the built work. Indeed, Wright's emergence in the American architectural literature was prompted by a textual event, not an architectural one: Schuyler's early article on the master was induced by, and devoted to, two volumes about Wright published in Germany in the preceding years.

In the Schuyler-Wright case the literary clue was explicit; more often it remains hidden. Banham once intimated that the names of Charles and Henry Greene, Irving Gill, Bernard Maybeck, and Rudolph M. Schindler were barely known to him and his fellow architectural historians through the 1950s.[16] "Then this extraordinary book [*Five California Architects*, by Esther McCoy] came out in 1960, and—suddenly—California architecture had heroes, history and character." The architects become objects of international pilgrimage. Their histograms (figure 5.8) suggest that Banham may have overestimated the impact of McCoy's book: by 1960 the West Coast architects were already on their way to becoming established in the literature. The book, however, consolidated their standing. As it is restricted to an area of the country, it is not referenced in this project, but some of the texts included in the corpus may have been equally consequential. Analysis of the indexes will show the influential works and the duration of their influence (chapter 6).

Wright appeared unusually late on the literary scene; by 1913 he had been practicing for approximately twenty-five years and had completed many seminal projects, including the Larkin Building, the Unity Temple, and the Robie House. His younger contemporaries Shreve, Lamb, & Harmon and Raymond Hood climbed to prominence earlier in their careers and more rapidly (figure 5.9), and that was true also for the masters of the next generation.

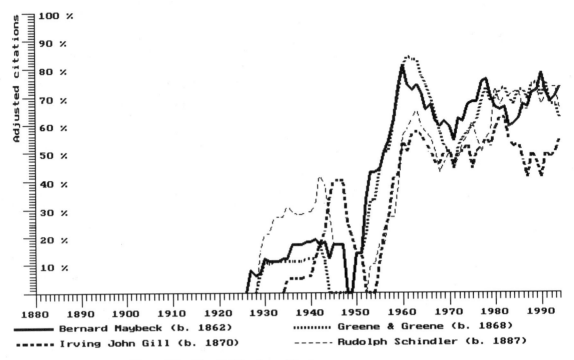

Figure 5.8   Five California architects

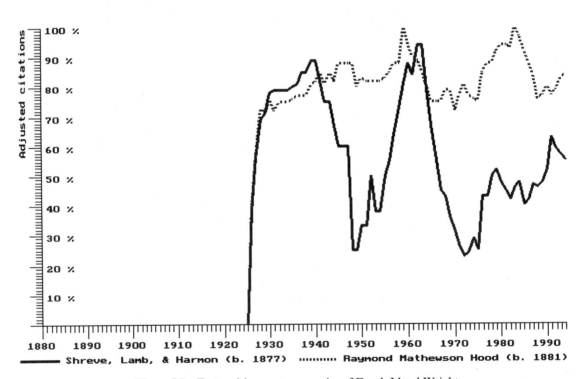

Figure 5.9   Faster-rising contemporaries of Frank Lloyd Wright

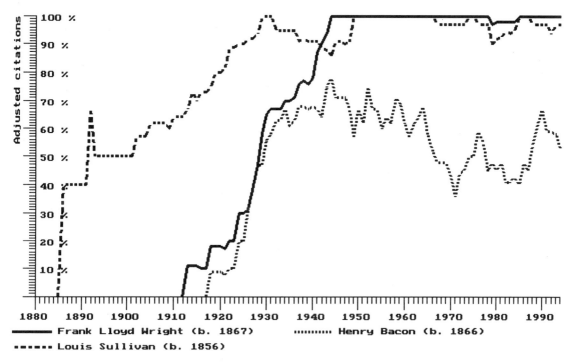

Figure 5.10   Road companions of Frank Lloyd Wright

The histograms for Shreve, Lamb, & Harmon and Hood are almost coincident during their early years. This is hardly surprising, as they worked in the same place (New York City), at the same time (the 1920s and 1930s), and in the same style—Shreve, Lamb, & Harmon as architects for the Empire State Building, and Hood for Rockefeller Center and the Daily News building.

Architects related in terms of style, chronology, regional affiliation, historical significance, or design philosophy often display similar histograms, but the reverse is not necessarily true: stylistic or historical congruence cannot be construed from parallelism, or even coincidence, of histograms. As the architect for the Lincoln Memorial in Washington and a champion of Beaux-Arts architecture, Henry Bacon was as far removed from Frank Lloyd Wright (who was only one year his junior) as it is possible to be; yet the histograms for the beginning of Bacon's and Wright's literary careers are almost coincident (figure 5.10). Their curves diverge near World War II, at the height of the struggle between Modernists and Classicists; it is clear who had the upper hand.

Close histograms reveal a common destiny in architectural discourse: the architects erupt onto the center stage of public consciousness or fade from the limelight hand in hand. They travel together, advancing at the same pace, making the same stops, traversing the same historiographical space. Polar opposites such as Wright and Bacon, even enemies, relate this way. Villains play as important a role in a narrative structure as heroes; each is required to define the place of the other. From a textual standpoint, God and the Devil often share the same territory: if one of them appears in discourse, the other is likely to emerge too; if one is ignored, so is the other.

A rising histogram does not necessarily bespeak positive treatment in the literature, any more than negative views are associated with declining curves. There is no correlation between histogram gradient and reference contents. Evaluations by critics and historians shift repeatedly; one generation's master often becomes the next generation's scoundrel. Rather than these fast-paced, changing evaluations, histograms portray the slower processes of a person's emergence into and then fading from collective interest.

Sullivan's and Wright's histograms become nearly indistinguishable since Wright's access to full dominance. The coincidence reflects still another type of connection. The architects were not contemporaries working in the same idiom, as were Shreve, Lamb, & Harmon and Hood, or opponents such as Wright and Bacon; they belonged to different generations and had their own stylistic orientation. But their relationship of mentor to apprentice, although strained at times, became one of the lasting legends in the mythology of modernism. Just as it was unthinkable to write about American architecture without dealing with Wright, it became impossible to speak of Wright without referring to his *Lieber Meister*. Wright pulled Sullivan along in his own rise, or at least delayed Sullivan's descent.

Proximity in discourse results from a variety of semantic relationships: similarity, opposition, temporal sequence, and so on. Any connection between architects, if endorsed by a significant number of writers, will make their histograms converge. Close histograms show only that the architects are related in discourse; the nature of the relationship cannot be derived from the shape of the histograms alone. Mies van der Rohe and Gropius, who brought the International Style to America after fleeing prewar Germany, followed parallel paths in their professional and academic careers and in the literature; their histograms are nearly indistinguishable (figure 5.11).

Such parallelism does not necessarily denote stylistic or ideological congruence. But analysis of indexes can be pushed further, to search not only for similar citation frequencies but also for citations occurring in the same texts. Because of their nearly coincidental arrival from Europe, Gropius and Mies burst onto the American architectural scene and into its literature almost exactly at the same time.[17] At first, however, they were not necessarily cited in the same texts. It was only after the midcentury, with the crystallization of the Modern Movement as a style and ideology, that they and their colleagues of similar persuasion became a solid block of names to be featured in toto, either all cited or all ignored. They became, like Adam and Eve, characters in the same story, elements of the same discourse. They became cotextual (chapter 9). Cotextuality entails a stronger connection between citation patterns than histogram parallelism or even histogram coincidence. The latter implies only citation in the same proportion of texts; the former requires citation in the same texts.

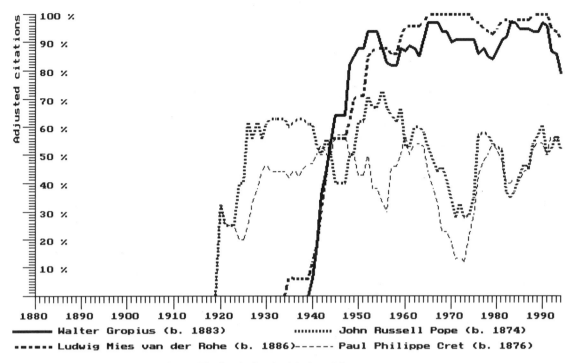

Figure 5.11   The battle for the Modern Movement

When Gropius and Mies arrived in this country, Neoclassical architects John Russell Pope and Paul Cret dominated the scene; their histograms (also included in figure 5.11) were running higher that that of either Wright or Bacon. The collapse of Neoclassicism starting at the midcentury is visible, as is the reversal of the trend during the mid-1970s when the aesthetic and ideological climate changed once again. Bacon's histogram follows the same pattern. The curves may be used to follow the changing fortunes not only of individuals but of styles or schools.

Histograms are powerful descriptive and analytical tools for more precise renderings of issues touched on in the preceding chapters. Architects were assigned time bars in figures 3.5 through 3.7 to represent their presence or absence in public awareness. Histograms are more informative: they disclose degrees of thereness. The bars of chapter 3 reveal that Hallet, Mangin, & McComb and Hoban fade away during the second half of the century, in contrast to a strong showing by their contemporary Jefferson; the histograms of figure 5.12 describe the process in more richness. (The information conveyed in the two graphs is not equivalent, however. The bars are based on all citations since the earliest text of the corpus. Histograms are drawn for citations in recent, active texts only.)

It was pointed out in chapter 4 that Colonial architecture started to receive substantial attention in the literature only after World War II. With access to histograms it is now possible to distinguish the fate of specific Colonial architects.

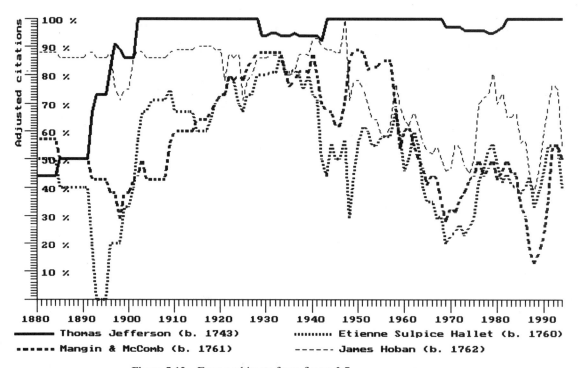

Figure 5.12 Four architects from figure 3.7

Superimposing the histograms of John Kearsley and Peter Harrison, one can see that they substituted each other as leading personalities several times (figure 5.13), with Kearsley being stronger during the early half of this century and Harrison becoming the mandatory reference during the second half.

Histograms for selected twentieth-century architects are furnished in figures 5.14 through 5.24. Not every one portrays a success story. The literary presence of prominent architects of the 1950s and 1960s, such as Carl Koch, a proponent of industrialized housing, and Victor Lundy was severely undercut in the ensuing years (figure 5.24). The histograms of every architect in the roster can be accessed through the electronic companion.

Early and Late Risers

It took Frank Lloyd Wright nearly thirty years to climb from the first citation to a position of dominance in the literature with 100 percent citations. Maya Lin, who was still an architectural student when she won the competition for the design of the Vietnam Memorial in Washington, achieved the same feat in two years (figure 5.25). This was influenced by individual circumstances, such as the extraordinary media attention garnered by the controversial memorial competition, and Wright's difficult personal struggles in the early stages of his career. But the contrast in climbing times also attests to the different perfor-

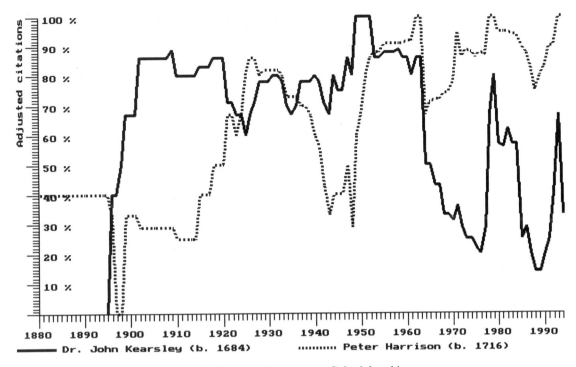

Figure 5.13   Shifting positions among Colonial architects

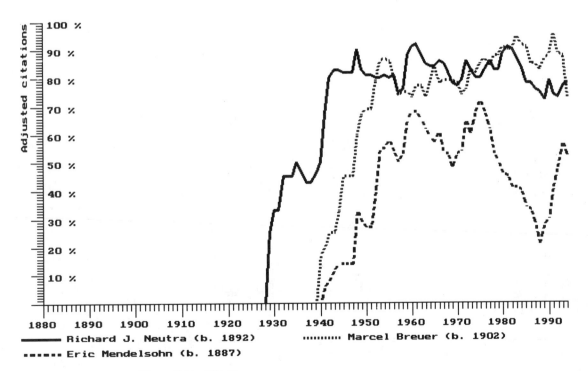

Figure 5.14   The Europeans

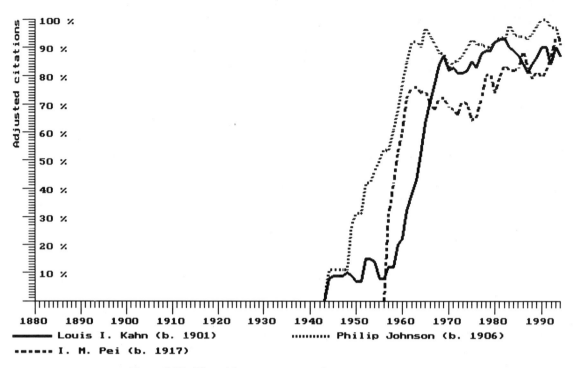

Figure 5.15   The mid-century masters I

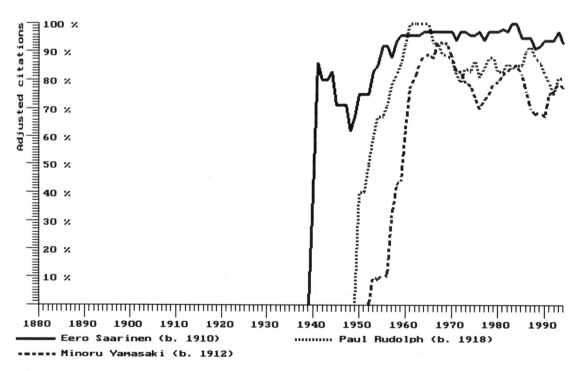

Figure 5.16   The mid-century masters II

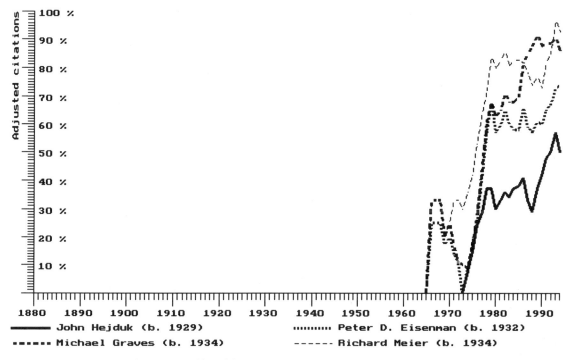

Figure 5.17   The whites

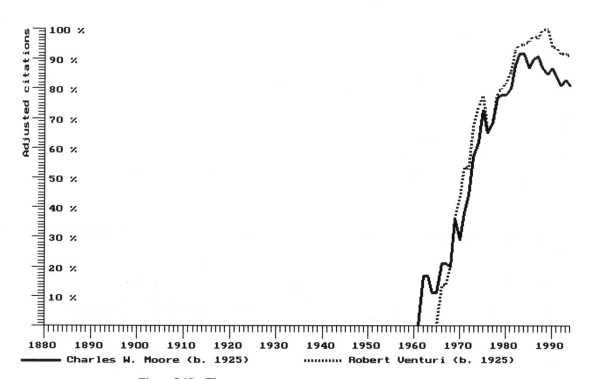

Figure 5.18   The grays

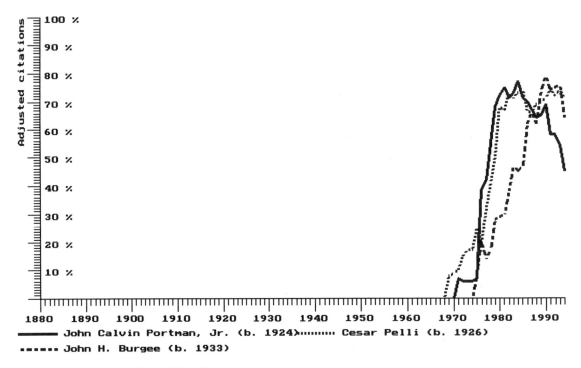

Figure 5.19   The recent past I

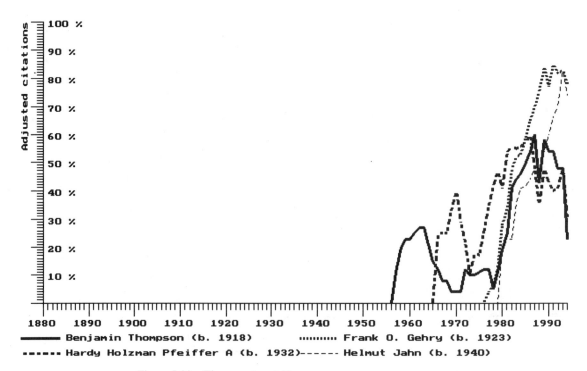

Figure 5.20   The recent past II

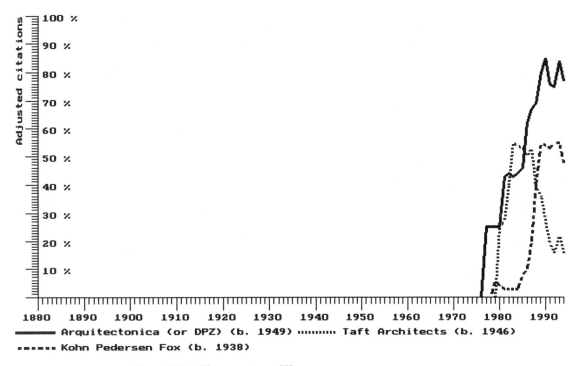

Figure 5.21   The recent past III

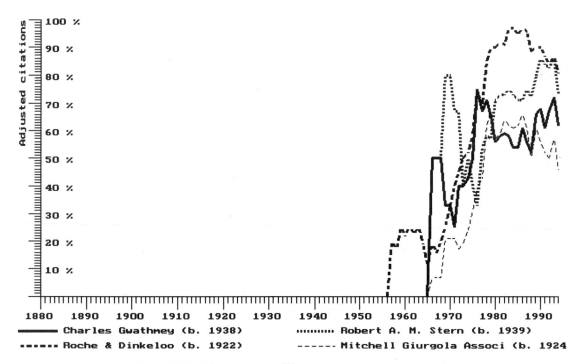

Figure 5.22   The recent past IV

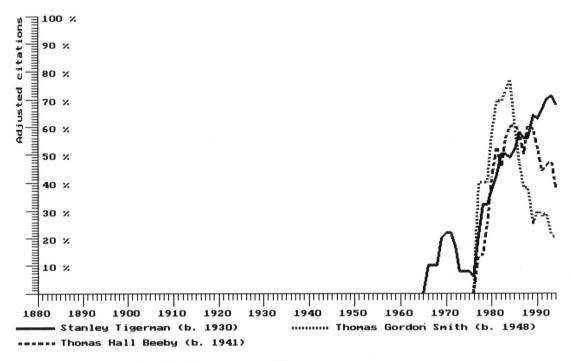

Figure 5.23   The recent past V

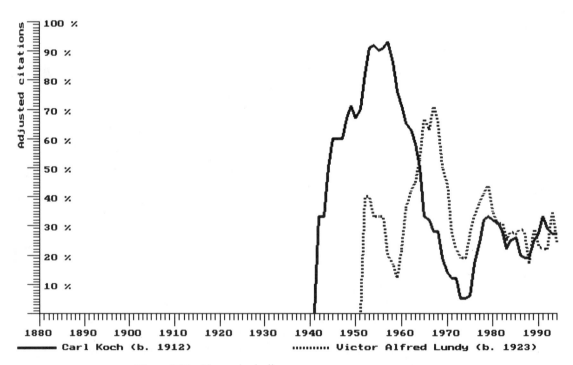

Figure 5.24   Names in decline

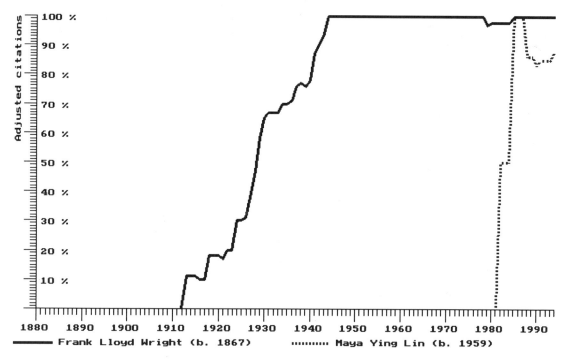

Figure 5.25 Different rise times

mance of the daily and professional presses at the beginning and the end of the century—their competitiveness, their willingness to assume risks, and their response time. Departures from the norm bespeak individual singularities, the norms themselves reveal societal standards, and both are amenable to index analytical scrutiny.

But there is also an internal, methodological reason behind the difference between the two histograms. The number of years a text remains in short-term memory limits the gradient at which curves may rise or plunge. If an architect were to burst into the literature with unsurpassable force (say, the person was never cited before, but after a momentous date is never ignored again), and if texts remained in memory for ten years, it would take full ten years for the histogram to rise from the bottom to the top of the diagram. The texts in memory could be renewed no sooner. According to our assumptions, writings remained effectual at the time Wright was emerging in the literature much longer than during the Lin years. Because of this factor alone, his curve could not possibly resemble hers, even if he had gained instant recognition.

Histogram users are interested only in external factors such as career paths and reaction time of the media; but as the curves are affected by internal factors as well, these must be acknowledged and their impact discounted. Steady histograms are helpful in achieving this. A steady histogram is the way an architect's curve would look if the citations were to be rearranged into a constant stream, altering their spacing but not their numbers. The real histogram may run above,

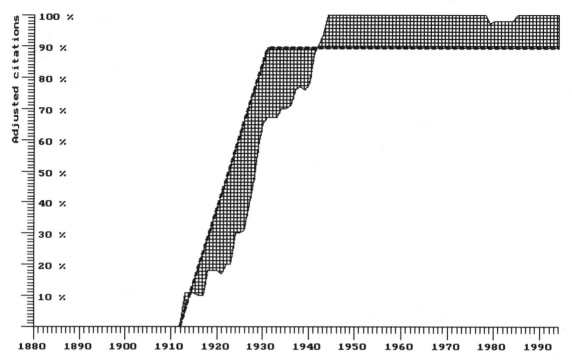

Figure 5.26 Steady histogram and deviations from steadiness: Frank Lloyd Wright (b. 1867)

below, or near the ideal curve; the divergence highlights deviations from constancy in the citation pattern, adding considerably to the meaning of the curve.

Steady histograms are composed of two straight lines: one rising from the first citation to a hypothetical stabilization point, followed by a constant (horizontal) line from there on. (See the appendix for a more detailed explanation.) Deviations from steadiness in Wright's and Lin's histograms are marked with shading in figures 5.26 and 5.27. In Wright's case, the real curve remains below the steady curve during the early part of his career. In view of his ultimate success, his early citations in the literature were indeed fewer than "normal." Lin, in contrast, achieved a peak sooner in her life and faster than most. The initial conclusions about the speed of their ascent are confirmed; the contrast between the two remains striking even after internal, methodological forces have been factored into the equation.

Access to steady histograms yields an additional payoff as well. Deviations from steadiness as represented by the shaded areas are easily measured so that architects can be ranked in terms of the steadiness of their literary careers. Latrobe, Gropius, Breuer, and Hejduk appear among the steadiest (figures 5.28–5.31). Two patterns are found at the opposite end of the scale: "early risers" such as Peabody and Sterns, Lescaze, and Lyndon (figures 5.32–5.34), and "late risers" such as Greene & Greene, Kahn, and Roche & Dinkeloo

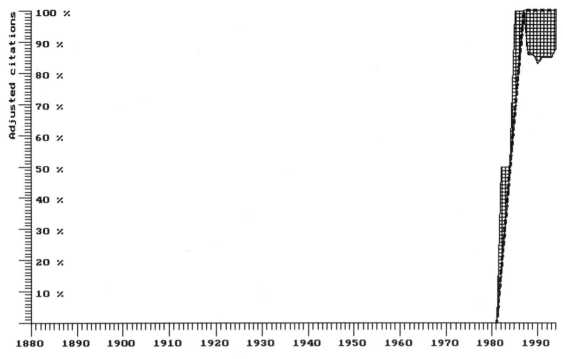

Figure 5.27   Steady histogram and deviations from steadiness: Maya Ying Lin (b. 1959)

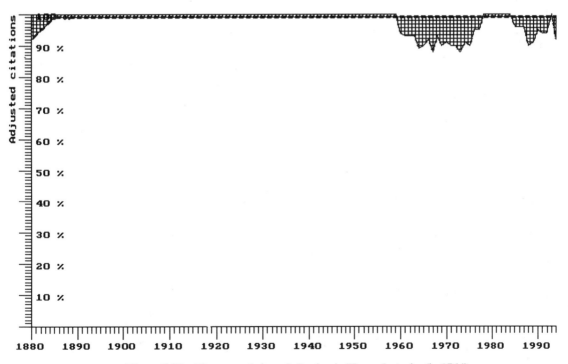

Figure 5.28   The normal risers I: Benjamin Henry Latrobe (b. 1764)

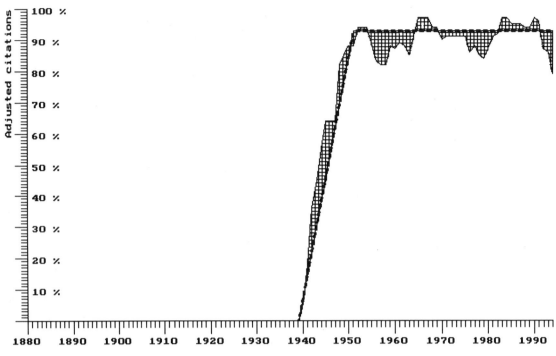

Figure 5.29   The normal risers II: Walter Gropius (b. 1883)

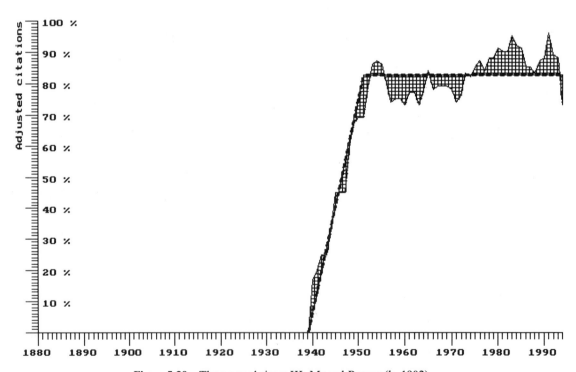

Figure 5.30   The normal risers III: Marcel Breuer (b. 1902)

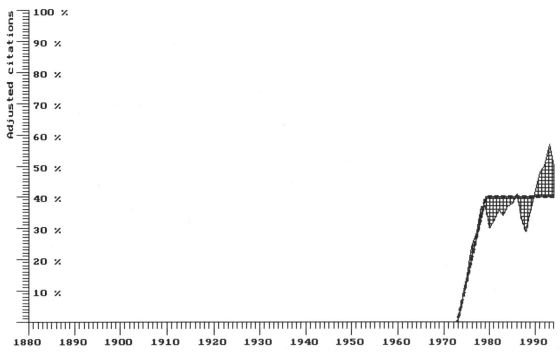

Figure 5.31   The normal risers IV: John Hejduk (b. 1929)

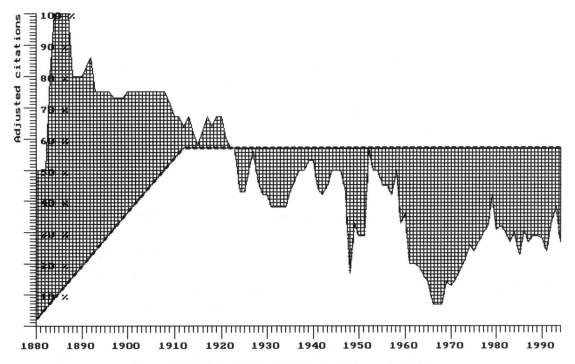

Figure 5.32   The early risers I: Peabody & Stearns (b. 1845)

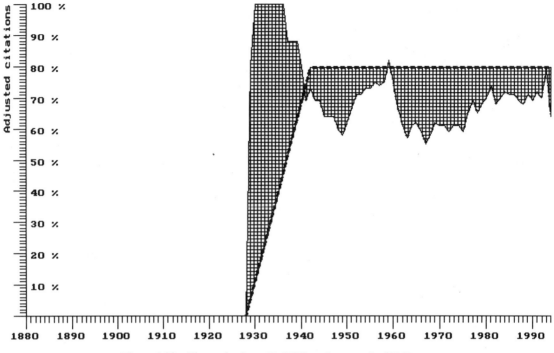

Figure 5.33   The early risers II: William Lescaze (b. 1896)

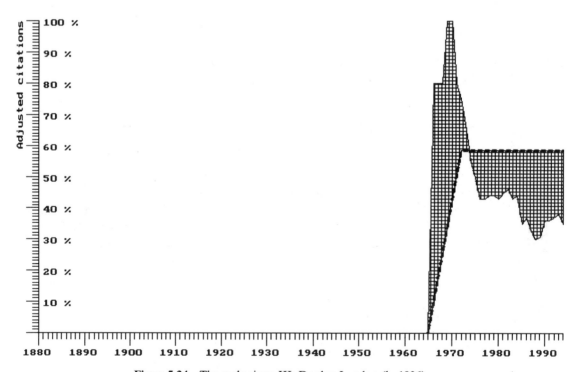

Figure 5.34   The early risers III: Donlyn Lyndon (b. 1936)

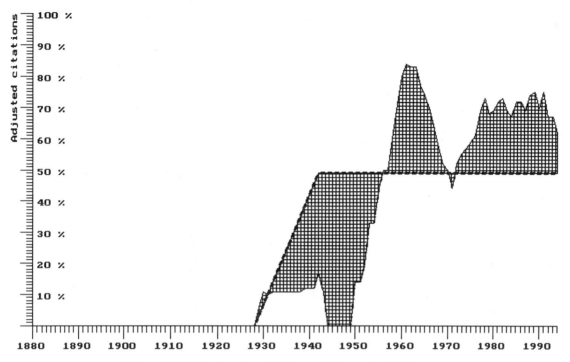

Figure 5.35   The late risers I: Greene & Greene (b. 1868)

(figures 5.35–5.37), and, of course, Wright himself. Early starters do better than steady climbers initially, and fall beyond later on; the opposite is true for late starters.

There is still another pattern. The literary careers of certain architects present a series of alternating periods of vigor and weakness. The firm of Shreve, Lamb, & Harmon underwent two periods of each type (figure 5.38). Bruce Goff went through a total of three peak periods, with more citations than normal, separated by two valleys (figure 5.39).

Remember Goff? He was mentioned in chapter 1 for his unusual citation pattern. We wondered at the time how unique his case really was; we did not know. Now we have at last a procedure to answer the question. Goff's citation pattern is very unusual indeed: in terms of average annual deviation from normalcy, his histogram is in the ninety-eighth percentile: 98 percent of the architects in the roster have steadier citation patterns!

The meaning of a histogram is best perceived if one traces it with queries at critical points in the curve such as the valleys and the peaks. Queries were used earlier for Frank Lloyd Wright's histogram (figures 5.3–5.7). Six queries for Goff's histogram are reported in figures 5.40 through 5.45.

In 1930 Cheney published *The New World Architecture* devoting one illustration and a brief line to 26-year-old Goff, and one of Goff's churches was included among Conant's selections for the *University Prints*. At that time no

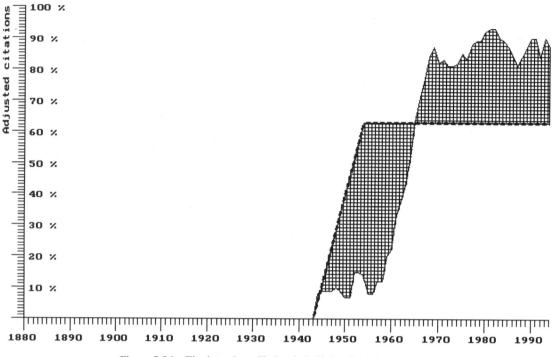

Figure 5.36   The late risers II: Louis I. Kahn (b. 1901)

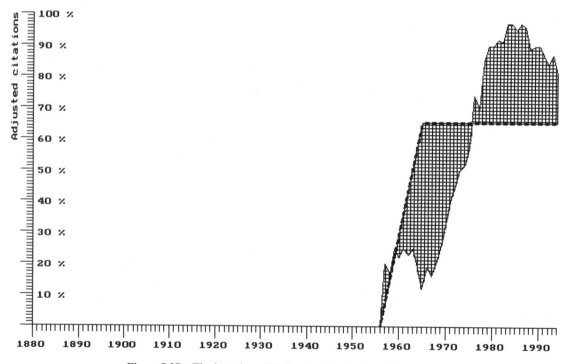

Figure 5.37   The late risers III: Roche & Dinkeloo (b. 1922)

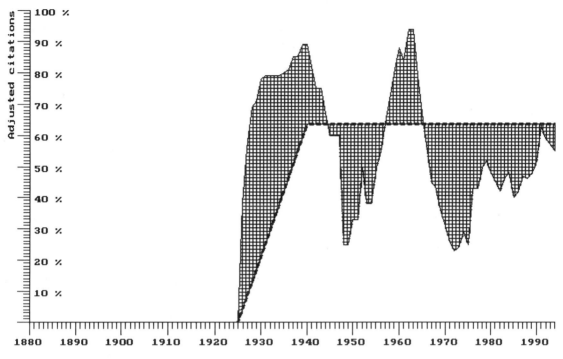

Figure 5.38   Mixed case I: Shreve, Lamb, & Harmon (b. 1877)

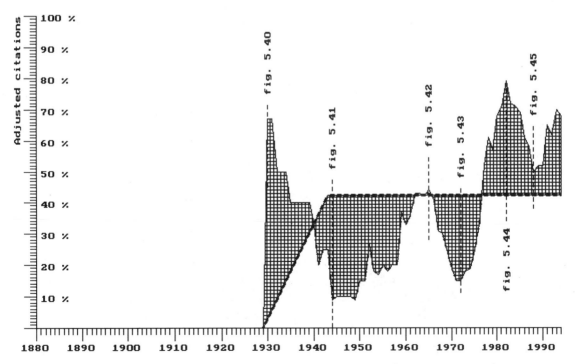

Figure 5.39   Mixed case II: Bruce Alonzo Goff (b. 1904)

Figure 5.40   Bruce Goff: Query for 1930 (pertinent texts from 1911 to 1930)

Citations: 2		
#58	1930	Cheney: *The New World Architecture*
#59	1930	Conant (ed.): *Modern Architecture*

Omissions: 1

One dummy omission introduced to compensate for insufficient relevant texts.

Adjusted citations: 0.67

Figure 5.41   Bruce Goff: Query for 1944 (pertinent texts from 1931 to 1944)

Citations: 1		
#80	1942	Newcomb: *History of Modern Architecture*

Omissions: 10		
#62	1932	Barr, Hitchcock, Johnson, & Mumford: *Modern Architects*
#63	1932	Hitchcock & Johnson: *The International Style*
#66	1935	Cahill & Barr: *Art in America*
#73	1940	Roth: *The New Architecture*
#74	1941	Architectural Record: "American Architecture 1891–1941"
#75	1941	Pencil Points: "Forty Under Forty"
#76	1941	Giedion: *Space, Time, and Architecture*
#77	1941	Johnson: "Architecture" (in *The American Year Book*)
#79	1942	Museum of Modern Art: *What Is Modern Architecture?*
#82	1944	Mock: *Built in America 1932–1944*

Adjusted citations: 0.09

other texts were in existence in which architects of his generation could expect to be featured. Goff's adjusted citations would be 100 percent—two citations of a possible total of two. Being based on too small a sample, the figure is deceiving. When faced with fewer than three pertinent texts, a few dummy omissions that do not correspond to real texts are automatically added by the system (see the appendix). With one dummy omission, Goff's adjusted citations for 1930 became 0.67.

Although books in which he could conceivably have been featured started to be published through the 1930s, Goff was not included in them at first. With each such new text the architect's curve drops one notch. An all-time low comes in 1944: Cheney's and Conant's aging books have faded away; ten newer texts cover his period, but he is cited in only one. Adjusted citations: 9 percent (figure 5.41).

Goff is acknowledged in almost one-half of the texts issued between 1958 and 1965, bringing up his standing to 0.44 (figure 5.42). This is, however, the beginning of a new descent. The architect is cited in only four of twenty-seven pertinent texts published between 1966 and 1972 (figure 5.43). The second rebirth in his literary career occurs between 1977 and 1982, with 79 percent of citations, Goff's all time high (figure 5.44). Another low point is established for 1988 at 50 percent (figure 5.45), at which time still one more ascent is starting.

Figure 5.42   Bruce Goff: Query for 1965 (pertinent texts from 1958 to 1965)

Citations: 11

#119	1959	Francastel: *Les Architects Celèbres*
#120	1959	Joedicke: *A History of Modern Architecture*
#122	1959	Kulterman: *Architecture of Today*
#123	1959	McCallum: *Architecture USA*
#129	1961	Burchard & Bush-Brown: *The Architecture of America*
#130	1961	*Contemporary Architecture of the World 1961*
#132	1961	Jones: *Architecture Today and Tomorrow*
#136	1962	Banham: *Guide to Modern Architecture*
#140	1964	Creighton: *American Architecture*
#146	1964	Pehnt: *Encyclopedia of Modern Architecture*
#149	1965	Drexler: *Modern Architecture USA*

Omissions: 14

#117	1958	Peter: *Masters of Modern Architecture*
#124	1959	Reed: *The Golden City*
#125	1960	Andrews: *Architecture in America*
#128	1960	Pierson & Davidson: *Arts in the United States*
#131	1961	Fletcher: *A History of Architecture* (ed. Cordingley)
#133	1961	Scully: *Modern Architecture*
#134	1961	Von Eckardt (ed.): *Mid-Century Architecture in America*
#139	1963	Jacobus: *Modern Architecture*
#141	1964	*Encyclopaedia Britannica*, 14th ed. (1964)
#145	1964	Muschenheim: *Elements of the Art of Architecture*
#147	1964	Tschacbasov: *Teachers Manual for the Study of Art History*
#148	1965	Collins: *Changing Ideals in Modern Architecture: 1750–1950*
#152	1965	Rogers: *What's Up in Architecture*
#153	1965	Ulanov: *The Two Worlds of American Art*

Adjusted citations: 0.44

Only the arithmetic of the histogram was followed here; not a very productive endeavor, since everything can be noted at a glance in the curve itself. A Goff scholar, however, might learn more by examining the texts listed in the queries. The nature of the successive citations (their content, length, illustrations, etc.) would give a fuller view of the evolution of Goff's place in the literature. Looking at the omissions is important too. Why was he left out? Perhaps he did not really belong to the subject matter; if so, the books should be ignored. Otherwise, the omissions stake out the outer limits of the man's literary impact.

The list of an important architect's citations and omissions is indicative about the texts themselves. Goff is a landmark in the evolution of American architectural culture; citation of his work means an endorsement of certain values and coolness toward others. Choosing to cite him or to ignore him reveals the writer's orientation and preferences, as well as sources. This idea is developed in chapter 9.

Figure 5.43   Bruce Goff: Query for 1972 (pertinent texts from 1966 to 1972)

Citations: 4

#157	1966	Heyer: *Architects on Architecture*
#160	1966	Read: *Encyclopedia of the Arts*
#178	1969	Whiffen: *American Architecture Since 1780*
#197	1972	Sharp: *Visual History of 20th Century Architecture*

Omissions: 23

#154	1966	Benevolo: *History of Modern Architecture*
#155	1966	Fitch: *American Building: The Historical Forces that Shaped It*
#156	1966	Green: *American Art. A Historical Survey*
#158	1966	Jacobus: *Twentieth Century Architecture: The Middle Years 1940–66*
#159	1966	Myers: *McGraw-Hill Dictionary of Art*
#162	1966	*The World Almanac and Book of Facts 1967*
#164	1967	Giedion: *Space, Time, and Architecture*, rev. ed.
#165	1967	Hillier: *From Tepees to Towers*
#168	1968	Condit: *American Building . . . from Beginning to the Present*
#171	1968	Norman: *Traveler's Guide to American Art*
#172	1968	Portoghesi: *Dizionario enciclopedico di architetture e urbanistica*
#173	1969	Joedicke: *Architecture Since 1945*
#174	1969	Jordan: *A Concise History of Western Architecture*
#176	1969	Scully: *American Architecture and Urbanism*
#179	1970	Hamilton: *19th & 20th Century Art: Painting, sculpture, architecture*
#180	1970	Hofmann & Kultermann: *Modern Architecture in Color*
#181	1970	Mendelowitz: *A History of American Art*
#183	1970	Osborne: *The Oxford Companion to Art* (main entries only)
#187	1971	*The World Almanac and Book of Facts 1972*
#188	1971	Jencks: *Architecture 2000*
#191	1972	*Encyclopaedia Britannica*, 14th ed. (1972)
#194	1972	Fitch: *American Building: The Environmental Forces that Shaped It*
#196	1972	Jordy: *American Buildings: Impact of European Modernism*

Adjusted citations: 0.15

Evaluation and Interpretation

Is it necessary to resort to index analysis to learn about all of this? Couldn't scholars determine by ordinary means which writers are sympathetic to which architects? They could, and the same is true about outlining the impact of an architect's work in the literature, or distinguishing steady citation patterns from early and late risers. The index analyst's findings are hardly unprecedented; the noteworthy aspect of the work is the speedy and effortless way in which it is possible to access the information. The analyst generates histograms for thousands of architects instantly and automatically. The system also measures deviations from steadiness in architects' literary fortunes, ranks the individuals accordingly, and flags typical as well as atypical citation patterns.

Scholars interested in specific architects could research their citation patterns working manually in libraries, but few of them do. This is hardly surprising: the

Figure 5.44   Bruce Goff: Query for 1982 (pertinent texts from 1977 to 1982)

Citations: 26

#225	1977	Jencks: *The Language of Post-Modern Architecture*
#226	1977	Jencks: *The Language of Post-Modern Architecture*, rev. ed.
#227	1977	Milwaukee Art Center: *An American Architecture*
#228	1977	Richards: *Who's Who in Architecture* (main entries only)
#229	1977	Richards: *Who's Who in Architecture*
#230	1977	Smith, C. R.: *Supermannerism*
#237	1978	Williamson: "An Architectural Family Tree"
#247	1980	Emanuel (ed.): *Contemporary Architects*
#249	1980	*GA Document Special Issue* 1970–1980
#250	1980	Hunt: *Encyclopedia of American Architecture*
#251	1980	Hunt: *Encyclopedia of American Architecture* (main entries only)
#253	1980	Nuttgens: *Pocket Guide to Architecture*
#255	1980	Raeburn: *Architecture of the Western World*
#256	1980	Reid: *The Book of Buildings*
#259	1981	Jencks: *The Language of Post-Modern Architecture*, 3rd ed.
#260	1981	Rugoff: *Encyclopedia of American Art*
#261	1981	Sanderson: *Int. Handbook of Contemporary Developments in Architecture*
#262	1981	Smith, K.: *The Architecture of the United States*
#266	1981	Thorndike: *Three Centuries of Notable American Architects*
#267	1981	Whiffen & Koepper: *American Architecture 1607–1976*
#268	1981	Wolfe: *From Bauhaus to Our House*
#271	1982	Curtis: *Modern Architecture Since 1900*
#272	1982	Jencks: *Architecture Today*
#273	1982	*Macmillan Encyclopedia of Architects* (Placzek, ed.)
#274	1982	McCoy & Goldstein: *Guide to U.S. Architecture 1940–1980*
#277	1982	Wright: *Highlights to Recent American Architecture 1945–1978*

Omissions: 7

#233	1977	Stierlin: *Encyclopaedia of World Architecture*
#235	1978	Burton: *A Choice Over Our Heads*
#243	1979	Roth: *A Concise History of American Architecture*
#248	1980	Frampton: *Modern Architecture*
#258	1981	*The New Encyclopaedia Britannica*, 15th ed.
#264	1981	*The World Almanac and Book of Facts 1982*
#270	1982	Condit: *American Building. Materials and Techniques*

Adjusted citations: 0.79

Figure 5.45   Bruce Goff: Query for 1988 (pertinent texts from 1984 to 1988)

Citations: 12

#285	1984	Hunt: *American Architecture. A Field Guide*
#286	1984	Jencks: *The Language of Post-Modern Architecture*, 4th ed.
#295	1985	Handlin: *American Architecture*
#300	1985	Maddex: *Master Builders*
#302	1985	Stimpson: *Fieldguide to Landmarks of Modern Architecture in United States*
#304	1986	Barford: *Understanding Modern Architecture*
#308	1986	Lampugnani: *Encyclopedia of 20th Century Architecture*
#315	1987	Musgrove (ed.): *Fletcher's History of Architecture*, 19th ed.
#316	1987	Oppenheimer Dean: "75 Turbulent Years of American Architecture"
#319	1988	Gibberd: *Architecture Source Book*
#320	1988	Hollingworth: *Architecture of the 20th Century*
#325	1988	Nuttgens: *Understanding Modern Architecture*

Omissions: 12

#284	1984	Flon (ed.): *The World Atlas of Architecture*
#287	1984	Jervis: *Design & Designers*
#293	1985	Crouch: *History of Architecture from Stonhenge to Skyscrapers*
#296	1985	Klein & Fogle: *Clues to American Architecture*
#297	1985	Kostof: *A History of Architecture. Settings & Rituals*
#305	1986	De Long, Searing, Stern: *American Architecture* (symposium)
#306	1986	De Long, Searing, Stern: *American Architecture* (exhibition)
#310	1986	Trachtenberg & Hyman: *Architecture from Prehistory to PostModernism*
#322	1988	Klotz: *The History of Postmodern Architecture*
#324	1988	Norberg-Schulz: *New World Architecture*
#326	1988	Pulos: *The American Design Adventure: 1940–1975*
#327	1988	Scully: *American Architecture and Urbanism*, new rev. ed.

Adjusted citations: 0.50

task is very laborious even for a single architect, and the findings would be of moderate interest because patterns become meaningful only by comparison with other patterns. The issue is not whether the results of index analysis could have been achieved by traditional means (they could, at a prohibitive cost), but whether quick and easy access to the data will further research in architectural history and criticism. I believe it will.

Histograms are susceptible to two types of interpretation. If the corpus is accepted as an embodiment of the entire literature, the curves, endowed with a wide significance, represent fluctuations in societal mood. But histograms may also be interpreted in a more restrictive albeit still useful way. Uncommon shapes in the curves are tell-tale signs of possible anomalies in a limited set of books. The anomalies are invisible to the naked eye in the texts themselves; only index analysis renders them noticeable.

Certain features in the histograms revealed Goff's early citation by Cheney and Conant, and Wright's absence in the Brooklyn Museum exhibit, which are significant events in themselves, regardless of whether or not the corpus is an acceptable representation of literature at large. Rises and falls in the curves are indicative of architects being cited or ignored in specific texts. That is what they mean—perhaps no more but certainly no less. This type of information is harvested without seductive generalizations about societal or historical trends, which may exceed what is supported by the data. To follow histograms point by point and find out what is behind the changes, it is necessary to access the electronic companion to this book.

Looser interpretations (the ones attaching a wider societal significance to the curves) are probably pertinent before major trends in the histograms; the more restrictive ones are most useful in considering short-term deviations. Other applications of histograms are presented in the ensuing chapters.

Notes

1. Los Teólogos, *El Aleph* 1949.

2. Regional texts could be included in the corpus if the data base were to comprise information about the regions in which each architect and firm worked. Lack of citation in a regional book would be counted only if the architect had worked in that region. Building types could be dealt with the same way. The software could be developed to include these factors, but the number of relevant texts and the data-collection task would expand significantly.

3. The idea can be worded another way. A text is pertinent to an architect if he is cited, or if he was born within the book's coverage span and was in the universe at publication time. Adjusted citations are the number of citations divided by the number of pertinent texts in the corpus.

4. Stevens, Garry: An Alliance Confirmed: Planning Literature and the Social Sciences. *Journal of the American Planning Association*, 1990, vol. 5, pp. 341–349.

5. The word *histogram* is used in statistics to refer to a graphic representation of a frequency distribution. My histograms, in contrast, result from collapsing into a single graph a series of binary frequency distributions (cited-not cited), one for each year. Nonstatisticians should disregard this note.

6. Duncan, Harry: The Permanence of Books. In *Doors of Perception. Essays in Book Typography*. Austin, TX: W. Thomas Taylor, 1987.

7. Perec, George: *Penser/Classer*. Paris: Hachette, 1985.

8. A friend in search of Camilo Sitte's *Die Stadtebau nach seinen kunstlerischen Grundsatzen* visited the store *Architectura & Natura* at the Leliegracht in Amsterdam. The storekeeper, informed of the date of publication of the book, proudly explained that they did not carry titles over ten years old.

9. If Perec's idea had been followed, the size of short-term memory would be constant and its duration would be aleatory, depending on the rate of publication. The dotted line would be horizontal and the line representing years in memory would be bumpy.

10. They are the *Science Citation Index*, the *Social Sciences Citation Index*, and the *Arts and Humanities Citation Index*, published by the Institute for Scientific Information in Philadelphia.

11. Hans Wellish, personal communication, 1983.

12. Texts are pertinent if the architect is or could have been cited, taking into account text coverage, the architect's birth date, and architect's entry into universe.

13. Schuyler published his *American Architecture—Studies* in 1891, without referring to Wright. *American Architecture and Other Writings*, edited by William H. Jordy and Ralph Coe, appeared in 1961, including the material of 1891 plus a selection of articles by Schuyler written between the 1870s and his death in 1914. For the purposes of this study, I dated the 1961 text as if it were of 1913, because all the material contained was first published on or before that date. The lengthiest reference to Wright is in an article of 1912.

14. Wright was featured in the book bearing the same title as the exhibition (#239), but not in the guide and catalogue, which was published first (#240).

15. Kanter, A., and G. Herbert: On Publishing Kahn: A Quantitative View. *Architectural Science Review*, December 1989, vol. 32, pp. 101–104.

16. Banham, Reyner: The Founding Mother. In *The Best of California. Some People, Places and Institutions of the Most Exciting State in the Nation, as Featured in California Magazine, 1976–86*. Santa Barbara: Capra Press, 1986 (pp. 122–125).

17. Mies's curve starts in 1935, before his arrival in this country in 1938. Philip Johnson, in his contribution to *Art in America* (#66), illustrated an apartment in New York with furniture by Mies. This is counted as American work and causes the early start of the curve.

6   The Foresight of Writers

Cheney's and Conant's early citations of the Goff were used in chapter 1 as examples of findings unveiled through the analysis of indexes. Such premature citations would be of little consequence if they were isolated episodes, due perhaps to personal connections between writer and architect. The matter acquires greater relevance, however, if certain texts consistently anticipate important personalities ahead of their time, and other writings feature important architects only after they have been recognized elsewhere, or trumpeted new names that later prove to be of limited or passing interest. Do certain texts fit into such categories? If so, is it possible to identify them merely from their indexes?

With access to histograms, the task is disarmingly simple, at least in principle; the key is to examine the histograms of the architects cited, comparing the evolution of the curves before and after the date of publication of the text.

In 1966 Robert Stern curated a show at the Architectural League of New York entitled *Forty Under Forty. An Exhibition of Young Talent in Architecture*. The histograms of the architects included in the catalog are displayed in figure 6.1,[1] with a dotted line marking the date of the exhibit and publication.[2] Judging by the curves, the architects were almost unknown before the exhibit; many of them, however, became very prominent afterward: Moore, Venturi, Graves, Meier, Turnbull, Lyndon, Gwathmey, and, of course, Stern himself. Except for Moore, who had been cited in the corpus once before, the others were absolute newcomers. Stern was exceptionally foresighted in his choices.

Millar's *The Architects of the American Colonies* (1968) presents a different case. By the time of publication, almost all architects featured had already been discussed in the literature, and some were rarely mentioned again (figure 6.2).

Two distinctly opposite types of texts do indeed exist. Comparing the evolution of the histograms before and after publication time seems a viable procedure to assign texts to one group or the other, or to place them somewhere in between.

There problems arise, however. The first one is practical. It is easy to look at histograms when few names are cited and most of them have been captured by the writer either early or late in their literary careers, as in the case of the

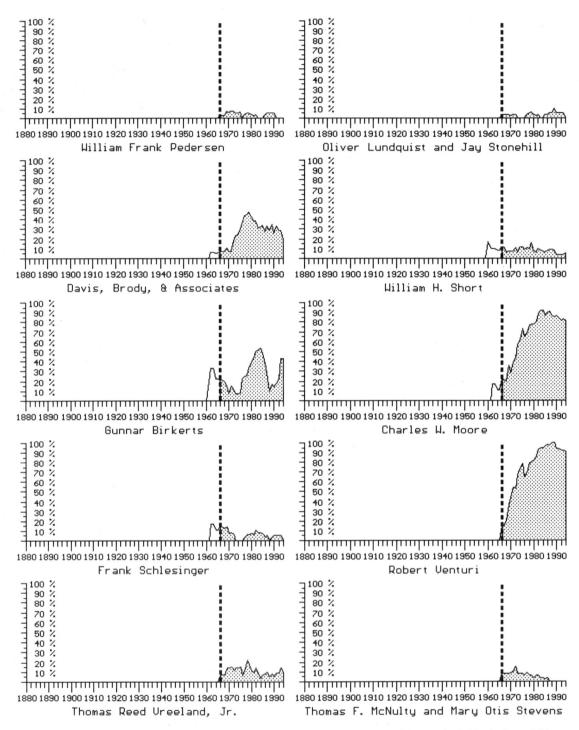

Figure 6.1 Stern: *Forty Under Forty* (1966). All architects cited. Evolution of histograms before and after publication date. Text foresight: 99th percentile

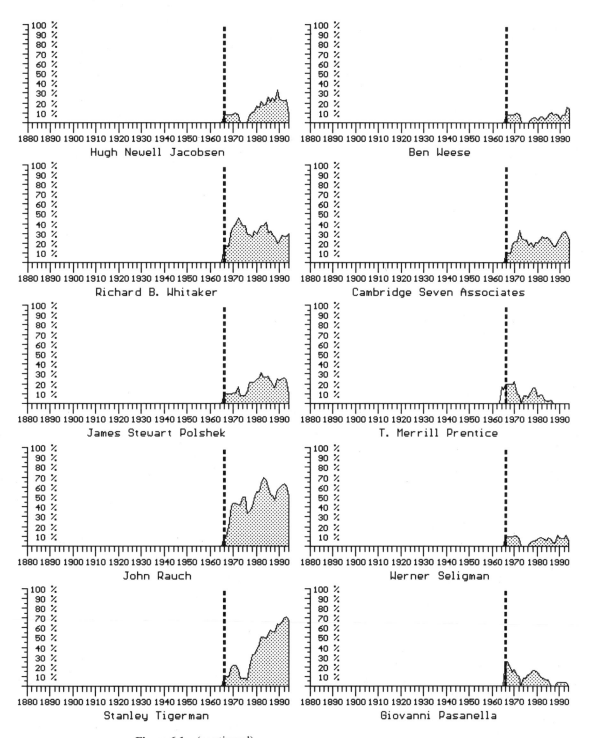

Figure 6.1   (continued)

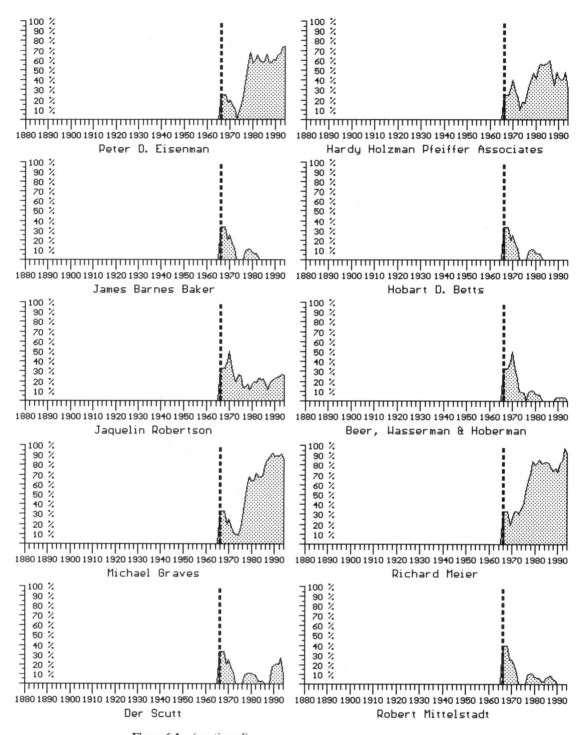

Figure 6.1   (continued)

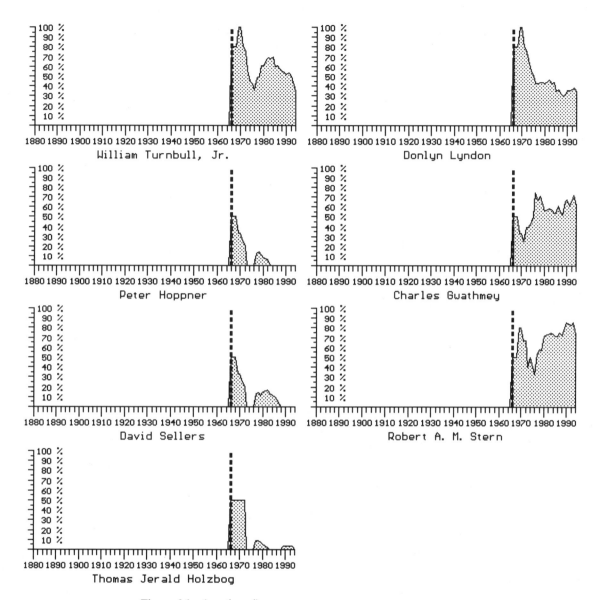

Figure 6.1   (continued)

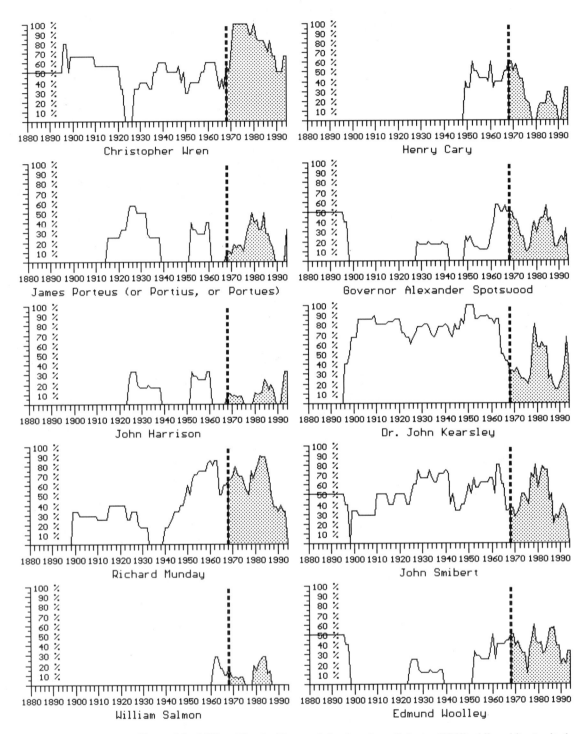

Figure 6.2 Millar: *The Architects of the American Colonies* (1968). All architects cited. Evolution of histograms before and after publication date. Text foresight: 0th percentile

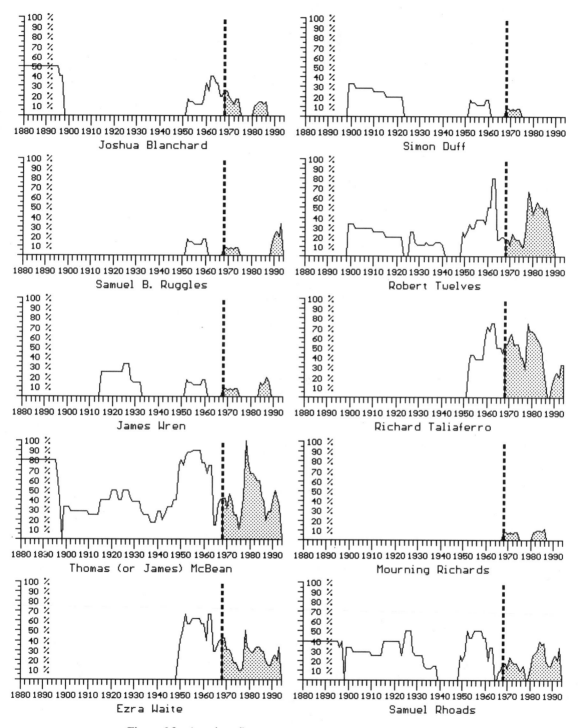

Figure 6.2   (continued)

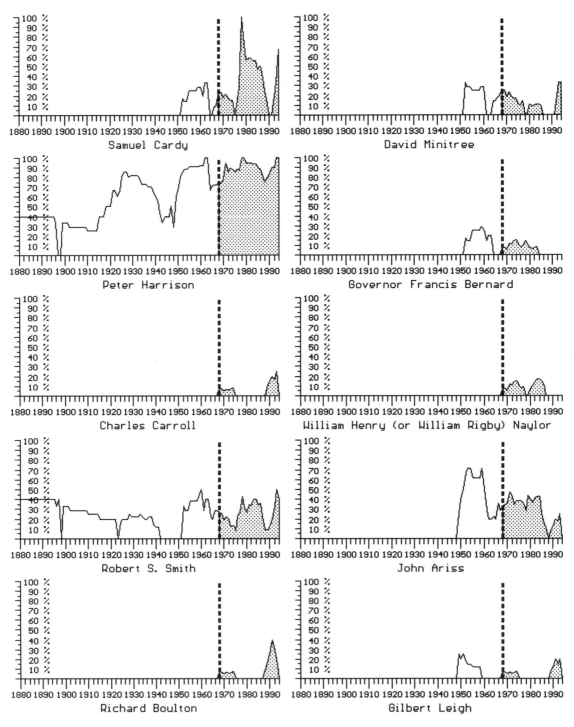

Figure 6.2   (continued)

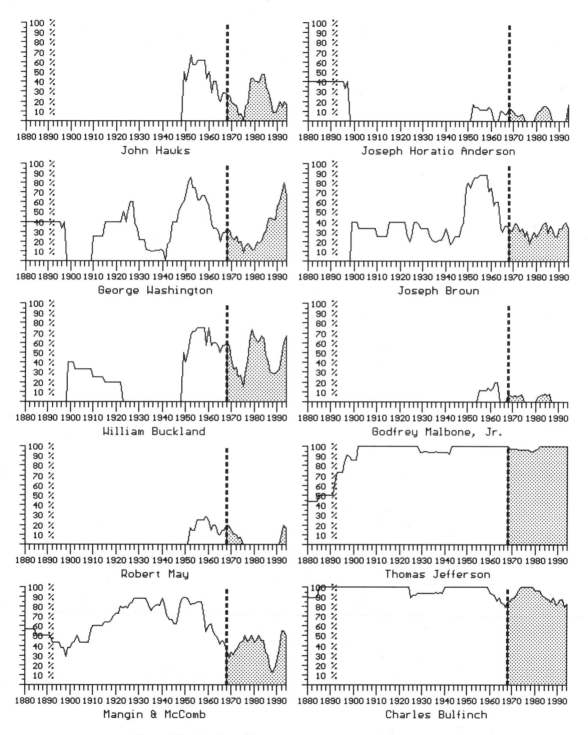

Figure 6.2   (continued)

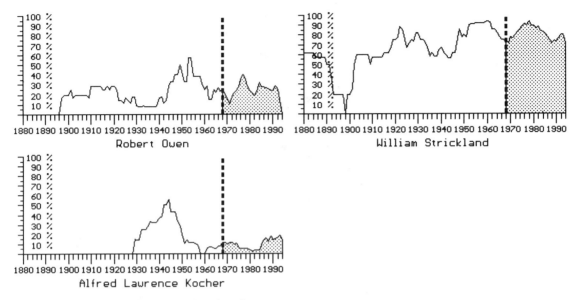

Figure 6.2   (continued)

opening examples; but with hundreds of architects by text and many different patterns for the curves, visual examination is in most cases too arduous. An automated, system-generated classification is called for, based on a comparison of the architects' citation frequencies before and after publication, as represented by the unshaded and shaded areas in figures 6.1 and 6.2.

The second problem is a propensity for skewed results with too early or too recent texts. Because of insufficient earlier publications, histograms start in 1880 at the very earliest. Books published shortly after that date invariably catch architects in the initial segment of their curves. Clever users will not be deceived into believing that they are also in the initial stages of their literary careers; but machines may. Assessing very recent publications poses a similar problem: it is not known yet who among the young emerging architects of today will become tomorrow's brightest stars. Attribution of foresight on the basis of a comparison of the areas under the histograms before and after publication would favor early texts and penalize recent ones.

The solution is, again, simple. Rather than comparing all the shaded and unshaded areas in the histograms, only fixed, predetermined periods—say, twenty years[3]—immediately before and after the publication dates are observed. Texts are assigned a *foresight index* that results from dividing the aggregate of such limited areas in the histograms of all architects cited, before and after publication. Texts are then ranked according to decreasing indexes (figure 6.3). *Forty Under Forty* of 1966, placed in the ninety-ninth percentile, heads the list; *The Architects of the American Colonies* ends it.[4]

Let us look at other foresighted texts. The Museum of Modern Art exhibition *The International Style* (1932) is generally credited with introducing America to

Figure 6.3   Texts ranked according to foresight

Column headings:
[1]   Percentile
[2]   Average age of cited architects at publication time
[3]   Text ID #
[4]   Publication date
[5]   Author and title
Note: texts in shaded areas are discussed in the chapter

[1]	[2]	[3]	[4]	[5]
99	36	161	1966	Stern: *40 Under 40. An Exhibition of Young Talent in Architecture*
99	40	63	1932	Hitchcock & Johnson: *The International Style*
99	60	48	1927	Reagan: *American Architecture of the Twentieth Century*
98	37	75	1941	*Pencil Points*: "Forty Under Forty"
98	47	77	1941	Johnson: "Architecture" (in *The American Year Book*)
97	58	56	1929	Sexton: Composite of books published in 1928–31
97	54	57	1929	Taut: *Modern Architecture*
97	50	83	1945	Reilly: *Some Contemporary American Buildings*
96	49	82	1944	Mock: *Built in America 1932–1944*
96	51	98	1952	Hitchcock & Drexler: *Built in USA: Post-war Architecture*
96	47	79	1942	Museum of Modern Art: *What is Modern Architecture?*
95	114	69	1937	Newcomb: *Spanish-Colonial Architecture in the United States*
95	67	73	1940	Roth: *The New Architecture*
95	54	58	1930	Cheney: *The New World Architecture*
94	53	74	1941	*Architectural Record*: "American Architecture 1891–1941"
94	51	91	1950	AIA: *Contemporary Architecture in the United States 1947–1949*
93	63	60	1930	Hoak & Church: *Masterpieces of Architecture in the United States*
93	51	95	1951	Giedion: *A Decade of Contemporary Architecture*
93	52	62	1932	Barr, Hitchcock, Johnson, & Mumford: *Modern Architects*
92	63	44	1926	Berlin: *Ausstellung Neuer Amerikanischer Baukunst*
92	55	33	1910	*Men and Women of America. A Biographical Dictionary*
92	41	232	1977	Stern (ed.): "Forty Under Forty"
91	52	105	1954	Giedion: *A Decade of Contemporary Architecture*, 2nd ed.
91	57	23	1897	*The Architectural Record Great American Architects Series*
90	71	21	1893	Baedecker: *The United States*
90	152	81	1944	Hamlin, T.: *Greek Revival Architecture in America*
90	54	238	1979	AIA J.: 1st to 3rd Annual Reviews of New American Architecture
89	43	265	1981	Stern: *American Architecture: After Modernism*
89	57	19	1892	Schuyler: *American Architecture—Studies*
89	53	27	1900	Mackson: *American Architecture Interiors & Furniture*
88	61	188	1971	Jencks: *Architecture 2000*
88	75	39	1920	Greber: *L'Architecture aux États-Unies*
88	70	50	1928	Edgell: *The American Architecture of To-day*
87	60	112	1957	McCallum: "Genetrix. Personal Contributions to American Architecture"
87	78	45	1926	Hamlin, T.: *The American Spirit in Architecture*
86	52	24	1897	Statham: *Modern Architecture*
86	58	226	1977	Jencks: *The Language of Post-Modern Architecture*, rev. ed.
86	60	177	1969	Stern: *New Directions in American Architecture*

Figure 6.3   (continued)

[1]	[2]	[3]	[4]	[5]
85	73	127	1960	Huxtable: *Twentieth-Century Architecture*
85	48	137	1962	Dixon: *Architectural Design Preview, USA*
85	63	246	1980	Diamondstein: *American Architecture Now*
84	45	263	1981	Searing: *Speaking a New Classicism: American Architecture Now*
84	59	130	1961	*Contemporary Architecture of the World 1961*
84	93	49	1927	Tallmadge: *The Story of Architecture in America*
83	71	31	1909	Bragdon: "Architecture in The United States"
83	58	249	1980	*GA Document Special Issue 1970–1980*
82	62	214	1976	Kulterman: *New Architecture in the World*
82	63	102	1953	Ferriss: *Power in Buildings*
82	72	54	1929	Hitchcock: *Modern Architecture*
81	76	47	1926	*The Architectural Record* American Architect Golden Anniversary Number
81	94	76	1941	Giedion: *Space, Time, and Architecture*
81	62	225	1977	Jencks: *The Language of Post-Modern Architecture*
80	67	117	1958	Peter: *Masters of Modern Architecture*
80	65	193	1972	Chermayeff: *Observations on American Architecture*
79	50	275	1982	Portoghesi: *After Modern Architecture*
79	68	121	1959	Jones: *Form Givers at Mid-century*
79	113	53	1928	Kimball: *American Architecture*
78	57	269	1982	*AIA J.*: 4th to 6th Annual Reviews of New American Architecture
78	66	122	1959	Kulterman: *Architecture of Today*
78	153	26	1899	Ware: *The Georgian Period*
77	56	230	1977	Smith, C. R.: *Supermannerism*
77	113	34	1910	*The Encyclopaedia Britannica*, 11th ed.
77	75	207	1974	Scully: *The Shingle Style Today*
76	66	242	1979	Drexler: *Transformations in Modern Architecture*
76	70	245	1980	Davern: *Architecture 1970–1980*
75	67	136	1962	Banham: *Guide to Modern Architecture*
75	61	259	1981	Jencks: *The Language of Post-Modern Architecture*, 3rd ed.
75	70	123	1959	McCallum: *Architecture USA*
74	66	93	1950	P/A: "United States Architecture 1900–1950"
74	79	88	1949	Conder: *An Introduction to Modern Architecture*
74	73	120	1959	Joedicke: *A History of Modern Architecture*
73	74	208	1975	Blake & Quint: *Modern Architecture America*
73	74	37	1916	Hamlin, A.D.F.: "25 Years of American Architecture"
73	88	52	1928	Jackman: *American Arts*
72	66	274	1982	McCoy & Goldstein: *Guide to U.S. Architecture 1940–1980*
72	75	97	1952	Hamlin, T.: *Forms and Functions of 20th Century Architecture*
71	91	133	1961	Scully: *Modern Architecture*
71	67	231	1977	Stern: *New Directions in American Architecture*, rev. ed.
71	97	92	1950	Egbert: *Organic Expression and American Architecture*
70	230	101	1952	Morrison: *Early American Architecture*
70	86	30	1905	Fletcher: *A History of Architecture*, 5th ed.
70	74	25	1897	Van Brunt: *Architecture and Society*
69	94	66	1935	Cahill & Barr: *Art in America*
69	136	72	1940	Hamlin, T.: *Architecture Through the Ages*
68	102	55	1929	LaFollette: *Art in America*

Figure 6.3   (continued)

[1]	[2]	[3]	[4]	[5]
68	100	90	1949	Lynes: *The Tastemakers*
68	107	42	1924	Mumford: *Sticks and Stones*
67	90	148	1965	Collins: *Changing Ideals in Modern Architecture: 1750–1950*
67	137	89	1949	Larkin: *Art and Life in America*
67	68	157	1966	Heyer: *Architects on Architecture*
66	113	85	1948	Kouwenhoven: *Made in America*
66	70	277	1982	Wright: *Highlights to Recent American Architecture 1945–1978*
66	94	84	1948	Fitch: *American Building: The Forces that Shape It*
65	92	61	1931	Fletcher: *A History of Architecture*, 9th ed.
65	68	247	1980	Emanuel (ed.): *Contemporary Architects*
64	107	262	1981	Smith, K.: *The Architecture of the United States*
64	98	59	1930	Conant (ed.): *Modern Architecture*
64	94	67	1936	Tallmadge: *The Story of Architecture in America*, rev. ed.
63	121	38	1918	Kimball & Edgell: *A History of Architecture*
63	64	252	1980	Kulterman: *Architecture in the Seventies*
63	77	223	1977	Blake: *Form Follows Fiasco*
62	75	18	1891	Fergusson: *History of Modern Styles of Architecture*
62	119	103	1953	Hamlin, T.: *Architecture Through the Ages*, rev. ed.
62	64	272	1982	Jencks: *Architecture Today*
61	61	278	1983	Colquhoun et al.: *Promising Directions in American Architecture*
61	82	35	1913	Schuyler: *American Architecture and Other Writings*
60	65	254	1980	Portoghesi: *Architecture 1980*
60	101	32	1909	Hamlin, A.D.F.: *A Text-Book of the History of Architecture*, 8th ed.
60	73	189	1971	Kulski: *Architecture in a Revolutionary Era*
59	65	149	1965	Drexler: *Modern Architecture USA*
59	70	132	1961	Jones: *Architecture Today and Tomorrow*
59	73	109	1956	Architectural Record: "100 Years of Significant Building"
58	101	80	1942	Newcomb: *History of Modern Architecture*
58	64	281	1983	Portoghesi: *Postmodern*
58	56	134	1961	Von Eckardt (ed.): *Mid-Century Architecture in America*
57	76	146	1964	Pehnt: *Encyclopedia of Modern Architecture*
57	74	202	1973	Jencks: *Modern Movements in Architecture*
56	86	68	1937	Behrendt: *Modern Building*
56	79	199	1973	Cook & Klotz: *Conversations with Architects*
56	82	201	1973	Jacobus: *American Art of the 20th Century*
55	85	114	1957	USIA: *Architecture USA* (ed.: Blake?)
55	135	218	1976	Smith, K.: *A Pictorial History of Architecture in America*
55	117	107	1955	Scully: *The Shingle Style and the Stick Style*
54	106	145	1964	Muschenheim: *Elements of the Art of Architecture*
54	78	64	1932	*The World Almanac and Book of Facts 1932*
53	103	51	1928	Hamlin, A.D.F.: *A Text-Book of the History of Architecture*, 18th pr.
53	124	28	1902	Schuyler: "United States Architecture"
53	99	29	1902	Sturgis: *A Dictionary of Architecture and Building*
52	109	250	1980	Hunt: *Encyclopedia of American Architecture*
52	181	36	1915	Eberlein: *The Architecture of Colonial America*
52	73	197	1972	Sharp: *Visual History of 20th C Architecture*
51	78	153	1965	Ulanov: *The Two Worlds of American Art*
51	154	46	1926	Jackson: *Development of American Architecture 1783–1830*

Figure 6.3   (continued)

[1]	[2]	[3]	[4]	[5]
51	72	261	1981	Sanderson: *International Handbook of Contemporary Developments in Architecture*
50	108	139	1963	Jacobus: *Modern Architecture*
50	63	286	1984	Jencks: *The Language of Post-Modern Architecture*, 4th ed.
49	79	268	1981	Wolfe: *From Bauhaus to Our House*
49	220	87	1949	Bannister: *From Colony to Nation*
49	102	220	1976	Tafuri & Dal Co.: *Modern Architecture*
48	136	106	1955	Andrews: *Architecture, Ambition, and Americans*
48	135	239	1979	*The American Renaissance 1876–1917* (without Catalogue)
48	117	266	1981	Thorndike: *Three Centuries of Notable American Architects*
47	131	104	1953	Tunnard: *The City of Man*
47	119	237	1978	Williamson: "An Architectural Family Tree"
47	102	248	1980	Frampton: *Modern Architecture*
46	96	124	1959	Reed: *The Golden City*
46	63	288	1984	Klotz: *Revision der Moderne*
45	227	41	1924	Jackson: *American Colonial Architecture*
45	139	243	1979	Roth: *A Concise History of American Architecture*
45	85	206	1974	Scully: *Modern Architecture*, 2nd ed. rev.
44	78	110	1957	Gutheim: *1857-1957: One Hundred Years of Architecture in America*
44	140	111	1957	Maas: *The Gingerbread Age*
44	131	125	1960	Andrews: *Architecture in America*
43	104	222	1976	Wodehouse: *American Architects from the Civil War to the Present*
43	99	221	1976	White: *The Architecture Book*
42	118	116	1958	Hitchcock: *Architecture: Nineteenth and Twentieth Centuries*
42	137	256	1980	Reid: *The Book of Buildings*
42	90	227	1977	Milwaukee Art Center: *An American Architecture*
41	232	96	1952	Eberlein & Hubbard: *American Georgian Architecture*
41	129	240	1979	*The American Renaissance 1876–1917* (Catalogue only)
41	95	211	1975	Varian: *American Art Deco Architecture*
40	108	126	1960	Condit: *American Building Art: The 19th & the 20th Centuries*
40	110	40	1921	Fletcher: *A History of Architecture*, 6th ed.
40	127	119	1959	Francastel: *Les Architects Celèbres*
39	119	20	1892	*The Dictionary of Architecture*
39	103	160	1966	Read: *Encyclopedia of the Arts*
38	92	271	1982	Curtis: *Modern Architecture Since 1900*
38	74	173	1969	Joedicke: *Architecture Since 1945*
38	154	241	1979	Brown et al.: *American Art*
37	125	216	1976	Platt: *America's Gilded Age*
37	127	273	1982	*Macmillan Encyclopedia of Architects* (Placzek, ed.)
37	112	253	1980	Nuttgens: *Pocket Guide to Architecture*
36	147	267	1981	Whiffen & Koepper: *American Architecture 1607–1976*
36	125	282	1983	Pulos: *American Design Ethic: A History of Industrial Design to 1940*
36	145	94	1950	Watterson: *Five Thousand Years of Building*
35	128	217	1976	Pevsner: *A History of Building Types*
35	117	255	1980	Raeburn: *Architecture of the Western World*
34	126	22	1896	Hamlin, A.D.F.: *A Text-Book of the History of Architecture*
34	118	43	1925	Kimball: *Three Centuries of American Architecture*

Figure 6.3   (continued)

[1]	[2]	[3]	[4]	[5]
34	172	244	1980	Ball: *Architecture and Interior Design*
33	110	213	1976	Hammett: *Architecture in the United States*
33	105	176	1969	Scully: *American Architecture and Urbanism*
33	130	285	1984	Hunt: *American Architecture: A Field Guide*
32	102	152	1965	Rogers: *What's Up in Architecture*
32	78	158	1966	Jacobus: *Twentieth Century Architecture: The Middle Years 1940–66*
32	158	234	1978	Andrews: *Architecture, Ambition and Americans*, rev. ed.
31	143	260	1981	Rugoff: *Encyclopedia of American Art*
31	96	70	1937	*The World Almanac and Book of Facts 1937*
30	123	251	1980	Hunt: *Encyclopedia of American Architecture* (main entries only)
30	132	258	1981	*The New Encyclopaedia Britannica*, 15th ed.
30	121	179	1970	Hamilton: *19th & 20th Century Art: Painting, sculpture, architecture*
29	124	128	1960	Pierson & Davidson: *Arts in the United States*
29	78	140	1964	Creighton: *American Architecture*
29	176	224	1977	Brown: *American Art to 1900*
28	95	180	1970	Hofmann & Kultermann: *Modern Architecture in Color*
28	119	287	1984	Jervis: *Design & Designers*
27	124	229	1977	Richards: *Who's Who in Architecture*
27	135	270	1982	Condit: *American Building: Materials and Techniques*
27	90	205	1974	Norberg-Schulz: *Meaning in Western Architecture*
26	147	215	1976	Panek: *American Architectural Styles 1600–1940*
26	178	236	1978	Pierson: *American Buildings: Technology & the Picturesque*
26	154	209	1975	Loth & Trousdale: *The Only Proper Style*
25	96	144	1964	Hilberseimer: *Contemporary Architecture*
25	148	71	1938	Richardson & Corfiato: *The Art of Architecture*
25	90	233	1977	Stierlin: *Encyclopaedia of World Architecture*
24	121	195	1972	Jordy: *American Buildings: Progressive and Academic Ideals*
24	143	86	1948	Pevsner: *An Outline of European Architecture*
23	87	194	1972	Fitch: *American Building: The Environmental Forces that Shaped It*
23	120	108	1955	Tunnard & Reed: *American Skyline*
23	124	65	1934	Whitaker: *The Story of Architecture*
22	97	284	1984	Flon (ed.): *The World Atlas of Architecture*
22	119	131	1961	Fletcher: *A History of Architecture* (ed. Cordingley)
22	165	175	1969	Norton: *The Arts in America: The 19th century*
21	144	171	1968	Norman: *Traveler's Guide to American Art*
21	157	257	1980	Rifkind: *A Field Guide to American Architecture*
21	117	279	1983	Frampton (w. Futagawa): *Modern Architecture 1851–1945*
20	117	147	1964	Tschacbasov: *Teachers Manual for the Study of Art History*
20	118	78	1941	Saint-Gaudens: *The American Artist and His Times*
19	99	129	1961	Burchard & Bush-Brown: *The Architecture of America*
19	97	196	1972	Jordy: *American Buildings: Impact of European Modernism*
19	113	219	1976	*The World Almanac and Book of Facts 1977*
18	128	228	1977	Richards: *Who's Who in Architecture* (main entries only)
18	111	204	1974	Kidney: *The Architecture of Choice: Eclecticism in America 1880–1930*
18	114	235	1978	Burton: *A Choice Over Our Heads*
17	115	264	1981	*The World Almanac and Book of Facts 1982*

Figure 6.3   (continued)

[1]	[2]	[3]	[4]	[5]
17	124	280	1983	Nuttgens: *The Story of Architecture*
16	121	165	1967	Hillier: *From Tepees to Towers*
16	103	187	1971	*The World Almanac and Book of Facts 1972*
16	121	141	1964	*Encyclopaedia Britannica*, 14th ed. (1964)
15	108	164	1967	Giedion: *Space, Time, and Architecture*, rev. ed.
15	130	174	1969	Jordan: *A Concise History of Western Architecture*
15	122	283	1983	Risebero: *Modern Architecture and Design*
14	122	203	1973	Rowland: *A History of the Modern Movement*
14	134	151	1965	Millon (ed.): *Key Monuments in the History of Architecture*
14	125	210	1975	Fletcher: *A History of Architecture* (ed. Palmes)
13	91	276	1982	Pothorn: *Architectural Styles*
13	141	181	1970	Mendelowitz: *A History of American Art*
12	83	113	1957	Morris: *A Century of AIA*
12	166	99	1952	Jones: *O Strange New World*
12	117	172	1968	Portoghesi: *Dizionario enciclopedico di architetture e urbanistica*
11	166	143	1964	Gowans: *Images of American Living*
11	109	289	1984	Pokinski: *Development of the American Modern Style*
11	97	154	1966	Benevolo: *History of Modern Architecture*
10	134	290	1984	Poppeliers et al.: *What Style Is It?*
10	129	156	1966	Green: *American Art: A Historical Survey*
10	124	198	1973	Boorstin: *The Americans: The Democratic Experience*
9	117	155	1966	Fitch: *American Building: The Historical Forces that Shaped It*
9	120	168	1968	Condit: *American Building ... from Beginning to the Present*
8	160	142	1964	*Encyclopaedia Britannica*, 14th ed. (main entries only)
8	116	178	1969	Whiffen: *American Architecture Since 1780*
8	147	185	1971	Cohen: *History of American Art*
7	129	191	1972	*Encyclopaedia Britannica*, 14th ed. (1972)
7	121	138	1962	Pevsner: "Architecture and Applied Arts"
7	156	192	1972	*Encyclopaedia Britannica*, 14th ed. (main entries only)
6	159	190	1972	Bacon: *Architecture and Townscape*
6	141	183	1970	Osborne: *The Oxford Companion to Art* (main entries only)
5	144	166	1967	Ross: *Taste in America*
5	110	159	1966	Myers: *McGraw-Hill Dictionary of Art*
5	114	162	1966	*The World Almanac and Book of Facts 1967*
4	77	212	1976	Brolin: *The Failure of Modern Architecture*
4	169	182	1970	Osborne: *The Oxford Companion to Art*
4	197	200	1973	Glubok: *Composite of books 1970–1973*
3	138	167	1967	Rosenblum: *Transformations in Late 18th Century Art*
3	160	115	1958	Gloag: *Guide to Western Architecture*
3	170	169	1968	McLanathan: *The American Tradition in the Arts*
2	205	184	1970	Pierson: *American Building: Colonial and Neo-classical Styles*
2	110	100	1952	*The World Almanac and Book of Facts 1952*
1	169	118	1959	Bode: *The Anatomy of American Popular Culture 1840–61*
1	168	150	1965	Early: *Romanticism in American Architecture*
1	238	163	1966	Tatum: *The Arts in America. The Colonial Period*
0	125	135	1962	*The World Almanac and Book of Facts 1962*
0	199	186	1971	Gillon: *Early Illustrations of American Architecture*
0	257	170	1968	Millar: *The Architects of the American Colonies*

Modernism, still essentially a European movement at the time. A few American architects were represented, some of whom had been cited previously in the corpus, but only very shortly before 1932. Hood, Neutra, the firm of Howe & Lescaze, and Albert Kahn constituted veritable scoops (figure 6.4).

Oliver Reagan's *American Architecture of the Twentieth Century* of 1927 also displays a high discovery index. With the exception of Hood, who is featured in both works, Reagan introduced an entirely different cast of characters; the big names in his book were Gilbert, Goodhue, Albert Kahn, Corbett, and Cret, and the firm Shreve, Lamb & Harmon (figure 6.5). With Gilbert and Goodhue already established, Reagan's foresight index is marginally lower.

Pencil Point's 1941 choice of *Forty Under Forty*, although still showing a higher discovery index than most other texts in the corpus, was less successful than Stern's. In 1941 the new names were Stone, H. H. Harris, and Eero Saarinen (figure 6.6).

Philip Johnson's article "Architecture" in *The American Year Book* of 1941 ranks as the next most foresighted. Gropius, Mies van der Rohe, Mendelsohn, the firm of Wurster, Bernardi & Emmons, Aalto, and Breuer are some of his discoveries (figure 6.7); perhaps this is the most impressive list of all because of the importance of the architects it introduced.

Despite their diverse publication dates, most of the texts in the highest ranks of figure 6.3 have certain common characteristics: they review recent developments in modern or American architecture; were prepared under the aegis of distinguished institutions (the Museum of Modern Art and the American Institute of Architects) or leading architectural journals (*Pencil Points*, *Architectural Record*, *AIA Journal*, and *Architectural Review*); and/or were written or curated by leading proponents of contemporary architecture at the time. The advocates of new architecture belong to four distinct generations: Montgomery Schuyler in the first generation; Reagan, Sexton, Taut, Hoak, and Church in the second; Johnson, Hitchcock, Drexler, Giedion, and Roth in the third; and Stern, Diamondstein, and Jencks in the fourth.

Foresightedness, however, is not restricted to just one type of publication. *Men and Women of America. A Biographical Dictionary* (1910), a reference work written neither for nor by architects, and not addressing architecture as a primary concern, does not fit the profile described, but ranks in the ninety-second percentile, ahead of many prominent architectural texts. It boosts important architects Flagg, Eyre, Cram, Carrère & Hastings, and Gilbert, most of whom were relatively unknown at the time (figure 6.8).[5] The same is true of the somewhat earlier 1893 edition of Karl Baedeker's *The United States* (90th percentile), another general reference work featuring important figures and firms such as Jefferson, John A. Roebling, Vaux, Hunt, Mullet, McKim, Mead & White, Root, Carrère & Hastings, and Gilbert, still in the early stages of their literary if not professional careers (figure 6.9).

Cheney's book ranks in the ninety-fifth percentile. Greene & Greene, Mac-Murray, Schindler, Neutra, Harrison, Howe, and Lescaze, and of course Goff,

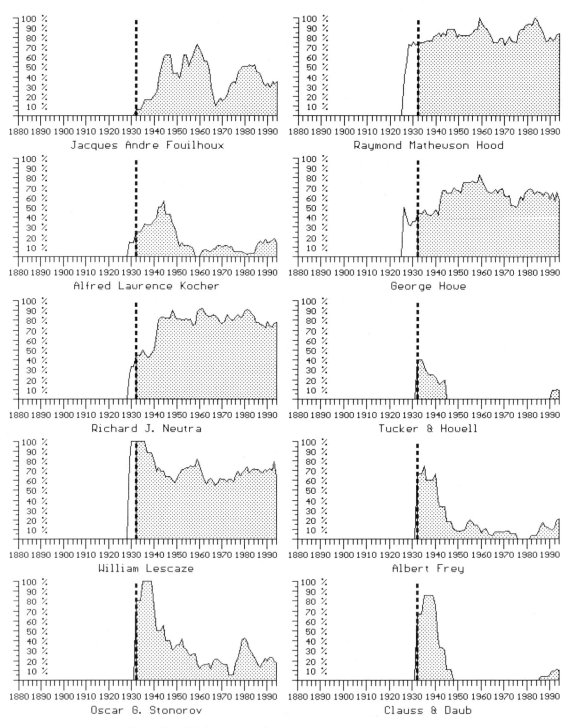

Figure 6.4 Hitchcock & Johnson: *The International Style* (1932). All architects cited. Evolution of histograms before and after publication date. Text foresight: 99th percentile

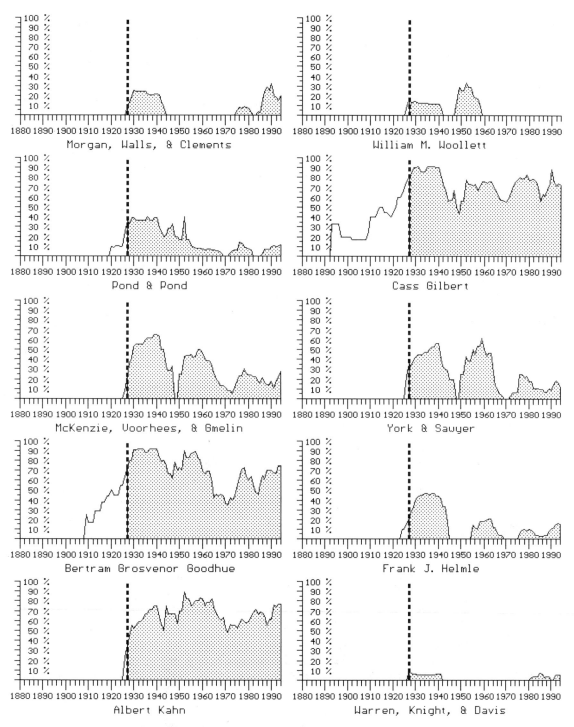

Figure 6.5 Reagan: *American Architecture of the 20th Century* (1927). All architects cited. Evolution of histograms before and after publication date. Text foresight: 99th percentile

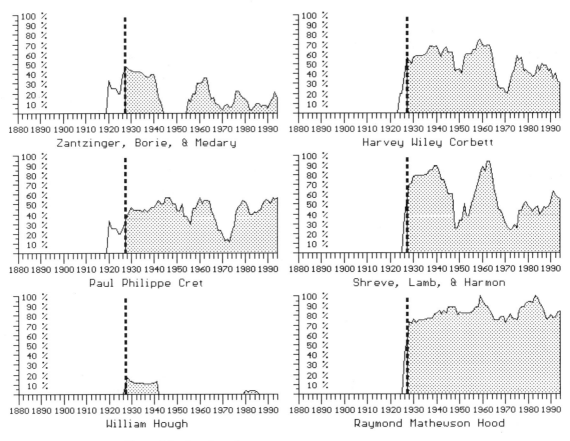

Figure 6.5   (continued)

are absolute scoops. Other important architects captured early in their textual history are Maybeck, Eliel Saarinen, Hood, and Frank Lloyd Wright (figure 6.10). Conant's *Modern Architecture*, the other text with an early Goff citation, commands a respectable but far lower foresight, in the sixty-fourth percentile. Goff is the only discovery; Wright, Goodhue, Eliel Saarinen, Pope, and Hood are featured early in their careers, but the text is also populated by many established architects (figure 6.11).

Readers may have identified the third problem with using histograms to assess foresight. Collections devoted to young architects such as *Forty Under Forty*, or publications on current architecture such as *The International Style*, *American Architecture of the Twentieth Century*, or the *Yearbook* article, travel less known ground than *The Architects of the American Colonies*. Millar deals with a period that has been under scrutiny for decades if not centuries; opportunities to uncover new names are here necessarily limited. Discovery indexes of texts with such different subject matters are hardly comparable. The ranking of figure 6.3 starts with books on recent events and ends with texts on Colonial

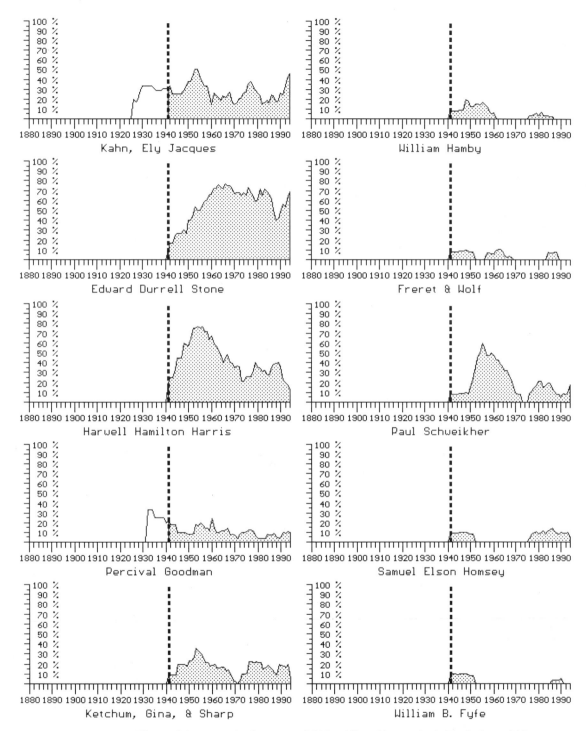

Figure 6.6 *Forty Under Forty* (1941). All architects cited. Evolution of histograms before and after publication date. Text foresight: 98th percentile

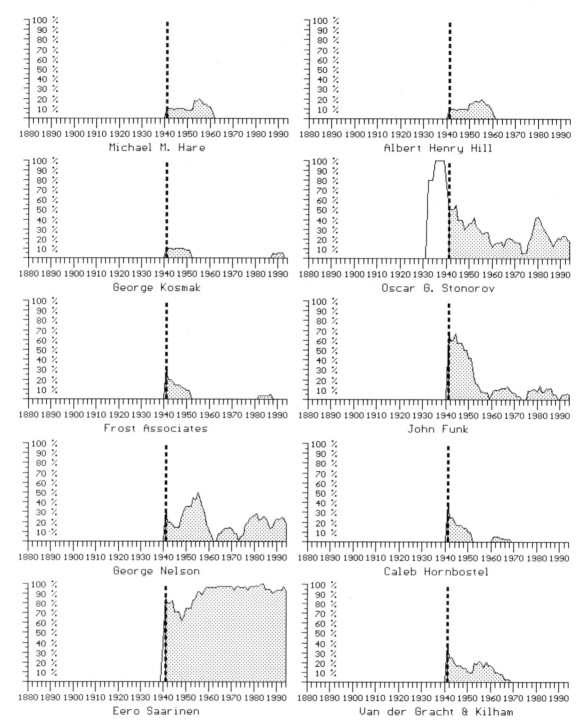

Figure 6.6 (continued)

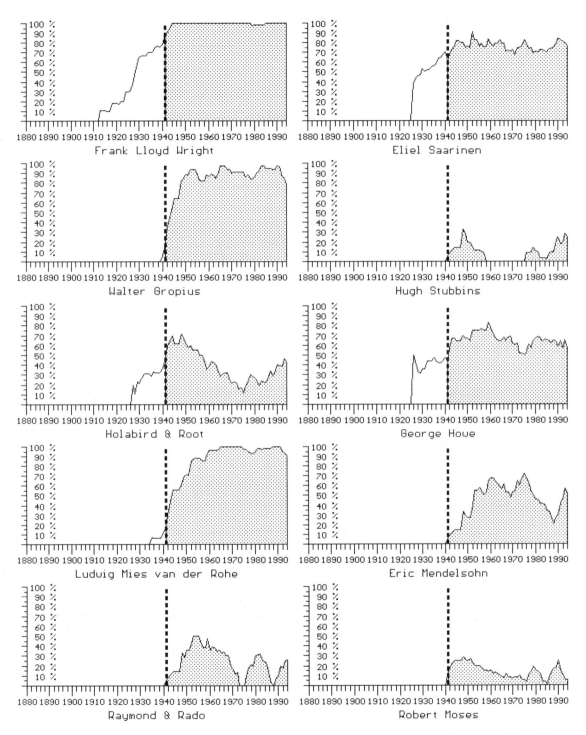

Figure 6.7 Johnson: Architecture (in *The American Yearbook*) (1941). All architects cited. Evolution of histograms before and after publication date. Text foresight: 98th percentile

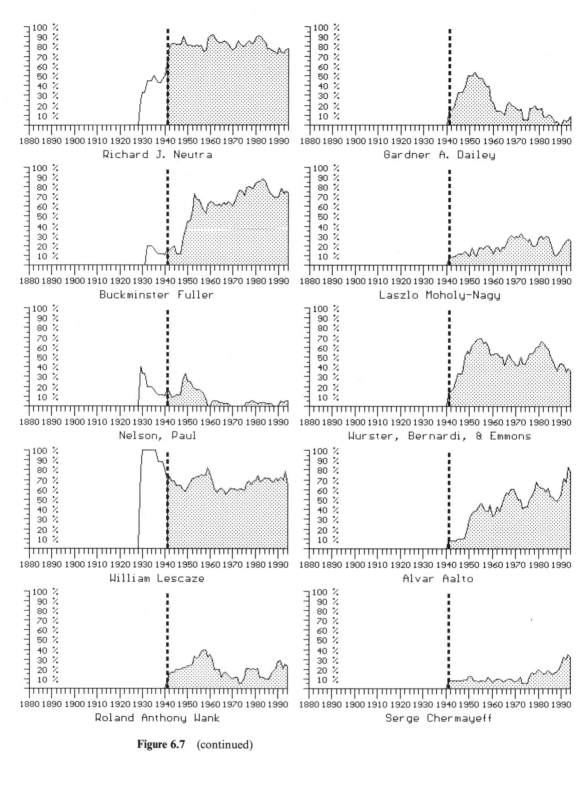

Figure 6.7 (continued)

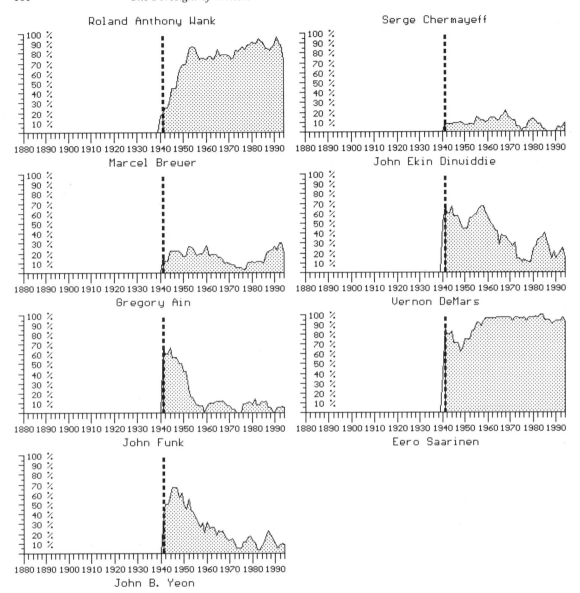

Figure 6.7   (continued)

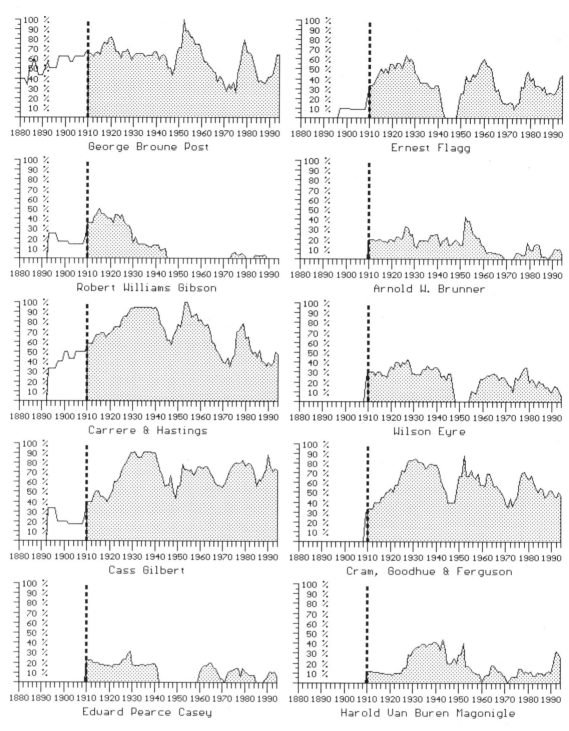

Figure 6.8 *Men and Women of America: A Biographical Dictionary of Contemporaries* (1910). Selected architects cited. Evolution of histograms before and after publication date. Text foresight: 92nd percentile

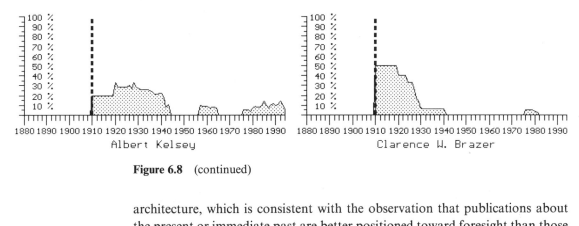

Figure 6.8   (continued)

architecture, which is consistent with the observation that publications about the present or immediate past are better positioned toward foresight than those devoted to more distant times. The differences between Cheney and Conant must be attributed at least in part to this factor: Cheney's coverage is 1844–1904; with coverage of 1658–1877, Conant reaches farther back and does not come that close to the present.

The fact remains, however, that certain texts are more innovative in their selection of architects than others written at the same time and dealing with the same period. A third *Forty Under Forty* (1977), in the ninety-second percentile in figure 6.3, falls short of its predecessors in foresight. And new names continue to emerge from time to time, even from the Colonial period.[6] Not all books about the past tread the same path. Recognizing this, we should look not at the rankings themselves, but rather at deviations from what would be expected if all texts were equally innovative (or repetitive) in their choices of architects. The potential to run into still uncharted territory is greater the less the time elapsed between the events chronicled and the timing of the chronicle itself. This time is reflected in the distance between text publication date and the average date of birth of all architects cited. Such distances are easily figured out in an electronic environment. In the case of recent architects, the value equals their average age at publication time. Assuming that age continues to accrue after death, the figure becomes the average age at publication time in every case. It is reported in the second column of figure 6.3.

Forty Under Forty at the top of the list has the youngest group of architects in the entire corpus—only thirty-six years of age as an average—which is consistent with the high name discovery rate. *The Architects of the American Colonies*, at the bottom of the table, shows an average age of 257 years, one of the longest spans between chronicler and chronicled. High foresight is expected with young average age and vice versa. If there were no significant foresight differences, the ages in column 2 would grow as the percentiles in column 1 decrease. Texts departing from the expectations are more noteworthy than those conforming to the rule. *Forty Under Forty* and *The Architects . . .* are not all that interesting.

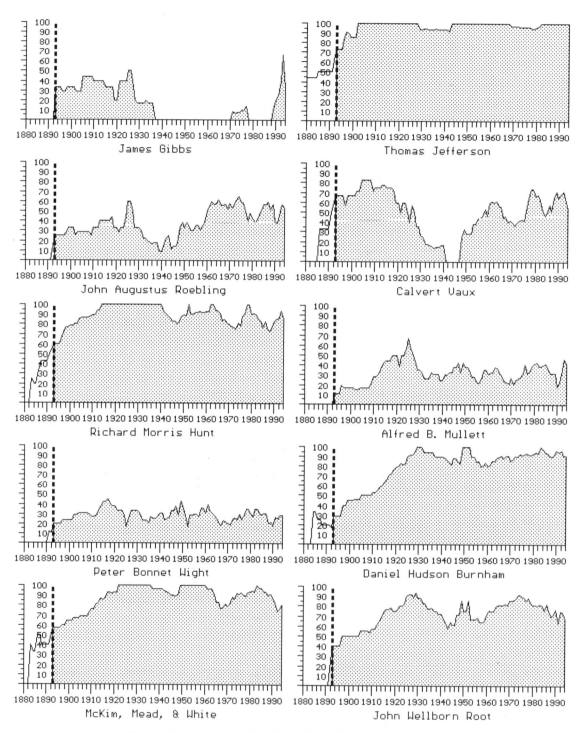

Figure 6.9 Baedecker: *The United States* (1893). Selected architects cited. Evolution of histograms before and after publication date. Text foresight: 90th percentile

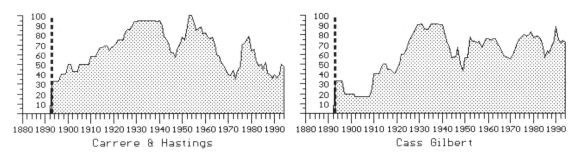

Figure 6.9   (continued)

Newcomb's *Spanish-Colonial Architecture in the United States* stands out in figure 6.3 with a high foresight (ninety-fifth percentile) coupled with an unusually high average architect age—114 years. Figure 6.12 shows that although many of the personalities referenced in the book reached only a moderate level of citation in the years after publication, twelve of the thirty-six names featured had never been cited before.

Talbot Hamlin (*Greek Revival Architecture in America*, 1944), William R. Ware (*The Georgian Period*, 1899), and Hugh S. Morrison (*Early American Architecture*, 1952) exhibit the same pattern: although dealing with the distant past, they wrote about architects later to be reckoned with but who had not yet reached their pinnacle of fame. Hamlin featured 154 architects who are in the universe today, 71 of whom were cited in his book for the first time; Ware cited a total of fifty-three, with twenty-six absolute newcomers; and Morrison introduced twenty-seven new names among the ninety-four he cited. These figures alone do not suffice to assess foresight, since certain new architects may seldom be cited again; to pass judgment, one must look at the histograms. With that many architects involved, however, printing all curves would be impractical. Histograms for selected citations of *Greek Revival* are shown in figure 6.13. When dealing with already established names, Hamlin often cleverly captured them shortly before their peak.

At the opposite end of the spectrum is *The Failure of Modern Architecture* by Brolin (1976), which placed near the bottom in figure 6.3 despite dealing with contemporary issues. The American architects featured were already well established in the literature (figure 6.14). Also singled out for limited foresight in dealing with relatively recent events are *History of Modern Architecture* by Leonardo Benevolo (1966), *Architectural Styles. An Historical Guide to World Design* (Pothorn, 1982) and *A Century of AIA*, prepared by E. B. Morris in 1957 for the ceramic tile industry. The foursome could not be more diverse: a polemical tract, a reputable scholarly work, a popular reference source, and a conservative, institutional pamphlet; yet from the perspective explored in this chapter they share a common attribute—they are at the antipodes Stern's *Forty Under Forty*, Hitchcock and Johnson's *The International Style*, and Johnson's 1941 *Yearbook* article.

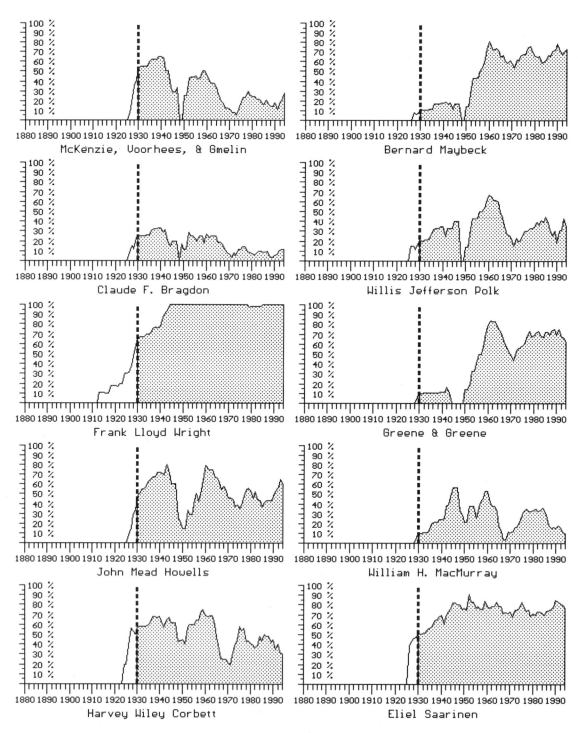

Figure 6.10   Cheney: *The New World Architecture* (1930). Selected architects cited. Evolution of histograms before and after publication date. Text foresight: 95th percentile

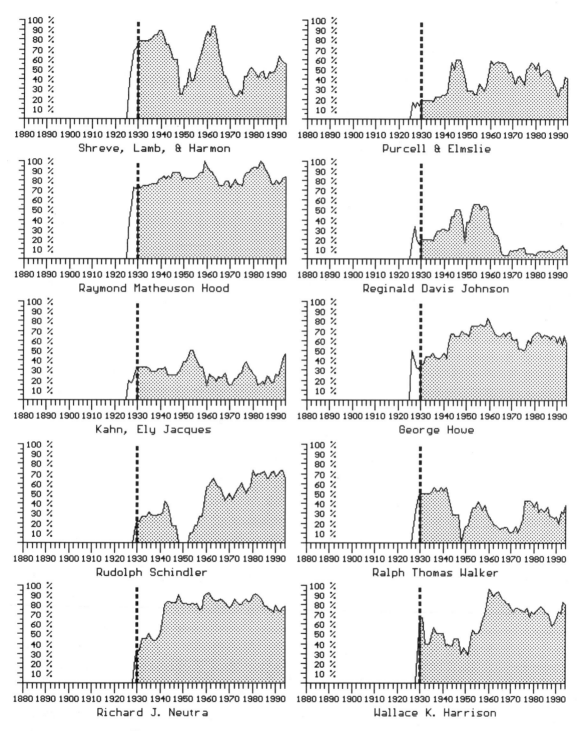

Figure 6.10   (continued)

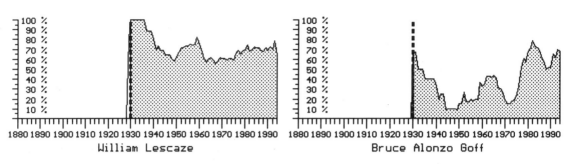

Figure 6.10   (continued)

Revised Editions

Updating and revising a text is challenging and difficult, regardless whether the job is done by the author or somebody else. The principles involved are beyond the scope of this study; but index analytical observations of specific instances are worth noting.

Giedion's extraordinarily influential *Space, Time, and Architecture* of 1941 had undergone several revisions by 1967 in a continual process of renewal. One can visualize the author carefully editing the manuscript, building up or compromising reputations, rewarding or punishing friends and foes. Strictly speaking this is not a private activity, as the results are a matter of public record; but tracing them before the advent of computers was too time consuming for most people to make the effort. Index analysts, in contrast, can instantly highlight the changes between successive editions; this privilege enables them to peak over the author's shoulders as he cuts and pastes, and second-guess him after examining not only what he left in but also what he threw into the wastebasket.

Giedion made three types of changes between the 1941 and 1967 editions. First, he inserted younger architects whose contributions could hardly have been acknowledged originally, for example, Rudolph, Yamasaki, Eero Saarinen, Bunshaft, Niemeyer, Sert, Breuer, Louis Kahn, and Aalto, and, to a lesser extent, Harrison and Sven Markelius. Second, he featured architects in the 1967 edition that could have been recognized in 1941, but for one reason or another were not: prominent among these are Mies van der Rohe and Eliel Saarinen. Third, and perhaps most revealing, he cut off personalities included in the original edition such as Irving Gill and the firm of McKim, Mead & White, whom he no longer saw fit to be included. The first type of change is typically an updating; the other two types are revisions, as they entail a changing evaluation of the subject matter. Revisions are as indicative of the writers as they are of the architects; in the case in point, one could focus on a change in Giedion's outlook between the two editions, or on a change in the architectural scene within the same period, with Classicism (McKim, Mead & White) and Regionalism (Gill) giving way before the onslaught of Modernism (Saarinen and Mies).

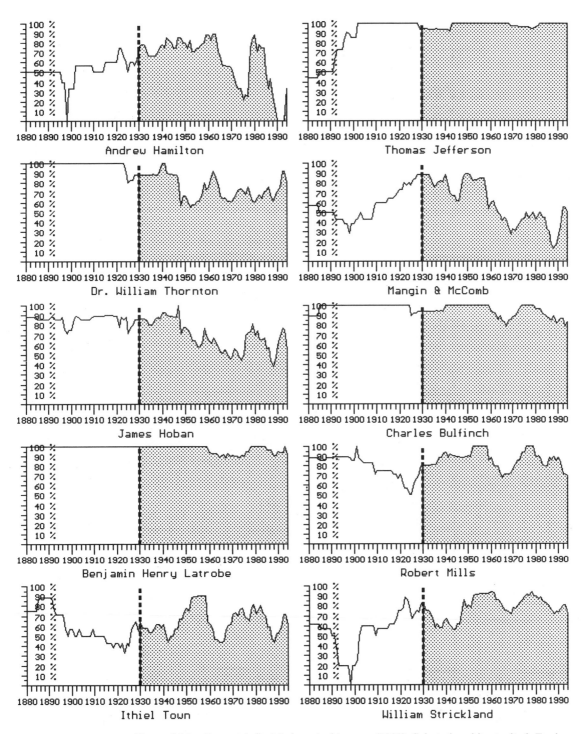

Figure 6.11 Conant (ed): *Modern Architecture* (1930). Selected architects cited. Evolution of histograms before and after publication date. Text foresight: 64th percentile

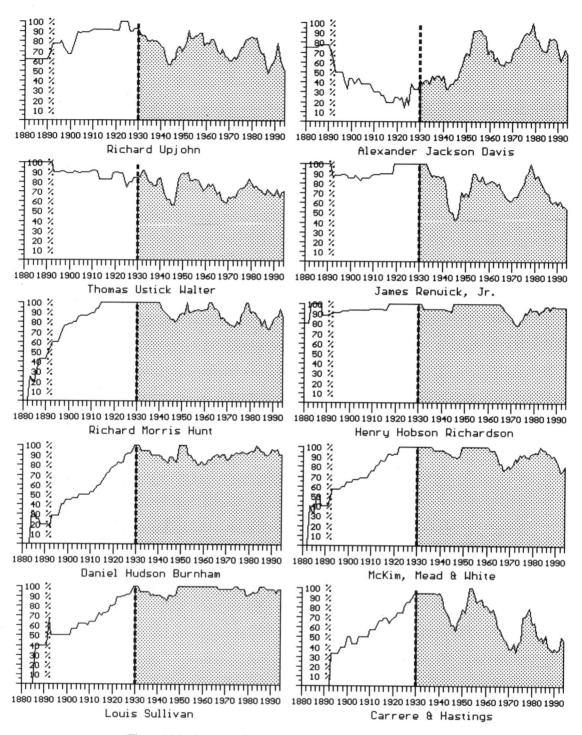

Figure 6.11   (continued)

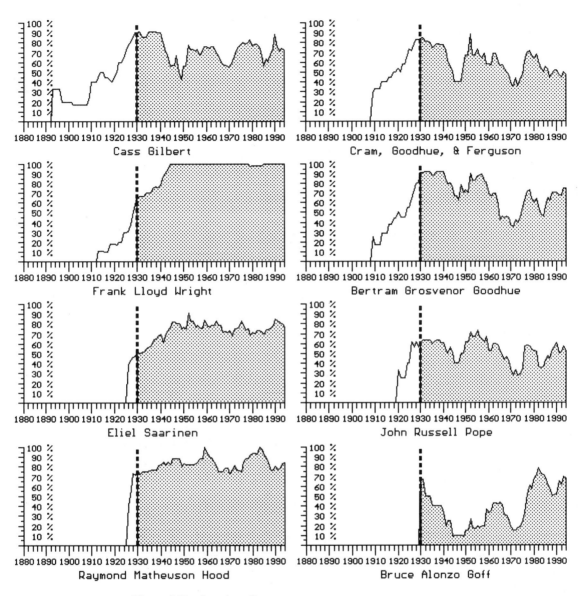

Figure 6.11   (continued)

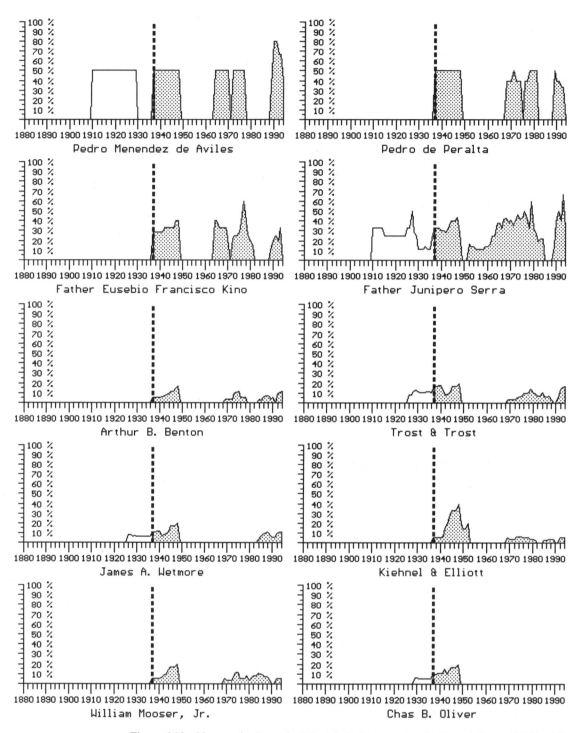

Figure 6.12 Newcomb: *Spanish-Colonial Architecture in the United States* (1937). All architects cited. Evolution of histograms before and after publication date. Text foresight: 95th percentile

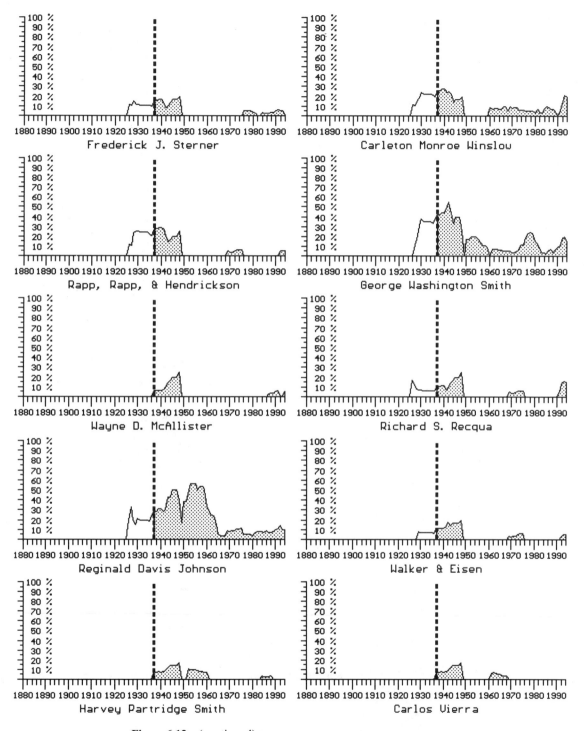

Figure 6.12   (continued)

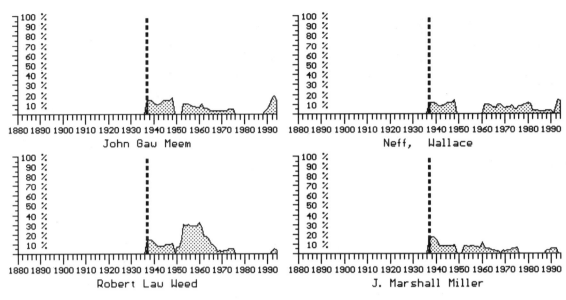

Figure 6.12 (continued)

In any case, *Space, Time, and Architecture* was updated and revised consistently with changing societal preferences, and as a result a new, somewhat different text emerged. The coverages suggest an effective *aggiornamento*: the span shifted from 1780–1906 in 1941 to 1797–1912 in 1967. The intervals are graphed in figure 6.15; the lines clearly shifted rightward.

A success story? Hardly! The original edition ranks in foresight in the eighty-first percentile; despite the changes, the revised edition drops precipitously to the fifteenth percentile (figures 6.3 and 6.16). In 1941 Giedion was setting trends; in 1967 he was following them. The foresight of the revised edition would have been even lower had the author refrained from making any changes. Foresight results from an intersection between the work and its circumstance, in the sense in which Ortega y Gasset used the term. The revised work is a new text, a new cultural event, and it must be judged in its new circumstance.

Like automobiles that devaluate the moment they are driven out of the showroom, manuscripts start aging the day the last T is crossed, the last I is dotted, or (more likely) the results of the last spell check are saved on disk. But there is a difference: significant publications change the circumstances in ways vehicles rarely do. The original insights of a book may hold valid several decades later; but what once was fresh, unexpected, or even revolutionary often becomes shared knowledge, if not commonplace. This is especially true in the case of successful works, perhaps as a result of their very impact. To correct or adjust details in an older text may be easy, and so is adding a postscript to account for events in the intervening years; but how can a newly influential and

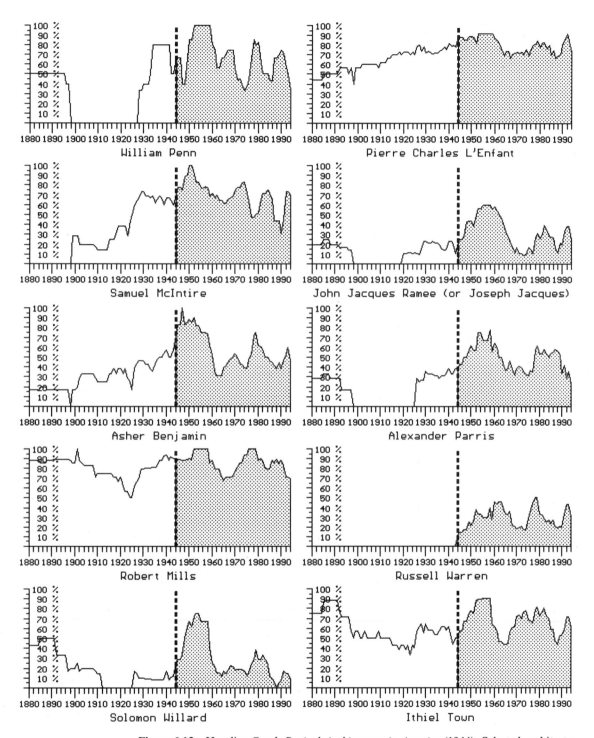

Figure 6.13 Hamlin: *Greek Revival Architecture in America* (1944). Selected architects cited. Evolution of histograms before and after publication date. Text foresight: 90th percentile

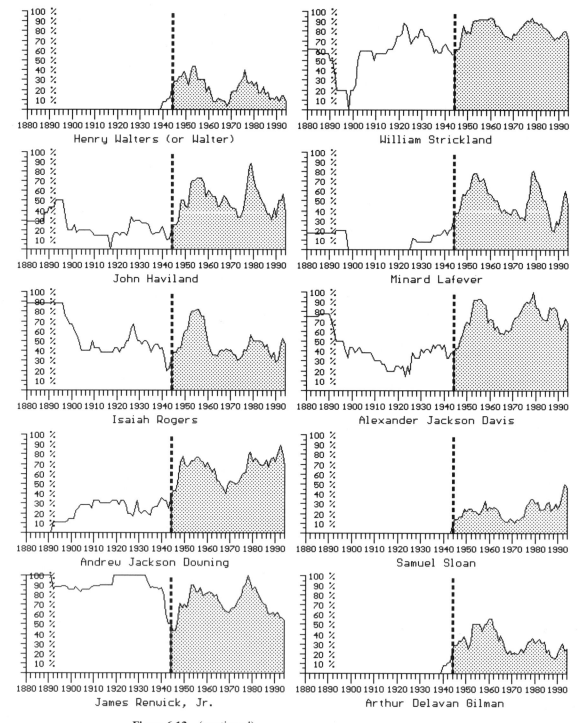

Figure 6.13 (continued)

100 %
90 %
80 %
70 %
60 %
50 %
40 %
30 %
20 %
10 %
1880 1890 1900 1910 1920 1930 1940 1950 1960 1970 1980 1990
Walter Gropius
Ludwig Mies van der Rohe
Eero Saarinen
Paul Rudolph

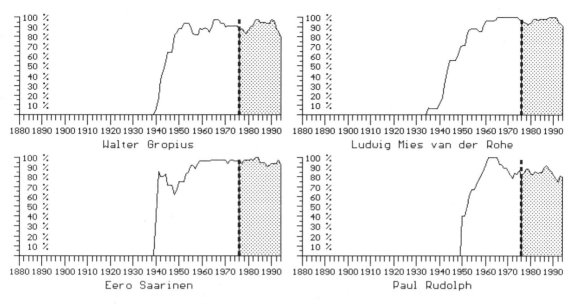

Figure 6.14 Brolin: *The Failure of Modern Architecture* (1976). All architects cited. Evolution of histograms before and after publication date. Text foresight: 4th percentile

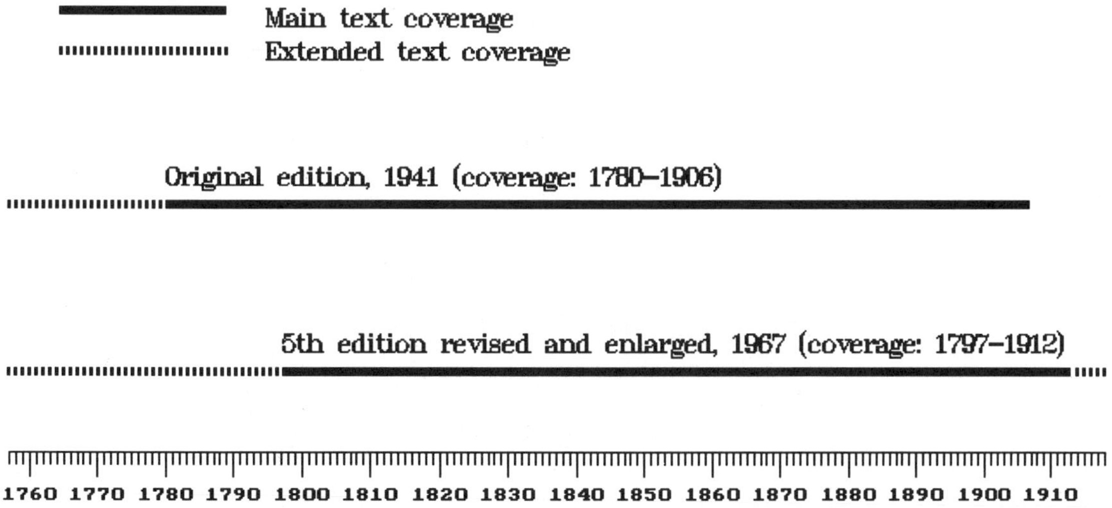

Main text coverage
Extended text coverage
Original edition, 1941 (coverage: 1780–1906)
5th edition revised and enlarged, 1967 (coverage: 1797–1912)
1760 1770 1780 1790 1800 1810 1820 1830 1840 1850 1860 1870 1880 1890 1900 1910

Figure 6.15 Giedion: *Space, Time, and Architecture*. Coverage comparison between original and revised editions

Figure 6.16   Foresight of successive revised editions of same work

Column headings:
[1]   Foresight percentile
[2]   Text ID #
[3]   Publication date
[4]   Author and title

[1]	[2]	[3]	[4]
81	76	1941	Giedion: *Space, Time, and Architecture*
15	164	1967	Giedion: *Space, Time, and Architecture*, rev. ed.
71	133	1961	Scully: *Modern Architecture*
45	206	1974	Scully: *Modern Architecture*, 2nd ed. rev.
86	177	1969	Stern: *New Directions in American Architecture*
71	231	1977	Stern: *New Directions in American Architecture*, rev. ed.
48	106	1955	Andrews: *Architecture, Ambition, and Americans*
32	234	1978	Andrews: *Architecture, Ambition, and Americans*, rev. ed.
84	49	1927	Tallmadge: *The Story of Architecture in America*
64	67	1936	Tallmadge: *The Story of Architecture in America*, rev. ed.
69	72	1940	Hamlin, T.: *Architecture Through the Ages*
62	103	1953	Hamlin, T.: *Architecture Through the Ages*, rev ed.
77	34	1910	*The Encyclopaedia Britannica*, 11th ed.
16	141	1964	*Encyclopaedia Britannica*, 14th ed. (1964)
7	191	1972	*Encyclopaedia Britannica*, 14th ed. (1972)
30	258	1981	*The New Encyclopaedia Britannica*, 15th ed.
54	64	1932	*The World Almanac and Book of Facts 1932*
31	70	1937	*The World Almanac and Book of Facts 1937*
2	100	1952	*The World Almanac and Book of Facts 1952*
0	135	1962	*The World Almanac and Book of Facts 1962*
5	162	1966	*The World Almanac and Book of Facts 1967*
16	187	1971	*The World Almanac and Book of Facts 1972*
19	219	1976	*The World Almanac and Book of Facts 1977*
17	264	1981	*The World Almanac and Book of Facts 1982*
93	95	1951	Giedion: *A Decade of Contemporary Architecture*
91	105	1954	Giedion: *A Decade of Contemporary Architecture*, 2nd ed.
70	30	1905	Fletcher: *A History of Architecture*, 5th ed.
40	40	1921	Fletcher: *A History of Architecture*, 6th ed.
65	61	1931	Fletcher: *A History of Architecture*, 9th ed.
22	131	1961	Fletcher: *A History of Architecture* (ed. Cordingley)
14	210	1975	Fletcher: *A History of Architecture* (ed. Palmes)

Figure 6.16   (continued)

[1]	[2]	[3]	[4]
34	22	1896	Hamlin, A.D.F.: *A Text-Book of the History of Architecture*
60	32	1909	Hamlin, A.D.F.: *A Text-Book of the History of Architecture*, 8th ed.
53	51	1928	Hamlin, A.D.F.: *A Text-Book of the History of Architecture*, 18th pr.
81	225	1977	Jencks: *The Language of Post-Modern Architecture*
86	226	1977	Jencks: *The Language of Post-Modern Architecture*, rev. ed.
75	259	1981	Jencks: *The Language of Post-Modern Architecture*, 3rd ed.
50	286	1984	Jencks: *The Language of Post-Modern Architecture*, 4th ed.

equally original work be created out of an old one that has become a standard reference?

Instances of successive editions of the same work dated between 1890 and 1983 (the boundaries of this study, cf. note 3) are tabulated in figure 6.16 for easy comparison of their foresight. (Indeed, successive editions of certain texts were included in the corpus to be able to perform this analysis.) Scully's *Modern Architecture*, Stern's *New Directions in American Architecture*, Andrews's *Architecture, Ambition, and Americans*, Tallmadge's *The Story of Architecture in America*, and, to a lesser extent, Hamlin's *Architecture Through the Ages* all follow the pattern of *Space, Time, and Architecture*. The same holds true for works with several editions, such as *The Encyclopaedia Britannica* and *The World Almanac and Book of Facts*. The earliest editions examined commanded respectable foresight, in the seventy-seventh percentile in the case of the 1910 version of the *Encyclopaedia* and in the fifty-fourth percentile for the 1932 *Almanac*, which is no mean achievement for a nonprofessional and nonacademic reference work. None of the ensuing editions examined of either work came close to this level of performance.

Giedion was more successful with *A Decade of Contemporary Architecture*, with the 1954 edition ranking almost at the same level as the original one of 1951. Although only three years elapsed between the two versions, eight new American architects were inserted in the latter.

Revisions with increased foresight are rare, and they invariably entail a substantial revamping in the list of citations, the more so the greater the time between editions. Foresight jumped between the 1921 (sixth) edition of Fletcher's *A History of Architecture on the Comparative Method* and the ninth edition of 1931; eight of the twenty-five American architects referenced in 1921 were dropped ten years later, and fifty-one new ones were inserted; as far as the American chapter is concerned, it was really a new text. The same holds for the first and second editions of Jencks's *The Language of Post-Modern Architecture*, which came out the same year, with the first one being, in fact, only a section of the second. The foresight of this celebrated work fell somewhat by the ensuing editions; the most recent edition has not yet been rated because of the ten-year cushion after publication required by the system to perform the calculations.

Foresight rankings, like all numerical abstractions, must be used with caution. They are helpful to identify general rules or unusual, potentially interesting items that depart from the norms. Prudent users, however, will recall the concepts and definitions behind the names, which often capture only imperfectly the meaning of the variables. This is true not only of foresight but of most the other terms used in this study—universe, coverage, normal histograms, and so on. In the case of foresight, it behooves one to examine the histograms themselves before drawing final conclusions. Discovery indexes are based only on the years immediately before and after publication; the tendencies revealed during that limited span may not hold for the rest of the duration of the histograms.

Often not even the curves suffice; one must return to the publications themselves, their goal, their structure. As already noted, the 1966 version of *Forty Under Forty* ranks number 1, with an extraordinarily high foresight. The 1977 edition, also curated by Stern, dropped several ranks in the chart to the ninety-second percentile. Did Stern lose his sagacity during the intervening years? Not at all; but he changed his authorial style. In 1977 he mentioned most of the architects of his previous selection, and for this reason alone the book's foresight index plummeted. Troubling? Perhaps; automatic procedures are bound to fall into such traps. Once the problem has been identified, however, it can easily be corrected. If only the new forty architects under forty are referenced, foresight index in 1977 is almost the same as it was in 1966.

Books must not be dismissed for attaining low discovery indexes. The latter measure increases in architects' citation frequencies immediately after publication; this may be completely irrelevant in the case of many texts. *The Failure of Modern Architecture* was an indictment of the architects whose careers had peaked during the 1960s and 1970s. By refocusing the terms of discussion, Brolin may have affected the architectural landscape of the 1970s and 1980s more effectively than by naming large groups of young practitioners.

Just as those who are cited more often than others are not necessarily better architects, writers who first mention often-cited architects are not necessarily more perspicacious. Unless the publication claims explicitly or implicitly to unearth new names, such as the *Forty Under Forty* selections or, more recently, *Emerging Voices* (1986), the intrinsic merit of the work is unrelated to its discovery ranking. Excellence is not what index analysts are after. *Men and Women of America* was not a better dictionary because of its high discovery index; for a while it may have been just the other way around, because readers may have encountered names they were not yet interested in, while failing to find the ones that mattered most for them at the time. But the indexes and the resulting rankings reveal something significant about the texts: by familiarizing a wider readership with the names and contributions of a group of emerging architects, *Men and Women* played a special role in the development of American architectural culture.

It is hard to tell solely from the analysis of indexes whether the texts propelled the architects, or the rising star of the latter raised the standing of the authors who first recognized them. But mutually connected texts and architects can be charted, and texts pointing toward emerging names can be distinguished from those associated with the status quo. This is helpful in understanding the fabric of architectural culture.

Notes

1. Architects featured in *Forty Under Forty* and nowhere else are not yet in the universe and are ignored in the figure. Having been cited neither before nor after, they have no incidence with respect to the issues discussed in this chapter in any case.

2. A certain symmetry can be seen between figure 6.1 and figures 4.38 through 4.41. In the latter, an architect's birth date was plotted in relation to the coverage of the texts in which he is cited; in the former, a text's publication date is marked as it relates to the histograms of the architects cited.

3. As histograms cover, at most, from 1880 to 1994, twenty-year periods are workable only for texts published between 1900 and 1973. The period is reduced as necessary up to a minimum of ten years for texts published between 1890 and 1984. Those published before 1890 or after 1984 are ignored in this chapter.

4. To circumvent to the extent possible the inconvenience of locating a specific item in a long list, the texts discussed are shaded in figure 6.3. Highlighting is easier in a computerized environment.

5. Only some architects featured in the *Dictionary* are included in figure 6.8. Please note the distinction between "selected architects" and "all architects" in the figure titles in this chapter.

6. Of 209 architects in the roster born before the middle of the eighteenth century, only thirty-five had entered the universe by 1950. Thirty-seven entered during the 1950s, the same number during the 1960s, twenty-two during the 1970s, and seventy-eight during the 1980s and early 1990's.

7   Predictable and Unpredictable Lists of Names

The Problem of the Missing Volume

The American Institute of Architect's *Encyclopedia of Architecture, Design, Engineering, & Construction* was distributed sequentially, volume by volume, starting in 1988, while I was working on this project. The fifth and last tome was still unavailable early in 1990. As the most important architectural reference work to be published in recent years, the *Encyclopedia* had to be included in the corpus sooner or later. Could this be accomplished at least partially, I wondered, before the release of the last installment? Entering the names of the first four volumes in the data base without any provisions for those in the fifth would have had undesirable effects: architects would be cast under the unfavorable light of the not-cited, when in fact their absence was merely due to their names starting with the last letters of the alphabet. This would have affected their histograms adversely, and would have distorted other statistics as well.

The *Encyclopedia* is assigned two slots in the corpus—one for names with individual articles only, and one for all the names. The problem with the first slot, I thought, was manageable. I conceived a list of persons who would probably be granted individual articles in the fifth volume, and used it temporarily to enter the text in the data base. The roster was amended as necessary on the release of the missing volume.

As behooves this project, the provisional list was not made up by premonition; it was generated using a systematic, computerized method. The data consisted of the names granted individual entries in the first four volumes, and the universe of architects. Two procedures were called for, one to determine how many individual entries to expect in the last volume, and the other to generate a ranked list of famous architects with last names starting with the appropriate letters, and born during or near the coverage span of the work. The first mechanism was based on the number of entries found in the first four volumes; the second looked for the architects in the universe with the highest adjusted citations. Both are described in the appendix.

Missing and Unexpected Names

Routines initially conceived for a limited purpose sometimes become useful in other contexts as well, yielding a payoff in excess of their original intent. This was the case with the method to anticipate the names in the fifth volume of the AIA encyclopedia. Comparing predictions with actual entries provided an opportunity not only to test the effectiveness of the method, but also to assess the orientation and philosophy of the editorial board and perhaps even the comprehensiveness of the work. Six of the thirteen architects and firms granted individual articles were correctly forecasted: The Architects' Collaborative, Robert Venturi, Harry Weese, Frank Lloyd Wright, William Wurster, and Minoru Yamasaki. The mismatches proved to be more revealing than the coincidences. The discrepancies consisted of two lists: certain unexpected architects appeared in the text but were not anticipated by the system, and certain missing ones were predicted but not found in the actual work. The unexpected entries were for Konrad Wachsman, Paul Weidlinger, the Tennessee Valley Authority, William Benjamin Tabler, Paul Thiry, Benjamin Thompson, and Oswald Mathias Ungers. The first three names suggest the emphasis on technical matters such as planning and structures that permeates the encyclopedia. The greatest surprises were Tabler, Thiry, and Weidlinger, who were, and remain, figures with a relatively modest standing in literature: their adjusted citations in 1989 were 20 percent or less, and they remained the same through 1994. The system mistakenly predicted articles for Stanley Tigerman, William Turnbull, Jr., William Van Alen, and Warren & Wetmore. The failure to feature Tigerman and Turnbull confirms the technological rather than more abstract "design" bent of the work.

It quickly became clear that if the technology was available and there was a pay-off, one might as well "predict" the names to be found in all four volumes, even the published ones. Forty-one architects (figure 7.1) were singled out by the system as missing among the main entries of the five volumes of the encyclopedia. The cases of Gill, Kallmann, McKinnell & Knowles, and Lyndon are remarkable because, whereas the system saw fit to grant them no less than individual articles, they were left out from the encyclopedia altogether, even from the small print. The two most prominent names among the missing main entries are those of William Le Baron Jenney and Richard Neutra. Jenney's work is discussed in an entry devoted to the Chicago School. Neutra's case is different: although mentioned in passing in other entries, his contributions are never discussed at length, which reinforces the notion that the encyclopedia shortchanges design-oriented architects to favor those who follow more traditionally professional activities, preferably with larger offices. This is consistent with the lack of a main entry for Frank Furness but the existence of one for the firm of Coolidge, Shepley, Bulfinch & Abbott.

Figure 7.1 *AIA Encyclopedia of Architecture, Design, Engineering & Construction.* Missing main entries

Max Abramovitz	William Le Baron Jenney
Arquitectonica (or DPZ)	Kallmann, McKinnell, & Knowles
Charles B. Atwood	Carl Koch
Thomas Hall Beeby	Maya Ying Lin
Gordon Bunshaft	Donlyn Lyndon
Carrère & Hastings	Eric Mendelsohn
Harvey Wiley Corbett	Charles W. Moore
Niels Diffrient	C. F. Murphy Associates
Peter D. Eisenman	Richard J. Neutra
Jacques André Fouilhoux	Cesar Pelli
Frank Furness	Willis Jefferson Polk
Irving John Gill	George Browne Post
Bertrand Goldberg	Bruce Price
Bertram Grosvenor Goodhue	Purcell & Elmslie
Victor Gruen	Reinhard & Hofmeister
Harwell Hamilton Harris	Shreve, Lamb, & Harmon
Holabird & Root	Stanley Tigerman
George Howe	William Turnbull, Jr.
John Mead Howells	William Van Alen
Steven Izenour	Warren & Wetmore
Helmut Jahn	

Architecture's sister disciplines of planning, structural design, landscape architecture, and furniture design are also favored, together with architectural writing. Missing among the architects of the current generation are Pelli, Eisenman, Hejduk, Jahn, and Beeby, in addition to Lyndon, Turnbull, and Tigerman, already mentioned. In contrast, Blake (writing), Bacon (writing and planning), Sasaki (landscape), Amman & Whitney (bridges), Salvadori (structures), and Florence Knoll and George Nelson (furniture) were all granted unexpected main articles (figure 7.2). The broad range of design activities covered in the encyclopedia is consistent with its title.

Inevitably, professionals from allied fields are included at the expense of "pure" architects who could have been featured in an encyclopedia of the same size planned with a more restrictive criterion. But who are the pure design architects? In fairness, there is no such thing as a pure architect; the term is used merely in contradistinction to the broader class of practitioners found in the encyclopedia. To the eye of the system, pure architects are those who are customarily cited in architectural literature; most, but not necessarily all, fit into what one would consider that category. James Bogardus, whose place in the literature is largely due to his technically innovating cast-iron commercial building facades in New York, is singled out by the system as a missing main entry of *Who's Who in Architecture* (1977). He is not a pure design architect, but he is an expected feature in the customary picture of nineteenth-century American architecture, at least since Giedion included a section on his work in his

Figure 7.2   *AIA Encyclopedia of Architecture, Design, Engineering & Construction.* Unexpected main entries

Amman & Whitney	Sven Markelius
Edmund N. Bacon	Julia Morgan
Peter Blake	George Nelson
Charles Bulfinch	Pier Luigi Nervi
Cambridge Seven Associates	Oscar Niemeyer
Caudill, Rowlett, & Scott	Eliot Noyes
Coolidge, Shepley, Bulfinch, & Abbott	Frederick Law Olmsted
Egon Eiermann	Raymond & Rado
Gustave Eiffel	Moshe Safdie
Arthur Erickson	Mario Salvadori
Charles M. Goodman	Sasaki, Dawson, & Demay Associates
George F. Hellmuth	Sasaki, Walker, & Associates
Reginald R. Isaacs	William Benjamin Tabler
Thomas Jefferson	Paul Thiry
Ketchum, Gina, & Sharp	Benjamin Thompson
Frederick Kiesler	Dr. William Thornton
Florence Knoll	TVA Tennessee Valley Authority
Pierre Charles L'Enfant	Oswald Mathias Ungers
Benjamin Henry Latrobe	Konrad Wachsmann
Fumihiko Maki	Paul Weidlinger

seminal *Space, Time, and Architecture*. The same is true of John A. Roebling, design engineer and builder of the Brooklyn Bridge, another missing figure in *Who's Who* according to the system.

Pure architects are those who do what most architects do; or, to express it from the perspective of an index analyst, they are those who are written about in texts dealing with architects. Although the emphasis shifts between the formulations, the epistemological status of the idea remains the same: purity rests on custom and consensus.

A knowledgeable editor furnished with the lists of unexpected and missing names early enough in the planning process (say, at the time of commissioning the articles) could correct a possible oversight or reconsider an occasional misevaluation. In chapter 4, when dealing with text coverage, we envisioned authors, editors, or publishers checking a draft to ensure that the subject matter was adequately covered. Now we have at hand a more penetrating procedure that returns specific names to be considered for inclusion, together with candidates for removal. The two procedures complement each other, one guaranteeing enough names from every period, and the other checking that the choices are not outlandish.

The search for missing and unexpected names is not necessarily limited to entries in dictionaries or encyclopedias: the technique yields the same benefits with any text, whether a history book, a guide book, or a collection of essays. Indeed, the general index of the *AIA Encyclopedia*, including hundreds of names cited in the work without individual entries, was also searched. Next to Gill, Kallmann, McKinnel & Knowles, and Purcell & Elmslie (already mentioned), the most prominent omissions are Mangin & McComb, Alexander Parris, Ralph Walker, Leopold Eidlitz, and the firm of Graham, Anderson, Probst & White.

It was anticipated in the introduction that the nature and slants of a text can be captured from unexpected name inclusions and omissions. My examples were a hypothetical bookstore browser and a book reviewer who, as far as I know, was not using computerized methods. Those were only conceptual examples; now we have the practical means to generate automatically the pertinent information.

The lack of main entries for Jenney or Neutra in the *AIA Encyclopedia* is comparable to Frank Lloyd Wright's absence from the catalogue to the Brooklyn Museum's exhibit *The American Renaissance*, discussed in chapter 5. The facts came to our attention, however, in different ways. News about the catalog surfaced almost accidentally while looking at an anomaly in Wright's histogram; the point about the encyclopedia originated in a technique capable of identifying systematically such oddities in every text of the corpus.

Variance from expectations based on precedent does not necessarily signal errors in the selection of architects; on the contrary, it may highlight one of the ways in which an opus is different. Entirely predictable works add little to the pool of knowledge; bringing new names to public attention or shunning established ones may well be the lasting contributions of an encyclopedia's editorial board. Used uncritically, index analysis may hamper change, promote tedium, and raise silliness to the level of an art form. Used cleverly, it nurtures individual judgment. Judgment must be recognized and described. Index analysis provides operational means to describe norms and averages as well as specific characteristics of each project.

Ranking Texts by Predictability

Some texts are very predictable in their choice of architects; others allow for few correct predictions and present several missing and unexpected citations. Intertext comparisons can be made by using a predictability index, approximately equal to the percentage of names in a text that are correctly predicted by the system. (For an exact definition, see the appendix.) With 63 entries forecast out of a total of 104, the predictability of the *AIA Encyclopedia* (main entries only) is 62 percent. Armed with the indexes, one builds a ranking, and with this comes a percentile scale to indicate the percentage of texts that are more predictable than a given one. The *AIA Encyclopedia* is in the seventy-seventh percentile, which means that it is more predictable than 77 percent of the texts in the corpus (figure 7.3).

Predictably, if I may be allowed to say so, none of the texts of the corpus is fully predictable. The one that comes closest to complete name predictability

Figure 7.3 Texts ranked according to predictability

Column headings:
[1] Percentile
[2] Predictability index (percentage of names predictable)
[3] Text ID #
[4] Publication date
[5] Author and title

Note: texts in shaded areas are discussed in the chapter

[1]	[2]	[3]	[4]	[5]
99	0.89	9	1862	Fergusson: *History of the Modern Styles of Architecture*
99	0.86	8	1856	Heck: *The Art of Building in Ancient and Modern Times*
99	0.76	4	1836	Cleveland: *Review of American Builder's General Price Book*
99	0.75	251	1980	Hunt: *Encyclopedia of American Architecture* (main entries only)
98	0.75	212	1976	Brolin: *The Failure of Modern Architecture*
98	0.74	228	1977	Richards: *Who's Who in Architecture* (main entries only)
98	0.74	135	1962	*The World Almanac and Book of Facts 1962*
98	0.74	187	1971	*The World Almanac and Book of Facts 1972*
97	0.73	264	1981	*The World Almanac and Book of Facts 1982*
97	0.73	219	1976	*The World Almanac and Book of Facts 1977*
97	0.72	284	1984	Flon (ed.): *The World Atlas of Architecture*
97	0.72	373	1993	Van Vynckt (ed.): *International Dictionary of Architects & Architecture*
96	0.71	276	1982	Pothorn: *Architectural Styles*
96	0.71	342	1990	*The World Almanac and Book of Facts 1991*
96	0.71	380	1994	Packard (ed.): *Encyclopedia of American Architecture*
96	0.71	210	1975	Fletcher: *A History of Architecture* (ed. Palmes)
95	0.71	237	1978	Williamson: "An Architectural Family Tree"
95	0.71	185	1971	Cohen: *History of American Art*
95	0.71	348	1991	Copplestone: *Twentieth-Century World Architecture*
94	0.70	165	1967	Hillier: *From Tepees to Towers*
94	0.70	320	1988	Hollingworth: *Architecture of the 20th Century*
94	0.70	96	1952	Eberlein & Hubbard: *American Georgian Architecture*
94	0.70	131	1961	Fletcher: *A History of Architecture* (ed. Cordingley)
93	0.69	46	1926	Jackson: *Development of American Architecture 1783–1830*
93	0.69	53	1928	Kimball: *American Architecture*
93	0.69	171	1968	Norman: *Traveler's Guide to American Art*
93	0.69	325	1988	Nuttgens: *Understanding Modern Architecture*
92	0.69	271	1982	Curtis: *Modern Architecture Since 1900*
92	0.68	16	1958	Hitchcock: *Architecture Nineteenth and Twentieth Centuries*
92	0.68	349	1991	Gossel & Lenhauser: *Architecture in the 20th Century*
92	0.68	67	1936	Tallmadge: *The Story of Architecture in America*, rev. ed.
91	0.68	169	1968	McLanathan: *The American Tradition in the Arts*
91	0.67	89	1949	Larkin: *Art and Life in America*
91	0.67	138	1962	Pevsner: "Architecture and Applied Arts"
90	0.67	308	1986	Lampugnani: *Encyclopedia of 20th Century Architecture*
90	0.66	181	1970	Mendelowitz: *A History of American Art*
90	0.66	159	1966	Myers: *McGraw-Hill Dictionary of Art*
90	0.66	42	1924	Mumford: *Sticks and Stones*
89	0.66	280	1983	Nuttgens: *The Story of Architecture*
89	0.66	29	1902	Sturgis: *A Dictionary of Architecture and Building*
89	0.66	162	1966	*The World Almanac and Book of Facts 1967*

Figure 7.3 (continued)

[1]	[2]	[3]	[4]	[5]
89	0.65	55	1929	LaFollette: *Art in America*
88	0.65	143	1964	Gowans: *Images of American Living*
88	0.65	153	1965	Ulanov: *The Two Worlds of American Art*
88	0.65	241	1979	Brown at al.: *American Art*
88	0.65	174	1969	Jordan: *A Concise History of Western Architecture*
87	0.65	222	1976	Wodehouse: *American Architects from the Civil War to the Present*
87	0.65	235	1978	Burton: *A Choice Over Our Heads*
87	0.64	197	1972	Sharp: *Visual History of 20th C Architecture*
87	0.64	144	1964	Hilberseimer: *Contemporary Architecture*
86	0.64	179	1970	Hamilton: *19th & 20th Century Art: Painting, Sculpture, Architecture*
86	0.64	182	1970	Osborne: *The Oxford Companion to Art*
86	0.64	267	1981	Whiffen & Koepper: *American Architecture 1607–1976*
85	0.64	156	1966	Green: *American Art: A Historical Survey*
85	0.64	40	1921	Fletcher: *A History of Architecture*, 6th ed.
85	0.64	247	1980	Emanuel (ed.): *Contemporary Architects*
85	0.64	311	1986	Watkin: *A History of Western Architecture*
84	0.64	49	1927	Tallmadge: *The Story of Architecture in America*
84	0.64	109	1956	*Architectural Record:* "100 Years of Significant Building"
84	0.64	302	1985	Stimpson: *Fieldguide to Landmarks of Modern Architecture in United States*
84	0.63	327	1988	Scully: *American Architecture and Urbanism*, new rev. ed.
83	0.63	253	1980	Nuttgens: *Pocket Guide to Architecture*
83	0.63	50	1928	Edgell: *The American Architecture of To-day*
83	0.63	129	1961	Burchard & Bush-Brown: *The Architecture of America*
83	0.63	369	1993	Kulterman: *Architecture in the 20th Century*
82	0.63	61	1931	Fletcher: *A History of Architecture*, 9th ed.
82	0.63	10	1864	Jarves: *The Art-idea*
82	0.63	163	1966	Tatum: *The Arts in America: The Colonial Period*
81	0.63	32	1909	Hamlin, A.D.F.: *A Text-Book of the History of Architecture*, 8th ed.
81	0.63	370	1993	LeBlanc: *20th Century American Architecture*
81	0.63	221	1976	White: *The Architecture Book*
81	0.63	35	1913	Schuyler: *American Architecture and Other Writings*
80	0.63	51	1928	Hamlin, A.D.F.: *A Text-Book of the History of Architecture*, 18th pr.
80	0.63	87	1949	Bannister: *From Colony to Nation*
80	0.63	99	1952	Jones: *O Strange New World*
80	0.63	147	1964	Tschacbasov: *Teachers Manual for the Study of Art History*
79	0.62	355	1991	Sharp: *Twentieth Century Architecture: A Visual History*
79	0.62	315	1987	Musgrove (ed.): *Fletcher's History of Architecture*, 19th ed.
79	0.62	354	1991	Sharp: *Illustrated Encyclopedia of Architects and Architecture*
79	0.62	176	1969	Scully: *American Architecture and Urbanism*
78	0.62	285	1984	Hunt: *American Architecture: A Field Guide*
78	0.62	252	1980	Kulterman: *Architecture in the Seventies*
78	0.62	316	1987	Oppenheimer Dean: "75 Turbulent Years of American Architecture"
78	0.62	234	1978	Andrews: *Architecture, Ambition and Americans*, rev. ed.
77	0.62	330	1989	*AIA Encyclopedia of Architecture, Design, Engineering...* (main entries only)
77	0.61	379	1994	Packard (ed.): *Encyclopedia of American Architecture* (main entries only)
77	0.61	5	1848	Tuthill: *History of Architecture from the Earliest Times*
76	0.61	38	1918	Kimball & Edgell: *A History of Architecture*

Figure 7.3 (continued)

[1]	[2]	[3]	[4]	[5]
76	0.61	97	1952	Hamlin, T.: *Forms and Functions of 20th Century Architecture*
76	0.60	201	1973	Jacobus: *American Art of the 20th Century*
76	0.60	152	1965	Rogers: *What's Up in Architecture*
75	0.60	106	1955	Andrews: *Architecture, Ambition, and Americans*
75	0.60	17	1888	Gwilt: *An Encyclopedia of Architecture*
75	0.60	31	1909	Bragdon: "Architecture in the United States"
75	0.60	63	1932	Hitchcock & Johnson: *The International Style*
74	0.60	203	1973	Rowland: *A History of the Modern Movement*
74	0.60	300	1985	Maddex: *Master Builders*
74	0.60	128	1960	Pierson & Davidson: *Arts in the United States*
74	0.60	310	1986	Trachtenberg & Hyman: *Architecture from Prehistory to PostModernism*
73	0.60	257	1980	Rifkind: *A Field Guide to American Architecture*
73	0.60	283	1983	Risebero: *Modern Architecture and Design*
73	0.60	249	1980	*GA Document Special Issue 1970–1980*
72	0.60	94	1950	Watterson: *Five Thousand Years of Building*
72	0.60	123	1959	McCallum: *Architecture USA*
72	0.59	317	1987	Yarwood: *A Chronology of Western Architecture*
72	0.59	295	1985	Handlin: *American Architecture*
71	0.59	173	1969	Joedicke: *Architecture Since 1945*
71	0.59	47	1926	*The Architectural Record American Architect Golden Anniversary Number*
71	0.59	72	1940	Hamlin, T.: *Architecture Through the Ages*
71	0.59	102	1953	Ferriss: *Power in Buildings*
70	0.59	117	1958	Peter: *Masters of Modern Architecture*
70	0.59	322	1988	Klotz: *The History of Postmodern Architecture*
70	0.59	229	1977	Richards: *Who's Who in Architecture*
70	0.59	59	1930	Conant (ed.): *Modern Architecture*
69	0.59	28	1902	Schuyler: "United States Architecture"
69	0.59	45	1926	Hamlin, T.: *The American Spirit in Architecture*
69	0.59	213	1976	Hammett: *Architecture in the United States*
69	0.59	120	1959	Joedicke: *A History of Modern Architecture*
68	0.59	158	1966	Jacobus: *Twentieth Century Architecture: The Middle Years 1940–66*
68	0.59	52	1928	Jackman: *American Arts*
68	0.58	170	1968	Millar: *The Architects of the American Colonies*
67	0.58	254	1980	Portoghesi: *Architecture 1980*
67	0.58	368	1993	Heyer: *American Architecture in the Late 20th Century*
67	0.58	140	1964	Creighton: *American Architecture*
67	0.58	132	1961	Jones: *Architecture Today and Tomorrow*
66	0.58	273	1982	*Macmillan Encyclopedia of Architects* (Placzek, ed.)
66	0.58	36	1915	Eberlein: *The Architecture of Colonial America*
66	0.58	172	1968	Portoghesi: *Dizionario enciclopedico di architetture e urbanistica*
66	0.57	208	1975	Blake & Quint: *Modern Architecture America*
65	0.57	44	1926	Berlin: *Ausstellung Neuer Amerikanischer Baukunst*
65	0.57	150	1965	Early: *Romanticism in American Architecture*
65	0.57	266	1981	Thorndike: *Three Centuries of Notable American Architects*
65	0.57	357	1991	Williamson: *American Architects and the Mechanics of Fame*
64	0.57	255	1980	Raeburn: *Architecture of the Western World*
64	0.56	184	1970	Pierson: *American Building: Colonial and Neo-classical Styles*
64	0.56	101	1952	Morrison: *Early American Architecture*

Figure 7.3 (continued)

[1]	[2]	[3]	[4]	[5]
63	0.56	79	1942	Museum of Modern Art: *What is Modern Architecture?*
63	0.56	141	1964	*Encyclopaedia Britannica*, 14th ed. (1964)
63	0.56	146	1964	Pehnt: *Encyclopedia of Modern Architecture*
63	0.56	202	1973	Jencks: *Modern Movements in Architecture*
62	0.56	260	1981	Rugoff: *Encyclopedia of American Art*
62	0.56	103	1953	Hamlin, T.: *Architecture Through the Ages,* rev ed.
62	0.56	233	1977	Stierlin: *Encyclopaedia of World Architecture*
62	0.56	336	1989	Russell: *Architecture and Design 1970–1990*
61	0.55	274	1982	McCoy & Goldstein: *Guide to U.S. Architecture 1940–1980*
61	0.55	250	1980	Hunt: *Encyclopedia of American Architecture*
61	0.55	329	1989	*AIA Encyclopedia of Architecture, Design, Engineering, and Construction*
61	0.55	256	1980	Reid: *The Book of Buildings*
60	0.55	78	1941	Saint-Gaudens: *The American Artist and His Times*
60	0.55	297	1985	Kostof: *A History of Architecture: Settings & Rituals*
60	0.55	160	1966	Read: *Encyclopedia of the Arts*
60	0.55	352	1991	Papadakis: *A Decade of Architectural Design*
59	0.55	366	1992	Whiffen: *American Architecture Since 1780*
59	0.55	226	1977	Jencks: *The Language of Post-Modern Architecture,* rev. ed.
59	0.55	155	1966	Fitch: *American Building: The Historical Forces that Shaped It*
58	0.55	230	1977	Smith, C. R.: *Supermannerism*
58	0.55	80	1942	Newcomb: *History of Modern Architecture*
58	0.55	178	1969	Whiffen: *American Architecture Since 1780*
58	0.55	68	1937	Behrendt: *Modern Building*
57	0.55	84	1948	Fitch: *American Building: The Forces that Shape It*
57	0.54	220	1976	Tafuri & Dal Co.: *Modern Architecture*
57	0.54	19	1892	Schuyler: *American Architecture—Studies*
57	0.54	166	1967	Ross: *Taste In America*
56	0.54	66	1935	Cahill & Barr: *Art in America*
56	0.54	37	1916	Hamlin, A.D.F.: "25 Years of American Architecture"
56	0.54	339	1990	AIA: *American Architecture of the 1980s.*
56	0.54	335	1989	Peel, Powell, & Garrett: *20th-Century Architecture*
55	0.54	3	1834	Dunlap: *History of the Arts of Design in the United States*
55	0.54	151	1965	Millon (ed.): *Key Monuments in the History of Architecture*
55	0.54	334	1989	Krantz: *American Architects*
54	0.53	350	1991	Jencks: *The Language of Post-Modern Architecture,* 6th ed.
54	0.53	56	1929	Sexton: Composite of books published in 1928–31
54	0.53	93	1950	P/A: "United States Architecture 1900–1950"
54	0.53	338	1989	Wright: *Sourcebook of Contemporary North American Architecture*
53	0.53	20	1892	*The Dictionary of Architecture*
53	0.53	60	1930	Hoak & Church: *Masterpieces of Architecture in the United States*
53	0.53	288	1984	Klotz: *Revision der Moderne*
53	0.53	191	1972	*Encyclopaedia Britannica*, 14th ed. (1972)
52	0.53	224	1977	Brown: *American Art to 1900*
52	0.53	243	1979	Roth: *A Concise History of American Architecture*
52	0.53	289	1984	Pokinski: *Development of the American Modern Style*
52	0.52	190	1972	Bacon: *Architecture and Townscape*
51	0.52	372	1993	Sarfatti Larson: *Behind the Postmodern Facade*
51	0.52	337	1989	Wodehouse & Moffett: *A History of Western Architecture*
51	0.52	23	1897	*The Architectural Record Great American Architects Series*
51	0.52	272	1982	Jencks: *Architecture Today*

Figure 7.3 (continued)

[1]	[2]	[3]	[4]	[5]
50	0.52	192	1972	*Encyclopaedia Britannica*, 14th ed. (main entries only)
50	0.52	304	1986	Barford: *Understanding Modern Architecture*
50	0.52	371	1993	Roth: *Understanding Architecture*
49	0.52	58	1930	Cheney: *The New World Architecture*
49	0.52	183	1970	Osborne: *The Oxford Companion to Art* (main entries only)
49	0.51	376	1994	Peter: *The Oral History of Modern Architecture*
49	0.51	341	1990	Jencks: *The New Moderns from Late to Neo-Modernism*
48	0.51	324	1988	Norberg-Schulz: *New World Architecture*
48	0.51	134	1961	Von Eckardt (ed.): *Mid-Century Architecture in America*
48	0.51	149	1965	Drexler: *Modern Architecture USA*
48	0.51	258	1981	*The New Encyclopaedia Britannica,* 15th ed.
47	0.51	306	1986	De Long, Searing, Stern: *American Architecture* (exhibition)
47	0.51	91	1950	AIA: *Contemporary Architecture in the United States 1947–1949*
47	0.51	286	1984	Jencks: *The Language of Post-Modern Architecture,* 4th ed.
47	0.50	262	1981	Smith, K.: *The Architecture of the United States*
46	0.50	15	1887	Longfellow: "The Course of American Architecture"
46	0.50	18	1891	Fergusson: *History of Modern Styles of Architecture*
46	0.50	22	1896	Hamlin, A.D.F.: *A Text-Book of the History of Architecture*
46	0.50	25	1897	Van Brunt: *Architecture and Society*
45	0.50	34	1910	*The Encyclopaedia Britannica*, 11th ed.
45	0.50	62	1932	Barr, Hitchcock, Johnson, & Mumford: *Modern Architects*
45	0.50	105	1954	Giedion: *A Decade of Contemporary Architecture,* 2nd ed.
44	0.50	115	1958	Gloag: *Guide to Western Architecture*
44	0.50	142	1964	*Encyclopaedia Britannica*, 14th ed. (main entries only)
44	0.50	180	1970	Hofmann & Kultermann: *Modern Architecture in Color*
44	0.50	232	1977	Stern (ed.): "Forty Under Forty"
43	0.50	246	1980	Diamondstein: *American Architecture Now*
43	0.50	279	1983	Frampton (w. Futagawa): *Modern Architecture 1851–1945*
43	0.50	333	1989	Kennedy (ed.): *Smithsonian Guide to Historic America*
43	0.50	277	1982	Wright: *Highlights to Recent American Architecture 1945–1978*
42	0.49	346	1990	Hays & Burns (eds.): *Thinking the Past: Recent American Architecture*
42	0.49	82	1944	Mock: *Built in America 1932–1944*
42	0.49	259	1981	Jencks: *The Language of Post-Modern Architecture,* 3rd ed.
42	0.49	26	1899	Ware: *The Georgian Period*
41	0.49	319	1988	Gibberd: *Architecture Source Book*
41	0.49	119	1959	Francastel: *Les Architects Celèbres*
41	0.49	361	1992	Gowans: *Styles and Types of North American Architecture*
40	0.48	110	1957	Gutheim: *1857–1957: One Hundred Years of Architecture in America*
40	0.48	218	1976	Smith, K.: *A Pictorial History of Architecture in America*
40	0.48	236	1978	Pierson: *American Buildings: Technology & the Picturesque*
40	0.48	65	1934	Whitaker: *The Story of Architecture*
39	0.48	145	1964	Muschenheim: *Elements of the Art of Architecture*
39	0.48	296	1985	Klein & Fogle: *Clues to American Architecture*
39	0.48	215	1976	Panek: *American Architectural Styles 1600–1940*
39	0.48	81	1944	Hamlin, T.: *Greek Revival Architecture in America*
38	0.48	133	1961	Scully: *Modern Architecture*
38	0.48	193	1972	Chermayeff: *Observations on American Architecture*
38	0.48	217	1976	Pevsner: *A History of Building Types*
38	0.48	291	1985	*AIA J.:* 7th to 9th Annual Reviews of New American Architecture

Figure 7.3 (continued)

[1]	[2]	[3]	[4]	[5]
37	0.48	154	1966	Benevolo: *History of Modern Architecture*
37	0.48	290	1984	Poppeliers et al.: *What Style Is It?*
37	0.48	199	1973	Cook & Klotz: *Conversations with Architects*
37	0.48	205	1974	Norberg-Schulz: *Meaning in Western Architecture*
36	0.47	98	1952	Hitchcock & Drexler: *Built in USA: Post-war Architecture*
36	0.46	275	1982	Portoghesi: *After Modern Architecture*
36	0.46	121	1959	Jones: *Form Givers at Mid-century*
35	0.46	200	1973	Glubok: Composite of books 1970–1973
35	0.46	130	1961	*Contemporary Architecture of the World 1961*
35	0.46	196	1972	Jordy: *American Buildings: Impact of European Modernism*
35	0.46	265	1981	Stern: *American Architecture: After Modernism*
34	0.45	125	1960	Andrews: *Architecture in America*
34	0.45	139	1963	Jacobus: *Modern Architecture*
34	0.45	303	1986	Allen: *Emerging Voices: New Generation of Architects in America*
34	0.45	332	1989	Kennedy: *Greek Revival America*
33	0.45	108	1955	Tunnard & Reed: *American Skyline*
33	0.45	100	1952	*The World Almanac and Book of Facts 1952*
33	0.45	309	1986	Stern: *Pride of Place: Building the American Dream*
33	0.45	14	1886	*L'Architecture Americaine*
32	0.45	225	1977	Jencks: *The Language of Post-Modern Architecture*
32	0.45	157	1966	Heyer: *Architects on Architecture*
32	0.45	261	1981	Sanderson: *Inernational Handbook of Contemporary Developments in Architecture*
31	0.44	353	1991	Scully: *Architecture: The Natural and the Manmade*
31	0.44	124	1959	Reed: *The Golden City*
31	0.44	312	1986	Wilson et al: *The Machine Age in America 1918–1941*
31	0.44	112	1957	McCallum: "Genetrix. Personal Contributions to American Architecture"
30	0.44	242	1979	Drexler: *Transformations in Modern Architecture*
30	0.44	6	1850	Sears: *A New and Popular Pictorial Description of the United States*
30	0.44	33	1910	*Men and Women of America: A Biographical Dictionary*
30	0.44	48	1927	Reagan: *American Architecture of the Twentieth Century*
29	0.44	71	1938	Richardson & Corfiato: *The Art of Architecture*
29	0.44	231	1977	Stern: *New Directions in American Architecture*, rev. ed.
29	0.43	30	1905	Fletcher: *A History of Architecture*, 5th ed.
29	0.43	111	1957	Maas: *The Gingerbread Age*
28	0.43	122	1959	Kulterman: *Architecture of Today*
28	0.43	209	1975	Loth & Trousdale: *The Only Proper Style*
28	0.43	245	1980	Davern: *Architecture 1970–1980*
28	0.43	126	1960	Condit: *American Building Art: The 19th & the 20th Centuries*
27	0.43	345	1990	Saunders: *Modern Architecture*
27	0.42	137	1962	Dixon: *Architectural Design Preview, USA*
27	0.42	318	1988	AIA J.: 10th to 12th Annual Reviews of New American Architecture
26	0.42	164	1967	Giedion: *Space, Time, and Architecture*, rev. ed.
26	0.42	86	1948	Pevsner: *An Outline of European Architecture*
26	0.42	148	1965	Collins: *Changing Ideals in Modern Architecture: 1750–1950*
26	0.42	363	1992	Reynolds: *Nineteenth Century Architecture*
25	0.42	358	1991	Wodehouse: *Roots of International Style Architecture*
25	0.41	328	1988	Stern: *Modern Classicism*
25	0.41	305	1986	De Long, Searing, Stern: *American Architecture* (symposium)
25	0.41	293	1985	Crouch: *History of Architecture from Stonhenge to Skyscrapers*

Figure 7.3 (continued)

[1]	[2]	[3]	[4]	[5]
24	0.41	360	1992	Garrett: *Classical America*
24	0.41	375	1994	Doremus: *Classical Styles in Modern Architecture*
24	0.41	204	1974	Kidney: *The Architecture of Choice: Eclecticism in America 1880–1930*
24	0.41	248	1980	Frampton: *Modern Architecture*
23	0.40	356	1991	*The Illustrated Dictionary of 20th Century Designers*
23	0.40	7	1851	Greenough: "American Architecture" and "Aesthetics at Washington"
23	0.40	95	1951	Giedion: *A Decade of Contemporary Architecture*
22	0.40	263	1981	Searing: *Speaking a New Classicism: American Architecture Now*
22	0.40	294	1985	Diamondstein: *American Architecture Now II*
22	0.40	364	1992	Thomas & Lewis: *American Architectural Masterpieces*
22	0.40	244	1980	Ball: *Architecture and Interior Design*
21	0.40	343	1990	Kennedy: *Rediscovering America*
21	0.39	299	1985	Maddex: *Built in the USA: American Buildings from A to Z*
21	0.39	70	1937	*The World Almanac and Book of Facts 1937*
21	0.39	281	1983	Portoghesi: *Postmodern*
20	0.39	216	1976	Platt: *America's Gilded Age*
20	0.38	177	1969	Stern: *New Directions in American Architecture*
20	0.38	195	1972	Jordy: *American Buildings: Progressive and Academic Ideals*
20	0.38	313	1987	Jencks: *Post-Modernism. The New Classicism in Art and Architecture*
19	0.38	90	1949	Lynes: *The Tastemakers*
19	0.38	104	1953	Tunnard: *The City of Man*
19	0.38	85	1948	Kouwenhoven: *Made in America*
19	0.38	118	1959	Bode: *The Anatomy of American Popular Culture 1840–61*
18	0.37	77	1941	Johnson: "Architecture" (in *The American Year Book*)
18	0.37	314	1987	Kostof: *America by Design*
18	0.37	298	1985	Macrae-Gibson: *The Secret Life of Buildings*
17	0.36	207	1974	Scully: *The Shingle Style Today*
17	0.36	186	1971	Gillon: *Early Illustrations of American Architecture*
17	0.35	307	1986	Duncan: *American Art Deco*
17	0.35	331	1989	Devlin: *Portraits of American Architecture*
16	0.35	114	1957	USIA: *Architecture USA* (ed.: Blake?)
16	0.35	268	1981	Wolfe: *From Bauhaus to our house*
16	0.35	282	1983	Pulos: *American Design Ethic. A History of Interior Design to 1940*
16	0.34	206	1974	Scully: *Modern Architecture*, 2nd ed. rev.
15	0.34	359	1992	Bayer: *Art Deco Architecture*
15	0.34	54	1929	Hitchcock: *Modern Architecture*
15	0.34	189	1971	Kulski: *Architecture in a Revolutionary Era*
15	0.33	21	1893	Baedecker: *The United States*
14	0.33	83	1945	Reilly: *Some Contemporary American Buildings*
14	0.33	113	1957	Morris: *A Century of AIA*
14	0.33	127	1960	Huxtable: *Twentieth-Century Architecture*
13	0.33	136	1962	Banham: *Guide to Modern Architecture*
13	0.33	223	1977	Blake: *Form Follows Fiasco*
13	0.33	347	1991	Cook & Llewellyn-Jones: *New Spirit in Architecture*
13	0.33	377	1994	Peter: *The Oral History of Modern Architecture* (interviewees only)
12	0.33	301	1985	Marder: *The Critical Edge: Controversy in American Architecture*

Figure 7.3 (continued)

[1]	[2]	[3]	[4]	[5]
12	0.32	362	1992	Newhouse: *The Builders: Marvels of Engineering*
12	0.32	107	1955	Scully: *The Shingle Style and the Stick Style*
12	0.32	238	1979	AIA J.: 1st to 3rd Annual Reviews of New American Architecture
11	0.31	326	1988	Pulos: *The American Design Adventure: 1940–1975*
11	0.31	374	1994	Byars: *The Design Encyclopedia*
11	0.30	39	1920	Greber: *L'Architecture aux États-Unies*
11	0.30	239	1979	*The American Renaissance 1876–1917* (without Catalogue)
10	0.30	168	1968	Condit: *American Building... from Beginning to the Present*
10	0.30	214	1976	Kulterman: *New Architecture in the World*
10	0.30	270	1982	Condit: *American Building: Materials and Techniques*
10	0.29	269	1982	AIA J.: 4th to 6th Annual Reviews of New American Architecture
9	0.29	12	1883	van Rensselaer: "Recent Architecture in America"
9	0.29	43	1925	Kimball: *Three Centuries of American Architecture*
9	0.29	73	1940	Roth: *The New Architecture*
8	0.29	76	1941	Giedion: *Space, Time, and Architecture*
8	0.29	92	1950	Egbert: *Organic Expression and American Architecture*
8	0.29	167	1967	Rosenblum: *Transformations in Late 18th Century Art*
8	0.29	194	1972	Fitch: *American Building: The Environmental Forces that Shaped It*
7	0.29	198	1973	Boorstin: *The Americans: The Democratic Experience*
7	0.28	378	1994	Striner: *Art Deco*
7	0.27	27	1900	Mackson: *American Architecture Interiors & Furniture*
7	0.27	278	1983	Colquhoun et al.: *Promising Directions in American Architecture*
6	0.27	13	1884	Levy: *Modern American Architecture*
6	0.27	188	1971	Jencks: *Architecture 2000*
6	0.26	211	1975	Varian: *American Art Deco Architecture*
6	0.25	16	1888	Arnold: *Studies in Architecture at Home and Abroad*
5	0.25	24	1897	Statham: *Modern Architecture*
5	0.25	57	1929	Taut: *Modern Architecture*
5	0.25	64	1932	*The World Almanac and Book of Facts 1932*
4	0.25	75	1941	*Pencil Points*: "Forty Under Forty"
4	0.25	367	1993	Economakis (ed.): *Building Classical: A Vision of Europe and America*
4	0.24	287	1984	Jervis: *Design & Designers*
4	0.24	41	1924	Jackson: *American Colonial Architecture*
3	0.24	344	1990	Papadakis & Watson (eds.): *New Classicism: Omnibus Volume*
3	0.23	240	1979	*The American Renaissance 1876–1917* (Catalogue only)
3	0.22	161	1966	Stern: *40 Under 40: An Exhibition of Young Talent in Architecture*
3	0.21	365	1992	Weber: *American Art Deco*
2	0.20	11	1880	Benjamin: *Art in America*
2	0.17	175	1969	Norton: *The Arts in America: The 19th Century*
2	0.16	74	1941	*Architectural Record*: "American Architecture 1891–1941"
2	0.16	292	1985	*Cross Currents of American Architecture* (AD Profile)
1	0.15	227	1977	Milwaukee Art Center: *An American Architecture*
1	0.14	321	1988	Johnson & Wigley: *Deconstructivist Architecture*
1	0.14	351	1991	Noever (ed.): *Architecture in Transition*
1	0.13	88	1949	Conder: *An Introduction to Modern Architecture*
0	0.04	69	1937	Newcomb: *Spanish-Colonial Architecture in the United States*
0	0.04	340	1990	Cottom-Winslow: *Environmental Design*
0	0.00	323	1988	Larkin et al.: *Colonial Design in the New World*

is the 1862 edition of Fergusson's *History of Modern Styles in Architecture*. Fergusson cites buildings, not architects. Compiling the list of architects on the basis of the list of buildings and comparing it with the predictions, it turns out that Town & Davis are missing, whereas buildings by James Renwick, Jr. and Thomas Cole, who were not expected, are there. Fergusson chastises Renwick's Smithsonian Institute in Washington for its "rude, irregular Medievalism," and he criticizes Cole (without naming him) for squeezing the Ohio State Capitol, a secular building, into the form of a temple "in order to save himself trouble and the necessity of thinking." The Englishman was disdainful of every example of American architecture, even the U.S. Capitol. He objected only to buildings he must have considered important; the recipients of his scorn were not praised, but at least they were singled out. Fergusson might be controversial because of his judgments, at least on this side of the Atlantic; but with a predictability index of 89 percent, the highest in the corpus, his choices of buildings remained well within the trodden paths.

Second-guessing the system is boring, because the choices are unprincipled and mechanical. Town & Davis had appeared in the corpus by 1862 more often than Renwick or Cole, and this is all the system sees when it makes its choices. Second-guessing Fergusson might (only might) be more fruitful. What prompted him to grant an illustration to the Ohio State Capitol, but not to the work of Town & Davis, who had two state capitols to their credit (Connecticut and Indiana), whose office was the biggest and busiest in the country, and who occupied a more prominent position in the literature? Perhaps he saw the Ohio building as more facile pray for criticism. Be that as it may, if any insight is gained in answering the question, index analysis deserves part of the credit for having posed it.

Standard reference works and noncontroversial history books predominate among the texts with highly predictable names, at the top of figure 7.3. Among the reference works is *The Art of Building in Ancient and Modern Times, or Architecture Illustrated*, which is an atlas of architecture, Hunt's *Encyclopedia of American Architecture* and the revised edition edited by Packard, *Who's Who in Architecture*, *The World Atlas of Architecture*, and *International Dictionary of Architects and Architecture*; the history books include those by Fletcher, Tallmadge, and Kimball. *The World Almanac and Book of Facts* is another example of the kind of texts appearing at this end of the scale. The almanacs include a brief section entitled "American Architects and Some of their Achievements," a mere list of past and present eminent individuals and their work. The list is substantially updated from time to time, and has been an accurate indicator of shifting fortunes as reflected in the entire body of literature. The success of the enterprise is measured by the fact that all editions of the almanac since 1962 rank consistently high on the scale. (Earlier releases were different.) One does not go to the almanac for emerging names; one goes for the consecrated ones.

Brolin's *The Failure of Modern Architecture* seems oddly placed among these books. No matter how premonitory his message, his list of names was not foresighted, as seen in the preceding chapter. Now we can add that no matter how disquieting in content, with predictability ranked in the ninety-ninth percentile, his names choices were not jolting. More about this book later.

Let us look at the opposite end of the scale. *Colonial Design in the New World* (Larkin, Sprigg, and Johnson, 1988) has zero predictability: not one of the names could be anticipated by the system. The book focuses on lesser figures who are credited in many cases only with the design of their own homes, ignoring established men such as Peter Harrison, Richard Munday, Andrew Hamilton, John Kearsley, Thomas McBean, and John Smibert, who were flagged by the system as missing. Readers more attuned to contemporary than to Colonial architecture may find the following example, next to the last in the ranking, more useful: Margaret Cottom-Winslow's *Environmental Design* of 1990, which carries the lofty subtitle of *The Best of Architecture and Technology*, features many architects in the second or third tiers of importance, but misses most of the leading names of the middle and late twentieth century: Saarinen, Johnson, Bunshaft, Pei, Roche, Venturi, Moore, Meier, Graves, Stern, and Eisenman, among others.

A ranking such as the one of figure 7.3 does not suffice to harvest the fruits of this chapter: one must also be able to access each text's list of missing names. With hundreds of lists and dozens of names in each list, however, the information can be shared only electronically.

At the lower end of the predictability scale are three distinct, different groups of texts. One consists of works devoted to specific groups of architects, linked by style, persuasion, or some other criterion that filters out some individuals. Readers are reminded of rules 10 and 11 governing the selection of texts (chapter 2). Texts dealing with just one chronological section of American architecture were deemed admissible even if the segmentation was stylistic, provided that the style name was used in a comprehensive, temporal sense.

A stylistic label is used comprehensively when any architect active during the period could, in principle, be included; it is used restrictively if it applies only to artists working in that particular style. In many cases it is hard to tell the difference. One way to assess whether a stylistic title is chronological or restrictive is by examining the list of missing names. A case in point is *Spanish-Colonial Architecture* (Newcomb, 1937), with twenty-three unexpected names out of a total of twenty-four, it ranks near the bottom in figure 7.3. Only a limited group of turn-of-the-century and early twentieth-century architects in America practiced in the Neocolonial style.

Many of those who did not pop up, nevertheless, among the expectations of a system that is blind to the difference, at least in its current state of development. This also explains the unpredictability of two recent works on Deconstructivism, those by Noever (1991) and by Johnson and Wigley (1988), and perhaps also of Weber's *American Art Deco* (1992), which is in the third percentile. Other books on Art Deco rank only marginally higher: in the sixth percentile (Varian), seventh (Striner), fifteenth (Bayer), or seventeenth (Duncan).

But there are counter-examples as well: Hitchcock and Johnson's famous *The International Style* of 1932 resembles recent publications on Deconstructivism in their intention to highlight the work of a rather unusual group of architects. Yet the book ranks in the seventy-fifth percentile, just barely below the *AIA Encyclopedia*: the system was on target with six of the ten names featured. Instead of Hood, Howe, Kocher, and Fouilhoux, the system expected to find Wallace K. Harrison (not a bad choice), Henry S. Churchill, Timothy L. Pflueger, and Bruce Goff. Only the last would have been utterly out of place in the Museum of Modern Art exhibit for stylistic reasons; but, again, the system does not yet understand this.

American Georgian Architecture by Eberlein and Hubbard (1952) ranks in the ninety-fourth percentile, proving conclusively that a stylistic label can be used in a chronological sense, excluding no one. Other comprehensive books on the Colonial period are those by Tatum (eighty-second percentile) and Eberlein (sixty-sixth percentile).

The second group of texts at the lower end of the predictability scale includes those that ignore or challenge the prevailing norms in name selection, and sets the stage for new, emerging ones. The 1966 and 1941 selections of *Forty Under Forty* are typical examples: they rank in the third and fourth percentile, respectively. More about these books in a moment.

Which is the third group? It includes texts that ignore important prevailing names and do not set the stage for new, emerging ones. The 1932 edition of *The World Almanac* ignores giants Sullivan, Richardson, and Burnham, but features the much more modest Donn Barber and Arnold W. Brunner.

Predictability and Foresight

Foresight and predictability represent complementary aspects of a text's insertion into the literary environment. Predictability depends on similarity between the names cited and the ones found in the preceding literature; the more similar, the easier to predict the architects. Foresight, measured by the discovery index, indicates connectedness with ensuing texts. The closer the linkage between a text and those following it, the higher the foresight. Predictability looks back, foresight looks ahead.

The World Almanac and Book of Facts for 1962 is a paradigm of a predictable, not foresighted, choice of architects: it ranks in the ninety-eighth percentile for predictability, and zero percentile for foresight! The values are consistent with the nature of the publications. (The *Almanac* was included in the corpus to test the system's ability to separate it from the mainstream literature.) *Forty Under*

Forty (1966) illustrates the opposite case, with the most foresighted text in the corpus (ninety-ninth percentile) and predictability only in the 3rd percentile. The contrast with the almanac published only four years earlier could not be starker. *Forty Under Forty* attempted to identify young, promising, still unrecognized talent. The numbers obtained underline the success of the exhibit when measured in relation to its goal, which is also true of the almanac. The results also demonstrate the accuracy and discrimination of the tool used.

Predictability and foresight are not necessarily mutually exclusive. Certain lists of names may have both characteristics, and others may display neither one. The system found fifth-five missing and fifty-five unexpected names in George H. Edgell's *The American Architecture of Today* (1928), which are not as many as it might seem at first if one takes into account that ninty-five names referenced in the work were correctly forecast. The book is in the eighty-third percentile in terms of predictability. The high prediction rate shows that Edgell was responsive co the earlier literature, but he also helped to set the direction of architectural scholarship in the years to come. Giants of the 1930s and 1940s such as Wright, Albert Kahn, Eliel Saarinen, Hood, and George Howe were granted exposure in *The American Architecture of Today* while still in the early stages of their careers. In consequence, the book ranks in the eighty-eighth percentile for foresight as well! Connected to the preceding texts and also to the ones to follow it, the work appears seamlessly inserted in the continuous evolutionary line of the architectural literature in this country.

With low predictability (17th percentile) and no foresight (zero percentile), *Early Illustrations and Views of American Architecture* (Gillon, 1971) is diametrically opposed to Edgell's book in the range of possibilities. It is a work almost completely disconnected from its historiographical context, which is not surprising in view of the fact that it is a mere compilation of nineteenth-century architectural illustrations, without any links to discourse as it unfolded during the 1970s. Once again, a text's connection (or, in this case, lack thereof) to contemporary literary trends is uncovered by the analysis of the index.

The *Almanac, Forty Under Forty*, and the books by Edgell and Gillon are archetypal works for each of the quadrants of a simple two-dimensional classification system, devised in function of their predictability and foresight. Using percentiles as a measurement, all texts in the corpus except those published before 1890 or after 1983 can be plotted as points in a two-dimensional cloud, or as lights in a starry sky (figure 7.4). (If foresight and predictability indexes had been used instead of percentiles, the points would tend to concentrate in a denser, central area, but their relative positioning would remain the same.) The four archetypal cases (marked on the graph with numbers) fall near the four corners of the diagram. Each text's position in the configuration is now triangulated in relation to those markers; their levels of predictability and foresight are appreciated at a glance. Constellations of nearby texts share similar levels of insertion into the preceding and subsequent literature.

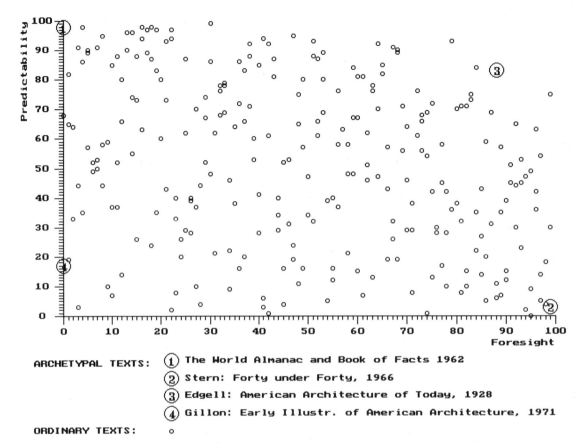

Figure 7.4   Texts scattered according to foresight and predictability (full picture)

By placing the cursor over a point on a computer screen, one can bring forth the identity of the text; or by entering its name from the keyboard, the machine will obligingly highlight the dot on the screen. The printed page is not so accommodating. To ameliorate the situation at least in part, the four corners of figure 7.4 (1/3 × 1/3) are enlarged in figures 7.5 through 7.8. Texts are identified by their numbers in the chronological list. Using the graphs as celestial charts, readers may explore the vicinities of the archetypal stars, which are the most mysterious parts of the firmament.

The Problem of the Missing Volume, Revisited

When predicting the architects and firms to be granted individual entries in the fifth volume of the *AIA Encyclopedia*, little consideration was paid to the already published volumes, except to determine the coverage of the work and the number of entries to be expected in the last one. The predictions themselves

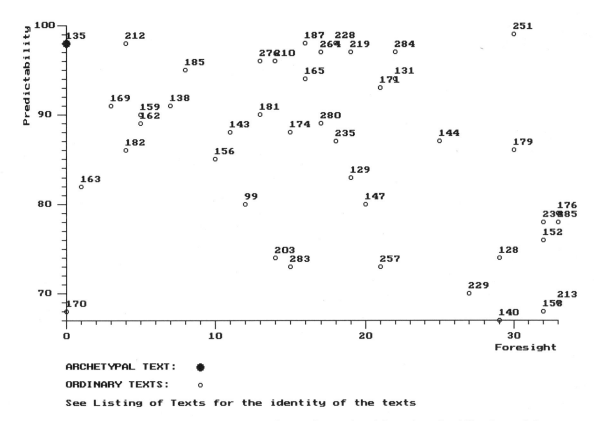

Figure 7.5 Texts scattered according to foresight and predictability (upper left corner of figure 7.4, enlarged)

were not influenced by the choices already made in the previous volumes. But certain commonalities ought to run through the entire encyclopedia; the editorial board surely leaves an imprint not only on the manner and level of treatment of the articles, but also on their selections.

Lesser known architects may take precedence over more famous ones if their work is in agreement with the editors' preferences and values. Those inclinations are likely to mold also the volume in preparation; not to take them into account for the prediction would be wasteful from the standpoint of effective use of the information. Having grasped the sensitivity and orientation of the editors, an index analyst may propose names for the missing volume that are consistent with, rather than indifferent or inimical to, the path already set. The procedure could be called predicting by affinity, in contradistinction to predicting by fame, as in the preceding sections.

Conceptually, the procedure rests on the use of implication tables between architects: for example, if Wright is cited in a text, the probability of Sullivan also being cited is raised by a certain margin; vice versa, a Sullivan citation raises the likelihood of a Wright citation, but not by the same margin. The

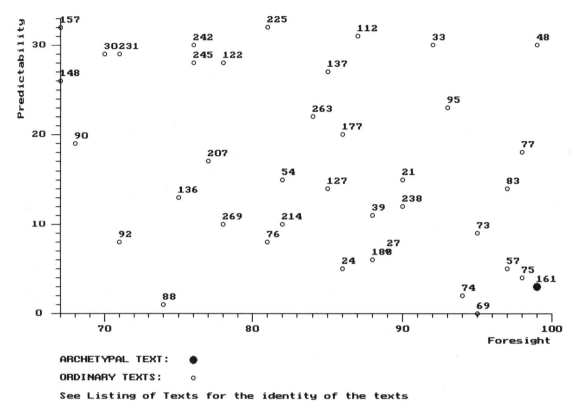

Figure 7.6 Texts scattered according to foresight and predictability (lower right corner of figure 7.4, enlarged)

names to be expected in the last volume are the ones whose last names start with the last letters of the alphabet, were born within or near the coverage span, and have the highest affinity (combination of implications) with the names in the other four volumes.

Five names in the fifth volume (Venturi, Weese, Wright, Wurster, Yamasaki) are correctly predicted either by fame or affinity; working by affinity, a sixth is anticipated—Paul Weidlinger's. Although not as famous as Turnbull (the sixth choice by fame), Weidlinger is more in line with the technical rather than the work's design orientation. A competent index analyst advising the editorial board around 1990 could have made the point clear.

The practical value of such advise is likely to be limited, so why pursue the undertaking? Because success means that authorial or editorial preferences are subject to computer-aided detection from the indexes, which as far as I know has not yet been achieved or possibly even attempted. For the effort to be successful, however, it is not enough to obtain good results in a single case; the procedure must be tested massively, and the overall accuracy must be significantly higher than when using fame alone. I used the alphabetical range of the

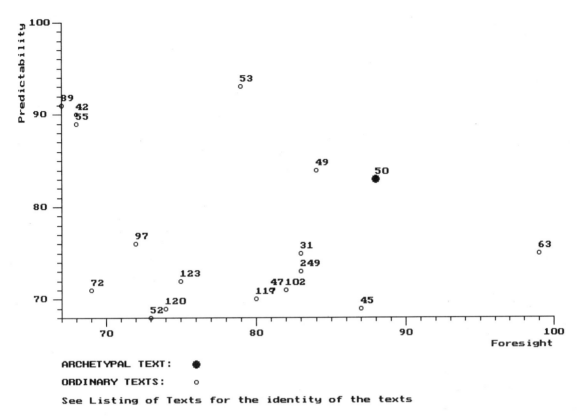

Figure 7.7   Texts scattered according to foresight and predictability (upper right corner of figure 7.4, enlarged)

AIA Encyclopedia volumes to test all the texts in the corpus. I assumed that the names of architects cited in a book starting from A to S were a given, and calculated those in the range T through Z. Predicting by fame the rate of correct responses is on average 49.5 percent. Working by affinity the results fluctuated from 50 to 53 percent, depending on the range of letters used as a given. (The overall probability of success with random guessing among names in the coverage span and the universe is only 7.5 percent.)

I did not pursue affinity predictions beyond this point because I do not see as much potential in the technique as in fame-based predictions. Guessing by fame it was possible to transcend the problem of the missing volume to produce, instead, a list of all the names expected in an entire oeuvre from the beginning to the end of the alphabet. No such generalization is viable when working by affinity, because a certain set of names (a range of the alphabet) must always be considered as given. With no overall affinity predictions there can be no overall affinity-generated missing or unexpected architects, and no predictability indexes or rankings. The implication tables between architects seemed intriguing at first, but they were eventually superseded by the more advanced concept of cotextuality (chapter 9).

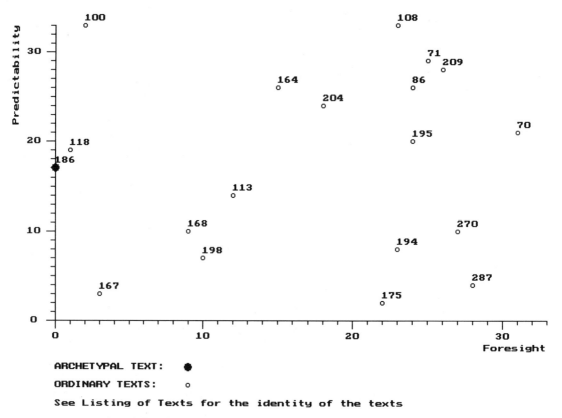

Figure 7.8 Texts scattered according to foresight and predictability (lower left corner of figure 7.4, enlarged)

8   Isonomy and Text Histograms

Measuring Distances Between Texts

In one of his short stories Borges describes an endless library with an infinite number of volumes. No two books are exactly alike; they always differ in at least a comma. The storyteller does not say whether the indexes diverge too; but the indexes of the texts of the corpus, like the books of the fictional library, are different. Some, however, are closer to each other than others. The distance between two indexes can be measured. It is argued throughout this book that indexes bear a nontrivial connection to the texts themselves; measuring distances between them opens the door to a variety of techniques to explore relationships between the items of the corpus.

A pair of indexes could be very close or very far apart. The closest possible contingency would be complete coincidence: every name included in one index is also in the other, and vice versa. Their distance would be zero, and the texts would be strictly isonomic: they would refer to the same names. At the opposite end of the spectrum is total disjunction, with not one name common to both indexes. Distance would be at a maximum, which could be assigned an arbitrary number such as 1 or 100. Although neither of these extremes occurs in the corpus, they are the poles of a continuum of possibilities against which every pair of indexes can be compared and measured. A number of statistical formulas can assign a numerical value to the distance between indexes.

Given two indexes, the system counts the names contained in both, if any. It also counts the names appearing in one index but not the other, and those in the latter but not the former. Finally, it tallies the names in neither one text nor the other. These four numbers are the building blocks for most formulas to measure distances between listings.

Association or correlation scales are similar to distance scales, except that they return values between one (for coincidence) and minus one (for complete disjunction). Although they have certain differences in their performance, several distance and association or correlation scales can be used, in principle, for the same purpose—to compare intertextual distances. Correlation and distance measurements can be converted into one another by monotonic transformations; it is therefore admissible to use language suggestive of distances (to say, for example, that two indexes are close to each other), even if the measurements are taken in an association scale. An association coefficient known in the literature as kappa is used in this chapter; it is described in the appendix.[1]

Once the scale has been set, the system has access to the distance between any two texts. Figure 8.1 shows the closest pairs of texts in the corpus. No surprise, most of the pairs, especially those at the top of the list, correspond to successive editions of the same work. But some unrelated works have very close indexes (e.g., pairs 14, 18, 25, 27, 30, 32). Successive versions of the same book are sometimes further apart than unconnected works, which confirms the validity of treating them as different texts.

The significance of high correlation is straightforward. When kappa equals 1, the texts are isonomic, the indexes are identical, and their distance is zero. Low or negative kappas signal considerable divergence, which may be due to one of the following reasons, or a combination thereof. First, the texts cover different chronological periods. Second, they deal with the same period, but were written at different times. Architects featured in the most recent one may not have been known at the time of writing the earlier one. Or third, the texts are close in coverage and publication time, but their authors espouse different aesthetic or philosophical orientations.

The most interesting factor is the third; the others can be detected effectively by means already discussed; coverages are identified by the coverage formula, and writing times are expressed directly by the publication dates. The goal in this chapter is to develop an instrument sensitive to similarities or differences between the orientations of texts. The kappa measurements must be refined to insulate them to the extent possible from the influence of the first two factors, and attune them to text direction or authorial attitudes alone.

A new correlation scale, called *adjusted kappas*, is developed. For each pair of texts one must figure out the overlap in their coverage. If no overlap exists, or if it does not reach a specified minimum, the texts are not regarded as comparable and their correlation is set to zero. If the overlap requirement is met, kappas are computed, but only architects pertinent to both texts are counted. Architects beyond the coverage of one of the texts or not yet in the universe at the time of publication of the oldest text, are flatly ignored. (See the appendix for details).

Name preference coincidence and divergence is measured only where it counts, in the universe common to both writers at the time they made their selections. The first two factors above are effectively neutralized. The association between pairs of texts given in chapter 1 (Examples of Applications) are expressed in adjusted kappas. These values reflect affinities between the writers' orientations and preferences more incisively than normal correlations. I would like to believe that if God were to use statistics to compare indexes, he would use only adjusted kappas.

Figure 8.1   Closest pairs of texts

Column headings:
[1] Pair number
[2] Kappa
[3] Text ID #
[4] Publication date
[5] Authors and titles

[1]	[2]	[3]	[4]	[5]
1	0.97	168	1968	Condit: *American Building ... from Beginning to the Present*
		270	1982	Condit: *American Building: Materials and Techniques*
2	0.96	187	1971	*The World Almanac and Book of Facts 1972*
		219	1976	*The World Almanac and Book of Facts 1977*
3	0.94	264	1981	*The World Almanac and Book of Facts 1982*
		342	1990	*The World Almanac and Book of Facts 1991*
4	0.91	178	1969	Whiffen: *American Architecture Since 1780*
		366	1992	Whiffen: *American Architecture Since 1780*
5	0.91	219	1976	*The World Almanac and Book of Facts 1977*
		264	1981	*The World Almanac and Book of Facts 1982*
6	0.91	187	1971	*The World Almanac and Book of Facts 1972*
		264	1981	*The World Almanac and Book of Facts 1982*
7	0.89	187	1971	*The World Almanac and Book of Facts 1972*
		342	1990	*The World Almanac and Book of Facts 1991*
8	0.89	131	1961	Fletcher: *A History of Architecture* (ed. Cordingley)
		210	1975	Fletcher: *A History of Architecture* (ed. Palmes)
9	0.88	219	1976	*The World Almanac and Book of Facts 1977*
		342	1990	*The World Almanac and Book of Facts 1991*
10	0.86	176	1969	Scully: *American Architecture and Urbanism*
		327	1988	Scully: *American Architecture and Urbanism*, new rev. ed.
11	0.84	135	1962	*The World Almanac and Book of Facts 1962*
		162	1966	*The World Almanac and Book of Facts 1967*
12	0.83	70	1937	*The World Almanac and Book of Facts 1937*
		100	1952	*The World Almanac and Book of Facts 1952*
13	0.81	95	1951	Giedion: *A Decade of Contemporary Architecture*
		105	1954	Giedion: *A Decade of Contemporary Architecture*, 2nd ed.
14	0.81	358	1991	Wodehouse: *Roots of International Style Architecture*
		359	1992	Bayer: *Art Deco Architecture*
15	0.81	226	1977	Jencks: *The Language of Post-Modern Architecture*, rev. ed.
		259	1981	Jencks: *The Language of Post-Modern Architecture*, 3rd ed.
16	0.77	76	1941	Giedion: *Space, Time, and Architecture*
		164	1967	Giedion: *Space, Time, and Architecture*, rev. ed.
17	0.76	64	1932	*The World Almanac and Book of Facts 1932*
		70	1937	*The World Almanac and Book of Facts 1937*
18	0.76	252	1980	Kulterman: *Architecture in the Seventies*
		254	1980	Portoghesi: *Architecture 1980*
19	0.75	142	1964	*Encyclopaedia Britannica*, 14th ed. (main entries only)
		192	1972	*Encyclopaedia Britannica*, 14th ed. (main entries only)

Figure 8.1 (continued)

[1]	[2]	[3]	[4]	[5]
20	0.74	251	1980	Hunt: *Encyclopedia of American Architecture* (main entries only)
		253	1980	Nuttgens: *Pocket Guide to Architecture*
21	0.73	49	1927	Tallmadge: *The Story of Architecture in America*
		67	1936	Tallmadge: *The Story of Architecture in America*, rev. ed.
22	0.73	286	1984	Jencks: *The Language of Post-Modern Architecture*, 4th ed.
		350	1991	Jencks: *The Language of Post-Modern Architecture*, 6th ed.
23	0.73	228	1977	Richards: *Who's Who in Architecture* (main entries only)
		229	1977	Richards: *Who's Who in Architecture*
24	0.72	141	1964	*Encyclopaedia Britannica*, 14th ed. (1964)
		191	1972	*Encyclopaedia Britannica*, 14th ed. (1972)
25	0.84	251	1980	Hunt: *Encyclopedia of American Architecture* (main entries only)
		378	1994	Striner: *Art Deco*
26	0.72	277	1982	Wright: *Highlights to Recent American Architecture 1945–1978*
		338	1989	Wright: *Sourcebook of Contemporary North American Architecture*
27	0.72	335	1989	Peel, Powell, & Garrett: *20th-Century Architecture*
		336	1989	Russell: *Architecture and Design 1970–1990*
28	0.71	197	1972	Sharp: *Visual History of 20th C Architecture*
		355	1991	Sharp: *Twentieth Century Architecture: A Visual History*
29	0.69	162	1966	*The World Almanac and Book of Facts 1967*
		187	1971	*The World Almanac and Book of Facts 1972*
30	0.68	106	1955	Andrews: *Architecture, Ambition, and Americans*
		234	1978	Andrews: *Architecture, Ambition and Americans*, rev. ed.
31	0.67	162	1966	*The World Almanac and Book of Facts 1967*
		264	1981	*The World Almanac and Book of Facts 1982*
32	0.66	121	1959	Jones: *Form Givers at Mid-century*
		276	1982	Pothorn: *Architectural Styles*
33	0.66	210	1975	Fletcher: *A History of Architecture* (ed. Palmes)
		315	1987	Musgrove (ed.): *Fletcher's History of Architecture*, 19th ed.
34	0.65	131	1961	Fletcher: *A History of Architecture* (ed. Cordingley)
		315	1987	Musgrove (ed.): *Fletcher's History of Architecture*, 19th ed.

Pairs of texts with a high adjusted kappa are said to be *isonomic*. This is less than strict isonomy as defined earlier, because the indexes are not coincident; but the writers, faced with the same array of possible names, made the same or similar choices.

Figure 8.2 shows the thirty-four closest pairs of isonomic texts. Successive editions of the same work have been eliminated from the ranking because they dominate the upper positions and are of limited consequence. Despite the steps taken to eliminate the influence of publication dates, most of the pairs of figure 8.2. are relatively close chronologically. This suggests the existence of constellations of names (and interests) predominating at certain times.

With access to the electronic companion, persons interested in a particular text can rank all the other ones in terms of their closeness to the one chosen.

Figure 8.2   Closest pairs of texts (adjusted)

Column headings:
[1] Pair number
[2] Adjusted kappa
[3] Text ID #
[4] Publication date
[5] Authors and titles

[1]	[2]	[3]	[4]	[5]
1	1.00	86	1948	Pevsner: *An Outline of European Architecture*
		111	1957	Maas: *The Gingerbread Age*
2	1.00	88	1949	Conder: *An Introduction to Modern Architecture*
		138	1962	Pevsner: "Architecture and Applied Arts"
3	1.00	121	1959	Jones: *Form Givers at Mid-century*
		144	1964	Hilberseimer: *Contemporary Architecture*
4	1.00	71	1938	Richardson & Corfiato: *The Art of Architecture*
		135	1962	*The World Almanac and Book of Facts 1962*
5	1.00	4	1836	Cleveland: *Review of American Builder's General Price Book*
		10	1864	Jarves: *The Art-idea*
6	1.00	100	1952	*The World Almanac and Book of Facts 1952*
		115	1958	Gloag: *Guide to Western Architecture*
7	1.00	54	1929	Hitchcock: *Modern Architecture*
		86	1948	Pevsner: *An Outline of European Architecture*
8	1.00	7	1851	Greenough: "American Architecture" and "Aesthetics at Washington"
		22	1896	Hamlin, A.D.F.: *A Text-Book of the History of Architecture*
9	1.00	7	1851	Greenough: "American Architecture" and "Aesthetics at Washington"
		200	1973	Glubok: Composite of books 1970–1973
10	1.00	121	1959	Jones: *Form Givers at Mid-century*
		127	1960	Huxtable: *Twentieth-Century Architecture*
11	1.00	43	1925	Kimball: *Three Centuries of American Architecture*
		92	1950	Egbert: *Organic Expression and American Architecture*
12	1.00	22	1896	Hamlin, A.D.F.: *A Text-Book of the History of Architecture*
		30	1905	Fletcher: *A History of Architecture*, 5th ed.
13	1.00	337	1989	Wodehouse & Moffett: *A History of Western Architecture*
		339	1990	AIA: *American Architecture of the 1980s.*
14	1.00	1	1815	Latrobe(?): "State of the Fine Arts in the United States"
		4	1836	Cleveland: *Review of American Builder's General Price Book*
15	1.00	3	1834	Dunlap: *History of the Arts of Design in the United States*
		10	1864	Jarves: *The Art-idea*
16	1.00	68	1937	Behrendt: *Modern Building*
		88	1949	Conder: *An Introduction to Modern Architecture*
17	1.00	3	1834	Dunlap: *History of the Arts of Design in the United States*
		4	1836	Cleveland: *Review of American Builder's General Price Book*
18	1.00	1	1815	Latrobe(?): "State of the Fine Arts in the United States"
		3	1834	Dunlap: *History of the Arts of Design in the United States*
19	0.97	335	1989	Peel, Powell, & Garrett: *20th-Century Architecture*
		336	1989	Russell: *Architecture and Design 1970–1990*

Figure 8.2   (continued)

[1]	[2]	[3]	[4]	[5]
20	0.95	182	1970	Osborne: *The Oxford Companion to Art*
		184	1970	Pierson: *American Building: Colonial and Neo-classical Styles*
21	0.95	284	1984	Flon (ed.): *The World Atlas of Architecture*
		289	1984	Pokinski: *Development of the American Modern Style*
22	0.91	358	1991	Wodehouse: *Roots of International Style Architecture*
		359	1992	Bayer: *Art Deco Architecture*
23	0.91	68	1937	Behrendt: *Modern Building*
		198	1973	Boorstin: *The Americans: The Democratic Experience*
24	0.90	92	1950	Egbert: *Organic Expression and American Architecture*
		148	1965	Collins: *Changing Ideals in Modern Architecture: 1750–1950*
25	0.90	115	1958	Gloag: *Guide to Western Architecture*
		151	1965	Millon (ed.): *Key Monuments in the History of Architecture*
26	0.88	22	1896	Hamlin, A.D.F.: *A Text-Book of the History of Architecture*
		28	1902	Schuyler: "United States Architecture"
27	0.87	252	1980	Kulterman: *Architecture in the Seventies*
		254	1980	Portoghesi: *Architecture 1980*
28	0.85	42	1924	Mumford: *Sticks and Stones*
		151	1965	Millon (ed.): *Key Monuments in the History of Architecture*
29	0.85	86	1948	Pevsner: *An Outline of European Architecture*
		151	1965	Millon (ed.): *Key Monuments in the History of Architecture*
30	0.84	68	1937	Behrendt: *Modern Building*
		144	1964	Hilberseimer: *Contemporary Architecture*
31	0.84	78	1941	Saint-Gaudens: *The American Artist and His Times*
		115	1958	Gloag: *Guide to Western Architecture*
32	0.84	151	1965	Millon (ed.): *Key Monuments in the History of Architecture*
		284	1984	Flon (ed.): *The World Atlas of Architecture*
33	0.84	68	1937	Behrendt: *Modern Building*
		203	1973	Rowland: *A History of the Modern Movement*
34	0.82	205	1974	Norberg-Schulz: *Meaning in Western Architecture*
		280	1983	Nuttgens: *The Story of Architecture*

Finding the most radically opposed one is potentially as interesting as searching for the closest.

Isonomy does not prove a deeper consonance any more than lack thereof demonstrates an underlying divergence; but they point in those directions. To confirm or disprove the presumption one must have the erudition and the familiarity with the literature of an architectural historian, the time availability of a patient reader, or the eye of God. If one is short of those attributes, one must rely on the fact that operating with intertextual distances generally leads to meaningful conclusions, as shown in the following sections.

Texts: The Influential and the Influenced

If two texts were to coincide in their appreciations about a group of architects or buildings, most people would posit a link between them or their writers. Depending on the extent of the resemblance, the link would be seen as an agreement in value judgment, a possible influence of the earlier text over the latter writer, or outright plagiarism. No sensible person would pay attention, however, if the correspondences were limited to a few names in the index. But the picture would change if the matches were very many.

Isonomy is inherently an asymmetrical relationship. One of the texts almost invariably predates the other, and the temporal sequence indicates the direction of the possible influence. The pairs of figure 8.2 are listed by order of publication. One isolated pair would not justify any assumptions about the earlier book having influenced the later one; but if a text were to appear consistently as the precedent in many such pairs, the case for its possible influence would be strengthened. Similarly, if a text were typically found occupying the second place in the relationship, the assumption of responsiveness (not to say indebtedness) toward the preceding literature would be stronger than if there were only an occasional, isolated connection.

Figure 8.2 contains too few cases to allow for significant conclusions. A better picture emerges after having the system examine nearly 8,000 pairs of isonomic texts, all those with adjusted kappas equal or greater than 1/3. Whenever a book appears as precedent in such a relationship, it is considered to have a *forward* link; if it is a follower, the link is regarded as *backward*. Horizontal links (those between texts with the same publication date) are also counted, but links between successive editions of the same work are ignored. Figure 8.3 shows the texts of the corpus with the highest number of forward links, backward links, and total links, and those with no links whatsoever. The works with many links toward the future are presumably the most influential. The ones following most closely precedents set in the existing literature can be regarded as the most bookish. A text can be both influential and bookish. (Forward and backward connectedness may be preferred as more neutral terms, without the overtones of influence and bookishness.) Texts are ranked by connectedness to the literature in function of their total number of links—back, forth, and horizontal. Texts with no connections are the most disconnected.

The number of possible linkages to past and future is affected by publication date: recent texts have few or no links forward, and very old ones can hardly have backward links. If the older books were the most influential and the more recent ones the most influenced, the findings would be trivial and inconsequential. The most influential texts in figure 8.3 are not, however, the oldest; they were for the most part published during the 1950s and 1960s. This is the body of literature that propelled to the world the extraordinary generation of American architects that entered the universe during the 1930s and 1940s (see chapter 3).

Figure 8.3   Texts ranked according to linkage

Column headings:
[1]   Total number of links
[2]   Forward links (to texts still to be written)
[3]   Backward links (to already existing texts)
[4]   Text ID #
[5]   Publication date
[6]   Author and title

[1]	[2]	[3]	[4]	[5]	[6]
Most "influential" texts (ranking by forward links):					
150	120	30	139	1963	Jacobus: *Modern Architecture*
127	116	11	109	1956	*Architectural Record:* "100 Years of Significant Building"
138	107	29	131	1961	Fletcher: *A History of Architecture* (ed. Cordingley)
116	104	11	55	1929	LaFollette: *Art in America*
120	102	18	94	1950	Watterson: *Five Thousand Years of Building*
159	101	56	165	1967	Hillier: *From Tepees to Towers*
106	101	5	103	1953	Hamlin, T.: *Architecture Through the Ages*, rev ed.
129	98	28	153	1965	Ulanov: *The Two Worlds of American Art*
128	98	26	152	1965	Rogers: *What's Up in Architecture*
111	97	10	120	1959	Joedicke: *A History of Modern Architecture*
107	97	8	53	1928	Kimball: *American Architecture*
138	96	38	159	1966	Myers: *McGraw-Hill Dictionary of Art*
106	96	10	117	1958	Peter: *Masters of Modern Architecture*
147	95	50	171	1968	Norman: *Traveler's Guide to American Art*
114	94	20	119	1959	Francastel: *Les Architects Celebres*
105	93	10	133	1961	Scully: *Modern Architecture*
Most "bookish" texts (ranking by backward links):					
143	0	142	380	1994	Packard (ed.): *Encyclopedia of American Architecture*
142	2	136	373	1993	Van Vynckt (ed.): *International Dictionary of Architects & Architecture*
146	10	131	354	1991	Sharp: *Illustrated Encyclopedia of Architects and Architecture*
140	11	124	348	1991	Copplestone: *Twentieth-Century World Architecture*
137	10	122	349	1991	Gossel & Lenhauser: *Architecture in the 20th Century*
130	13	116	342	1990	*The World Almanac and Book of Facts 1991*
149	30	113	311	1986	Watkin: *A History of Western Architecture*
120	3	113	369	1993	Kulterman: *Architecture in the 20th Century*
141	26	110	320	1988	Hollingworth: *Architecture of the 20th Century*
118	3	110	370	1993	LeBlanc: *20th Century American Architecture*
126	18	106	330	1989	*AIA Encyclopedia of Architecture, Design, Engineering ...* (main entries only)
121	9	106	355	1991	Sharp: *Twentieth Century Architecture: A Visual History*
128	24	101	315	1987	Musgrove (ed.): *Fletcher's History of Architecture*, 19th ed.
119	18	99	327	1988	Scully: *American Architecture and Urbanism*, new rev. ed.
122	23	97	317	1987	Yarwood: *A Chronology of Western Architecture*
137	34	96	308	1986	Lampugnani: *Encyclopedia of 20th Century Architecture*
Most "connected" texts (ranking by total links):					
159	101	56	165	1967	Hillier: *From Tepees to Towers*
159	70	89	228	1977	Richards: *Who's Who in Architecture* (main entries only)
152	76	76	210	1975	Fletcher: *A History of Architecture* (ed. Palmes)
150	120	30	139	1963	Jacobus: *Modern Architecture*
149	66	81	237	1978	Williamson: "An Architectural Family Tree"

Figure 8.3   (continued)

[1]	[2]	[3]	[4]	[5]	[6]
149	30	113	311	1986	Watkin: *A History of Western Architecture*
147	95	50	171	1968	Norman: *Traveler's Guide to American Art*
147	56	86	251	1980	Hunt: *Encyclopedia of American Architecture* (main entries only)
146	85	57	179	1970	Hamilton: *19th & 20th Century Art: Painting, Sculpture, Architecture*
146	10	131	354	1991	Sharp: *Illustrated Encyclopedia of Architects and Architecture*
144	57	85	271	1982	Curtis: *Modern Architecture Since 1900*
143	0	142	380	1994	Packard (ed.): *Encyclopedia of American Architecture*
142	85	53	181	1970	Mendelowitz: *A History of American Art*
142	78	63	185	1971	Cohen: *History of American Art*
142	2	136	373	1993	Van Vynckt (ed.): *International Dictionary of Architects & Architecture*
141	44	94	284	1984	Flon (ed.): *The World Atlas of Architecture*

Most "disconnected" texts (ranking by total links):

[1]	[2]	[3]	[4]	[5]	[6]
0	0	0	2	1830	*American Journal of Science & Arts:* "Architecture in the United States"
0	0	0	6	1850	Sears: *A New and Popular Pictorial Description of the United States*
0	0	0	11	1880	Benjamin: *Art in America*
0	0	0	12	1883	van Rensselaer: "Recent Architecture in America"
0	0	0	13	1884	Levy: *Modern American Architecture*
0	0	0	14	1886	*L'Architecture Americaine*
0	0	0	16	1888	Arnold: *Studies in Architecture at Home and Abroad*
0	0	0	26	1899	Ware: *The Georgian Period*
0	0	0	27	1900	Mackson: *American Architecture Interiors & Furniture*
0	0	0	33	1910	*Men and Women of America: A Biographical Dictionary*
0	0	0	39	1920	Greber: *L'Architecture aux États-Unies*
0	0	0	41	1924	Jackson: *American Colonial Architecture*
0	0	0	45	1926	Hamlin, T.: *The American Spirit in Architecture*
0	0	0	50	1928	Edgell: *The American Architecture of To-day*
0	0	0	56	1929	Sexton: Composite of books published in 1928–31
0	0	0	62	1932	Barr, Hitchcock, Johnson, & Mumford: *Modern Architects*
0	0	0	63	1932	Hitchcock & Johnson: *The International Style*
0	0	0	69	1937	Newcomb: *Spanish-Colonial Architecture in the United States*
0	0	0	74	1941	*Architectural Record:* "American Architecture 1891–1941"
0	0	0	75	1941	*Pencil Points:* "Forty Under Forty"
0	0	0	81	1944	Hamlin, T.: *Greek Revival Architecture in America*
0	0	0	91	1950	AIA: *Contemporary Architecture in the United States 1947–1949*
0	0	0	97	1952	Hamlin, T.: *Forms and Functions of 20th Century Architecture*
0	0	0	101	1952	Morrison: *Early American Architecture*
0	0	0	112	1957	McCallum: "Genetrix. Personal Contributions to American Architecture"
0	0	0	137	1962	Dixon: *Architectural Design Preview, USA*
0	0	0	161	1966	Stern: *40 Under 40: An Exhibition of Young Talent in Architecture*
0	0	0	230	1977	Smith, C. R.: *Supermannerism*
0	0	0	232	1977	Stern (ed.): "Forty Under Forty"
0	0	0	303	1986	Allen: *Emerging Voices. New Generation of Architects in America*
0	0	0	323	1988	Larkin et al.: *Colonial Design in the New World*
0	0	0	328	1988	Stern: *Modern Classicism*
0	0	0	367	1993	Economakis (ed.): *Building Classical: A Vision of Europe and America*

It is not surprising that reference works predominate among the bookish texts. The most connected works are rather recent, and many of the most disconnected ones are very old. American architectural literature at its inception pointed in many directions; agreement about the leading architects evolved gradually, as a result of decades of collective work.

Figure 8.3 would be bulky and inconvenient if all books were included. Persons with access to the electronic companion can select a text and obtain all those that precede and follow it, sorted by their proximity to the one chosen; the text's connections with the entire corpus can thus be apprehended.

Forward connectedness as discussed here and foresightedness as presented in chapter 6 have a certain similarity. To distinguish them one must think of the concepts behind the labels. Foresightedness measures a writer's ability to capture still relatively unknown architects with a brilliant future; influence depends on focusing on a cluster of names that will remain present, as a group, in future texts. Similarly, a certain convergence can be seen between predictability (chapter 7) and bookishness, backward connectedness, or the condition of being influenced. As the definitions and measurement criteria differ, the results will not match.

Families, Tribes, Nations

Let us look at pairings numbers 5, 14, 15, 17, and 18 in figure 8.2: they involve a cluster of four tightly interconnected texts, those by Latrobe (1815), Dunlap (1834), Cleveland (1836), and Jarves (1984). Numerous links exist among these texts, but no links between them and other texts in the corpus, at least not within the links reported in figure 8.2. The figure has other clusters of interconnected texts; readers inclined to do so may find them in minutes. As the number of texts and links increases, finding the clusters becomes cumbersome.

Various computer algorithms exist to generate a clustering of texts on the basis of intertextual distances. The one used for this section starts by considering each text as a separate cluster. The two closest texts are then joined to form a larger cluster. The amalgamating process continues in a stepwise fashion, joining texts or clusters of texts, until a single cluster is formed containing all the texts in the corpus.[2] The outcome is a tree with as many branches as texts, voluminous and unwieldy. To facilitate use I reformatted the results into a series of arbitrary hierarchical levels. Texts are arranged into families, which are grouped into tribes, which constitute nations (figure 8.4). The nations can be conceived, in turn, as constituting a federation of nations—the entire corpus. Individual texts may appear at any of the levels, as indicated by the indentations in the figure. For example, a tribe may be composed of families of texts and texts that do not belong to any family. Families, tribes, and nations are defined not by size, but by their degree of internal similarity. The texts in a tribe are closer in their choice of architects than those in a nation, but not as similar as those in a family.

Figure 8.4   Texts clustered into nations, tribes, and families

---

Nation 1
1815   Latrobe(?): "State of the Fine Arts in the United States"
  Tribe 1
    Family 1
      1834   Dunlap: *History of the Arts of Design in the United States*
      1836   Cleveland: *Review of American Builder's General Price Book*
      1864   Jarves: *The Art-idea*
Nation 2
  Tribe 1
    Family 1
      1862   Fergusson: *History of the Modern Styles of Architecture*
      1888   Gwilt: *An Encyclopedia of Architecture*
Nation 3
1892   The Dictionary of Architecture
  Tribe 1
    1848   Tuthill: *History of Architecture from the Earliest Times*
    1856   Heck: *The Art of Building in Ancient and Modern Times*
  Tribe 2
    Family 1
      1851   Greenough: "American Architecture" and "Aesthetics at Washington"
      1973   Glubok: Composite of books 1970–1973
Nation 4
1886   *L'Architecture Americaine*
1891   Fergusson: *History of Modern Styles of Architecture*
Nation 5
  Tribe 1
    1887   Longfellow: "The Course of American Architecture"
    1897   Statham: *Modern Architecture*
Nation 6
  Tribe 1
    1893   Baedecker: *The United States*
    1910   *The Encyclopaedia Britannica*, 11th ed.
Nation 7
  Tribe 1
    1892   Schuyler: *American Architecture—Studies*
    1913   Schuyler: *American Architecture and Other Writings*
Nation 8
1897   *The Architectural Record Great American Architects Series*
1909   Bragdon: "Architecture in The United States"
Nation 9
  Tribe 1
    1902   Schuyler: "United States Architecture"
    Family 1
      1909   Hamlin, A.D.F.: *A Text-Book of the History of Architecture*, 8th ed.
      1928   Hamlin, A.D.F.: *A Text-Book of the History of Architecture*, 18th pr.
  Tribe 2
  1902   Sturgis: *A Dictionary of Architecture and Building*
  1928   Kimball: *American Architecture*

Figure 8.4   (continued)

Nation 10
  Tribe 1
    Family 1
    1896   Hamlin, A.D.F.: *A Text-Book of the History of Architecture*
    1905   Fletcher: *A History of Architecture*, 5th ed.
  Tribe 2
  1921   Fletcher: *A History of Architecture*, 6th ed.
  1952   Jones: *O Strange New World*

Nation 11
1929   Taut: *Modern Architecture*
  Tribe 1
  1929   Hitchcock: *Modern Architecture*
  1930   Cheney: *The New World Architecture*

Nation 12
1926   *The Architectural Record* American Architect Golden Anniversary Number
  Tribe 1
    Family 1
    1932   *The World Almanac and Book of Facts 1932*
    1937   *The World Almanac and Book of Facts 1937*

Nation 13
  Tribe 1
  1897   Van Brunt: *Architecture and Society*
  1931   Fletcher: *A History of Architecture*, 9th ed.
  Tribe 2
  1916   Hamlin, A.D.F.: "25 Years of American Architecture"
  1934   Whitaker: *The Story of Architecture*
  1949   Lynes: *The Tastemakers*
  Tribe 3
    Family 1
    1952   *The World Almanac and Book of Facts 1952*
    1958   Gloag: *Guide to Western Architecture*

Nation 14
  Tribe 1
  1915   Eberlein: *The Architecture of Colonial America*
  1938   Richardson & Corfiato: *The Art of Architecture*
  1949   Bannister: *From Colony to Nation*

Nation 15
  Tribe 1
    Family 1
    1925   Kimball: *Three Centuries of American Architecture*
    1950   Egbert: *Organic Expression and American Architecture*

Nation 16
  Tribe 1
  1940   Roth: *The New Architecture*
  1945   Reilly: *Some Contemporary American Buildings*

Nation 17
  Tribe 1
    Family 1
    1942   Museum of Modern Art: *What is Modern Architecture?*
    1944   Mock: *Built in America 1932–1944*

Figure 8.4   (continued)

Nation 18
1926   Berlin: *Ausstellung Neuer Amerikanischer Baukunst*
1926   Hamlin, T.: *The American Spirit in Architecture*
1928   Edgell: *The American Architecture of To-day*
1957   Morris: *A Century of AIA*
1967   Rosenblum: *Transformations in Late 18th Century Art*
  Tribe 1
  1928   Jackman: *American Arts*
    Family 1
    1930   Hoak & Church: *Masterpieces of Architecture in the United States*
    1992   Thomas & Lewis: *American Architectural Masterpieces*

Nation 19
1952   Hamlin, T.: *Forms and Functions of 20th Century Architecture*
  Tribe 1
  1950   P/A: "United States Architecture 1900–1950"
  1953   Ferriss: *Power in Buildings*

Nation 20
1950   AIA: *Contemporary Architecture in the United States 1947–1949*
  Tribe 1
  1952   Hitchcock & Drexler: *Built in USA: Post-war Architecture*
    Family 1
    1951   Giedion: *A Decade of Contemporary Architecture*
    1954   Giedion: *A Decade of Contemporary Architecture*, 2nd ed.

Nation 21
1959   Bode: *The Anatomy of American Popular Culture 1840–61*
  Tribe 1
  1965   Early: *Romanticism in American Architecture*
    Family 1
    1948   Pevsner: *An Outline of European Architecture*
    1957   Maas: *The Gingerbread Age*

Nation 22
  Tribe 1
  1941   Saint-Gaudens: *The American Artist and His Times*
  Family 1
    1918   Kimball & Edgell: *A History of Architecture*
    1924   Mumford: *Sticks and Stones*
    1965   Millon (ed.): *Key Monuments in the History of Architecture*
  Family 2
    1962   *The World Almanac and Book of Facts 1962*
    1966   *The World Almanac and Book of Facts 1967*
    1971   *The World Almanac and Book of Facts 1972*
    1976   *The World Almanac and Book of Facts 1977*
    1981   *The World Almanac and Book of Facts 1982*
    1990   *The World Almanac and Book of Facts 1991*
  Tribe 2
  1942   Newcomb: *History of Modern Architecture*
  1972   Jordy: *American Buildings: Progressive and Academic Ideals*
    Family 1
    1927   Tallmadge: *The Story of Architecture in America*
    1936   Tallmadge: *The Story of Architecture in America*, rev. ed.

Figure 8.4   (continued)

Tribe 3
1979   *The American Renaissance 1876–1917* (without Catalogue)
1979   *The American Renaissance 1876–1917* (Catalogue only)

Nation 23
  Tribe 1
    Family 1
    1937   Behrendt: *Modern Building*
    1973   Boorstin: *The Americans: The Democratic Experience*
    1973   Rowland: *A History of the Modern Movement*
  Tribe 2
    Family 1
    1949   Conder: *An Introduction to Modern Architecture*
    1962   Pevsner: "Architecture and Applied Arts"

Nation 24
1952   Morrison: *Early American Architecture*
  Tribe 1
    1952   Eberlein & Hubbard: *American Georgian Architecture*
    1966   Tatum: *The Arts in America: The Colonial Period*
    1968   Millar: *The Architects of the American Colonies*

Nation 25
1949   Larkin: *Art and Life in America*
1969   Norton: *The Arts in America: The 19th century*
  Tribe 1
    1929   LaFollette: *Art in America*
    1930   Conant (ed.): *Modern Architecture*
    1950   Watterson: *Five Thousand Years of Building*
    1959   Francastel: *Les Architects Celèbres*
    1990   Kennedy: *Rediscovering America*
    Family 1
    1940   Hamlin, T.: *Architecture Through the Ages*
    1953   Hamlin, T.: *Architecture Through the Ages*, rev ed.
    Family 2
    1970   Osborne: *The Oxford Companion to Art*
    1970   Pierson: *American Building: Colonial and Neo-classical Styles*
  Tribe 2
    1948   Fitch: *American Building: The Forces that Shape It*
    1966   Fitch: *American Building: The Historical Forces that Shaped It*
    1967   Ross: *Taste In America*
    1980   Ball: *Architecture and Interior Design*
    1992   Reynolds: *Nineteenth Century Architecture*
  Tribe 3
    1953   Tunnard: *The City of Man*
    1970   Osborne: *The Oxford Companion to Art* (main entries only)
    1978   Pierson: *American Buildings: Technology & the Picturesque*
    Family 1
    1963   Jacobus: *Modern Architecture*
    1989   Devlin: *Portraits of American Architecture*

Nation 26
1992   Garrett: *Classical America*

Figure 8.4   (continued)

Tribe 1
1926   Jackson: *Development of American Architecture 1783–1830*
1971   Gillon: *Early Illustrations of American Architecture*

Nation 27
1957   McCallum: "Genetrix. Personal Contributions to American Architecture"
  Tribe 1
  1966   Jacobus: *Twentieth Century Architecture: The Middle Years 1940–66*
    Family 1
    1960   Huxtable: *Twentieth-Century Architecture*
    1973   Jencks: *Modern Movements in Architecture*

Nation 28
1955   Scully: *The Shingle Style and the Stick Style*
1977   Milwaukee Art Center: *An American Architecture*

Nation 29
1944   Hamlin, T.: *Greek Revival Architecture in America*
1989   Kennedy: *Greek Revival America*

Nation 30
1966   Stern: *40 Under 40: An Exhibition of Young Talent in Architecture*
1977   Stern (ed.): "Forty Under Forty"

Nation 31
1961   Von Eckardt (ed.): *Mid-Century Architecture in America*
1982   McCoy & Goldstein: *Guide to U.S. Architecture 1940–1980*
1992   Newhouse: *The Builders Marvels of Engineering*
  Tribe 1
  1956   *Architectural Record:* "100 Years of Significant Building"
  1957   Gutheim: *1857–1957. One Hundred Years of Architecture in America*
  1957   USIA: *Architecture USA* (ed: Blake?)
  Tribe 2
  1959   Joedicke: *A History of Modern Architecture*
  1959   Kulterman: *Architecture of Today*
  1961   *Contemporary Architecture of the World 1961*
  1973   *Jacobus: American Art of the 20th Century*
  1982   *Curtis: Modern Architecture Since 1900*
  1991   Gossel & Lenhauser: *Architecture in the 20th Century*
    Family 1
    1964   Pehnt: *Encyclopedia of Modern Architecture*
    1975   Blake & Quint: *Modern Architecture America*
  Tribe 3
  1964   Muschenheim: *Elements of the Art of Architecture*
  1984   Jervis: *Design & Designers*
    Family 1
    1962   Banham: *Guide to Modern Architecture*
    1991   *The Illustrated Dictionary of 20th Century Designers*
  Tribe 4
  1964   Creighton: *American Architecture*
  1966   Heyer: *Architects on Architecture*
  1976   White: *The Architecture Book*
  Tribe 5
  1964   Tschacbasov: *Teachers Manual for the Study of Art History*

Figure 8.4   (continued)

1965   Drexler: *Modern Architecture USA*
1965   Rogers: *What's Up in Architecture*
1965   Ulanov: *The Two Worlds of American Art*
1969   Joedicke: *Architecture Since 1945*
1972   Fitch: *American Building: The Environmental Forces that Shaped It*
1972   Jordy: *American Buildings: Impact of Europeam Modernism*
1983   Risebero: *Modern Architecture and Design*
  Family 1
  1968   Norman: *Traveler's Guide to American Art*
  1991   Copplestone: *Twentieth-Century World Architecture*
  Family 2
  1972   Sharp: *Visual History of 20th C Architecture*
  1991   Sharp: *Twentieth Century Architecture: A Visual History*
  Family 3
  1987   Yarwood: *A Chronology of Western Architecture*
  1990   Saunders: *Modern Architecture*

Nation 32
  Tribe 1
  1961   Scully: *Modern Architecture*
  1970   Hofmann & Kultermann: *Modern Architecture in Color*
  1976   Brolin: *The Failure of Modern Architecture*
  1977   Stierlin: *Encyclopaedia of World Architecture*
    Family 1
    1959   Jones: *Form Givers at Mid-century*
    1964   Hilberseimer: *Contemporary Architecture*
    1982   Pothorn: *Architectural Styles*
  Tribe 2
    Family 1
    1965   Collins: *Changing Ideals in Modern Architecture: 1750–1950*
    1991   Scully: *Architecture: The Natural and the Manmade*
    Family 2
    1974   Norberg-Schulz: *Meaning in Western Architecture*
    1983   Nuttgens: *The Story of Architecture*

Nation 33
  Tribe 1
    Family 1
    1969   Stern: *New Directions in American Architecture*
    1977   Stern: *New Directions in American Architecture*, rev. ed.

Nation 34
  Tribe 1
  1974   Scully: *Modern Architecture*, 2nd ed. rev.
  1974   Scully: *The Shingle Style Today*

Nation 35
1929   Sexton: Composite of books published in 1928–31
1974   Kidney: *The Architecture of Choice: Eclecticism in America 1880–1930*
1975   Varian: *American Art Deco Architecture*
  Tribe 1
  1986   Duncan: *American Art Deco*

Figure 8.4   (continued)

Family 1
1991   Wodehouse: *Roots of International Style Architecture*
1992   Bayer: *Art Deco Architecture*

Nation 36
1955   Tunnard & Reed: *American Skyline*
1959   Reed: *The Golden City*
1966   Benevolo: *History of Modern Architecture*
1976   Pevsner: *A History of Building Types*
1980   Frampton: *Modern Architecture*
1985   Klein & Fogle: *Clues to American Architecture*
1985   Maddex: *Built in the USA: American Buildings from A to Z*
1989   Kennedy (ed.): *Smithsonian Guide to Historic America*
1992   Gowans: *Styles and Types of North American Architecture*

Tribe 1
Family 1
1935   Cahill & Barr: *Art in America*
1958   Peter: *Masters of Modern Architecture*

Tribe 2
Family 1
1941   Giedion: *Space, Time, and Architecture*
1967   Giedion: *Space, Time, and Architecture*, rev. ed.

Tribe 3
1958   Hitchcock: *Architecture: Nineteenth and Twentieth Centuries*
1960   Pierson & Davidson: *Arts in the United States*
1966   Green: *American Art: A Historical Survey*
1966   Myers: *McGraw-Hill Dictionary of Art*
1976   Panek: *American Architectural Styles 1600–1940*
1977   Brown: *American Art to 1900*
1981   Whiffen & Koepper: *American Architecture 1607–1976*

Family 1
1955   Andrews: *Architecture, Ambition, and Americans*
1978   Andrews: *Architecture, Ambition and Americans*, rev. ed.

Family 2
1969   Whiffen: *American Architecture Since 1780*
1992   Whiffen: *American Architecture Since 1780*

Tribe 4
1959   McCallum: *Architecture USA*
1961   Jones: *Architecture Today and Tomorrow*
1976   Hammett: *Architecture in the United States*
1984   Poppeliers et al.: *What Style Is It?*

Tribe 5
1960   Andrews: *Architecture in America*
1978   Williamson: "An Architectural Family Tree"
1980   Reid: *The Book of Buildings*
1981   Rugoff: *Encyclopedia of American Art*
1986   De Long, Searing, Stern: *American Architecture* (exhibition)
1989   *AIA Encyclopedia of Architecture, Design, Engineering* ... (main entries only)

Family 1
1979   Brown et al.: *American Art*
1986   Lampugnani: *Encyclopedia of 20th Century Architecture*

Figure 8.4   (continued)

Tribe 6
1960   Condit: *American Building Art: The 19th & the 20th Centuries*
   Family 1
1968   Condit: *American Building ... from Beginning to the Present*
1982   Condit: *American Building: Materialas and Techniques*
Tribe 7
1961   Burchard & Bush-Brown: *The Architecture of America*
1964   Gowans: *Images of American Living*
1976   Wodehouse: *American Architects from the Civil War to the Present*
Tribe 8
1969   Jordan: *A Concise History of Western Architecture*
1970   Hamilton: *19th & 20th Century Art: Painting, Sculpture, Architecture*
1978   Burton: *A Choice Over Our Heads*
1980   Raeburn: *Architecture of the Western World*
1985   Crouch: *History of Architecture from Stonhenge to Skyscrapers*
1986   Trachtenberg & Hyman: *Architecture from Prehistory to PostModernism*
1988   Gibberd: *Architecture Source Book*
1988   Norberg-Schulz: *New World Architecture*
   Family 1
   1961   Fletcher: *A History of Architecture* (ed. Cordingley)
   1975   Fletcher: *A History of Architecture* (ed. Palmes)
   1987   Musgrove (ed.): *Fletcher's History of Architecture*, 19th ed.
   Family 2
   1966   Read: *Encyclopedia of the Arts*
   1988   Nuttgens: *Understanding Modern Architecture*
   Family 3
   1967   Hillier: *From Tepees to Towers*
   1971   Cohen: *History of American Art*
   Family 4
   1980   Hunt: *Encyclopedia of American Architecture* (main entries only)
   1980   Nuttgens: *Pocket Guide to Architecture*
   Family 5
   1984   Flon (ed.): *The World Atlas of Architecture*
   1984   Pokinski: *Development of the American Modern Style*
   1986   Watkin: *A History of Western Architecture*
Tribe 9
1968   McLanathan: *The American Tradition in the Arts*
1968   Portoghesi: *Dizionario enciclopedico di architetture e urbanistica*
1972   Bacon: *Architecture and Townscape*
1977   Richards: *Who's Who in Architecture*
1980   Rifkind: *A Field Guide to American Architecture*
1981   *The New Encyclopaedia Britannica*, 15th ed.
1981   Thorndike: *Three Centuries of Notable American Architects*
1985   Handlin: *American Architecture*
1985   Maddex: *Master Builders*
   Family 1
   1964   *Encyclopaedia Britannica*, 14th ed. (1964)
   1972   *Encyclopaedia Britannica*, 14th ed. (1972)
   Family 2
   1964   *Encyclopaedia Britannica*, 14th ed. (main entries only)
   1972   *Encyclopaedia Britannica*, 14th ed. (main entries only)

Figure 8.4   (continued)

Family 3
1977   Richards: *Who's Who in Architecture* (main entries only)
1991   Sharp: *Illustrated Encyclopedia of Architects and Architecture*
Tribe 10
1970   Mendelowitz: *A History of American Art*
1973   Cook & Klotz: *Conversations with Architects*
    Family 1
    1969   Scully: *American Architecture and Urbanism*
    1988   Scully: *American Architecture and Urbanism*, new rev. ed.
Tribe 11
1975   Loth & Trousdale: *The Only Proper Style*
1976   Platt: *America's Gilded Age*
Tribe 12
1976   Tafuri & Dal Co: *Modern Architecture*
1979   Roth: *A Concise History of American Architecture*
Tribe 13
1980   Hunt: *Encyclopedia of American Architecture*
1989   *AIA Encyclopedia of Architecture, Design, Engineering, and Construction*
Tribe 14
1982   *Macmillan Encyclopedia of Architects* (Placzek, ed.)
1991   Williamson: *American Architects and the Mechanics of Fame*
Tribe 15
1983   Frampton (w. Futagawa): *Modern Architecture 1851–1945*
1985   Kostof: *A History of Architecture. Settings & Rituals*
1988   Klotz: *The History of Postmodern Architecture*
Tribe 16
1986   De Long, Searing, Stern: *American Architecture* (symposium)
1986   Stern: *Pride of Place. Building the American Dream*
1987   Kostof: *America by Design*

Nation 37
1971   Jencks: *Architecture 2000*
1976   Kulterman: *New Architecture in the World*
1990   Cottom-Winslow: *Environmental Design*
    Tribe 1
    1971   Kulski: *Architecture in a Revolutionary Era*
    1972   Chermayeff: *Observations on American Architecture*

Nation 38
1985   Stimpson: *Fieldguide to Landmarks of Modern Architecture in United States*
    Tribe 1
    1976   Smith, K.: *A Pictorial History of Architecture in America*
    1981   Smith, K.: *The Architecture of the United States*
    1984   Hunt: *American Architecture: A Field Guide*

Nation 39
1977   Smith, C. R.: *Supermannerism*
    Tribe 1
    1979   Drexler: *Transformations in Modern Architecture*
    1980   Davern: *Architecture 1970–1980*
        Family 1
        1982   Wright: *Highlights to Recent American Architecture 1945–1978*
        1989   Wright: *Sourcebook of Contemporary North American Architecture*

Figure 8.4   (continued)

Tribe 2
  Family 1
    1980 Emanuel (ed.): *Contemporary Architects*
    1989 Krantz: *American Architects*

Nation 40
  Tribe 1
  1981 Searing: *Speaking a New Classicism: American Architecture Now*
  1981 Stern: *American Architecture: After Modernism*
  Family 1
    1980 Kulterman: *Architecture in the Seventies*
    1980 Portoghesi: *Architecture 1980*
  Tribe 2
  1982 Portoghesi: *After Modern Architecture*
  1990 Papadakis & Watson (eds): *New Classicism: Omnibus Volume*
  Family 1
    1983 Portoghesi: *Postmodern*
    1987 Jencks: *Post-Modernism: The New Classicism in Art and Architecture*

Nation 41
1979 AIA J.: *1st to 3rd Annual Reviews of New American Architecture*
1980 Diamondstein: *American Architecture Now*
  Tribe 1
  1982 AIA J.: 4th to 6th Annual Reviews of New American Architecture
  1983 Colquhoun et al: *Promising Directions in American Architecture*
  1985 AIA J.: 7th to 9th Annual Reviews of New American Architecture
  Tribe 2
  1985 Diamondstein: *American Architecture Now II*
  1991 Papadakis: *A Decade of Architectural Design*

Nation 42
  Tribe 1
    Family 1
    1985 *Cross Currents of American Architecture* (AD Profile)
    1985 Macrae-Gibson: *The Secret Life of Buildings*

Nation 43
  Tribe 1
  1977 Blake: *Form Follows Fiasco*
  1985 Marder: *The Critical Edge: Controversy in American Architecture*
  Tribe 2
  1980 *GA Document Special Issue 1970–1980*
  1981 Sanderson: *Int. Handbook of Contemporary Developments in Architecture*
  1982 Jencks: *Architecture Today*
  1984 Klotz: *Revision der Moderne*
  1993 Heyer: *American Architecture in the Late 20th Century*
  Family 1
    1977 Jencks: *The Language of Post-Modern Architecture*
    1977 Jencks: *The Language of Post-Modern Architecture*, rev. ed.
    1981 Jencks: *The Language of Post-Modern Architecture*, 3rd ed.
    1981 Wolfe: *From Bauhaus to Our House*
    1984 Jencks: *The Language of Post-Modern Architecture*, 4th ed.
    1991 Jencks: *The Language of Post-Modern Architecture*, 6th ed.

Figure 8.4   (continued)

Tribe 3
1986   Barford: *Understanding Modern Architecture*
1987   Oppenheimer Dean: "75 Turbulent Years of American Architecture"
1990   Hays & Burns (eds.): *Thinking the Past: Recent American Architecture*
    Family 1
    1988   Hollingworth: *Architecture of the 20th Century*
    1990   Jencks: *The New Moderns from Late to Neo-Modernism*
Tribe 4
1988   *AIA J.:* 10th to 12th Annual Reviews of New American Architecture
    Family 1
    1989   Peel, Powell, & Garrett: *20th-Century Architecture*
    1989   Russell: *Architecture and Design 1970–1990*
    Family 2
    1989   Wodehouse & Moffett: *A History of Western Architecture*
    1990   AIA: *American Architecture of the 1980s.*

Nation 44
1992   Weber: *American Art Deco*
    Tribe 1
    1986   Wilson et al.: *The Machine Age in America 1918–1941*
        Family 1
        1983   Pulos: *American Design Ethic. A History of Interior Design to 1940*
        1988   Pulos: *The American Design Adventure: 1940–1975*

Nation 45
    Tribe 1
    1988   Johnson & Wigley: *Deconstructivist Architecture*
    1991   Cook & Llewellyn-Jones: **New Spirit in Architecture**
    1991   Noever (ed.): **Architecture in Transition**

Nation 46
1830   *American Journal of Science & Arts*: "Architecture in the United States"

Nation 47
1850   Sears: *A New and Popular Pictorial Description of the United States*

Nation 48
1880   Benjamin: *Art in America*

Nation 49
1883   van Rensselaer: "Recent Architecture in America"

Nation 50
1884   Levy: *Modern American Architecture*

Nation 51
1888   Arnold: *Studies in Architecture at Home and Abroad*

Nation 52
1899   Ware: *The Georgian Period*

Nation 53
1900   Mackson: *American Architecture Interiors & Furniture*

Nation 54
1910   *Men and Women of America: A Biographical Dictionary*

Nation 55
1920   Greber: *L'Architecture aux États-Unies*

Figure 8.4 (continued)

Nation 56
1924   Jackson: *American Colonial Architecture*
Nation 57
1927   Reagan: *American Architecture of the Twentieth Century*
Nation 58
1932   Hitchcock & Johnson: *The International Style*
Nation 59
1932   Barr, Hitchcock, Johnson, & Mumford: *Modern Architects*
Nation 60
1937   Newcomb: *Spanish-Colonial Architecture in the United States*
Nation 61
1941   Johnson: "Architecture" (in *The American Year Book*)
Nation 62
1941   *Architectural Record:* "American Architecture 1891–1941"
Nation 63
1941   *Pencil Points:* "Forty Under Forty"
Nation 64
1948   Kouwenhoven: *Made in America*
Nation 65
1962   Dixon: *Architectural Design Preview, USA*
Nation 66
1986   Allen: *Emerging Voices. New Generation of Architects in America*
Nation 67
1988   Stern: *Modern Classicism*
Nation 68
1988   Larkin et al.: *Colonial Design in the New World*
Nation 69
1993   Economakis (ed.): *Building Classical: A Vision of Europe and America*

Predictably, families are often composed of successive editions of the same work. There are, however, also families of supposedly unrelated works, and instances of several editions of the same book not placed within the same family. Sometimes the clustering seems more attuned to publication date than to authorship or even work. The 1905 edition of Fletcher's *History of Architecture* is in the same family as A. D. F. Hamlin's *History of Architecture* of 1896 (nation 10, tribe 1, family 1, or, more succinctly, 10.1.1). The 1921 edition of Fletcher's text is in the same nation, but not the same family or even tribe, and other editions are scattered in still other nations. Cheney's *The New World Architecture* is indeed closer to Hitchcock's *Modern Architecture* (11.1) than to Conant's *Modern Architecture*, which in turn bears a stronger connection to LaFollette's *Art in America* and to Talbot Hamlin's *Architecture Through the Ages* (25.1) (Cheney and Conant were used as early examples in chapter 1).

Sometimes the commonalities in a unit are clear, including close dating, authorship, related subject matter, cultural or institutional affiliation of the writers, or type of text. The classification reads so naturally that one must be reminded of the fact that it was performed by a machine oblivious to content, title, date, and authorship, and fed only with the indexes.

What are the practical uses of such a classification? I can think of two; persons with a pragmatic bent will foresee more. First, it allows one to perform quick, automatic categorizations of texts, most productive when faced with unfamiliar works, in classrooms, libraries, and bookstores. Second, one can generate clues to investigate more profoundly hitherto unsuspected relationships among well-known texts. Texts lumped together without an obvious connection are, from this perspective, the most promising. One must remember that the clusters are not intuitive pronouncements of some dreamy guru; they are based on factual relationships present in the data. If invisible to the naked eye, they can be brought to light by focused observation.

Let us look at an example. Someone might be surprised to find *Modern Architecture 1851–1945*, by Kenneth Frampton in the same tribe as *The History of Postmodern Architecture*, by Klotz (36.15). With one of the books picking up the story precisely at the point where the other one leaves it, at least if one is to believe in titles, these are unlikely candidates for a close association. According to the system, however, the two overlap in coverage from 1883 to 1902, and the coincidental names outnumber the pertinent differences: Sullivan, Maybeck, Wright, Gropius, Mies van der Rohe, Le Corbusier, Schindler, Neutra, Breuer, and Eero Saarinen are in both lists. confirming the validity of the connection. (Lists of common and divergent names for particular texts can be accessed through the electronic companion.)

Instead of performing cluster analysis on all texts of the corpus, the technique could be applied to the subgroups of texts active year by year. As the number of texts involved would be smaller, the number of levels could be reduced, perhaps to tribes and families, or families only. Newly published texts would pop up in an already existing cluster, increasing its size; similarly, texts no longer active would disappear. With the shifting configurations of texts year by year, the clusters would occasionally split amoeba-like (with a larger entity breaking up into two or more smaller ones) or unite (smaller units constituting a larger one). The picture would acquire a dynamic dimension lacking in the clusters of figure 8.4. Computationally, generating such a series of clusters would be trivial; but much ingenuity would be required to deliver and interpret the results in view of their bulkiness. A more elegant technique to portray changing textual alignments is presented in the next section.

Proximity to the Sun: Text Histograms

Assuming that some rule is used to convert kappa measurements (which equal one for coincidence) into distance measurements (which equal zero for coincidence), given any pair of texts it is always possible to represent them by two

Figure 8.5   Diagram showing coverage overlap among three texts

points such that the length of the segment they define is proportional to the distance between their indexes. When three texts are at stake and their intertextual distances are known, it is sometimes, but not necessarily always, possible to draw a triangle in which the vertexes represent the texts and the lengths of the sides are proportional to their distances. For the representation to be possible, the sides of the triangle must "close"; in other words, each side (or distance) must measure less than the sum of the other two.

Let us assume that the coverage span of three texts, A, B, and C, overlaps in the way represented in figure 8.5. Let us further suppose that when two of these texts overlap, they deal with the same or very similar lists of architects. If adjusted kappas were used to measure their proximity, A and B would be very close, and the same would be true of B and C; but A and C, with no overlap, would be assigned an association of zero, which would translate into a considerable distance. Closeness is not a transitive relationship when using adjusted kappas, and as a consequence it cannot be represented geometrically. This limitation forces us to use nonadjusted kappas in the ensuing discussion.

Converting ordinary kappas into distances by a simple rule described in the appendix, and testing very large numbers of triads of texts, I found that a triangular representation like the one described in the first paragraph is viable in 99 percent of cases. If four texts are at stake the geometric representation would be three dimensional (a pyramid), and in the general case of N texts the representation would be a construct of points and segments deployed in a hyperspace of $N - 1$ dimensions. Such constructs cannot be visualized or drawn by ordinary means, but they are clearly defined geometric entities that can be subjected to a number of mathematical operations. Of particular interest here is the identification of their centroid, which is defined in a multidimensional space the same way as in two or three dimensions: the center of gravity of a configuration of points is a privileged point such that if one were to place there a mass equal to the sum of the mass of all the points, its static properties would be equivalent to those of the entire system. If all interpoint distances are defined and all masses are known (say, they are made equal to one), the position of the centroid of a configuration can be determined by repeated application of the Pythagorean theorem (see the appendix).

The texts of the corpus can be conceived as forming one such multidimensional "cloud." The cloud has a well-defined center; and the distance of every text to the center is a simple, linear measurement. Certain texts are close to the center, or perhaps they are sitting at the center itself; others are placed near the fringes of the cloud. The centrality-periphery dimension lends itself to a clear interpretation in terms of text theory. Discourse is a collective entity in the Saussurian sense, and so is the literature; no text can be singled out as the embodiment of the entire literature, just as no individual or utterance can be picked as the repository of discourse. Certain texts, however, present a selection of architects that are also found in many other works. A text with a typical choice provides a closer glimpse on collective discourse than one with highly personal or idiosyncratic choices.

It is not surprising that the most typical indexes are those of reference works: *The World Atlas of Architecture* (Flon, ed., 1984), *Who's Who in Architecture from 1400 to the Present* (Richards, ed., 1977), *Encyclopedia of Modern Architecture* (Pehnt, ed., 1964), and the architecture section of *Traveler's Guide to America's Art* (Norman, 1968). They embody whatever consensus exists in the literature about who are the leading American architects. Next come three general histories (Mendelowitz, *A History of American Art*, 1970; Curtis, *Modern Architecture Since 1900*, 1982; and Cohen, *A History of American Art*, 1971). They differ in many regards, but not in their selections, which are almost as typical of average discourse as those of the preceding reference works.

At the opposite end of the spectrum are texts with highly personal choices; the most unusual is *Forms and Functions of 20th Century Architecture* (Hamlin, ed., 1952). Focusing on building types rather than following a conventional historical narrative, Hamlin and his colleagues brought to the limelight the work of architects who had seldom been discussed in the general literature earlier or since. Gowans's *Images of American Living* (1964), Burchard and Bush-Brown's *The Architecture of America* (1961), and Condit's *American Building* (1968) also have atypical choices. This is neither to be commended nor censured; it is a characteristic of the works that may help us better to understand their nature.

Atypical texts disagree not only with common discourse but also with each other. Gowans is far more considered in his treatment of seventeenth- and eighteenth-century American architecture than in that of the nineteenth and twentieth centuries, whereas the opposite is true for Burchard and Bush-Brown. Condit, in his study of the materials and building techniques from the Colonial settlements to the present, traverses the same material once more, but with a different cast of characters.

Multidimensional clouds are particularly intriguing when they represent the subset of texts active at any one time. With new texts continually added to the set and older ones removed, the cloud is constantly taking new shapes, as if swept by the wind. Although the position of a text in the cloud remains fixed while it stays there, as other texts are added and removed the gravity center changes and so does the distance of every text to the center. As the Copernican and Ptolemaic representations of the world are ultimately equivalent, we are free to conceive of a center moving among fixed points, or (my preferred image)

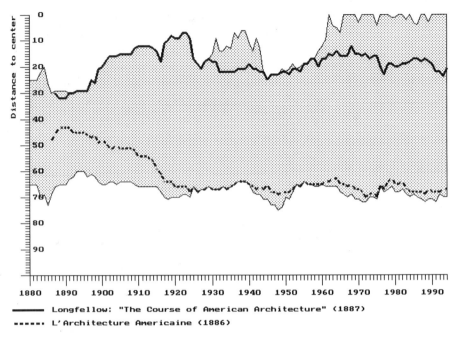

Figure 8.6   Two early, extreme cases

of texts sailing through the multidimensional skies, coming closer or drifting farther away from a sun sitting at the center. Their complex trail in the hyperspace cannot be visualized by ordinary means, but their distance to the core can be plotted precisely year after year.

Figures 8.6 and following contain several examples of what I will call text histograms. Unlike the architect histograms introduced in chapter 5, these do not graph citation frequencies. Years are represented horizontally, as usual. Distance to the centroid of active texts is plotted vertically, from zero to 100. The maximum is never attained, although zero sometimes is. I had imagined that no text can ever reach the center of gravity; colliding with the sun, like looking into the face of God, would entail immediate annihilation. It does not.

The significance of the curves is enhanced by shading the range of values actually encountered in the corpus. When a curve reaches the upper limit of the range (smaller distances), the text is the closest one to the center of the configuration; its choice of architects is as characteristic of the set of active texts as any. When it reaches the lower limit (larger distances), the text is floating in the outer edges of the galaxy; the names cited are most idiosyncratic, at least from the vantage point of the norm defined by the active texts. Every book is active for the first few years after publication. Histograms are continued beyond its point of fading, however, just as an architect's histogram extends beyond the person's retirement and death.

Figure 8.6 shows two widely divergent histograms for almost contemporary texts. W. P. P. Longfellow's article "The Course of American Architecture" in the *New Princeton Review* (1887) features only two architects—Richard Morris Hunt and Henry Hobson Richardson. The extraordinary prominence of these names at the time of publication and thereafter ensured them a central position in the cloud; in fact, the curve for this index defined the upper edge of the range of possible histograms for many years to come. At the opposite end of the spectrum is *L'Architecture Americaine* of 1886 (reprinted as *American Victorian Architecture* in 1975). Although giants such as Richardson, Hunt, and Sullivan were mentioned, the list of sixty-eight architects and firms comprised many whose reputation was short lived, including some who have never been cited before or heard about again. Although the histogram was near the middle of the range shortly after publication time, it quickly lost ground, and the book drifted toward the fringes of the system.

Texts dealing with a narrow coverage period are inherently pushed toward the periphery, especially if the period is at either extreme of the time scale—the Colonial times or recent years. This is a consequence of the inability to use adjusted kappas; with ordinary kappas, texts at either extreme of the time scale tend to have a low association with most other texts. Figure 8.7 shows the consistently low positions of the histograms of several books devoted to Colonial architecture, and figure 8.8 does the same for selected titles on the recent past by Stern. *L'Architecture Americaine* (figure 8.6) is also affected by this factor. The work of Jencks (figure 8.9) is placed higher up in the diagram than

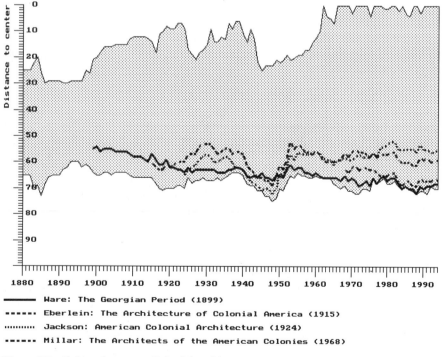

Figure 8.7   Selected texts on Colonial architecture

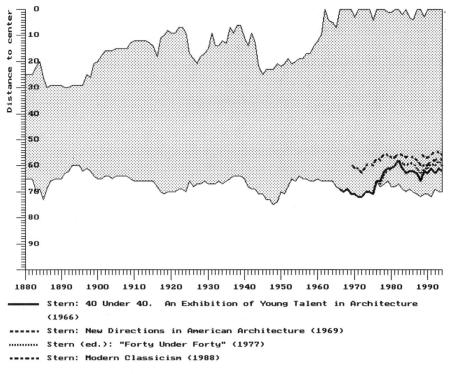

Figure 8.8   Selected works by Robert A. M. Stern

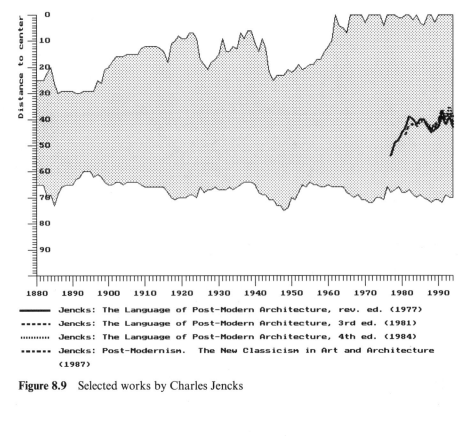

Figure 8.9   Selected works by Charles Jencks

that of Stern merely because he cites, in addition to recent architects, earlier persons such as Wright, Mies, and Gropius.

The distances to the center and their evolution are most meaningful for texts devoted to the entire temporal gamut. In principle, it would be feasible to generate another series of histograms devoted exclusively to the earliest centuries or the latest decades; texts would be considered only to the extent that they dealt with these periods. The idea is not implemented because it adds little to the scope of the argument, and because there would be a shortage of active books meeting the temporal criteria at certain points of the curve.

A typical, recurrent pattern appears in slight variations in the histograms of more than one-half of the texts of the corpus. Several examples are shown in figures 8.10 through 8.15. The curves start on or near the upper edge of the range. They may follow the edge or run parallel to it for a while, or they may start their descent immediately; but sooner or later the curves plunge, indicating that the text is propelled toward the outer limits of the solar system. The older books actually reach the lower edge; the most recent ones still have a long way to go, but the pattern is unmistakable: one gets the distinct impression that it is only a matter of time before even the newest texts will loose steam.

Text revisions and updates almost invariably have the effect of raising the beginning of the histogram closer to the upper edge, even in cases when originally the curve was not there (figures 8.16–8.20). The shifts may be minimal (figure 8.16) or very significant (figure 8.18).

Another pattern frequently encountered among text histograms is composed of an ascending stretch of variable length, followed by a descending curve. The change often occurs abruptly, through an acute inflection point (figures 8.21–8.26). The date signals a shift in the relationship of the text with its cultural milieu: a work that was marking directions stops doing so or, to word it differently, the direction it marks is no longer followed by those coming behind.

An initially ascending pattern is reinforced by the fact that during the first few years after publication, while the text is still active, it contributes with its gravitational pull to define the position of the centroid; as it ages it looses this power, which contributes to its drifting toward the fringes. To the extent that this is true, the phenomenon observed, governed by method rather than reality, is trivial. But the explanation does not fully account for the pattern, for the following reasons. First, the point of inflection does not necessarily coincide with the work's exit from the set of active texts. This can be verified in figure 8.21, where texts with different publication dates reach the inflection point at the same time, and the curves of texts published nearly simultaneously inflect at different points. Second, with more than forty active texts at any one time after 1960 (see figure 5.2), the pull of a single text is negligible. Third, and most important, the majority of text histograms lack an ascending stretch. This would not be possible if the ascent were merely a consequence of the method used.

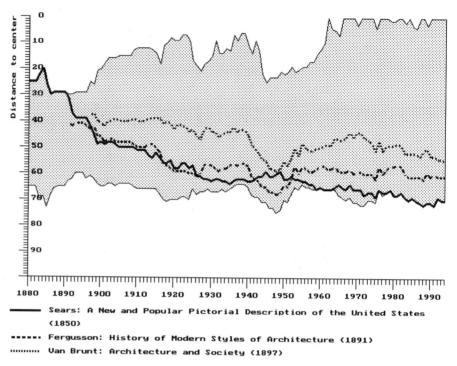

Figure 8.10   Descending pattern: selected examples

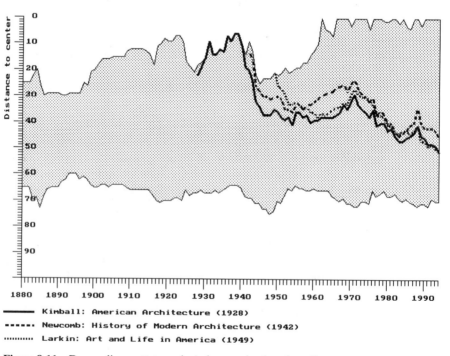

Figure 8.11   Descending pattern: selected examples (continued)

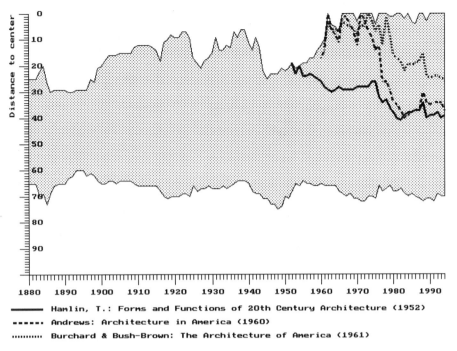

Figure 8.12   Descending pattern: selected examples (continued)

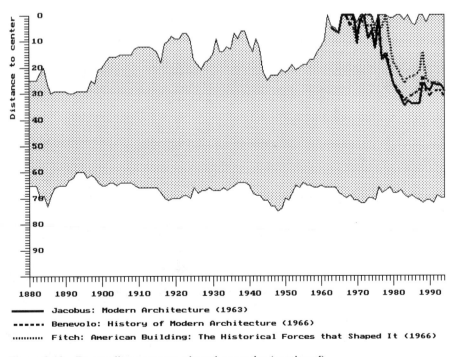

Figure 8.13   Descending pattern: selected examples (continued)

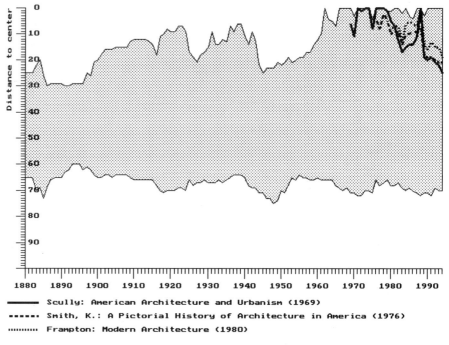

Figure 8.14   Descending pattern: selected examples (continued)

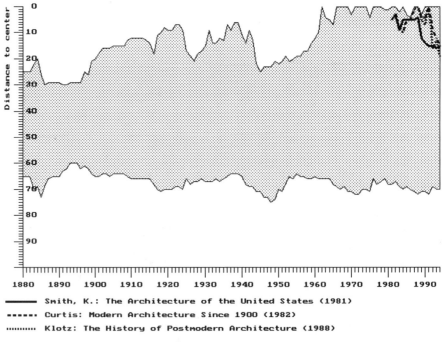

Figure 8.15   Descending pattern: selected examples (continued)

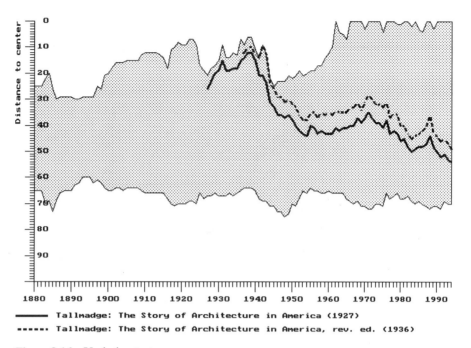

Figure 8.16   Updating texts

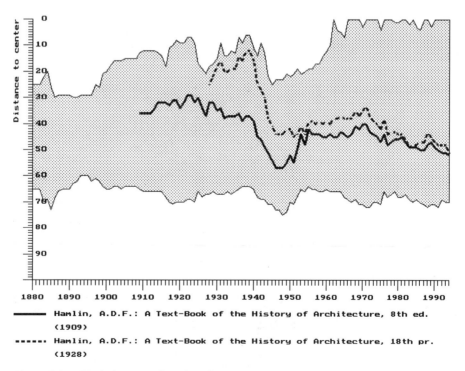

Figure 8.17   Updating texts (continued)

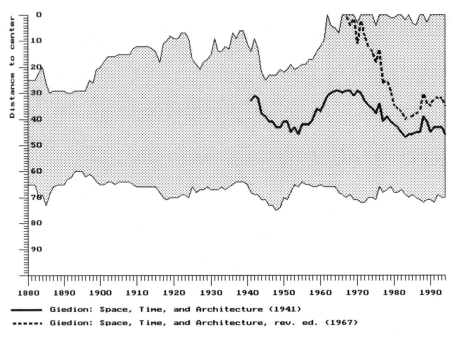

Figure 8.18   Updating texts (continued)

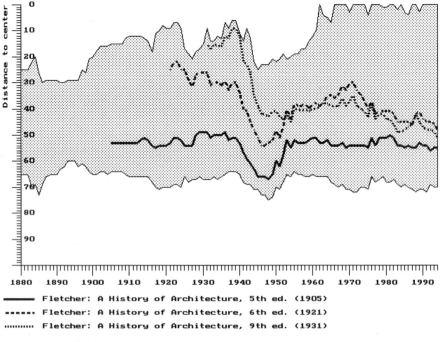

Figure 8.19   Updating texts (continued)

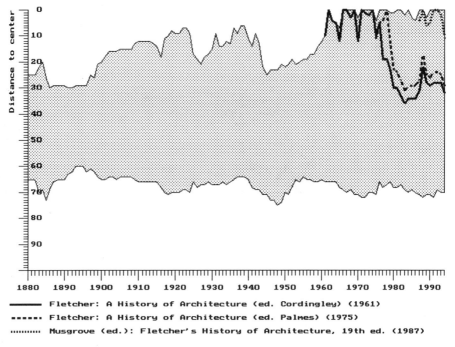

Figure 8.20 Updating texts (continued)

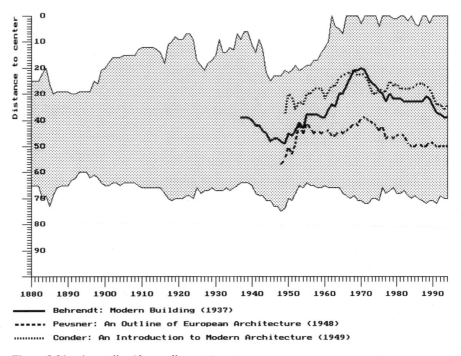

Figure 8.21 Ascending/descending pattern

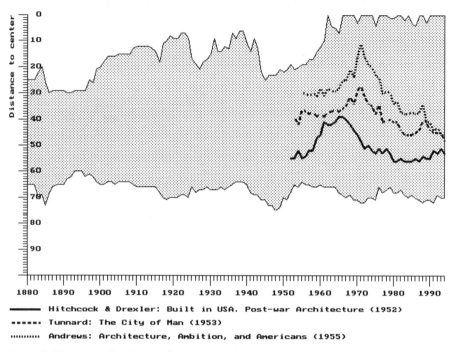

Figure 8.22   Ascending/descending pattern (continued)

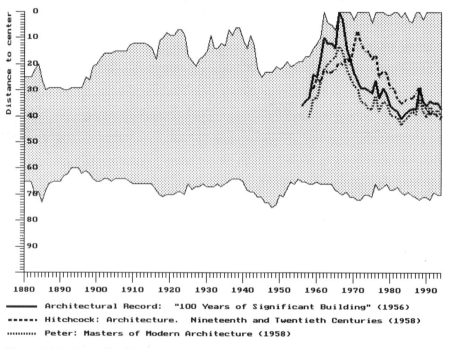

Figure 8.23   Ascending/descending pattern (continued)

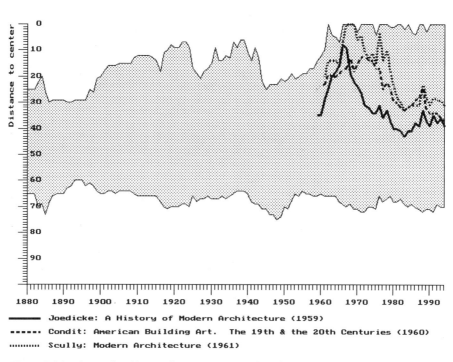

Figure 8.24   Ascending/descending pattern (continued)

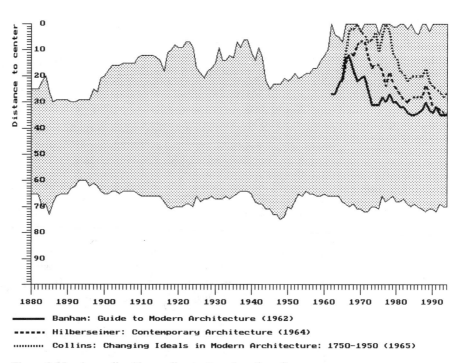

Figure 8.25   Ascending/descending pattern (continued)

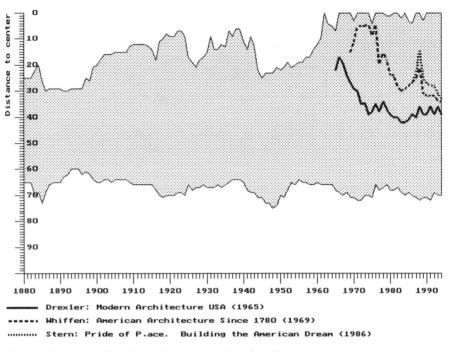

Figure 8.26 Ascending/descending pattern (continued)

We all know of books that were marginal to current preoccupations and interests at the time of their writing but, once published, attracted followers who developed the ideas further. What was once outlandish eventually became part of normal knowledge. When I began this chapter I was looking for two types of texts: those that are solidly based on up-to-date, current knowledge, but fail to affect the thoughts of ensuing generations; and those that by exploring marginal areas and little known names open up new directions for future investigation. I expected to find texts with falling histograms, as well as some with curves rising over an extended period of time. The latter type do not exist, or if they do, I could not find them. The ascending histograms I encountered are invariably too short to regard them as anything but the first stretch in an ascending-descending pattern, with the inflection point still to come (figures 8.27 and 8.28).

This is not an indictment of the literature. The corpus contains many influential works that transformed the landscape of architectural ideas. But within the limited range of phenomena addressed in this study, the situation is different. A basic asymmetry is built into the system. Centripetal forces are scarce and short lived. Notwithstanding a few superstars who remained in the literature for long stretches of time, most of the architects come and go in successive waves. As a consequence, indexes of texts naturally tend to drift outward. The multidimensional textual system is subject to unstoppable centrifugal forces.

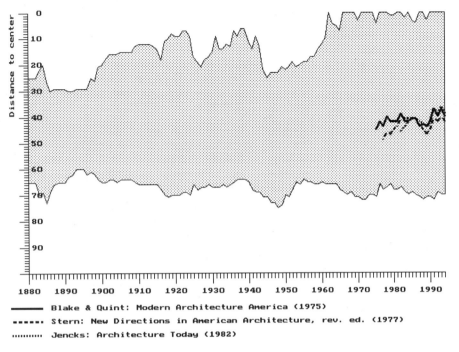

Figure 8.27   Early ascending pattern

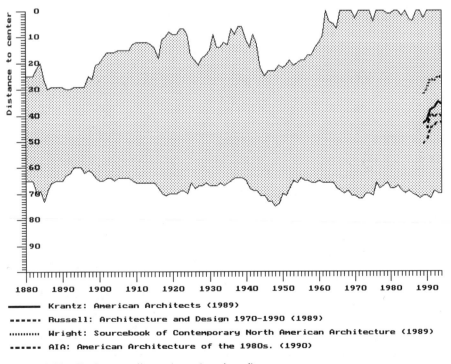

Figure 8.28   Early ascending pattern (continued)

Notes

1. Statements such as, "The distance between texts A and B is twice the distance between C and D" are scale dependent; they may be true in one scale and false in another. The statement, "The distance between A and B is greater than the distance between C and D," on the other hand, has greater, but not necessarily absolute, interscale validity. If one refrains from the first type of statement, scale selection becomes less critical.

2. The statistical package employed was SPSS/PC+. Adjusted kappas were used as similarity coefficients, and the amalgamation procedure specified was by average linkage. See Norusis, Marija J., and SPSS, Inc.: *SPSS/PC+ Advanced Statistics for the IBM PC/XT/AT and PS2*. Chicago: SPSS, 1988. For a discussion of cluster analysis, see John A. Hartigan: *Clustering Algorithms*. New York: Wiley, 1975.

9   Cotextuality

Books can be classified into the following categories: (i) those in which Adam and Eve are mentioned; (ii) those in which they are not; (iii) those in which Adam is mentioned but not Eve; and (iv) those in which Eve is featured and Adam is ignored. The taxonomy is improbable but consistent; every book fits into one, and only one, of the groups. Whether a library is religious or secular, public or private, large or small, most of the books contained (if not all) will fit in categories (i) and (ii). Adam and Eve belong to the same discourse. They are cotextual: they are either copresent or coabsent in most texts.

Now consider the following statements:

(i)   Jane and Jim are jumping rope.

(ii)   Jim is jumping rope, Jane is sick in bed.

The first sentence conjures an image of kids engaged in interactive play; as in a choreographed dance, if Jane jumps higher so does Jim, and if Jim stumbles it brings down Jane. The kids are together in (i), separated in (ii). From a discursive standpoint, however, they are together in both sentences. Even if no connection is stated explicitly, their copresence begets a series of possible relationships, such as

(iii) Jane would like to be playing with Jim, but she must stay home because she is sick,

(iv)   Jim should be visiting Jane, but he was jumping rope instead.

When curtains rise in the theater and actors are seen sharing the stage, their joint presence signals a relationship between them even before anyone has moved or any line has been uttered. If the play is fuzzy or the acting is poor, the connection may never become clear; but the expectation of a linkage is there because of theatrical convention. It is not necessary that two characters share a scene for a connection to be posited. Some personages will embrace and kiss on stage, others will cross their swords; still others may never meet face to face, but this does not prevent them from being part of the network of interpersonal relationships that is the basis of the plot.

A text is like a stage, and the subjects spoken about are like characters in a play. Narrative conventions generate an expectation for connections, some of which are established by the playwright and others are projected by the audience. For Adam and Eve to be linked in a discursive relationship, it is not necessary to have them pictured in the garden of Eden or sharing a game like Jim and Jane. The presence of them both in the index is sufficient to generate an expectation, and the presumption of a connectedness is strengthened if their cotextuality is extended over many or most of the titles of a corpus.

Architects may be cotextual too. Many histories read like drama, with heroes and villains and a finite cast of characters. A dictionary arranged into unrelated entries governed by the alphabet is seemingly the antithesis of a Shakespearian play in terms of relationships among the performers. But even a reference work in its cool detachment invariably establishes interconnections among architects based on such matters as chronology, geography, or building type: A and B were contemporaries, they worked in the same part of the country, they built houses.

The specific nature of what is predicated is irrelevant to cotextuality; it will vary from text to text, and many times there will be no explicit predicate at all. If the names appear in the same sentence, as Jane and Jim, the relationship is defined by what is being said. When such is not the case but the names are in the same chapter, the title of the chapter often determines the commonality. But even if the architects were to appear in the opening and closing chapters, respectively, and no statement involving both were to be found anywhere, readers would be entitled to presume that, one way or another, both are pertinent to the subject matter of the book.

Some might object that the connection is much too weak in the latter case to mean anything at all; in doing so, however, they would be placing under attack the very concept of text. When the connections cementing together the chapters of a book are too tenuous to warrant an assumption of unity, the chapter, not the book, should perhaps become the basic textual unit. This is, of course, feasible, and in many cases it is legitimate: when assembling the corpus, segments of volumes were sometimes regarded as texts (see chapter 2). The textuality of each element of the corpus, based on unity and consistency, supports the inferences of this chapter.

Pairs of Close and Distant Architects

Cotextuality between architects resembles isonomy between texts, discussed in the preceding chapter. Their parallelism becomes apparent if citations are visualized as arranged in a matrix with as many columns as texts and as many rows as architects, with ones and zeros distributed appropriately to indicate who is cited (or ignored). The zeros and ones in a column represent the citations in a text; similarly, the values in a row contain the citations of an architect. If two columns coincide, the texts are isonomic; when two rows are equal, the architects are cotextual. Full cotextuality is a rare occurrence, like complete isonomy. Being a matter of degrees, it is subject to measurement, like isonomy. The same kappa value, and the same adjustment, is used to measure cotextuality and isonomy. Unadjusted kappas between two architects are a function of the number of texts of the corpus in which both individuals are respectively cited and ignored. Adjusted values (used for figures 9.1–9.5) are based on texts pertinent to both architects only.

Figure 9.1 shows the closest pairs among the 100 most frequently cited architects (from figure 5.1). It is no surprise that there are many instances of partnerships, especially among the upper ranks of the list (pairs 1, 3, 4, 5, 11). These are the names that one would expect to see closely associated, since each mention of their collaboration (or merely of the name of the firm) triggers a joint citation. In addition, some architects were not associated but worked in the same style (e.g., Maybeck and the Greene brothers, Bacon and Pope, Moore and Venturi), were active during the same period (e.g., Mills and Renwick, Roche and Moore), worked in the same regions of the country (e.g., Jenney and Root, Maybeck and Wurster), or had similar practices (e.g., the firms of Carrère & Hastings, and Cram, Goodhue & Ferguson). Then, architects may be unrelated by style, location, of chronology, but linked by the scale of their interventions and the concerns they raised; for example, Washington city planner Pierre L'Enfant, and park designer and landscape architect Frederick Law Olmsted. Cotextuality is tantamount to copresence in the same discourse; in the examples here, the reasons for the joint occurrence of the names are immediately apparent.

The most intriguing instances of cotextuality, however, are those not directly dependent on such external factors: case in point, the connection between Calvert Vaux and Romualdo Giurgola, born exactly 100 years apart (pair 18 in figure 9.1). Theirs is a purely discursive, textual relationship. The men are featured together in twenty-one texts and jointly ignored in seventeen relevant works; one is cited and the other ignored in only twelve instances. Scholars with access to the electronic companion can generate a list of the texts involved and examine them for a cause of the connection. Discovering such factual links either in the life and work of the architects concerned or, more likely, in the interests of the writers would be illuminating. I am not sure, however, that specific links exist; nor do I believe that it is necessary to find them to validate the connection. The connection operates in the abstract plane in which it is defined, and it provides a platform for more complex constructs, as will be shown in ensuing sections of this chapter.

Pairs of textually distant architects are as provocative and worth examining as close ones. Distant architects tend not to be cited (or jointly ignored) in the same texts; their citation histories return negative or low kappas. The most interesting cases of cotextuality involve architects of different historical periods. The reverse is true with distant pairs: architects who lived and worked centuries

Figure 9.1   Closest pairs of architects (adjusted)

Column headings:
[1]   Pair number
[2]   Adjusted kappa
[3]   Birth date
[4]   Name

[1]	[2]	[3]	[4]
1	0.80	1886	George Howe
		1896	William Lescaze
2	0.77	1862	Bernard Maybeck
		1868	Greene & Greene
3	0.64	1863	Cram, Goodhue, & Ferguson
		1869	Bertram Grosvenor Goodhue
4	0.61	1784	Ithiel Town
		1803	Alexander Jackson Davis
5	0.60	1895	Wallace K. Harrison
		1908	Max Abramovitz
6	0.58	1866	Henry Bacon
		1874	John Russell Pope
7	0.58	1754	Pierre Charles L'Enfant
		1822	Frederick Law Olmsted
8	0.57	1869	Albert Kahn
		1896	William Lescaze
9	0.57	1858	Carrère & Hastings
		1863	Cram, Goodhue, & Ferguson
10	0.56	1803	Alexander Jackson Davis
		1868	Greene & Greene
11	0.56	1815	Andrew Jackson Downing
		1824	Calvert Vaux
12	0.55	1925	Charles W. Moore
		1925	Robert Venturi
13	0.55	1764	Benjamin Henry Latrobe
		1827	Richard Morris Hunt
14	0.55	1922	Roche & Dinkeloo
		1925	Charles W. Moore
15	0.54	1863	Cram, Goodhue, & Ferguson
		1874	John Russell Pope
16	0.54	1844	Dankmar Adler
		1850	John Wellborn Root
17	0.53	1881	Raymond Mathewson Hood
		1896	William Lescaze
18	0.53	1824	Calvert Vaux
		1924	Mitchell Giurgola Associates
19	0.53	1895	Wurster, Bernardi, & Emmons
		1935	William Turnbull, Jr.

Figure 9.1   (continued)

[1]	[2]	[3]	[4]
20	0.53	1874	John Russell Pope
		1895	Wurster, Bernardi, & Emmons
21	0.53	1858	Carrère & Hastings
		1874	John Russell Pope
22	0.53	1685c	Richard Munday
		1716	Peter Harrison
23	0.53	1858	Carrère & Hastings
		1869	Bertram Grosvenor Goodhue
24	0.52	1895	Wurster, Bernardi, & Emmons
		1924	Mitchell Giurgola Associates
25	0.52	1895	Wurster, Bernardi, & Emmons
		1899	Pietro Belluschi
26	0.51	1862	Bernard Maybeck
		1895	Wurster, Bernardi, & Emmons
27	0.51	1832	William Le Baron Jenney
		1850	John Wellborn Root
28	0.51	1846	Daniel Hudson Burnham
		1850	John Wellborn Root
29	0.51	1802	Richard Upjohn
		1869	Bertram Grosvenor Goodhue
30	0.51	1868	John Mead Howells
		1877	Shreve, Lamb, & Harmon
31	0.51	1917	I. M. Pei
		1934	Richard Meier
32	0.50	1685c	Richard Munday
		1710?	Thomas (or James) McBean
33	0.50	1827	Richard Morris Hunt
		1896	William Lescaze
34	0.50	1781	Robert Mills
		1818	James Renwick, Jr.

apart are unlikely to appear in the same discussion, and are therefore expected to be far apart. The noteworthy occurs when contemporary architects register as distant. Figure 9.2, listing selected instances of distant architects, is restricted to pairs born no more than fifteen years apart.

Every pair signals a possible cultural fracture, with writers impelled to consider the work of one architect or the other, but not both. Sometimes, as in the case of Paul Cret and Mies van der Rohe, the members of the pair represent different artistic or philosophical orientations. But this is not the rule, because opposition or conflict between personalities often draws them into the same discourse. Landscape painter Thomas Cole, designer of the Ohio State Capitol but most often cited in the literature for *The Architect's Dream*, an idyllic pictorial fantasy about Classical styles, and John Augustus Roebling, one of the

Figure 9.2   Selected distant pairs of architects

Column headings:
[1]   Pair number
[2]   Adjusted kappa
[3]   Birth date
[4]   Name

[1]	[2]	[3]	[4]
1	−0.33	1948	Thomas Gordon Smith
		1949	Michael Rotondi
2	−0.29	1933	John H. Burgee
		1942	Rodolfo Machado
3	−0.29	1685c	Richard Munday
		1696	James Edward Oglethorpe
4	−0.27	1933	Schipporeit & Heinrich
		1938	Allan Greenberg
5	−0.25	1941	Thomas Hall Beeby
		1946	Daniel Libeskind
6	−0.22	1938	Charles Gwathmey
		1942	Stuart Cohen
7	−0.20	1929	Herb Greene
		1940	Steven Izenour
8	−0.19	1930	John Rauch
		1942	Jorge Silvetti
9	−0.18	1949	Arquitectonica (or DPZ)
		1959	Maya Ying Lin
10	−0.17	1930	Cambridge Seven Associates
		1932	Peter D. Eisenman
11	−0.15	1939	Robert A. M. Stern
		1944	Thom Mayne
12	−0.13	1801	Thomas Cole
		1806	John Augustus Roebling
13	−0.11	1700?	Robert Twelves
		1713	Father Junipero Serra
14	−0.09	1893	Raymond Loewy
		1907	George F. Hellmuth
15	−0.09	1845	Bruce Price
		1848	Louis Comfort Tiffany
16	−0.08	1868	William H. MacMurray
		1883	Walter Dorwin Teague, Sr.
17	−0.08	1760c	Étienne Sulpice Hallet
		1770?	Robert Owen
18	−0.08	1895	Lászlo Moholy-Nagy
		1909	William L. Pereira
19	−0.07	1931	Denise Scott Brown
		1943	Emilio Ambasz

Figure 9.2   (continued)

[1]	[2]	[3]	[4]
20	−0.07	1859 1867	Cass Gilbert Frank Lloyd Wright
21	−0.07	1933 1940?	Jaquelin Robertson John S. Hagmann
22	−0.07	1901 1903	Walt Disney Paul Schweikher
23	−0.06	1876 1886	Paul Philippe Cret Ludwig Mies van der Rohe
24	−0.06	1886 1901	Holabird & Root Louis I. Kahn
25	−0.06	1915 1925	Harry Weese Robert Venturi
26	−0.06	1926 1929	Henry N. Cobb Richard B. Whitaker
27	−0.05	1722 1734	Charles Louis Clérisseau William Buckland
28	−0.05	1822 1833	Frederick Law Olmsted William Ralph Emerson
29	−0.05	1890 1891	Frederick Kiesler Reinhard & Hofmeister
30	−0.05	1845 1856	Peabody & Stearns Louis Sullivan
31	−0.04	1876 1883	Walter B. Griffin William Van Alen
32	−0.04	1827 1832	Richard Mitchell Upjohn William Le Baron Jenney
33	−0.03	1895 1903	Buckminster Fuller Harwell Hamilton Harris
34	−0.03	1922 1923	Roche & Dinkeloo Victor Alfred Lundy

chief designers and structural engineers for the Brooklyn Bridge, provide a better illustration of low, or negative, cotextuality. The two men could hardly be more distant in their artistic visions and historical significance. They are not at war with each other; they simply belong to different worlds, if one is to believe what transpires from the analysis of indexes. The surprise is not their distance in the literature, but the realization that Cole and Roebling were born only five years apart.

Buckminster Fuller and Harwell Hamilton Harris are another revealing example of persons close agewise but populating different universes of interests and ideas. One was open to the wide world of technology and internationalism, and the other nurtured more traditional values in the realm of the local and the regional.

Robert Twelves, the designer of Old South Meeting House in Boston, and Fray Junipero Serra, founder of nine Franciscan missions, are also at the antipodes, not only geographically (the Northeast vs. the Southwest), culturally, and stylistically (the English vs. the Spanish), but also, it now turns out, textually.

Clusters

With hundreds of famous architects and thousands of lesser known ones in the data base, pairing architects one to one is too inefficient a technique to produce an overall picture. Clustering is more effective. Two hundred twenty architects with the highest adjusted citations are grouped into families, tribes, and nations on the basis of their adjusted kappas (figure 9.3). The remarks made in connection to figure 9.1 also apply here, and so do many of the comments raised in the preceding chapter when arranging texts in a similar clustering.

Pairs of architects who were partners appear in the same family; for example, Roebling and Roebling (nation 2, tribe 2, family 1), Town and Davis (3.7.1), Downing and Vaux (3.7.2), Howe and Lescaze (3.18.1), Harrison and Abramovitz (3.18.2), and Mayne and Rotondi (6.1.1). Architects with similar interests are also together, such as Moore and Venturi (3.20.1) and Goff and Soleri (3.7.4). Such couples can be identified by simple pairing; but clustering is more powerful, because it sometimes leads to groups of more than two members who often worked together—cases in point, Whitaker, Turnbull, and Lyndon (5.8.1), and Corbett, Fouilhoux, and Reinhard & Hofmeister (3.19.1))—or participated in similar cultural or stylistic endeavors, such as Maybeck, Greene & Greene, and Gill (3.7.3). In fact, the logic of the grouping is so obvious and the results read so smoothly that one must be reminded again that this was done blindly by a machine.

The most significant difference between clustering and pairings such as those of figures 9.1 and 9.2, however, is not the number of elements in a group, but the overall level of organization of the outcome. The pairs in these figures are unrelated; they are listed merely by increasing or decreasing adjusted kappas. In contrast, groups of related families in figure 9.3 are arranged into tribes, which in turn are structured into nations, as was discussed in the preceding chapter. Nations, tribes, and families effectively capture in an abstract fashion the fabric of American architectural culture at various scales as it appears in the literature. Let as look, for instance, at nation 3, the largest one, that encapsulates a widely held image of the entire history and extension of American architecture. Jefferson, Bulfinch, Sullivan, Wright, Mies van der Rohe, and the two Saarinens are the common points of reference in this nation. Countless narratives of American architecture can be triangulated on these names alone. But these individuals are not in a vacuum; they are connected to smaller pockets of more closely related architects who may or may not be a part of the narrative.

Figure 9.3   Selected architects clustered into nations, tribes, and families

Nation 1
1688   John Smibert
1716   Peter Harrison
1786   Nicholas Biddle
  Tribe 1
  1676   Andrew Hamilton
  1705   Richard Taliaferro
  Tribe 2
  1710   Thomas (or James) McBean
  1712   Samuel Cardy
    Family 1
    1676   Governor Alexander Spotswood
    1710   Ezra Waite
    Family 2
    1684   Dr. John Kearsley
    1810   John Notman
    Family 3
    1700   Robert Twelves
    1783   Russell Warren
  Tribe 3
  1761   Mangin & McComb
  1764   John Jacques Ramée (or Joseph Jacques)
  1804   Henry Austin
  1867   Willis Jefferson Polk
    Family 1
    1685   Richard Munday
    1880   Purcell & Elmslie
    Family 2
    1734   William Buckland
    1860   Shepley, Rutan, & Coolidge
    Family 3
    1765   Maximilien Godefroy
    1780   Alexander Parris
    Family 4
    1771   Asher Benjamin
    1798   Minard Lafever
  Tribe 4
  1696   Edmund Woolley
  1732   George Washington
  Tribe 5
    Family 1
    1722   Robert S. Smith
    1731   John Hawks
    1733   Joseph Brown
    1916   Lawrence Halprin
  Tribe 6
  1725   John Ariss
  1760   Étienne Sulpice Hallet
  1762   James Hoban

Figure 9.3   (continued)

Nation 2
  Tribe 1
  1713   Father Junípero Serra
  1811   Elisha Graves Otis
  Tribe 2
    Family 1
    1806   John Augustus Roebling
    1837   Washington Augustus Roebling

Nation 3
  1743   Thomas Jefferson
  1763   Charles Bulfinch
  1856   Louis Sullivan
  1867   Frank Lloyd Wright
  1873   Eliel Saarinen
  1886   Ludwig Mies van der Rohe
  1897   Skidmore, Owings, & Merrill
  1910   Eero Saarinen
  Tribe 1
  1722   Charles Louis Clérisseau
  1839   Frank Furness
  Tribe 2
    Family 1
    1754   Pierre Charles L'Enfant
    1822   Frederick Law Olmsted
  Tribe 3
  1757   Samuel McIntire
  1759   Dr. William Thornton
  Tribe 4
  1837   George Browne Post
  1845   Bruce Price
  1848   Charles B. Atwood
  1883   The Architects' Collaborative
  1895   Wurster, Bernardi, & Emmons
  1903   Harwell Hamilton Harris
  1910   Matthew Nowicki
  Family 1
  1763   George Hadfield
  1915   Harry Weese
  Family 2
  1798   Ammi Burnham Young
  1800   Isaiah Rogers
  1916   John Maclane Johansen
  Family 3
  1802   Gideon Shryock
  1923   Victor Alfred Lundy
  Family 4
  1821   Arthur Delavan Gilman
  1907   Perkins & Will
  1914   Caudill, Rowlett, & Scott

Figure 9.3   (continued)

Family 5
1832   Henry Van Brunt
1832   William Robert Ware
1903   Victor Gruen
Family 6
1834   Alfred B. Mullett
1902   Josep Lluis Sert
Family 7
1838   Peter Bonnet Wight
1920   Walter A. Netsch
Family 8
1847   Ernest Flagg
1905   Oscar G. Stonorov
Family 9
1861   Day & Klauder
1911   Ernest J. Kump
Family 10
1861   Charles Adams Platt
1874   Delano & Aldrich
Family 11
1908   Vernon DeMars
1912   Carl Koch
1914   Ralph R. Rapson
Tribe 5
1847   McKim, Mead, & White
Family 1
1764   Benjamin Henry Latrobe
1827   Richard Morris Hunt
Tribe 6
1781   Robert Mills
1802   Richard Upjohn
1818   James Renwick, Jr.
1859   Cass Gilbert
Family 1
1858   Carrère & Hastings
1863   Cram, Goodhue, & Ferguson
1869   Bertram Grosvenor Goodhue
Family 2
1866   Henry Bacon
1874   John Russell Pope
Tribe 7
1887   Rudolph Schindler
1907   Charles Osmand Eames
Family 1
1784   Ithiel Town
1803   Alexander Jackson Davis
Family 2
1815   Andrew Jackson Downing
1824   Calvert Vaux

Figure 9.3   (continued)

Family 3
1862   Bernard Maybeck
1868   Greene & Greene
1870   Irving John Gill
Family 4
1904   Bruce Alonzo Goff
1919   Paolo Soleri
Tribe 8
1788   William Strickland
1804   Thomas Ustick Walter
Tribe 9
1887   Eric Mendelsohn
1898   Alvar Aalto
  Family 1
  1792   John Haviland
  1909   Gordon Bunshaft
Tribe 10
1800   James Bogardus
1832   William Le Baron Jenney
1854   Holabird & Roche
  Family 1
  1844   Dankmar Adler
  1850   John Wellborn Root
Tribe 11
1823   Leopold Eidlitz
1836   Russell Sturgis
1845   Peabody & Stearns
Tribe 12
1823   John McArthur, Jr.
  Family 1
  1857   Reed & Stem
  1864   Warren & Wetmore
Tribe 13
1838   Henry Hobson Richardson
1883   Walter Gropius
1902   Marcel Breuer
1906   Philip Johnson
Tribe 14
1846   Daniel Hudson Burnham
1901   Louis I. Kahn
Tribe 15
1884   Kahn, Ely Jacques
  Family 1
  1861   McKenzie, Voorhees, & Gmelin
  1889   Ralph Thomas Walker
Tribe 16
1867   James Gamble Rogers
1882   Clarence S. Stein

Figure 9.3 (continued)

Tribe 17
1868 John Mead Howells
1877 Shreve, Lamb, & Harmon
1886 Holabird & Root
Tribe 18
1869 Albert Kahn
1881 Raymond Mathewson Hood
1892 Richard J. Neutra
1899 Pietro Belluschi
  Family 1
  1886 George Howe
  1896 William Lescaze
  Family 2
  1895 Wallace K. Harrison
  1908 Max Abramovitz
Tribe 19
  Family 1
  1873 Harvey Wiley Corbett
  1879 Jacques André Fouilhoux
  1891 Reinhard & Hofmeister
Tribe 20
1889 Hugh Ferriss
1890 Frederick Kiesler
1893 Norman Bel Geddes
Tribe 21
1922 Roche & Dinkeloo
  Family 1
  1925 Charles W. Moore
  1925 Robert Venturi

Nation 4
1895 Buckminster Fuller
Tribe 1
1868 Graham, Anderson, Probst, & White
1933 John H. Burgee
Tribe 2
1885 Philip Lippincott Goodwin
1912 Hugh Asher Stubbins, Jr.
1917 Davis, Brody, & Associates
1922 Craig Ellwood
  Family 1
  1871 Emery Roth & Sons
  1890 C. F. Murphy Associates
  Family 2
  1907 George F. Hellmuth
  1925 Gunnar Birkerts
  Family 3
  1914 Joseph Esherick
  1924 Mitchell Giurgola Associates

Figure 9.3   (continued)

    Family 4
    1915   Edward Larrabee Barnes
    1921   Ulrich Franzen
    Family 5
    1918   Benjamin Thompson
    1932   Hardy Holzman Pfeiffer Associates
Tribe 3
1876   Paul Philippe Cret
1883   William Van Alen
Tribe 4
1876   Walter B. Griffin
1929   Herb Greene
Tribe 5
1887   Le Corbusier (Charles Eduard Jeanneret)
1915   Kallmann, McKinnell, & Knowles
Tribe 6
1902   Edward Durrell Stone
1938   Charles Gwathmey
Tribe 7
1912   Minoru Yamasaki
1924   John Calvin Portman, Jr.
Tribe 8
1913   Bertrand Goldberg
    Family 1
    1929   Richard B. Whitaker
    1935   William Turnbull, Jr.
    1936   Donlyn Lyndon
Tribe 9
1917   I. M. Pei
1918   Paul Rudolph
1934   Richard Meier

Nation 5
1940   Steven Izenour
1946   Taft Architects
    Tribe 1
    1932   James Wines
    1934   Michael Graves
    1940   Helmut Jahn
      Family 1
      1923   Frank O. Gehry
      1930   Stanley Tigerman
      Family 2
      1929   John Hejduk
      1932   Peter D. Eisenman
    Tribe 2
      Family 1
      1926   Henry N. Cobb
      1943   Emilio Ambasz
      1947   Steven Holl

Figure 9.3   (continued)

> **Family 2**
> 1938   Kohn Pedersen Fox
> 1941   Thomas Hall Beeby
> **Tribe 3**
> 1926   Cesar Pelli
> 1930   John Rauch
> 1931   Denise Scott Brown
> **Tribe 4**
> 1938   Allan Greenberg
> 1942   Jorge Silvetti
> 1948   Thomas Gordon Smith
> **Tribe 5**
> 1939   Robert A. M. Stern
> 1949   Arquitectonica (or DPZ)
>
> **Nation 6**
> 1950   Zaha Hadid
> **Tribe 1**
> **Family 1**
> 1944   Thom Mayne
> 1949   Michael Rotondi
> **Tribe 2**
> 1944   OMA (Office for Metropolitan Architecture)
> **Family 1**
> 1946   Daniel Libeskind
> 1950   Bernard Tschumi

Writers are not really aware of this cultural geography, but the system functions as if they were. One can picture them at the crossroads, choosing between one route or another, engaging their attention and interest toward one tribe of connected architects or another, and within tribes, visiting this family or that. Writers may fail to pursue the trodden paths, insert new names, and explore new configurations of the names already in the roster; in fact, they do this all the time. This does not negate the validity of the mapping strategy, but it may change the map. As writers continue generating texts, index analysts must continue updating the clusters. It is in this sense that clustering captures certain features of the cultural fabric.

A Dynamic Picture

The distances of figures 9.1 and 9.2, and the clusters of figure 9.3, such as the ones presented in the preceding chapter, are insensitive to changes due to the passage of time. Although the position of the center of gravity of a cloud of active texts has been shown to vary, the texts themselves, once published, remain unchanged, and so do intertextual distances. Things are different when

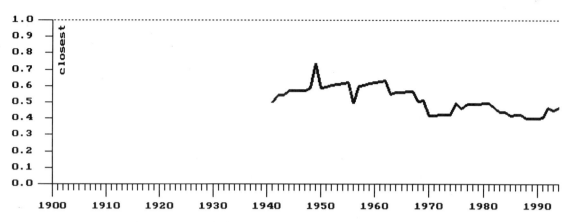

Figure 9.4 Proximity between Walter Gropius and Mies van der Rohe

dealing with distances between architects. Each time a book is published, every pair of architects in the roster becomes a little closer or drifts a little farther apart, depending on whether the two are jointly cited, jointly ignored, or one is cited but not the other.

To get a dynamic picture of changing discursive relationships between architects, distances can be computed on the basis of active texts only. Architects can be represented, like texts, as points in a multidimensional space: those with a high level of cotextuality occupy close positions, and the ones with low cotextuality are very far apart. With new texts being continually published and older ones fading away, the points in the configuration are permanently shifting positions, much like swarming bees.

The proximity between any two architects can be plotted year by year. The curve of figure 9.4, for example, shows the evolution of the distance between Gropius and Mies. There are two periods of maximum proximity, first from the mid-1950s to the late 1960s, during the heyday of their ascendancy, and then again around 1980, when they became the targets of attacks by the next generation of architects and writers. Although no longer dominant, they still represented, together with their kindred, an active pole in the alignment of architectural forces. But their closeness did not outlast the dominance of the Modern Movement. The demise of their ideology by 1980 is signaled in the charts not by a decrease in the frequency of their citations (their histograms did not start to plunge until 1990) but by the fact that they are no longer necessarily cited in the same texts. Although still on the stage, rather than sharing the center as in yesteryear, they retreated to the solitude of separate corners. Instead of a common, monolithic, and often somewhat uncritical following among most writers, now each one has his individual admirers.

A clustering like the one in figure 9.3 could also be generated year by year on the basis of active texts only, but the outcome would be too bulky to be useful. A more succinct but conceptually similar result is presented in figure 9.5. The twelve most frequently cited architects (or more in the case of ties) within the

Figure 9.5   Clusters of co-textual architects at various times

1880
William Thornton
Charles Bulfinch
Benjamin Latrobe
William Strickland
Thomas U. Walter

James Hoban
Robert Mills
Isaiah Rogers

Ithiel Town
Richard Upjohn

Alexander J. Davis
James Renwick, Jr.

1890
William Thornton
Charles Bulfinch
Benjamin Latrobe
Isaiah Rogers
Thomas U. Walter
James Renwick, Jr.

James Hoban
Robert Mills
William Strickland
Richard Upjohn

Ithiel Town
Alexander J. Davis

Henry H. Richardson

1900
James Hoban
Robert Mills
James Renwick, Jr.
Richard M. Hunt
Benjamin Latrobe
Richard Upjohn

Ithiel Town
Alexander J. Davis

William Thornton
Thomas U. Walter
George B. Post
Peabody & Stearns

Charles Bulfinch
Richard M. Hunt
Henry H. Richardson
Isaiah Rogers

1910
Thomas Jefferson
William Thornton
Thomas U. Walter
William Thornton
Henry H. Richardson
McKim, Mead, & White
Charles Bulfinch
Benjamin Latrobe
James Renwick, Jr.

James Hoban
Richard Upjohn

Robert Mills

George B. Post

1920
Thomas Jefferson
Richard M. Hunt
Henry H. Richardson

James Renwick, Jr.
McKim, Mead, & White
Charles Bulfinch
Benjamin Latrobe
Thomas U. Walter

James Hoban
Richard Upjohn

Robert Mills

1930
William Thornton
Thomas U. Walter
James Hoban

Charles Bulfinch
Benjamin Latrobe
Richard Upjohn
James Renwick, Jr.
Richard M. Hunt
Henry H. Richardson
Daniel H. Burnham

Thomas Jefferson

McKim, Mead, & White

1940
William Thornton
Charles Bulfinch
Henry H. Richardson
Benjamin Latrobe
Richard M. Hunt
Daniel H. Burnham
McKim, Mead, & White
Louis Sullivan

James Hoban
Thomas U. Walter

Thomas Jefferson
Richard Upjohn

1950
Thomas Jefferson
Benjamin Latrobe
Henry H. Richardson
Louis Sullivan
Frank Lloyd Wright
Charles Bulfinch
Daniel H. Burnham
McKim, Mead, & White

Robert Mills
Thomas U. Walter
Richard M. Hunt
Richard Upjohn

William Thornton
James Hoban

1960
William Thornton
Robert Mills

Thomas Jefferson
Henry H. Richardson
McKim, Mead, & White
Louis Sullivan
Frank Lloyd Wright

Charles Bulfinch
Benjamin Latrobe
Daniel H. Burnham

Richard M. Hunt

Richard Upjohn

1970
Thomas Jefferson
Frank Lloyd Wright
Mies van der Rohe

Benjamin Latrobe
Richard M. Hunt
McKim, Mead, & White
William Thornton
Henry H. Richardson

Charles Bulfinch
Louis Sullivan

Daniel H. Burnham
John W. Root

1980
Charles Bulfinch
Richard M. Hunt

Benjamin Latrobe
Mies van der Rohe
Eero Saarinen
Daniel H. Burnham
McKim, Mead, & White
Walter Gropius

Henry H. Richardson
Louis Sullivan

Thomas Jefferson

Frank Lloyd Wright

1990
Henry H. Richardson
Walter Gropius

Thomas Jefferson
Frank Lloyd Wright
Mies van der Rohe

McKim, Mead, & White
Louis Sullivan

Benjamin Latrobe
Eero Saarinen
Skidmore, Owings & Merrill

Philip Johnson

active texts chosen at ten-year intervals have been clustered using one level of clustering, rather than the three of figure 9.3. The architects involved are almost the same as the ones appearing among the twelve leading positions in figure 3.7, except that cumulative citations were used in that chapter because the concept of active texts had not yet been introduced. Although a few new names enter into the picture of figure 9.5 from time to time and others disappear, the most significant changes are not in the names but in their grouping.

Cotextuality, unlike isonomy, is not a fixed quantity. Like real families, families of architects are subject to divorce and remarrying. Ithiel Town and Alexander J. Davis lived in different clusters if one is to go by the literature of 1880; they became a couple only by the next decade, and they remained strongly cotextual ever since. James Renwick, who was Davis's "partner" in 1880, joined by the next decade the cluster listed at the top of the column. At the same time, Richard Upjohn lost his connection with Town to go to the second cluster in the list, and so on.

Despite differences in generation method and subject matter, the picture emerging from figure 9.5 bears some similarity with an evolutionary tree used by Jencks some time ago (figure 9.6).[1] He, too, envisioned historical units continually splitting amoeba-like and regrouping in new configurations. Architects, though, are pinned onto one spot of the diagram in Jencks's model; in figure 9.5 they may run through the entire duration, because it is not the names but the connections that are represented.

Blocks of Texts and Architects

When looking at a cluster of isonomic texts, it would sometimes be desirable to see the architects common to their indexes. Similarly, when facing a cluster of cotextual architects, one sometimes wishes to access the list of texts in which they are jointly cited. Block clustering[2] allows for exactly that: rather than clustering texts in terms of architects or vice versa, it returns blocks on interconnected architects and texts. The input for block clustering is citation lists, not kappa distances. The distinction between regular and adjusted kappas is therefore not applicable; however, as the clustering algorithm ignores all matters of relevancy, conceptually block clustering is akin to the use of nonadjusted kappas. Unlike the clustering algorithms used earlier, block clustering allows for overlaps. Texts as well as architects may appear in more than one block, or in none. Figure 9.7 shows seven blocks generated for the 220 most frequently cited architects.

To examine the output, it is best to start with the lists of architects that appear sorted by birth date. As mentioned in chapter 1, each such list telegraphs in a brief but revealing code a particular historical vision—from Jefferson to Yamasaki, Pei, and Rudolph in the case of block 1, from Wright to Helmuth

Jahn in block 2, and so on. The opening and closing names and dates for each narrative arch, the number of intermediate names visited, and their particular selection indicate to a knowledgeable person a general outline of the approach. The texts of a block do not cite every one of the block architects; but they cite a substantial number, and therefore the outline mentioned is generally applicable to all of them.

The lists of texts in each block are also sorted chronologically. Each list defines a citation pattern that is approximately common to all architects in the block. It is intuitively easier to accept that citations define a text than the other way around—that architects are "defined" by a citation pattern. Writers choose whom to cite, and in the process they leave a little bit of their individuality in their choices. Architects have no control over who is going to cite them, and to that extent, it seems silly or unfair to classify them accordingly. But architects as well as other cultural units are categorized into discrete discursive groups by society at large, whether they can control it or not. Figures 9.1, 9.3, and 9.5 show who are the cotextual architects; figure 9.7 starts revealing their common citation patterns. The outcome of block clustering can be read both ways, wherein lies its beauty.

Blocks carry the seeds of important cultural units. By finding them and using them as conceptual entities, it could one day become possible to remap the entire architectural culture and its history from a new perspective. One block of related architects and texts was identified in the closing section of chapter 3, to which readers are kindly requested to refer. The writers and architects listed in that section were foresighted and influential, which is not necessarily the case for all those listed in the blocks of figure 9.7. However, as shown in preceding chapters, the study of foresight and influence is not beyond the grasp of an index analyst. By using techniques that I have not yet been able to implement effectively, one could conceivably search for progressive as well as for conservative or regressive blocks of architects and texts. Achieving this goal requires not only further refinement of data-processing algorithms, but also larger and better data bases, and a keen empirical insight into the nature and location of those units.

But the most important difference between the blocks of chapter 3 and those of figure 9.7, one that speaks in favor of the latter, is that to identify the Young Turks, or to draw Jencks's diagram reprinted in figure 9.6, it is necessary to know about history. I fantasize about the young Jencks traveling extensively and spending long days in sites, offices and libraries, taking copious notes about contemporary architecture and its evolution. Later, in the calm of his study, he begins harboring vague intuitions about the amoeba-like nature of architectural movements, with separations and aggregations taking place in a complex pattern. Eventually, as the concept becomes clearer, he starts thinking of the graphic means to convey his findings. He toils with various ways or organizing the variables on paper, selects scales and line qualities, and eventually renders the actual diagram. Perhaps he vacillates between placing certain names in this

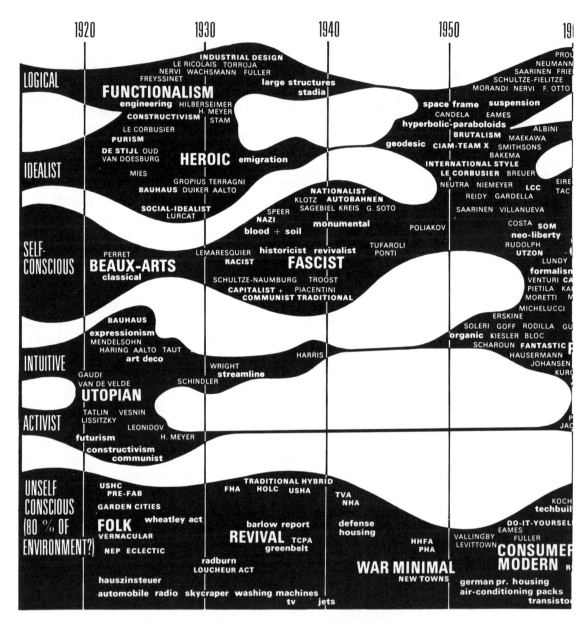

Figure 9.6   Evolutionary tree to the year 2000 (from Charles Jencks: *Architecture 2000*)

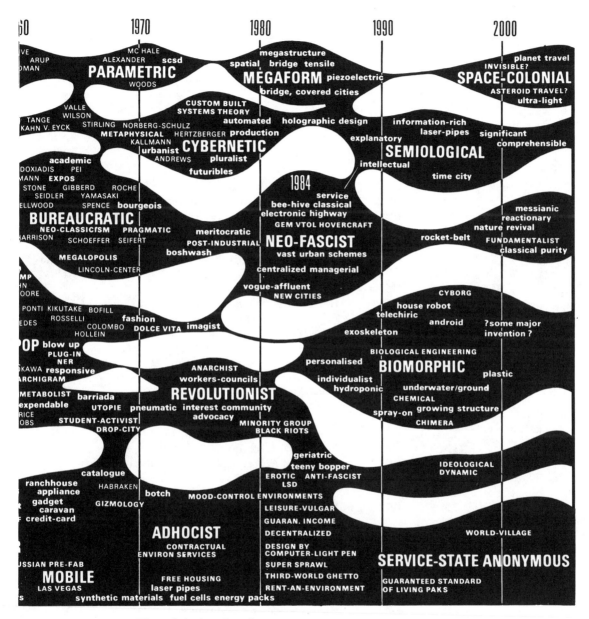

Figure 9.6   (continued)

Figure 9.7　Blocks of related texts and architects

Column headings:
[1]　Text ID #
[2]　Publication date
[3]　Author and title
[4]　Birth date
[5]　Name

Block #1
Texts:

[1]	[2]	[3]
108	1955	Tunnard & Reed: *American Skyline*
109	1956	*Architectural Record:* "100 Years of Significant Building"
110	1957	Gutheim: *1857–1957: One Hundred Years of Architecture in America*
112	1957	McCallum: "Genetrix. Personal Contributions to American Architecture"
114	1957	USIA: *Architecture USA* (ed.: Blake?)
116	1958	Hitchcock: *Architecture. Nineteenth and Twentieth Centuries*
117	1958	Peter: *Masters of Modern Architecture*
119	1959	Francastel: *Les Architects Celèbres*
120	1959	Joedicke: *A History of Modern Architecture*
122	1959	Kulterman: *Architecture of Today*
123	1959	McCallum: *Architecture USA*
124	1959	Reed: *The Golden City*
125	1960	Andrews: *Architecture in America*
126	1960	Condit: *American Building Art: The 19th & the 20th Centuries*
128	1960	Pierson & Davidson: *Arts in the United States*
129	1961	Burchard & Bush-Brown: *The Architecture of America*
131	1961	Fletcher: *A History of Architecture* (ed. Cordingley)
132	1961	Jones: *Architecture Today and Tomorrow*
133	1961	Scully: *Modern Architecture*
224	1977	Brown: *American Art to 1900*
228	1977	Richards: *Who's Who in Architecture* (main entries only)
229	1977	Richards: *Who's Who in Architecture*
230	1977	Smith, C. R.: *Supermannerism*
245	1980	Davern: *Architecture 1970–1980*
247	1980	Emanuel (ed.): *Contemporary Architects*
248	1980	Frampton: *Modern Architecture*
250	1980	Hunt: *Encyclopedia of American Architecture*
253	1980	Nuttgens: *Pocket Guide to Architecture*
255	1980	Raeburn: *Architecture of the Western World*
256	1980	Reid: *The Book of Buildings*
257	1980	Rifkind: *A Field Guide to American Architecture*
258	1981	*The New Encyclopaedia Britannica*, 15th ed.
260	1981	Rugoff: *Encyclopedia of American Art*
261	1981	Sanderson: *International Handbook of Contemporary Developments in Architecture*
262	1981	Smith, K.: *The Architecture of the United States*
264	1981	*The World Almanac and Book of Facts 1982*

Figure 9.7   (continued)

[1]	[2]	[3]
283	1983	Risebero: *Modern Architecture and Design*
284	1984	Flon (ed.): *The World Atlas of Architecture*
285	1984	Hunt: *American Architecture: A Field Guide*
290	1984	Poppeliers et al.: *What Style Is It?*
295	1985	Handlin: *American Architecture*
296	1985	Klein & Fogle: *Clues to American Architecture*
297	1985	Kostof: *A History of Architecture: Settings & Rituals*
299	1985	Maddex: *Built in the USA: American Buildings from A to Z*
300	1985	Maddex: *Master Builders*
302	1985	Stimpson: *Fieldguide to Landmarks of Modern Architecture in United States*
304	1986	Barford: *Understanding Modern Architecture*
305	1986	De Long, Searing, Stern: *American Architecture* (symposium)
306	1986	De Long, Searing, Stern: *American Architecture* (exhibition)
307	1986	Duncan: *American Art Deco*
308	1986	Lampugnani: *Encyclopedia of 20th Century Architecture*
309	1986	Stern: *Pride of Place: Building the American Dream*
310	1986	Trachtenberg & Hyman: *Architecture from Prehistory to PostModernism*
311	1986	Watkin: *A History of Western Architecture*
312	1986	Wilson et al.: *The Machine Age in America 1918–1941*
314	1987	Kostof: *America by Design*
315	1987	Musgrove (ed.): *Fletcher's History of Architecture*, 19th ed.
316	1987	Oppenheimer Dean: "75 Turbulent Years of American Architecture"
317	1987	Yarwood: *A Chronology of Western Architecture*
319	1988	Gibberd: *Architecture Source Book*
320	1988	Hollingworth: *Architecture of the 20th Century*

61 texts in block #1

Architects:

[4]	[5]
1743	Thomas Jefferson
1763	Charles Bulfinch
1764	Benjamin Henry Latrobe
1781	Robert Mills
1788	William Strickland
1804	Thomas Ustick Walter
1818	James Renwick, Jr.
1827	Richard Morris Hunt
1832	William Le Baron Jenney
1838	Henry Hobson Richardson
1844	Dankmar Adler
1846	Daniel Hudson Burnham
1847	McKim, Mead, & White
1850	John Welborn Root
1854	Holabird & Roche
1856	Louis Sullivan
1859	Cass Gilbert
1862	Bernard Maybeck

Figure 9.7   (continued)

Architects:

[4]	[5]
1867	Frank Lloyd Wright
1868	Greene & Greene
1869	Albert Kahn
1873	Eliel Saarinen
1881	Raymond Mathewson Hood
1883	Walter Gropius
1886	George Howe
1886	Ludwig Mies van der Rohe
1887	Rudolph Schindler
1892	Richard J. Neutra
1895	Buckminster Fuller
1895	Wallace K. Harrison
1896	William Lescaze
1897	Skidmore, Owings, & Merrill
1899	Pietro Belluschi
1901	Louis I. Kahn
1902	Marcel Breuer
1902	Edward Durrell Stone
1906	Philip Johnson
1908	Max Abramovitz
1910	Eero Saarinen
1912	Minoru Yamasaki
1917	I. M. Pei
1918	Paul Rudolph

42 architects in block #1

Block #2
Texts:

[1]	[2]	[3]
202	1973	Jencks: *Modern Movements in Architecture*
206	1974	Scully: *Modern Architecture*, 2nd ed. rev.
207	1974	Scully: *The Shingle Style Today*
208	1975	Blake & Quint: *Modern Architecture America*
210	1975	Fletcher: *A History of Architecture* (ed. Palmes)
213	1976	Hammett: *Architecture in the United States*
218	1976	Smith, K.: *A Pictorial History of Architecture in America*
219	1976	*The World Almanac and Book of Facts 1977*
220	1976	Tafuri & Dal Co.: *Modern Architecture*
221	1976	White: *The Architecture Book*
222	1976	Wodehouse: *American Architects from the Civil War to the Present*
223	1977	Blake: *Form Follows Fiasco*
230	1977	Smith, C. R.: *Supermannerism*
231	1977	Stern: *New Directions in American Architecture*, rev. ed.
244	1980	Ball: *Architecture and Interior Design*
253	1980	Nuttgens: *Pocket Guide to Architecture*
254	1980	Portoghesi: *Architecture 1980*
255	1980	Raeburn: *Architecture of the Western World*

Figure 9.7   (continued)

Block #2
Texts:

[1]	[2]	[3]
256	1980	Reid: *The Book of Buildings*
258	1981	*The New Encyclopaedia Britannica*, 15th ed.
259	1981	Jencks: *The Language of Post-Modern Architecture*, 3rd ed.
260	1981	Rugoff: *Encyclopedia of American Art*
261	1981	Sanderson: *International Handbook of Contemporary Developments in Architecture*
262	1981	Smith, K.: *The Architecture of the United States*
306	1986	De Long, Searing, Stern: *American Architecture* (exhibition)
308	1986	Lampugnani: *Encyclopedia of 20th Century Architecture*
309	1986	Stern: *Pride of Place: Building the American Dream*
310	1986	Trachtenberg & Hyman: *Architecture from Prehistory to PostModernism*
311	1986	Watkin: *A History of Western Architecture*
313	1987	Jencks: *Post-Modernism: The New Classicism in Art and Architecture*
320	1988	Hollingworth: *Architecture of the 20th Century*
322	1988	Klotz: *The History of Postmodern Architecture*
324	1988	Norberg-Schulz: *New World Architecture*
325	1988	Nuttgens: *Understanding Modern Architecture*
327	1988	Scully: *American Architecture and Urbanism*, new rev. ed.
328	1988	Stern: *Modern Classicism*
329	1989	*AIA Encyclopedia of Architecture, Design, Engineering, and Construction*
330	1989	*AIA Encyclopedia of Architecture, Design, Engineering and Construction* (main entries only)
333	1989	Kennedy (ed.): *Smithsonian Guide to Historic America*
334	1989	Krantz: *American Architects*
336	1989	Russell: *Architecture and Design 1970–1990*

42 texts in block #2

Architects:

[4]	[5]
1867	Frank Lloyd Wright
1883	Walter Gropius
1886	Ludwig Mies van der Rohe
1887	Le Corbusier (Charles Eduard Jeanneret)
1890	C. F. Murphy Associates
1895	Buckminster Fuller
1897	Skidmore, Owings, & Merrill
1898	Alvar Aalto
1901	Louis I. Kahn
1902	Marcel Breuer
1904	Bruce Alonzo Goff
1906	Philip Johnson
1909	Gordon Bunshaft
1910	Eero Saarinen

Figure 9.7 (continued)

Architects:

[4]	[5]
1912	Minoru Yamasaki
1915	Edward Larrabee Barnes
1915	Kallmann, McKinnell, & Knowles
1916	John Maclane Johansen
1917	I. M. Pei
1918	Paul Rudolph
1919	Paolo Soleri
1921	Ulrich Franzen
1922	Roche & Dinkeloo
1923	Frank O. Gehry
1924	Mitchell Giurgola Associates
1924	John Calvin Portman, Jr.
1925	Charles W. Moore
1925	Robert Venturi
1926	Cesar Pelli
1929	John Hejduk
1930	John Rauch
1930	Walker Gee Design Group
1931	Denise Scott Brown
1932	Peter D. Eisenman
1932	Hardy Holzman Pfeiffer Associates
1932	James Wines
1933	John H. Burgee
1834	Michael Graves
1934	Richard Meier
1935	William Turnbull, Jr.
1936	Donlyn Lyndon
1938	Charles Gwathmey
1939	Robert
1940	Helmut Jahn

44 architects in block #2

Block #3
Texts:

[1]	[2]	[3]
135	1962	*The World Almanac and Book of Facts 1962*
140	1964	Creighton: *American Architecture*
141	1964	*Encyclopaedia Britannica*, 14th ed. (1964)
142	1964	*Encyclopaedia Britannica*, 14th ed. (main entries only)
143	1964	Gowans: *Images of American Living*
150	1965	Early: *Romanticism in American Architecture*
244	1980	Ball: *Architecture and Interior Design*
258	1981	*The New Encyclopaedia Britannica*, 15th ed.
260	1981	Rugoff: *Encyclopedia of American Art*
262	1981	Smith, K.: *The Architecture of the United States*
264	1981	*The World Almanac and Book of Facts 1982*
266	1981	Thorndike: *Three Centuries of Notable American Architects*

Figure 9.7   (continued)

Block #3
Texts:

[1]	[2]	[3]
267	1981	Whiffen & Koepper: *American Architecture 1607–1976*
270	1982	Condit: *American Building: Materials and Techniques*
273	1982	*Macmillan Encyclopedia of Architects* (Placzek, ed.)
282	1983	Pulos: *American Design Ethic: A History of Industrial Design to 1940*
283	1983	Risebero: *Modern Architecture and Design*
285	1984	Hunt: *American Architecture: A Field Guide*
290	1984	Poppeliers et al.: *What Style Is It?*
295	1985	Handlin: *American Architecture*
296	1985	Klein & Fogle: *Clues to American Architecture*
297	1985	Kostof: *A History of Architecture: Settings & Rituals*
299	1985	Maddex: *Built in the USA: American Buildings from A to Z*
300	1985	Maddex: *Master Builders*
306	1986	De Long, Searing, Stern: *American Architecture* (exhibition)
309	1986	Stern: *Pride of Place: Building the American Dream*
311	1986	Watkin: *A History of Western Architecture*
314	1987	Kostof: *America by Design*
315	1987	Musgrove (ed.): *Fletcher's History of Architecture*, 19th ed.
317	1987	Yarwood: *A Chronology of Western Architecture*

30 texts in block #3

Architects:

[4]	[5]
1716	Peter Harrison
1743	Thomas Jefferson
1754	Pierre Charles L'Enfant
1757	Samuel McIntire
1759	Dr. William Thornton
1760	Étienne Sulpice Hallet
1761	Mangin & McComb
1762	James Hoban
1763	Charles Bulfinch
1764	Benjamin Henry Latrobe
1764	John Jacques Ramée (or Joseph Jacques)
1771	Asher Benjamin
1780	Alexander Parris
1781	Robert Mills
1788	William Strickland
1792	John Haviland
1800	Isaiah Rogers
1802	Richard Upjohn
1803	Alexander Jackson Davis
1804	Thomas Ustick Walter
1815	Andrew Jackson Downing
1818	James Renwick, Jr.
1822	Frederick Law Olmsted

Figure 9.7   (continued)

Architects:

[4]	[5]
1827	Richard Morris Hunt
1838	Henry Hobson Richardson
1858	Carrère & Hastings
1863	Cram, Goodhue, & Ferguson
1869	Bertram Grosvenor Goodhue

28 architects in block #3

Block #4
Texts:

[1]	[2]	[3]
133	1961	Scully: *Modern Architecture*
135	1962	*The World Almanac and Book of Facts 1962*
138	1962	Pevsner: "Architecture and Applied Arts"
139	1963	Jacobus: *Modern Architecture*
140	1964	Creighton: *American Architecture*
141	1964	*Encyclopaedia Britannica*, 14th ed. (1964)
142	1964	*Encyclopaedia Britannica*, 14th ed. (main entries only)
143	1964	Gowans: *Images of American Living*
144	1964	Hilberseimer: *Contemporary Architecture*
145	1964	Muschenheim: *Elements of the Art of Architecture*
146	1964	Pehnt: *Encyclopedia of Modern Architecture*
147	1964	Tschacbasov: *Teachers Manual for the Study of Art History*
148	1965	Collins: *Changing Ideals in Modern Architecture: 1750–1950*
150	1965	Early: *Romanticism in American Architecture*
151	1965	Millon (ed.): *Key Monuments in the History of Architecture*
153	1965	Ulanov: *The Two Worlds of American Art*
154	1966	Benevolo: *History of Modern Architecture*
155	1966	Fitch: *American Building: The Historical Forces that Shaped It*
156	1966	Green: *American Art: A Historical Survey*
157	1966	Heyer: *Architects on Architecture*
158	1966	Jacobus: *Twentieth Century Architecture: The Middle Years 1940–66*
159	1966	Myers: *McGraw-Hill Dictionary of Art*
160	1966	Read: *Encyclopedia of the Arts*
162	1966	*The World Almanac and Book of Facts 1967*
164	1967	Giedion: *Space, Time, and Architecture*, rev. ed.
165	1967	Hillier: *From Tepees to Towers*
166	1967	Ross: *Taste In America*
168	1968	Condit: *American Building ... from Beginning to the Present*
169	1968	McLanathan: *The American Tradition in the Arts*
171	1968	Norman: *Traveler's Guide to American Art*
172	1968	Portoghesi: *Dizionario enciclopedico di architettura e urbanistica*
174	1969	Jordan: *A Concise History of Western Architecture*
176	1969	Scully: *American Architecture and Urbanism*
178	1969	Whiffen: *American Architecture Since 1780*

Figure 9.7   (continued)

Block #4
Texts:

[1]	[2]	[3]
179	1970	Hamilton: *19th & 20th Century Art: Painting, Sculpture, Architecture*
180	1970	Hofmann & Kultermann: *Modern Architecture in Color*
181	1970	Mendelowitz: *A History of American Art*
184	1970	Pierson: *American Building: Colonial and Neo-classical Styles*
185	1971	Cohen: *History of American Art*
187	1971	*The World Almanac and Book of Facts 1972*
190	1972	Bacon: *Architecture and Townscape*
191	1972	*Encyclopaedia Britannica*, 14th ed. (1972)
192	1972	*Encyclopaedia Britannica*, 14th ed. (main entries only)
193	1972	Chermayeff: *Observations on American Architecture*
194	1972	Fitch: *American Building: The Environmental Forces that Shaped It*
195	1972	Jordy: *American Buildings: Progressive and Academic Ideals*
196	1972	Jordy: *American Buildings: Impact of European Modernism*
198	1973	Boorstin: *The Americans: The Democratic Experience*
199	1973	Cook & Klotz: *Conversations with Architects*
201	1973	Jacobus: *American Art of the 20th Century*
203	1973	Rowland: *A History of the Modern Movement*
241	1979	Brown at al.: *American Art*
243·	1979	Roth: *A Concise History of American Architecture*
244	1980	Ball: *Architecture and Interior Design*
245	1980	Davern: *Architecture 1970–1980*
324	1988	Norberg-Schulz: *New World Architecture*
325	1988	Nuttgens: *Understanding Modern Architecture*
327	1988	Scully: *American Architecture and Urbanism*, new rev. ed.

58 texts in block #4

Architects:

[4]	[5]
1743	Thomas Jefferson
1838	Henry Hobson Richardson
1844	Dankmar Adler
1846	Daniel Hudson Burnham
1847	McKim, Mead, & White
1850	John Welborn Root
1856	Louis Sullivan
1867	Frank Lloyd Wright

8 architects in block #4

Block #5
Texts:

[1]	[2]	[3]
245	1980	Davern: *Architecture 1970–1980*
247	1980	Emanuel (ed.): *Contemporary Architects*
248	1980	Frampton: *Modern Architecture*

Figure 9.7   (continued)

Block #5
Texts:

[1]	[2]	[3]
262	1981	Smith, K.: *The Architecture of the United States*
253	1980	Nuttgens: *Pocket Guide to Architecture*
254	1980	Portoghesi: *Architecture 1980*
255	1980	Raeburn: *Architecture of the Western World*
256	1980	Reid: *The Book of Buildings*
258	1981	*The New Encyclopaedia Britannica*, 15th ed.
259	1981	Jencks: *The Language of Post-Modern Architecture*, 3rd ed.
260	1981	Rugoff: *Encyclopedia of American Art*
306	1986	De Long, Searing, Stern: *American Architecture* (exhibition)
307	1986	Duncan: *American Art Deco*
308	1986	Lampugnani: *Encyclopedia of 20th Century Architecture*
309	1986	Stern: *Pride of Place: Building the American Dream*
310	1986	Trachtenberg & Hyman: *Architecture from Prehistory to PostModernism*
311	1986	Watkin: *A History of Western Architecture*
312	1986	Wilson et al.: *The Machine Age in America 1918–1941*
313	1987	Jencks: *Post-Modernism: The New Classicism in Art and Architecture*
315	1987	Musgrove (ed.): *Fletcher's History of Architecture*, 19th ed.
316	1987	Oppenheimer Dean: *"75 Turbulent Years of American Architecture"*
317	1987	Yarwood: *A Chronology of Western Architecture*
319	1988	Gibberd: *Architecture Source Book*
320	1988	Hollingworth: *Architecture of the 20th Century*
322	1988	Klotz: *The History of Postmodern Architecture*
325	1988	Nuttgens: *Understanding Modern Architecture*
326	1988	Pulos: *The American Design Adventure: 1940–1975*
327	1988	Scully: *American Architecture and Urbanism*, new rev. ed.
328	1988	Stern: *Modern Classicism*
329	1989	*AIA Encyclopedia of Architecture, Design, Engineering, and Construction*
330	1989	*AIA Encyclopedia of Architecture, Design, Engineering and Construction* (main entries only)
333	1989	Kennedy (ed.): *Smithsonian Guide to Historic America*
334	1989	Krantz: *American Architects*
347	1991	Cook & Llewellyn-Jones: *New Spirit in Architecture*

34 texts in block #5

Architects:

[4]	[5]
1867	Frank Lloyd Wright
1873	Harvey Wiley Corbett
1883	Walter Gropius
1883	The Architects' Collaborative
1886	Ludwig Mies van der Rohe
1887	Eric Mendelsohn

Figure 9.7   (continued)

Architects:

[4]	[5]
1892	Richard J. Neutra
1895	Buckminster Fuller
1895	Wallace K. Harrison
1895	Wurster, Bernardi, & Emmons
1897	Skidmore, Owings, & Merrill
1898	Alvar Aalto
1899	Pietro Belluschi
1901	Louis I. Kahn
1902	Marcel Breuer
1902	Edward Durrell Stone
1906	Philip Johnson
1907	Charles Osmand Eames
1908	Max Abramovitz
1909	Gordon Bunshaft
1910	Eero Saarinen
1912	Minoru Yamasaki
1917	I. M. Pei
1914	Paul Weidlinger

24 architects in block #5

Block #6
Texts:

[1]	[2]	[3]
228	1977	Richards: *Who's Who in Architecture* (main entries only)
229	1977	Richards: *Who's Who in Architecture*
231	1977	Stern: *New Directions in American Architecture*, rev. ed.
234	1978	Andrews: *Architecture, Ambition and Americans*, rev. ed.
235	1978	Burton: *A Choice Over Our Heads*
237	1978	Williamson: "An Architectural Family Tree"
241	1979	Brown et al.: *American Art*
243	1979	Roth: *A Concise History of American Architecture*
244	1980	Ball: *Architecture and Interior Design*
247	1980	Emanuel (ed.): *Contemporary Architects*
248	1980	Frampton: *Modern Architecture*
250	1980	Hunt: *Encyclopedia of American Architecture*
253	1980	Nuttgens: *Pocket Guide to Architecture*
254	1980	Portoghesi: *Architecture 1980*
255	1980	Raeburn: *Architecture of the Western World*
256	1980	Reid: *The Book of Buildings*
257	1980	Rifkind: *A Field Guide to American Architecture*
258	1981	*The New Encyclopaedia Britannica*, 15th ed.
260	1981	Rugoff: *Encyclopedia of American Art*
261	1981	Sanderson: *Int. Handbook of Contemporary Developments in Architecture*
262	1981	Smith, K.: *The Architecture of the United States*
264	1981	*The World Almanac and Book of Facts 1982*

Figure 9.7   (continued)

Block #6
Texts:

[1]	[2]	[3]
266	1981	Thorndike: *Three Centuries of Notable American Architects*
267	1981	Whiffen & Koepper: *American Architecture 1607–1976*

74 texts in block #6

Architects:

[4]	[5]
1856	Louis Sullivan
1867	Frank Lloyd Wright
1868	John Mead Howells
1869	Bertram Grosvenor Goodhue
1869	Albert Kahn
1873	Harvey Wiley Corbett
1873	Eliel Saarinen
1877	Shreve, Lamb, & Harmon
1879	Jacques André Fouilhoux
1881	Raymond Mathewson Hood
1883	Walter Gropius
1886	George Howe
1886	Ludwig Mies van der Rohe
1891	Reinhard & Hofmeister
1891	Gio Ponti
1895	Wallace K. Harrison
1896	William Lescaze

17 architects in block #6

Block #7
Texts:

[1]	[2]	[3]
221	1976	White: *The Architecture Book*
222	1976	Wodehouse: *American Architects from the Civil War to the Present*
320	1988	Hollingworth: *Architecture of the 20th Century*
322	1988	Klotz: *The History of Postmodern Architecture*
327	1988	Scully: *American Architecture and Urbanism*, new rev. ed.
328	1988	Stern: *Modern Classicism*
329	1989	*AIA Encyclopedia of Architecture, Design, Engineering, and Construction*
330	1989	*AIA Encyclopedia of Architecture, Design, Engineering and Construction* (main entries only)
334	1989	Krantz: *American Architects*
336	1989	Russell: *Architecture and Design 1970–1990*
338	1989	Wright: *Sourcebook of Contemporary North American Architecture*
339	1990	AIA: *American Architecture of the 1980s*
341	1990	Jencks: *The New Moderns from Late to Neo-Modernism*

13 texts in block #7

Figure 9.7   (continued)

| Architects: | |
[4]	[5]
1871	Emery Roth & Sons
1882	Clarence S. Stein
1890	Frederick Kiesler
1907	George F. Hellmuth
1907	Perkins & Will
1912	Carl Koch
1912	Hugh Asher Stubbins, Jr.
1914	Caudill, Rowlett, & Scott
1916	Lawrence Halprin
1917	Davis, Brody, & Associates
1918	Benjamin Thompson
1920	Walter A. Netsch
1921	Ulrich Franzen
1922	Craig Ellwood
1923	Frank O. Gehry
1923	Victor Alfred Lundy
1926	Henry N. Cobb
1929	John Hejduk
1930	John Rauch
1930	Stanley Tigerman
1931	Denise Scott Brown
1932	Peter D. Eisenman
1932	Hardy Holzman Pfeiffer Associates
1932	James Wines
1933	John H. Burgee
1938	Allan Greenberg
1938	Kohn Pedersen Fox
1939	Robert A. M. Stern
1940	Steven Izenour
1940	Helmut Jahn
1941	Thomas Hall Beeby
1943	Emilio Ambasz
1944	Thom Mayne
1944	OMA (Office for Metropolitan Architecture)
1946	Daniel Libeskind
1948	Thomas Gordon Smith
1949	Arquitectonica (or DPZ)
1950	Bernard Tschumi
1959	Maya Ying Lin
39 architects in block #7	

position of the stream or that, or decides, as an afterthought, to replace one architect with another.

This is not at all the way the figures of this and preceding chapters were developed; literally, it was the other way around. Once the data were made accessible to the system, many types of analyses were performed at whim. Some ideas led to dead ends; the fruitful ones brought to light certain regularities or patterns. Whenever this happened the outcome was, conceptually if not exactly, a diagram like the one of figure 9.7. Only afterward was it possible to mull over its significance and whether or not it was worth reporting. The diagrams (and the connections between variables they represent) preceded the understanding, rather than following it; they were the mechanism of discovery, not the result. Digital technology is transforming the practice of research in the humanities. It is empowering the ignorant to come up with findings previously restricted to the cognoscenti. Herein lies its promise, and perhaps its danger.

Notes

1. Jencks, Charles: *Architecture 2000. Predictions and Methods.* New York, Washington, DC: Praeger, 1971 (pp. 46–47).

2. The statistical package used was BMDP. The program is called P3M. See Dixon, W. J. (ed.): *BMDP Statistical Software.* Berkeley, Los Angeles, London: University of California Press, 1985. The output was simplified by the author.

10   International and Domestic Frames of Reference

American architecture is the set of all buildings erected in this country. Similarly, twentieth-century architecture is composed of all buildings raised or designed during this century. (The statements can be qualified, if desired, to include only significant or consequential buildings.) Common sense suggests that twentieth-century American architecture consists, in turn, of the buildings in both of those categories. A logician might affirm that the third set is the intersection of the other two.

Examination of the indexes reveals a more complex, fuzzier picture. Certain buildings in the United States are often featured in the literature devoted to world architecture but rarely in texts about America. Le Corbusier's Carpenter Center in Harvard University and Alvar Aalto's Baker Dormitory at Massachusetts Institute of Technology are conspicuous examples. As their architects were European, it might be argued that the buildings are less than fully American, despite their location in Massachusetts. The work of American born and American based Louis Kahn, however, is in this regard in the same category, and so is that of Gordon Bunshaft. Other contemporary buildings and architects display the opposite characteristic: they shine in the literature about American architecture, but are often neglected in texts devoted to the contemporary scene internationally.

There exist a discourse about American architecture, a discourse about contemporary architecture, and a discourse about contemporary American architecture, each with its own literary traditions. Like religions, the traditions comprise myths, heroes and villains, a visual imagery, established and predictable issues of concern, preferred narrators (writers, prophets), and favored canonical narrations (texts). The traditions are partially overlapping and partially divergent. Not all contemporary American architects, buildings, or writers participate in them to the same extent. Carpenter Center and the Baker Dormitory are important points of reference in the images and traditions associated with modern architecture, but not in those of American architecture. The works of William Wurster in the West, Harwell Hamilton Harris in the South, and, more recently, Charles Gwathmey in the Northeast are significant landmarks in outlines of American architecture, but are frequently bypassed from a transatlantic frame of reference, when their geographic location and regional characteristics become blurry. Buckminster Fuller occupies a more important position in the mythology of modern American architecture than he does in either American architecture or contemporary world architecture.

Other frames of reference in architectural literature are anchored in a territory (region, state, city), a building type, or an issue (sustainability, historic preservation, aging), each with their own traditions and mythologies. As America grows more complex, diverse, and fragmentary, so does the need for more compartmentalized discourses; but this remains beyond the scope of our study.

Archetypal Domestic and International Narratives

The texts of the corpus can be separated into two groups. On one hand we have books and articles specifically devoted to the United States. Some of them deal only with architecture, others refer also to other arts or activities; in the case of the latter, the nonarchitectural names were excised before entering the index in the data base. On the other hand are universal histories, dictionaries, and encyclopedias in which the architecture of this country is approached from the larger perspective of the architecture of the world. Again, some texts are devoted to architecture only, others cover other fields as well. In the case of these works, non-American names were expunged from the indexes along with the nonarchitectural ones. Let us call the first group the national or domestic literature, and the other international or worldwide. It is not their origin that counts, but their frame of reference. Every text in the corpus unequivocally belongs to one category or the other. The corpus contains 171 international texts and 209 domestic ones.

Figure 10.1 shows the names featured in the greatest number of international texts; figure 10.2 contains those featured most often in domestic texts. The names are arranged by date of birth. The lists resemble the one printed on pages 8–9. Faced with such an enumeration, it was said in chapter 1, knowledgeable persons could surmise a developmental line linking the names into a narrative; they could conceive an ideal text whose index would match the list. Performing that mental operation with these lists it is possible to gain initial insight into archetypal discourses on American architecture with one frame of reference or the other, and their differences.

Jefferson, Richardson, Wright, and other outstanding giants are included in both lists; they cannot be ignored in any discourse on American architecture, no matter what the frame of reference. The distinctive names, the ones that define the specific realm of each discourse, are those appearing in one list but not the other. They are marked with asterisks in figures 10.1 and 10.2.

If the index of a book includes the names of Holabird & Roche, Howe & Lescaze, Fuller, Harrison, Aalto, Kahn, Bunshaft, Yamasaki, Rudolph, and Venturi, the text deals with the architecture of the world, or it is atypical.

Figure 10.1 Typical American architects in discourse with an international frame of reference

Column headings:
[1] Birth date
[2] Name

[1]	[2]
1743	Thomas Jefferson
1763	Charles Bulfinch
1764	Benjamin Henry Latrobe
1804	Thomas Ustick Walter
1827	Richard Morris Hunt
1832	William Le Baron Jenney
1838	Henry Hobson Richardson
1844	Dankmar Adler
1846	Daniel Hudson Burnham
1847	McKim, Mead, & White
1850	John Wellborn Root
1854	*Holabird & Roche
1856	Louis Sullivan
1867	Frank Lloyd Wright
1873	Eliel Saarinen
1881	Raymond Mathewson Hood
1883	Walter Gropius
1886	*George Howe
1886	Ludwig Mies van der Rohe
1892	Richard J. Neutra
1895	*Buckminster Fuller
1895	Wallace K. Harrison
1896	*William Lescaze
1897	Skidmore, Owings, & Merrill
1898	*Alvar Aalto
1901	*Louis I. Kahn
1902	Marcel Breuer
1906	Philip Johnson
1909	*Gordon Bunshaft
1910	Eero Saarinen
1912	*Minoru Yamasaki
1917	I. M. Pei
1918	*Paul Rudolph
1925	*Robert Venturi

* typical only in an international frame of reference

Figure 10.2 Typical American architects in discourse with a domestic frame of reference

Column headings:
[1] Birth date
[2] Name

[1]	[2]
1743	Thomas Jefferson
1754	*Pierre Charles L'Enfant
1759	*Dr. William Thornton
1763	Charles Bulfinch
1764	Benjamin Henry Latrobe
1781	*Robert Mills
1788	*William Strickland
1802	*Richard Upjohn
1803	*Alexander Jackson Davis
1804	Thomas Ustick Walter
1818	*James Renwick, Jr.
1827	Richard Morris Hunt
1832	William Le Baron Jenney
1838	Henry Hobson Richardson
1844	Dankmar Adler
1846	Daniel Hudson Burnham
1847	McKim, Mead, & White
1850	John Wellborn Root
1856	Louis Sullivan
1859	*Cass Gilbert
1867	Frank Lloyd Wright
1869	*Bertram Grosvenor Goodhue
1873	Eliel Saarinen
1881	Raymond Mathewson Hood
1883	Walter Gropius
1886	Ludwig Mies van der Rohe
1892	Richard J. Neutra
1895	Wallace K. Harrison
1897	Skidmore, Owings, & Merrill
1902	Marcel Breuer
1906	Philip Johnson
1910	Eero Saarinen
1917	I. M. Pei

* typical only in a domestic frame of reference

Similarly, if L'Enfant, Thornton, Mills, Strickland, Upjohn, Davis, Renwick, Gilbert, and Goodhue are featured, the text is devoted to the United States only, or it is anomalous. Texts that do not follow the rule are covered in a special section at the end of this chapter.

All but two architects specific to figure 10.1 were born since 1895 and started their careers around or after World War II. All but two with asterisks in figure 10.2 were born before 1820 and died before the end of the century, and the other two died by 1934. Twentieth-century American architects left the strongest mark in international discourse; earlier architects fared better in the domestic literature.

The Guessing Game

Although useful as illustrations, the lists in figures 10.1 and 10.2 are inconclusive; if longer (or shorter) lists had been used, the overlaps and the names would have been different. To demonstrate that certain names do have a measurable association with one frame of reference or the other, we must labor a little harder.

Suppose that you are told who is cited in a text. Then, without any additional information whatsoever—no title, author, or list of contents—you are challenged to guess whether the text is national or international in scope. (Only American architects are listed for you; names of foreign architects, if present, are withheld. The quiz would be trivial otherwise.) Could you respond? How accurate would you be?

The solution to the puzzle, if one exists, is unlikely to have practical applications. When, you might ask, will anyone be faced with such an implausible problem? The motivation to find an answer is theoretical. If no differences in the names were to be expected between the two types of discourses, the riddle would be unsolvable; but if a solution exists, it would prove that the frame of reference of a text, domestic or worldwide, does indeed affect the choice of American architects to be cited. How else could the former be derived from the latter?

To be convincing, the solution must yield substantially better results than what could be achieved by chance or by clever guessing. The procedure must be tested against real cases, and the only way to do this in significant numbers is to apply it to the texts of the corpus itself. The task therefore is reformulated to predict the frame of reference of every text in the corpus, on the basis of the lists of American architects cited.

An index analyst can discharge the assignment with startling effectiveness. The first step is to figure out the *international coefficient* of every architect cited (see the appendix for the formula and for a more detailed description of the guessing game). Coefficients greater than one identify architects who are cited

Figure 10.3 Predicting the frame of reference for Brolin: *The Failure of Modern Architecture* (1976)

Column headings:
[1] Index
[2] Architects cited

[1]	[2]
1.41	Paul Rudolph
1.38	Ludwig Mies van der Rohe
1.37	Eero Saarinen
1.29	Walter Gropius
Predictor (average of indexes):	1.36
Prediction:	International
Result:	Correct

more often in the international literature. Next, the analyst will find the text's *international predictor*, which is the product of the coefficients of all architects cited. If the predictor is greater than a threshold close to one, the analyst will confidently guess that the text is international, and otherwise will predict a domestic frame of reference. (More about the threshold later.)

Let us see some examples. The American architects cited in *The Failure of Modern Architecture* (Brolin, 1976) are Gropius, Mies, Rudolph, and Eero Saarinen. They are listed in figure 10.3 according to decreasing coefficients. The text predictor—the product of the coefficients—is 1.36. As it is greater than the threshold, it accurately signals that the text deals with modern architecture worldwide. The predictor for *From Colony to Nation; An Exhibition of American Painting, Silver, and Architecture from 1650 to the War of 1812* (1949), on the other hand, is 0.60 (figure 10.4). The text has a domestic frame of reference.

Figure 10.5 lists all texts according to decreasing international predictor (column [1]). Most texts at the top of the ranking are international, and most at the other end are domestic; texts of both types appear intermingled in the middle area of the ranking. A cut-off point of 0.955 maximizes the number of correct predictions and becomes the threshold. The predictions appear in column [2]. The real nature of the text is in column [3]. The prediction is successful when columns [2] and [3] coincide; a running count of successful guesses is performed in column [4].

The system yields 291 correct guesses from a total of 380 cases, for a 77 percent rate of success. The odds of equating this performance merely by chance are of the order of one divided by a number represented by one followed by thirty-five zeros (see the appendix). The frame of reference can be deduced from the list of citations, which proves that the architects and buildings discussed depend on the frame of reference—*quod erat demonstrandum*, which is what was to be demonstrated, as my geometry teacher used to say with a triumphant look in his eyes.

Figure 10.4 Predicting the frame of reference for Bannister: *From Colony to Nation* (1949)

Column headings:	
[1] Index	
[2] Architects cited	

[1]	[2]
1.02	Thomas Jefferson
0.96	Gilbert Leigh
0.96	Peter and John A. Horlbeck
0.92	William Byrd II
0.89	Joseph Clark
0.86	Benjamin Henry Latrobe
0.81	James Diamond
0.77	James Hoban
0.72	Charles Bulfinch
0.72	Robert Mills
0.65	Pierre Charles L'Enfant
0.64	John Ariss
0.64	Dr. William Thornton
0.61	Christopher Wren
0.60	Andrew Hamilton
0.55	Étienne Sulpice Hallet
0.55	Dr. John Kearsley
0.53	Samuel McIntire
0.50	Thomas (or James) McBean
0.48	Henry Cary
0.48	Peter Harrison
0.48	Ezra Waite
0.45	Samuel Rhoads
0.43	Joseph Brown
0.39	Mangin & McComb
0.39	Governor Alexander Spotswood
0.36	George Washington
0.35	John Hawks
0.34	George Hadfield
0.30	William Buckland
0.30	David Manigault

Predictor (average of indexes):	0.60
Prediction:	Domestic
Result:	Correct

Figure 10.5   Texts ranked according to international predictor

Column headings:
[1]   International predictor
[2]   Prediction (INTernational or DOMestic)
[3]   Real nature of text (INTernational or DOMestic)
[4]   Count of successful predictions (or *** if unsuccessful)
[5]   Text identifier number
[6]   Author and title

[1]	[2]	[3]	[4]	[5]	[6]
1.49	INT	INT	1	321	Johnson & Wigley: *Deconstructivist Architecture*
1.36	INT	INT	2	212	Brolin: *The Failure of Modern Architecture*
1.35	INT	INT	3	352	Papadakis: *A Decade of Architectural Design*
1.31	INT	INT	4	275	Portoghesi: *After Modern Architecture*
1.31	INT	INT	5	144	Hilberseimer: *Contemporary Architecture*
1.29	INT	INT	6	188	Jencks: *Architecture 2000*
1.29	INT	INT	7	226	Jencks: *The Language of Post-Modern Architecture*, rev. ed.
1.27	INT	INT	8	121	Jones: *Form Givers at Mid-century*
1.27	INT	INT	9	276	Pothorn: *Architectural Styles*
1.27	INT	INT	10	148	Collins: *Changing Ideals in Modern Architecture: 1750–1950*
1.27	INT	INT	11	136	Banham: *Guide to Modern Architecture*
1.26	INT	INT	12	259	Jencks: *The Language of Post-Modern Architecture*, 3rd ed.
1.25	INT	INT	13	351	Noever (ed.): *Architecture in Transition*
1.25	INT	INT	14	233	Stierlin: *Encyclopaedia of World Architecture*
1.25	INT	INT	15	341	Jencks: *The New Moderns from Late to Neo-Modernism*
1.24	INT	INT	16	225	Jencks: *The Language of Post-Modern Architecture*
1.24	INT	INT	17	173	Joedicke: *Architecture Since 1945*
1.24	INT	INT	18	322	Klotz: *The History of Postmodern Architecture*
1.24	INT	INT	19	347	Cook & Llewellyn-Jones: *New Spirit in Architecture*
1.23	INT	INT	20	254	Portoghesi: *Architecture 1980*
1.23	INT	INT	21	356	*The Illustrated Dictionary of 20th Century Designers*
1.22	INT	INT	22	288	Klotz: *Revision der Moderne*
1.22	INT	INT	23	367	Economakis (ed.): *Building Classical: A Vision of Europe and America*
1.21	INT	INT	24	252	Kulterman: *Architecture in the Seventies*
1.21	INT	INT	25	286	Jencks: *The Language of Post-Modern Architecture*, 4th ed.
1.21	INT	INT	26	281	Portoghesi: *Postmodern*
1.20	INT	INT	27	325	Nuttgens: *Understanding Modern Architecture*
1.20	INT	INT	28	350	Jencks: *The Language of Post-Modern Architecture*, 6th ed.
1.20	INT	INT	29	313	Jencks: *Post-Modernism: The New Classicism in Art and Architecture*
1.18	INT	INT	30	105	Giedion: *A Decade of Contemporary Architecture*, 2nd ed.
1.18	INT	INT	31	95	Giedion: *A Decade of Contemporary Architecture*
1.16	INT	INT	32	284	Flon (ed.): *The World Atlas of Architecture*
1.16	INT	INT	33	272	Jencks: *Architecture Today*
1.15	INT	INT	34	344	Papadakis & Watson (eds.): *New Classicism: Omnibus Volume*
1.15	INT	DOM	***	263	Searing: *Speaking a New Classicism: American Architecture Now*
1.14	INT	INT	35	202	Jencks: *Modern Movements in Architecture*
1.14	INT	INT	36	355	Sharp: *Twentieth Century Architecture: A Visual History*
1.14	INT	DOM	***	268	Wolfe: *From Bauhaus to Our House*
1.14	INT	INT	37	348	Copplestone: *Twentieth-Century World Architecture*

Figure 10.5   (continued)

[1]	[2]	[3]	[4]	[5]	[6]
1.13	INT	INT	38	205	Norberg-Schulz: *Meaning in Western Architecture*
1.13	INT	INT	39	180	Hofmann & Kultermann: *Modern Architecture in Color*
1.13	INT	INT	40	145	Muschenheim: *Elements of the Art of Architecture*
1.12	INT	INT	41	271	Curtis: *Modern Architecture Since 1900*
1.12	INT	INT	42	376	Peter: *The Oral History of Modern Architecture*
1.12	INT	INT	43	354	Sharp: *Illustrated Encyclopedia of Architects and Architecture*
1.11	INT	DOM	***	92	Egbert: *Organic Expression and American Architecture*
1.11	INT	DOM	***	278	Colquhoun et al.: *Promising Directions in American Architecture*
1.11	INT	DOM	***	292	*Cross Currents of American Architecture* (AD Profile)
1.11	INT	DOM	***	265	Stern: *American Architecture: After Modernism*
1.11	INT	INT	44	160	Read: *Encyclopedia of the Arts*
1.10	INT	INT	45	223	Blake: *Form Follows Fiasco*
1.10	INT	DOM	***	346	Hays & Burns (eds.): *Thinking the Past: Recent American Architecture*
1.10	INT	INT	46	255	Raeburn: *Architecture of the Western World*
1.10	INT	INT	47	235	Burton: *A Choice Over Our Heads*
1.10	INT	INT	48	261	Sanderson: *International Handbook of Contemporary Developments in Architecture*
1.10	INT	INT	49	374	Byars: *The Design Encyclopedia*
1.09	INT	INT	50	158	Jacobus: *Twentieth Century Architecture: The Middle Years 1940–66*
1.09	INT	INT	51	146	Pehnt: *Encyclopedia of Modern Architecture*
1.09	INT	INT	52	345	Saunders: *Modern Architecture*
1.09	INT	INT	53	349	Gossel & Lenhauser: *Architecture in the 20th Century*
1.08	INT	INT	54	122	Kulterman: *Architecture of Today*
1.08	INT	INT	55	183	Osborne: *The Oxford Companion to Art* (main entries only)
1.08	INT	INT	56	164	Giedion: *Space, Time, and Architecture*, rev. ed.
1.08	INT	INT	57	130	*Contemporary Architecture of the World 1961*
1.08	INT	INT	58	197	Sharp: *Visual History of 20th C Architecture*
1.07	INT	INT	59	335	Peel, Powell, & Garrett: *20th-Century Architecture*
1.07	INT	INT	60	253	Nuttgens: *Pocket Guide to Architecture*
1.07	INT	INT	61	308	Lampugnani: *Encyclopedia of 20th Century Architecture*
1.07	INT	INT	62	167	Rosenblum: *Transformations in Late 18th Century Art*
1.07	INT	INT	63	279	Frampton (w. Futagawa): *Modern Architecture 1851–1945*
1.06	INT	INT	64	120	Joedicke: *A History of Modern Architecture*
1.06	INT	INT	65	320	Hollingworth: *Architecture of the 20th Century*
1.05	INT	INT	66	319	Gibberd: *Architecture Source Book*
1.05	INT	DOM	***	336	Russell: *Architecture and Design 1970–1990*
1.05	INT	INT	67	117	Peter: *Masters of Modern Architecture*
1.05	INT	INT	68	249	*GA Document Special Issue 1970–1980*
1.05	INT	INT	69	304	Barford: *Understanding Modern Architecture*
1.05	INT	DOM	***	208	Blake & Quint: *Modern Architecture America*
1.05	INT	INT	70	206	Scully: *Modern Architecture*, 2nd ed. rev.
1.05	INT	INT	71	369	Kulterman: *Architecture in the 20th Century*
1.05	INT	INT	72	151	Millon (ed.): *Key Monuments in the History of Architecture*
1.04	INT	INT	73	133	Scully: *Modern Architecture*
1.04	INT	INT	74	375	Doremus: *Classical Styles in Modern Architecture*
1.04	INT	INT	75	127	Huxtable: *Twentieth-Century Architecture*
1.04	INT	INT	76	287	Jervis: *Design & Designers*

Figure 10.5　(continued)

[1]	[2]	[3]	[4]	[5]	[6]
1.04	INT	DOM	***	368	Heyer: *American Architecture in the Late 20th Century*
1.04	INT	INT	77	362	Newhouse: *The Builders: Marvels of Engineering*
1.03	INT	DOM	***	153	Ulanov: *The Two Worlds of American Art*
1.03	INT	DOM	***	339	AIA: *American Architecture of the 1980s.*
1.03	INT	DOM	***	77	Johnson: "Architecture" (in *The American Year Book*)
1.03	INT	INT	78	132	Jones: *Architecture Today and Tomorrow*
1.03	INT	INT	79	248	Frampton: *Modern Architecture*
1.02	INT	INT	80	203	Rowland: *A History of the Modern Movement*
1.02	INT	DOM	***	194	Fitch: *American Building: The Environmental Forces that Shaped It*
1.02	INT	DOM	***	330	*AIA Encyclopedia of Architecture, Design, Engineering and Construction* (main entries only)
1.02	INT	INT	81	283	Risebero: *Modern Architecture and Design*
1.02	INT	DOM	***	198	Boorstin: *The Americans: The Democratic Experience*
1.02	INT	INT	82	152	Rogers: *What's Up in Architecture*
1.02	INT	INT	83	371	Roth: *Understanding Architecture*
1.02	INT	DOM	***	372	Sarfatti Larson: *Behind the Postmodern Facade*
1.02	INT	DOM	***	294	Diamondstein: *American Architecture Now II*
1.01	INT	INT	84	310	Trachtenberg & Hyman: *Architecture from Prehistory to PostModernism*
1.01	INT	INT	85	353	Scully: *Architecture: The Natural and the Manmade*
1.01	INT	DOM	***	326	Pulos: *The American Design Adventure: 1940–1975*
1.01	INT	INT	86	192	*Encyclopaedia Britannica*, 14th ed. (main entries only)
1.01	INT	INT	87	147	Tschacbasov: *Teachers Manual for the Study of Art History*
1.01	INT	DOM	***	149	Drexler: *Modern Architecture USA*
1.00	INT	INT	88	73	Roth: *The New Architecture*
1.00	INT	DOM	***	301	Marder: *The Critical Edge: Controversy in American Architecture*
1.00	INT	INT	89	68	Behrendt: *Modern Building*
1.00	INT	DOM	***	98	Hitchcock & Drexler: *Built in USA. Post-war Architecture*
1.00	INT	INT	90	280	Nuttgens: *The Story of Architecture*
1.00	INT	INT	91	328	Stern: *Modern Classicism*
1.00	INT	INT	92	377	Peter: *The Oral History of Modern Architecture* (interviewees only)
1.00	INT	INT	93	337	Wodehouse & Moffett: *A History of Western Architecture*
0.99	INT	INT	94	358	Wodehouse: *Roots of International Style Architecture*
0.99	INT	INT	95	154	Benevolo: *History of Modern Architecture*
0.99	INT	INT	96	247	Emanuel (ed.): *Contemporary Architects*
0.99	INT	INT	97	220	Tafuri & Dal Co.: *Modern Architecture*
0.99	INT	INT	98	63	Hitchcock & Johnson: *The International Style*
0.99	*INT*	*INT*	*99*	*174*	Jordan: *A Concise History of Western Architecture*
0.99	INT	INT	100	157	Heyer: *Architects on Architecture*
0.99	INT	INT	101	228	Richards: *Who's Who in Architecture* (main entries only)
0.99	INT	INT	102	57	Taut: *Modern Architecture*
0.98	INT	DOM	***	201	Jacobus: *American Art of the 20th Century*
0.98	INT	DOM	***	199	Cook & Klotz: *Conversations with Architects*
0.98	INT	DOM	***	232	Stern (ed.): "Forty Under Forty"
0.98	INT	INT	103	317	Yarwood: *A Chronology of Western Architecture*
0.98	INT	INT	104	359	Bayer: *Art Deco Architecture*
0.98	INT	INT	105	79	Museum of Modern Art: *What is Modern Architecture?*
0.97	INT	INT	106	138	Pevsner: "Architecture and Applied Arts"

Figure 10.5 (continued)

[1]	[2]	[3]	[4]	[5]	[6]
0.97	INT	DOM	***	230	Smith, C. R.: *Supermannerism*
0.97	INT	DOM	***	303	Allen: *Emerging Voices: New Generation of Architects in America*
0.96	INT	DOM	***	298	Macrae-Gibson: *The Secret Life of Buildings*
0.96	INT	INT	107	179	Hamilton: *19th & 20th Century Art: Painting, Sculpture, Architecture*
0.96	INT	INT	108	210	Fletcher: *A History of Architecture* (ed. Palmes)
0.96	INT	INT	109	62	Barr, Hitchcock, Johnson, & Mumford: *Modern Architects*
0.96	INT	DOM	***	370	LeBlanc: *20th Century American Architecture*
0.95	INT	DOM	***	316	Oppenheimer Dean: "75 Turbulent Years of American Architecture"
0.95	INT	INT	110	88	Conder: *An Introduction to Modern Architecture*
0.95	INT	DOM	***	312	Wilson et al.: *The Machine Age in America 1918–1941*
0.95	INT	INT	111	242	Drexler: *Transformations in Modern Architecture*
0.95	INT	INT	112	258	*The New Encyclopaedia Britannica*, 15th ed.
0.95	INT	INT	113	229	Richards: *Who's Who in Architecture*
0.95	DOM	DOM	114	207	Scully: *The Shingle Style Today*
0.95	DOM	DOM	115	123	McCallum: *Architecture USA*
0.94	DOM	INT	***	142	*Encyclopaedia Britannica*, 14th ed. (main entries only)
0.94	DOM	DOM	116	193	Chermayeff: *Observations on American Architecture*
0.94	DOM	DOM	117	307	Duncan: *American Art Deco*
0.94	DOM	DOM	118	365	Weber: *American Art Deco*
0.94	DOM	INT	***	139	Jacobus: *Modern Architecture*
0.94	DOM	INT	***	189	Kulski: *Architecture in a Revolutionary Era*
0.94	DOM	DOM	119	251	Hunt: *Encyclopedia of American Architecture* (main entries only)
0.94	DOM	INT	***	378	Striner: *Art Deco*
0.94	DOM	DOM	120	318	AIA J.: *10th to 12th Annual Reviews of New American Architecture*
0.94	DOM	INT	***	245	Davern: *Architecture 1970–1980*
0.94	DOM	DOM	121	112	McCallum: "Genetrix: Personal Contributions to American Architecture"
0.94	DOM	INT	***	340	Cottom-Winslow: *Environmental Design*
0.93	DOM	INT	***	293	Crouch: *History of Architecture from Stonhenge to Skyscrapers*
0.93	DOM	INT	***	329	AIA *Encyclopedia of Architecture, Design, Engineering, and Construction*
0.93	DOM	DOM	122	231	Stern: *New Directions in American Architecture*, rev. ed.
0.93	DOM	DOM	123	282	Pulos: *American Design Ethic: A History of Industrial Design to 1940*
0.93	DOM	DOM	124	334	Krantz: *American Architects*
0.93	DOM	DOM	125	227	Milwaukee Art Center: *An American Architecture*
0.93	DOM	DOM	126	274	McCoy & Goldstein: *Guide to U.S. Architecture 1940–1980*
0.93	DOM	INT	***	165	Hillier: *From Tepees to Towers*
0.93	DOM	INT	***	131	Fletcher: *A History of Architecture* (ed. Cordingley)
0.92	DOM	DOM	127	246	Diamondstein: *American Architecture Now*
0.92	DOM	INT	***	76	Giedion: *Space, Time, and Architecture*
0.92	DOM	DOM	128	177	Stern: *New Directions in American Architecture*
0.92	DOM	DOM	129	91	AIA: *Contemporary Architecture in the United States 1947–1949*
0.91	DOM	DOM	130	161	Stern: *40 Under 40: An Exhibition of Young Talent in Architecture*
0.91	DOM	DOM	131	302	Stimpson: *Fieldguide to Landmarks of Modern Architecture in United States*
0.91	DOM	INT	***	191	*Encyclopaedia Britannica*, 14th ed. (1972)
0.91	DOM	DOM	132	291	AIA J.: *7th to 9th Annual Reviews of New American Architecture*
0.91	DOM	DOM	133	102	Ferriss: *Power in Buildings*

Figure 10.5   (continued)

[1]	[2]	[3]	[4]	[5]	[6]
0.91	DOM	DOM	134	338	Wright: *Sourcebook of Contemporary North American Architecture*
0.91	DOM	DOM	135	140	Creighton: *American Architecture*
0.91	DOM	DOM	136	323	Larkin et al.: *Colonial Design in the New World*
0.91	DOM	DOM	137	15	Longfellow: "The Course of American Architecture"
0.91	DOM	DOM	138	238	*AIA J.:* 1st to 3rd Annual Reviews of New American Architecture
0.91	DOM	DOM	139	380	Packard (ed.): *Encyclopedia of American Architecture*
0.90	DOM	DOM	140	364	Thomas & Lewis: *American Architectural Masterpieces*
0.90	DOM	DOM	141	109	*Architectural Record:* "100 Years of Significant Building"
0.90	DOM	INT	***	141	*Encyclopaedia Britannica*, 14th ed. (1964)
0.90	DOM	DOM	142	75	*Pencil Points:* "Forty Under Forty"
0.90	DOM	DOM	143	264	*The World Almanac and Book of Facts 1982*
0.90	DOM	DOM	144	342	*The World Almanac and Book of Facts 1991*
0.90	DOM	DOM	145	196	Jordy: *American Buildings: Impact of European Modernism*
0.90	DOM	DOM	146	305	De Long, Searing, Stern: *American Architecture* (symposium)
0.90	DOM	DOM	147	244	Ball: *Architecture and Interior Design*
0.89	DOM	DOM	148	324	Norberg-Schulz: *New World Architecture*
0.89	DOM	DOM	149	187	*The World Almanac and Book of Facts 1972*
0.89	DOM	INT	***	297	Kostof: *A History of Architecture: Settings & Rituals*
0.89	DOM	DOM	150	134	Von Eckardt (ed.): *Mid-Century Architecture in America*
0.89	DOM	INT	***	172	Portoghesi: *Dizionario enciclopedico di architettura e urbanistica*
0.89	DOM	INT	***	58	Cheney: *The New World Architecture*
0.89	DOM	DOM	151	277	Wright: *Highlights to Recent American Architecture 1945–1978*
0.88	DOM	DOM	152	219	*The World Almanac and Book of Facts 1977*
0.88	DOM	DOM	153	306	De Long, Searing, Stern: *American Architecture* (exhibition)
0.88	DOM	INT	***	97	Hamlin, T.: *Forms and Functions of 20th Century Architecture*
0.88	DOM	DOM	154	56	Sexton: Composite of books published in 1928–31
0.88	DOM	INT	***	124	Reed: *The Golden City*
0.88	DOM	DOM	155	296	Klein & Fogle: *Clues to American Architecture*
0.88	DOM	INT	***	373	Van Vynckt (ed.): *International Dictionary of Architects & Architecture*
0.88	DOM	DOM	156	74	*Architectural Record:* "American Architecture 1891–1941"
0.87	DOM	INT	***	363	Reynolds: *Nineteenth Century Architecture*
0.87	DOM	DOM	157	221	White: *The Architecture Book*
0.87	DOM	INT	***	119	Francastel: *Les Architects Celèbres*
0.87	DOM	DOM	158	211	Varian: *American Art Deco Architecture*
0.87	DOM	DOM	159	185	Cohen: *History of American Art*
0.87	DOM	DOM	160	266	Thorndike: *Three Centuries of Notable American Architects*
0.87	DOM	DOM	161	182	Osborne: *The Oxford Companion to Art*
0.87	DOM	DOM	162	114	USIA: *Architecture USA* (ed.: Blake?)
0.86	DOM	DOM	163	361	Gowans: *Styles and Types of North American Architecture*
0.86	DOM	INT	***	214	Kulterman: *New Architecture in the World*
0.86	DOM	DOM	164	155	Fitch: *American Building: The Historical Forces that Shaped It*
0.86	DOM	DOM	165	137	Dixon: *Architectural Design Preview, USA*
0.86	DOM	INT	***	315	Musgrove (ed.): *Fletcher's History of Architecture*, 19th ed.
0.86	DOM	INT	***	256	Reid: *The Book of Buildings*
0.86	DOM	DOM	166	83	Reilly: *Some Contemporary American Buildings*
0.86	DOM	DOM	167	84	Fitch: *American Building: The Forces that Shape It*
0.86	DOM	INT	***	311	Watkin: *A History of Western Architecture*

Figure 10.5   (continued)

[1]	[2]	[3]	[4]	[5]	[6]
0.86	DOM	INT	***	159	Myers: *McGraw-Hill Dictionary of Art*
0.86	DOM	DOM	168	171	Norman: *Traveler's Guide to American Art*
0.86	DOM	DOM	169	314	Kostof: *America by Design*
0.86	DOM	INT	***	54	Hitchcock: *Modern Architecture*
0.86	DOM	DOM	170	269	*AIA J.:* 4th to 6th Annual Reviews of New American Architecture
0.85	DOM	INT	***	90	Lynes: *The Tastemakers*
0.85	DOM	DOM	171	289	Pokinski: *Development of the American Modern Style*
0.85	DOM	DOM	172	126	Condit: *American Building Art: The 19th & the 20th Centuries*
0.85	DOM	DOM	173	295	Handlin: *American Architecture*
0.85	DOM	DOM	174	270	Condit: *American Building: Materials and Techniques*
0.85	DOM	DOM	175	262	Smith, K.: *The Architecture of the United States*
0.85	DOM	DOM	176	113	Morris: *A Century of AIA*
0.85	DOM	DOM	177	327	Scully: *American Architecture and Urbanism*, new rev. ed.
0.85	DOM	DOM	178	309	Stern: *Pride of Place: Building the American Dream*
0.85	DOM	DOM	179	168	Condit: *American Building . . . from Beginning to the Present*
0.85	DOM	DOM	180	69	Newcomb: *Spanish-Colonial Architecture in the United States*
0.85	DOM	DOM	181	93	P/A: "United States Architecture 1900–1950"
0.85	DOM	DOM	182	379	Packard (ed.): *Encyclopedia of American Architecture* (main entries only)
0.84	DOM	INT	***	104	Tunnard: *The City of Man*
0.84	DOM	DOM	183	285	Hunt: *American Architecture: A Field Guide*
0.84	DOM	DOM	184	250	Hunt: *Encyclopedia of American Architecture*
0.84	DOM	DOM	185	357	Williamson: *American Architects and the Mechanics of Fame*
0.84	DOM	DOM	186	82	Mock: *Built in America 1932–1944*
0.84	DOM	DOM	187	43	Kimball: *Three Centuries of American Architecture*
0.83	DOM	INT	***	273	*Macmillan Encyclopedia of Architects* (Placzek, ed.)
0.83	DOM	DOM	188	181	Mendelowitz: *A History of American Art*
0.83	DOM	DOM	189	129	Burchard & Bush-Brown: *The Architecture of America*
0.83	DOM	INT	***	217	Pevsner: *A History of Building Types*
0.83	DOM	DOM	190	195	Jordy: *American Buildings: Progressive and Academic Ideals*
0.83	DOM	INT	***	34	*The Encyclopaedia Britannica*, 11th ed.
0.83	DOM	DOM	191	166	Ross: *Taste In America*
0.82	DOM	DOM	192	176	Scully: *American Architecture and Urbanism*
0.82	DOM	DOM	193	299	Maddex: *Built in the USA: American Buildings from A to Z*
0.82	DOM	DOM	194	237	Williamson: "An Architectural Family Tree"
0.82	DOM	DOM	195	162	*The World Almanac and Book of Facts 1967*
0.82	DOM	DOM	196	213	Hammett: *Architecture in the United States*
0.82	DOM	DOM	197	27	Mackson: *American Architecture Interiors & Furniture*
0.82	DOM	DOM	198	243	Roth: *A Concise History of American Architecture*
0.82	DOM	DOM	199	333	Kennedy (ed.): *Smithsonian Guide to Historic America*
0.82	DOM	DOM	200	218	Smith, K.: *A Pictorial History of Architecture in America*
0.82	DOM	DOM	201	222	Wodehouse: *American Architects from the Civil War to the Present*
0.81	DOM	INT	***	80	Newcomb: *History of Modern Architecture*
0.81	DOM	DOM	202	23	*The Architectural Record Great American Architects Series*
0.81	DOM	DOM	203	260	Rugoff: *Encyclopedia of American Art*
0.81	DOM	DOM	204	290	Poppeliers et al.: *What Style Is It?*
0.81	DOM	INT	***	103	Hamlin, T.: *Architecture Through the Ages*, rev ed.
0.81	DOM	DOM	205	241	Brown at al.: *American Art*

Figure 10.5   (continued)

[1]	[2]	[3]	[4]	[5]	[6]
0.81	DOM	DOM	206	300	Maddex: *Master Builders*
0.81	DOM	INT	***	30	Fletcher: *A History of Architecture*, 5th ed.
0.81	DOM	DOM	207	366	Whiffen: *American Architecture Since 1780*
0.80	DOM	DOM	208	66	Cahill & Barr: *Art in America*
0.80	DOM	DOM	209	204	Kidney: *The Architecture of Choice: Eclecticism in America 1880–1930*
0.80	DOM	INT	***	17	Gwilt: *An Encyclopedia of Architecture*
0.80	DOM	DOM	210	190	Bacon: *Architecture and Townscape*
0.80	DOM	DOM	211	21	Baedecker: *The United States*
0.80	DOM	DOM	212	110	Gutheim: *1857–1957: One Hundred Years of Architecture in America*
0.80	DOM	DOM	213	78	Saint-Gaudens: *The American Artist and His Times*
0.80	DOM	DOM	214	175	Norton: *The Arts in America: The 19th Century*
0.79	DOM	DOM	215	239	*The American Renaissance 1876–1917* (without Catalogue)
0.79	DOM	DOM	216	13	Levy: *Modern American Architecture*
0.79	DOM	DOM	217	343	Kennedy: *Rediscovering America*
0.79	DOM	DOM	218	143	Gowans: *Images of American Living*
0.79	DOM	DOM	219	41	Jackson: *American Colonial Architecture*
0.79	DOM	INT	***	71	Richardson & Corfiato: *The Art of Architecture*
0.78	DOM	DOM	220	178	Whiffen: *American Architecture Since 1780*
0.78	DOM	INT	***	116	Hitchcock: *Architecture: Nineteenth and Twentieth Centuries*
0.78	DOM	DOM	221	50	Edgell: *The American Architecture of To-day*
0.78	DOM	INT	***	40	Fletcher: *A History of Architecture*, 6th ed.
0.78	DOM	DOM	222	33	*Men and Women of America: A Biographical Dictionary*
0.78	DOM	DOM	223	25	Van Brunt: *Architecture and Society*
0.78	DOM	DOM	224	14	*L'Architecture Americaine*
0.78	DOM	DOM	225	267	Whiffen & Koepper: *American Architecture 1607–1976*
0.77	DOM	DOM	226	7	Greenough: "American Architecture" and "Aesthetics at Washington"
0.77	DOM	INT	***	86	Pevsner: *An Outline of European Architecture*
0.77	DOM	DOM	227	45	Hamlin, T.: *The American Spirit in Architecture*
0.77	DOM	DOM	228	44	Berlin: *Ausstellung Neuer Amerikanischer Baukunst*
0.77	DOM	DOM	229	200	Glubok: Composite of books 1970–1973
0.77	DOM	DOM	230	85	Kouwenhoven: *Made in America*
0.77	DOM	DOM	231	81	Hamlin, T.: *Greek Revival Architecture in America*
0.77	DOM	DOM	232	35	Schuyler: *American Architecture and Other Writings*
0.77	DOM	DOM	233	37	Hamlin, A.D.F.: "25 Years of American Architecture"
0.77	DOM	DOM	234	156	Green: *American Art: A Historical Survey*
0.77	DOM	DOM	235	216	Platt: *America's Gilded Age*
0.77	DOM	DOM	236	28	Schuyler: "United States Architecture"
0.77	DOM	DOM	237	47	*The Architectural Record* American Architect Golden Anniversary Number
0.76	DOM	DOM	238	128	Pierson & Davidson: *Arts in the United States*
0.76	DOM	DOM	239	107	Scully: *The Shingle Style and the Stick Style*
0.76	DOM	DOM	240	209	Loth & Trousdale: *The Only Proper Style*
0.76	DOM	INT	***	59	Conant (ed.): *Modern Architecture*
0.76	DOM	INT	***	94	Watterson: *Five Thousand Years of Building*
0.76	DOM	INT	***	20	*The Dictionary of Architecture*
0.76	DOM	DOM	241	135	*The World Almanac and Book of Facts 1962*

Figure 10.5 (continued)

[1]	[2]	[3]	[4]	[5]	[6]
0.76	DOM	DOM	242	125	Andrews: *Architecture in America*
0.76	DOM	INT	***	115	Gloag: *Guide to Western Architecture*
0.75	DOM	DOM	243	240	*The American Renaissance 1876–1917* (Catalogue only)
0.75	DOM	DOM	244	118	Bode: *The Anatomy of American Popular Culture 1840–61*
0.75	DOM	DOM	245	108	Tunnard & Reed: *American Skyline*
0.75	DOM	DOM	246	331	Devlin: *Portraits of American Architecture*
0.75	DOM	INT	***	29	Sturgis: *A Dictionary of Architecture and Building*
0.75	DOM	DOM	247	10	Jarves: *The Art-idea*
0.74	DOM	INT	***	22	Hamlin, A.D.F.: *A Text-Book of the History of Architecture*
0.74	DOM	DOM	248	332	Kennedy: *Greek Revival America*
0.74	DOM	DOM	249	360	Garrett: *Classical America*
0.74	DOM	DOM	250	89	Larkin: *Art and Life in America*
0.74	DOM	DOM	251	101	Morrison: *Early American Arschitecture*
0.74	DOM	DOM	252	236	Pierson: *American Buildings: Technology & the Picturesque*
0.74	DOM	DOM	253	234	Andrews: *Architecture, Ambition and Americans*, rev. ed.
0.74	DOM	DOM	254	42	Mumford: *Sticks and Stones*
0.74	DOM	DOM	255	48	Reagan: *American Architecture of the Twentieth Century*
0.73	DOM	INT	***	9	Fergusson: *History of the Modern Styles of Architecture*
0.73	DOM	DOM	256	3	Dunlap: *History of the Arts of Design in the United States*
0.73	DOM	DOM	257	169	McLanathan: *The American Tradition in the Arts*
0.73	DOM	DOM	258	39	Greber: *L'Architecture aux États-Unies*
0.73	DOM	DOM	259	52	Jackman: *American Arts*
0.73	DOM	INT	***	51	Hamlin, A.D.F.: *A Text-Book of the History of Architecture*, 18th pr.
0.73	DOM	INT	***	61	Fletcher: *A History of Architecture*, 9th ed.
0.73	DOM	DOM	260	111	Maas: *The Gingerbread Age*
0.73	DOM	INT	***	65	Whitaker: *The Story of Architecture*
0.73	DOM	DOM	261	99	Jones: *O Strange New World*
0.72	DOM	INT	***	18	Fergusson: *History of Modern Styles of Architecture*
0.72	DOM	DOM	262	67	Tallmadge: *The Story of Architecture in America*, rev. ed.
0.72	DOM	INT	***	72	Hamlin, T.: *Architecture Through the Ages*
0.72	DOM	DOM	263	257	Rifkind: *A Field Guide to American Architecture*
0.72	DOM	DOM	264	55	LaFollette: *Art in America*
0.72	DOM	DOM	265	19	Schuyler: *American Architecture—Studies*
0.72	DOM	DOM	266	31	Bragdon: "Architecture in The United States"
0.71	DOM	DOM	267	11	Benjamin: *Art in America*
0.71	DOM	DOM	268	224	Brown: *American Art to 1900*
0.71	DOM	DOM	269	184	Pierson: *American Building: Colonial and Neo-classical Styles*
0.71	DOM	DOM	270	49	Tallmadge: *The Story of Architecture in America*
0.71	DOM	INT	***	38	Kimball & Edgell: *A History of Architecture*
0.70	DOM	INT	***	5	Tuthill: *History of Architecture from the Earliest Times*
0.70	DOM	DOM	271	106	Andrews: *Architecture, Ambition, and Americans*
0.70	DOM	INT	***	32	Hamlin, A.D.F.: *A Text-Book of the History of Architecture*, 8th ed.
0.69	DOM	DOM	272	60	Hoak & Church: *Masterpieces of Architecture in the United States*
0.69	DOM	DOM	273	6	Sears: *A New and Popular Pictorial Description of the United States*
0.68	DOM	DOM	274	53	Kimball: *American Architecture*
0.68	DOM	DOM	275	100	*The World Almanac and Book of Facts 1952*
0.68	DOM	INT	***	8	Heck: *The Art of Building in Ancient and Modern Times*
0.68	DOM	DOM	276	170	Millar: *The Architects of the American Colonies*

Figure 10.5   (continued)

[1]	[2]	[3]	[4]	[5]	[6]
0.68	DOM	DOM	277	26	Ware: *The Georgian Period*
0.67	DOM	INT	***	16	Arnold: *Studies in Architecture at Home and Abroad*
0.67	DOM	DOM	278	2	*American Journal of Science & Arts:* "Architecture in the United States"
0.67	DOM	INT	***	24	Statham: *Modern Architecture*
0.66	DOM	DOM	279	150	Early: *Romanticism in American Architecture*
0.66	DOM	DOM	280	36	Eberlein: *The Architecture of Colonial America*
0.65	DOM	DOM	281	215	Panek: *American Architectural Styles 1600–1940*
0.65	DOM	DOM	282	1	Latrobe(?): "State of the Fine Arts in the United States"
0.64	DOM	DOM	283	186	Gillon: *Early Illustrations of American Architecture*
0.64	DOM	DOM	284	46	Jackson: *Development of American Architecture 1783–1830*
0.64	DOM	DOM	285	70	*The World Almanac and Book of Facts 1937*
0.63	DOM	DOM	286	12	van Rensselaer: "Recent Architecture in America"
0.62	DOM	DOM	287	4	Cleveland: *Review of American Builder's General Price Book*
0.61	DOM	DOM	288	163	Tatum: *The Arts in America: The Colonial Period*
0.60	DOM	DOM	289	96	Eberlein & Hubbard: *American Georgian Architecture*
0.60	DOM	DOM	290	87	Bannister: *From Colony to Nation*
0.58	DOM	DOM	291	64	*The World Almanac and Book of Facts 1932*

Domestic and International American Architects

An architect's international coefficient reveals another still unrecognized dimension of his record, and by extension, of his or her historical profile and cultural significance.

A series of prominent architects are listed in figure 10.6, ranked by their international coefficients, from the most international to the most domestic. Very large and very small coefficients denote names with a strong correlation to one frame of reference or the other; these are the names that play a significant role in the outcome of the prediction game. Coefficients close to one, on the other hand, identify architects whose presence in a text has little impact one way or the other. Very famous architects generally command this type of value, because they are equally prominent in national and international discourse.

Alvar Aalto and Le Corbusier head the list as the most international. With their gigantic roles in the world scene but only limited commissions in the United States, it was only to be expected that they would be cited more often in the literature about the world than about America; this is trivial, and it is not what the table reveals. Le Corbusier and Aalto are counted in the data base only if their American works—the Baker Dormitory, the 1939 New York Fair Swedish Pavilion, the Carpenter Center, the United Nations Secretariat—are referenced. It is not the names of the masters what is at stake, but only the

Figure 10.6 Selected famous architects sorted according to their international coefficients

Column headings:
[1] International coefficient
[2] Birth date
[3] Name

[1]	[2]	[3]
2.00	1898	Alvar Aalto
1.97	1887	Le Corbusier (Charles Eduard Jeanneret)
1.75	1904	Bruce Alonzo Goff
1.61	1909	Gordon Bunshaft
1.53	1932	Peter D. Eisenman
1.48	1901	Louis I. Kahn
1.45	1887	Eric Mendelsohn
1.43	1940	Helmut Jahn
1.41	1918	Paul Rudolph
1.40	1939	Robert A. M. Stern
1.38	1886	Ludwig Mies van der Rohe
1.37	1907	Charles Osmand Eames
1.37	1910	Eero Saarinen
1.36	1895	Buckminster Fuller
1.34	1902	Josep Lluis Sert
1.29	1883	Walter Gropius
1.27	1923	Frank O. Gehry
1.24	1925	Robert Venturi
1.22	1902	Marcel Breuer
1.22	1892	Richard J. Neutra
1.21	1934	Michael Graves
1.21	1897	Skidmore, Owings, & Merrill
1.21	1915	Kallmann, McKinnell, & Knowles
1.21	1926	Cesar Pelli
1.20	1867	Frank Lloyd Wright
1.16	1941	Thomas Hall Beeby
1.15	1856	Louis Sullivan
1.14	1906	Philip Johnson
1.13	1912	Minoru Yamasaki
1.12	1883	The Architects' Collaborative
1.12	1931	Denise Scott Brown
1.10	1930	Stanley Tigerman
1.09	1922	Roche & Dinkeloo
1.09	1908	Max Abramovitz
1.08	1896	William Lescaze
1.08	1838	Henry Hobson Richardson
1.08	1949	Arquitectonica (or DPZ)
1.08	1934	Richard Meier
1.04	1895	Wallace K. Harrison
1.04	1924	John Calvin Portman, Jr.
1.03	1887	Rudolph Schindler
1.03	1846	Daniel Hudson Burnham

Figure 10.6   (continued)

[1]	[2]	[3]
1.02	1925	Charles W. Moore
1.02	1743	Thomas Jefferson
1.02	1930	John Rauch
1.00	1886	George Howe
1.00	1873	Eliel Saarinen
0.99	1917	I. M. Pei
0.99	1854	Holabird & Roche
0.99	1868	Greene & Greene
0.99	1806	John Augustus Roebling
0.99	1916	John Maclane Johansen
0.97	1844	Dankmar Adler
0.97	1902	Edward Durrell Stone
0.96	1850	John Wellborn Root
0.95	1832	William Le Baron Jenney
0.94	1883	William Van Alen
0.94	1862	Bernard Maybeck
0.92	1890	C. F. Murphy Associates
0.90	1800	James Bogardus
0.90	1868	John Mead Howells
0.88	1933	John H. Burgee
0.88	1935	William Turnbull, Jr.
0.86	1764	Benjamin Henry Latrobe
0.84	1881	Raymond Mathewson Hood
0.83	1804	Thomas Ustick Walter
0.80	1788	William Strickland
0.80	1869	Albert Kahn
0.78	1847	McKim, Mead, & White
0.77	1864	Warren & Wetmore
0.77	1762c	James Hoban
0.76	1839	Frank Furness
0.75	1866	Henry Bacon
0.74	1827	Richard Morris Hunt
0.73	1880	Purcell & Elmslie
0.72	1763	Charles Bulfinch
0.72	1781	Robert Mills
0.72	1899	Pietro Belluschi
0.72	1915	Edward Larrabee Barnes
0.72	1873	Harvey Wiley Corbett
0.71	1877	Shreve, Lamb, & Harmon
0.70	1818	James Renwick, Jr.
0.68	1924	Mitchell Giurgola Associates
0.68	1784	Ithiel Town
0.68	1859	Cass Gilbert
0.67	1870	Irving John Gill
0.66	1803	Alexander Jackson Davis
0.65	1802	Richard Upjohn
0.65	1959	Maya Ying Lin
0.65	1754	Pierre Charles L'Enfant

Figure 10.6   (continued)

[1]	[2]	[3]
0.64	1837	George Browne Post
0.64	1759	Dr. William Thornton
0.64	1938	Charles Gwathmey
0.61	1895	Wurster, Bernardi, & Emmons
0.61	1792	John Haviland
0.61	1688	John Smibert
0.60	1676c	Andrew Hamilton
0.60	1800	Isaiah Rogers
0.59	1869	Bertram Grosvenor Goodhue
0.59	1874	John Russell Pope
0.58	1858	Carrère & Hastings
0.58	1822	Frederick Law Olmsted
0.58	1815	Andrew Jackson Downing
0.57	1780	Alexander Parris
0.57	1863	Cram, Goodhue, & Ferguson
0.55	1760c	Étienne Sulpice Hallet
0.55	1684c	Dr. John Kearsley
0.54	1848	Charles B. Atwood
0.53	1876	Paul Philippe Cret
0.53	1757	Samuel McIntire
0.51	1722	Charles Louis Clérisseau
0.50	1710?	Thomas (or James) McBean
0.48	1716	Peter Harrison
0.47	1771	Asher Benjamin
0.47	1824	Calvert Vaux
0.39	1761?	Mangin & McComb
0.34	1685c	Richard Munday

citations of those four buildings. Featured in one type of text and ignored in the other, discursively the buildings seem not to be in America, no matter where they are geographically.

The names that follow at the top of the list are those of some of the most conspicuous American architects of the generation who made their impact after World War II. This group was identified at the end of chapter 3 for their extraordinary impact on the literature; now it can be added that the literature they conquered and directed was strongly international in its frame of reference. This was consistent with their personal and professional orientations: the stylistic, social, urban, technical, and ideological problems they addressed in their buildings, teaching, and writing were of a global scale. Local, regional, and national issues were secondary to their preoccupations. (It is not surprising that many architects of the group are also cotextual: see, for example, nation 3, tribe 9, family 1, and nation 4, especially tribe 9, in figure 3, chapter 9. By the same token, many pairs of textually distant architects listed in figure 9.2 contain names from different frame of reference.)

Figure 10.6 includes only very prominent architects. To see some additional names at both ends of the scale, figures 10.7 and 10.8 list less frequently cited architects with very high or very low international coefficients.

Besides Aalto and Le Corbusier, several architects near the top in figure 10.6 are not American born: Mendelsohn, Jahn, Mies, Gropius, Sert, Breuer, Neutra, and Pelli. The same is true for eleven of the first fourteen individuals in figure 10.7. Seven of the eleven did very limited work in or for America. Did their nationality determine the outcome? Not necessarily. Pierre L'Enfant, from France, appears almost twice as often in the domestic is in the international literature; and another Frenchman, Charles Louis Clérisseau, who never set his foot on this land, is almost three times more likely to be cited in the national literature.[1] Because of his purported association with Jefferson for the design of the Virginia State Capitol, and because of Jefferson's importance to America, Clérisseau enjoys a privileged place in American literature, nowhere near his weight in a wider context. Discourse, not birthplace, controls an architect's international coefficient.

The international character of the literature of midcentury Europeans and the domestic frame of reference for the eighteenth-century Frenchmen comes as no surprise to those familiar with their orientation and work. Index analysis, however, not only confirms the known, but makes it more readily accessible and sometimes pushes the limits of the knowable a little farther.

The most important difference between typical architects from one frame of reference or the other is not where they were born, but when. With few exceptions, the American architects most often featured in the international literature were born in the twentieth or late nineteenth century; the average year of birth of those listed in figure 10.7 (including those of figure 10.6 with comparable coefficients) is 1907. Most of those at the other end of the spectrum were born before the midnineteenth century; their average date of birth is 1795. The age distribution is congruent with the fact that the architecture of the United States, like the nation itself, played a modest role in the world up to the midtwentieth century. (Tallmadge was a bit rushed in 1927 when he proclaimed that the United States "recently achieved world supremacy in architecture."[2])

Perhaps as a consequence of this state of affairs, much attention is paid in America to its architectural heritage. Such efforts are, and will necessarily remain, provincial. They resemble struggles in developing countries to rediscover, reevaluate, and, if necessary, invent local and national cultural identities. In America, however, the situation is more remarkable. It is not that American architects of the eighteenth, nineteenth, and early twentieth centuries are ignored by foreign writers, as happens to architects from culturally peripheral countries, past and present; rather, Colonial and early Republican architects *are overlooked by American scholars* when they write about the architecture of the world. The lesser standing of early American architecture worldwide is indelibly etched into the fabric of architectural literature, even that produced in this country.

Figure 10.7 Selected architects with high international coefficients (names reported in figure 10.6 excluded)

Column headings:
[1] International coefficient
[2] Birth date
[3] Name

[1]	[2]	[3]
2.95	1926	Oswald Mathias Ungers
2.59	1870	Adolf Loos
2.29	1885	Ludwig K. Hilberseimer
2.21	1944	OMA (Office for Metropolitan Architecture)
2.02	1907	Oscar Niemeyer
1.97	1948	Thomas Gordon Smith
1.80	1932	James Wines
1.75	1890	Frederick Kiesler
1.69	1832	Gustave Eiffel
1.56	1895	Lászlo Moholy-Nagy
1.49	1929	John Hejduk
1.47	1950	Zaha Hadid
1.46	1889	Sven Markelius
1.46	1900	Serge Chermayeff
1.44	1811	Elisha Graves Otis
1.39	1940	Steven Izenour
1.39	1770?	Robert Owen
1.39	1920	Walter A. Netsch
1.38	1942	Jorge Silvetti
1.38	1946	Daniel Libeskind
1.35	1940?	John S. Hagmann
1.33	1950?	Bernard Tschumi
1.30	1942	Rodolfo Machado
1.30	1943	Emilio Ambasz
1.28	1893	Norman Bel Geddes
1.28	1918	Benjamin Thompson
1.27	1901	Konrad Wachsmann
1.26	1807	John Kellum
1.26	1938	Allan Greenberg
1.23	1942	Stuart Cohen
1.23	1848	Louis Comfort Tiffany
1.22	1901	Walt Disney
1.21	1929	Herb Greene
1.20	1940	Batey & Mack
1.17	1888	Raymond & Rado
1.12	1910	Matthew Nowicki
1.12	1949	Michael Rotondi

Figure 10.8 Selected architects with low international coefficients (names reported in figure 10.6 excluded)

Column headings:
[1]   International coefficient
[2]   Birth date
[3]   Name

[1]	[2]	[3]
0.44	1842	William Appleton Potter
0.43	1895	Gardner A. Dailey
0.43	1733	Joseph Brown
0.43	1806	Colonel James Harrison Dakin
0.42	1712?	Samuel Cardy
0.42	1847	Ernest Flagg
0.41	1903	Whittlesey, Conklin, & Rossant
0.41	1801	James C. Bucklin
0.41	1872	Addison Mizner
0.40	1810	John Notman
0.40	1705	Richard Taliaferro
0.40	1809	Orson Squire Fowler
0.40	1912	William Wesley Peters
0.39	1833	William Ralph Emerson
0.39	1847	Henry Janeway Hardenbergh
0.39	1676	Governor Alexander Spotswood
0.39	1874	Delano & Aldrich
0.38	1861	Day & Klauder
0.36	1732	George Washington
0.36	1798	James Gallier, Sr.
0.35	1731	John Hawks
0.34	1763	George Hadfield
0.34	1815	Samuel Sloan
0.33	1845	Peabody & Stearns
0.31	1793c	William Jay
0.30	1734	William Buckland
0.30	1722	Robert S. Smith
0.30	1758	David Manigault (or Gabriel)
0.29	1859	Henry Ives Cobb
0.28	1696	Edmund Woolley

Shifting Frames of Reference

John Hejduk appears in figure 10.7 near the international pole with a coefficient of 1.49; Michael Graves, with 1.21, is nearer to the middle (figure 10.6), and Charles Gwathmey, with a coefficient of only 0.64, is closer to the domestic end of the spectrum (figure 10.6). The stylistic, generational, and historical links among these men became obvious since joint appearance, with Meier and Eisenman, in the famous *Five Architects* of 1972.[3] Why are their coefficients so far apart?

An architect's position in the spectrum is not carved in stone; with new texts appearing and old ones loosing currency, the placing is bound to shift. Histograms similar to the ones of chapter 6 are drawn for selected architects in figures 10.9 through 10.11, distinguishing the citations by frame of reference of the text with appropriate hues of shading. Citation percentages are measured as usual along the left side vertical scale.

International coefficients are computed again, looking at active texts only rather than at the architect's entire citation record. Instead of a single value for a whole life span, we obtain arrays of yearly coefficients reflecting the dynamic evolution in international standing during the person's lifetime and beyond. The coefficients are also graphed on the diagram using a logarithmic scale drawn along the right side edge. The value 1, which indicates neutrality, is placed in the middle of the graph. When the dotted line is in the upper part the predominant citations are international; in the lower part the prevailing citations are domestic.

The curves open to scrutiny still another dimension in the career of an architect through the literature. Even if we knew nothing else about his literary or architectural record, the position of the curve in relation to the middle horizontal would tell us whether his contributions were discussed and evaluated within the context of ideas relevant to domestic or international discourse. We do not know what is being said about him unless we read the texts; but we can assume that whatever is being predicated, the predicate involves a relationship with other architects whose work he is said to have supported, equaled, developed, modified, or opposed, as the case might be. We can tell from the graph whether his position in the universe is triangulated in the texts by relations of similarity or opposition to architects belonging to one frame of reference or the other.

The curves sometimes follow peculiar, recognizable patterns. A pattern is characterized by starting, developing, and concluding always in the same band, upper, middle, or lower. When the pattern is shared by several American architects, it tells us something about the ways in which the group achieved literary notoriety.

Figure 10.9 shows the curves for architects with high international standing, from figure 10.6. Le Corbusier's early citations are related to his participation

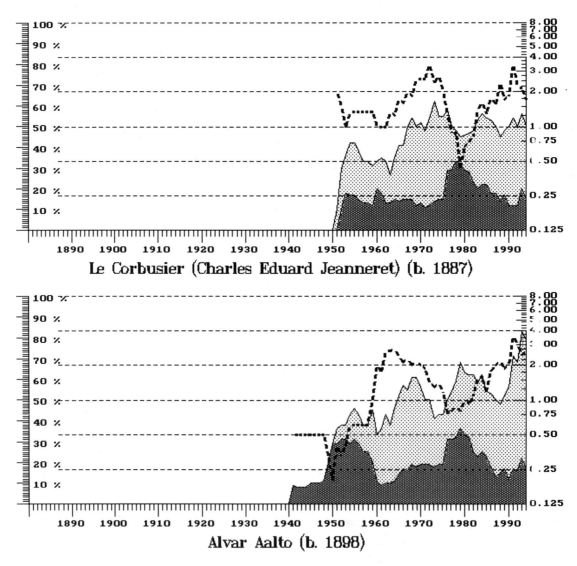

Figure 10.9   Selected modern architects

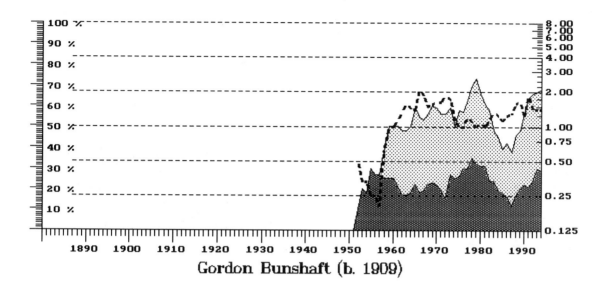

Gordon Bunshaft (b. 1909)

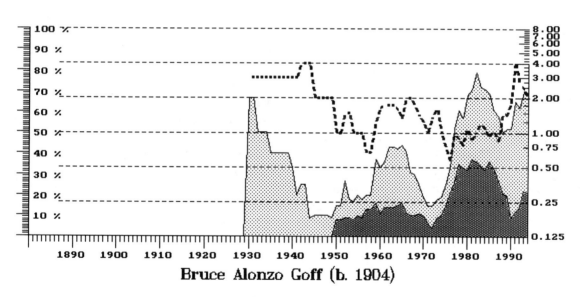

Bruce Alonzo Goff (b. 1904)

Figure 10.9   (continued)

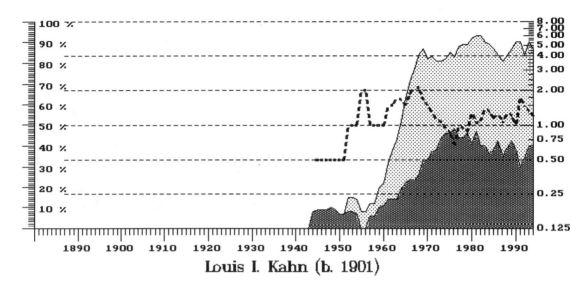

Figure 10.9   (continued)

in the design of the United Nations Headquarters in New York, his only architectural work in the United States until the 1960s. Giedion's *A Decade of Contemporary Architecture* (1951) is the first text in the corpus to acknowledge him, and it is international. Another text of the same orientation follows the next year (Hamlin's *Forms and Functions of Twentieth-Century Architecture*), along with one of a domestic frame of reference: Hitchcock and Johnson's *Built in USA* (1952). A few other publications ensue during the decade, keeping approximately the same profile—a slight preponderance of international texts. Then comes the commission for the Carpenter Center for the Visual Arts at Harvard University (1961–1964). Its literary impact is quick and significant, but only in international texts. The curve peaks in 1972, with a maximum in the international literature and an all-time low in the local scene. Domestic interest in the Carpenter Center grows a little bit during the middle and late 1970s, briefly bringing down the index toward the neutral area. This is followed by a decline in domestic interest and a clear tilting of the curve toward the international pole.

Aalto's early American work in New York, on the other hand, was initially only noticed in the domestic context. His standing in the international literature, largely based on the MIT Baker Dormitory, peaked in 1960 when Le Corbusier's was at its lowest, and then again in recent years.

A common pattern can be seen among the trajectories portrayed in figure 10.9: with the exception of Goff, the architects were first noticed in the domestic arena, and made their impact in international discourse only after a number of years. The pattern is present, although not as markedly, in the textual career of Louis Kahn. It started in the domestic arena and rose through the 1960s,

Citations in international texts	(left side scale)
Citations in domestic texts	(left side scale)
International index	(right side scale)

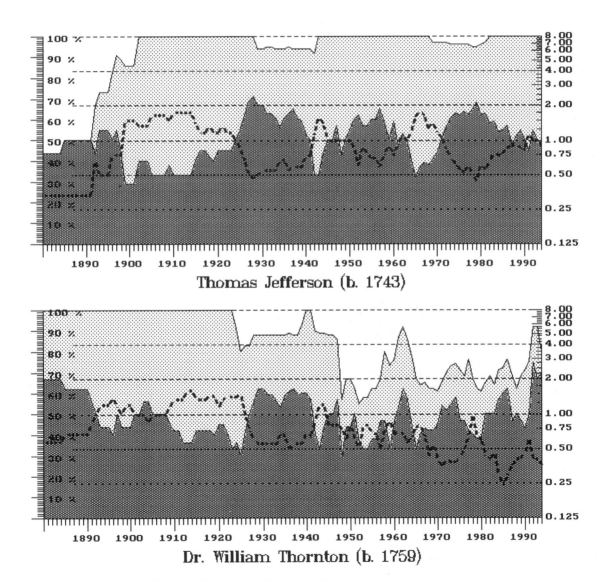

Figure 10.10   Selected federal architects

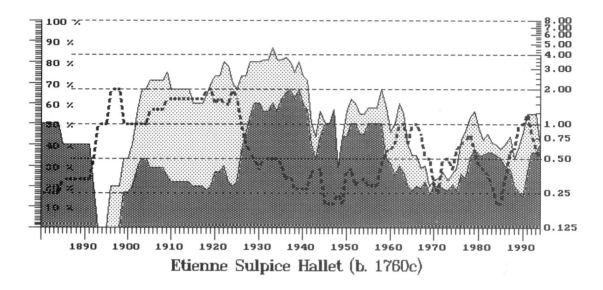

Etienne Sulpice Hallet (b. 1760c)

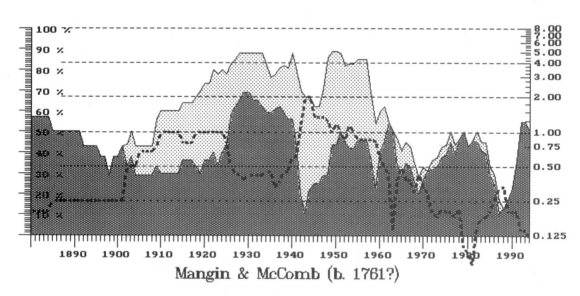

Mangin & McComb (b. 1761?)

Figure 10.10   (continued)

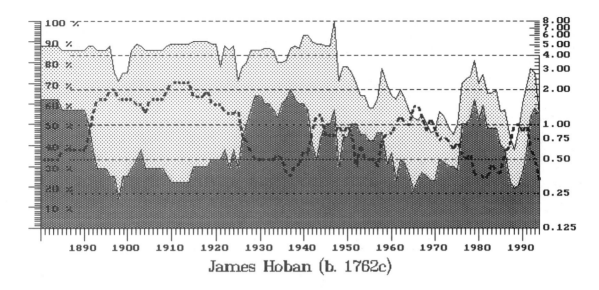

James Hoban (b. 1762c)

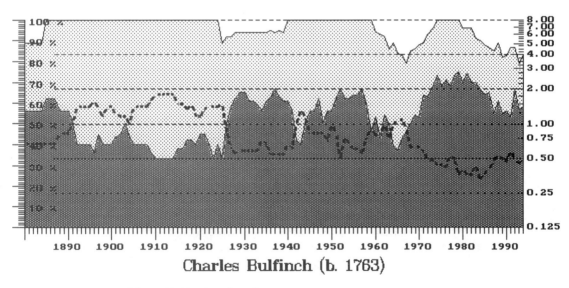

Charles Bulfinch (b. 1763)

Figure 10.10   (continued)

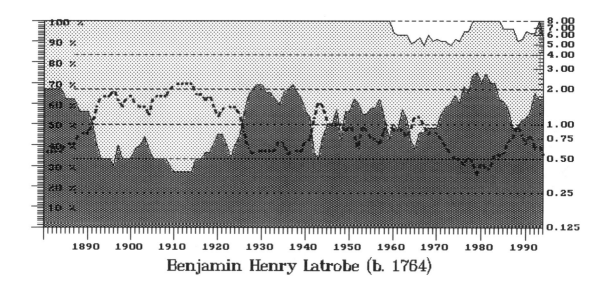

Benjamin Henry Latrobe (b. 1764)

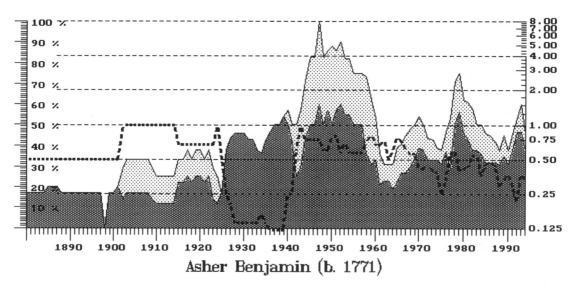

Asher Benjamin (b. 1771)

Figure 10.10   (continued)

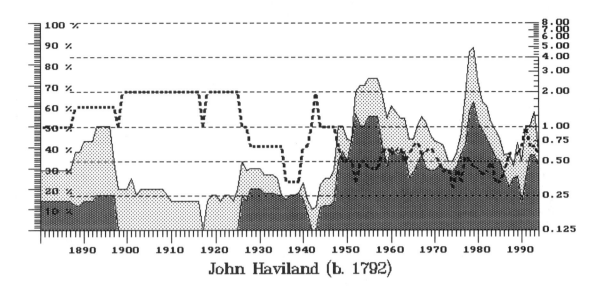

John Haviland (b. 1792)

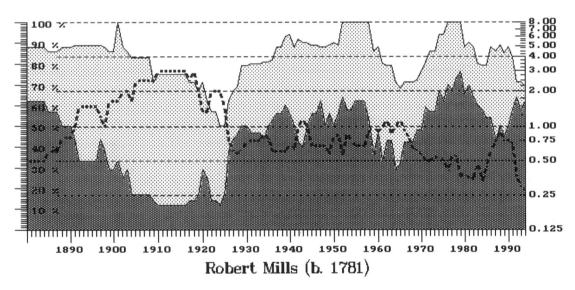

Robert Mills (b. 1781)

Figure 10.10   (continued)

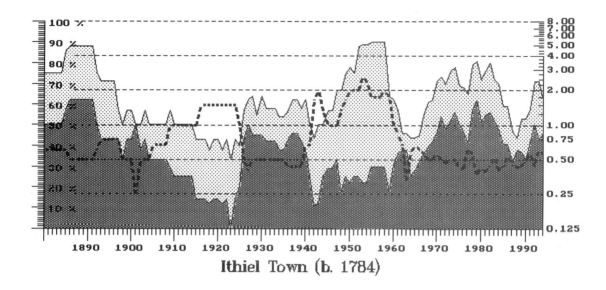

Ithiel Town (b. 1784)

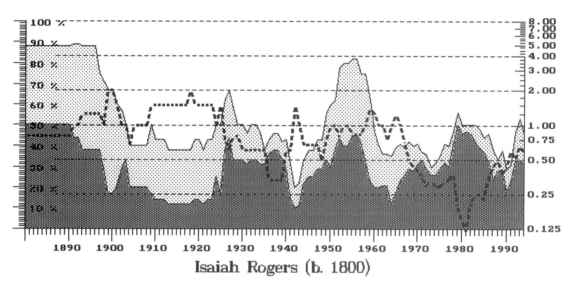

Isaiah Rogers (b. 1800)

Figure 10.10   (continued)

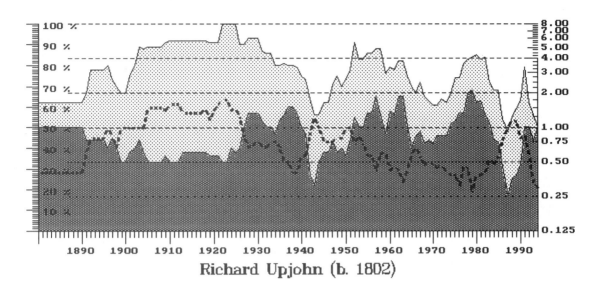

Richard Upjohn (b. 1802)

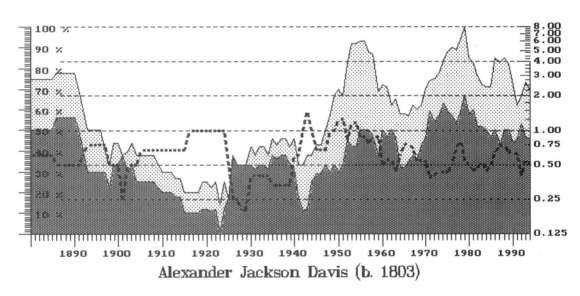

Alexander Jackson Davis (b. 1803)

Figure 10.10   (continued)

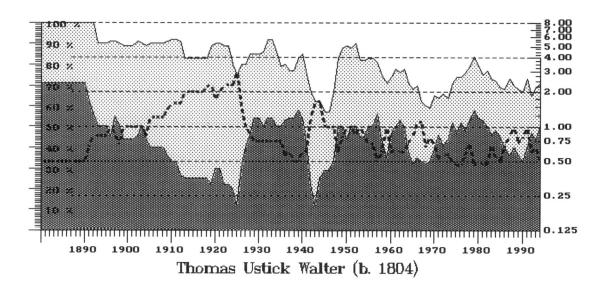

Thomas Ustick Walter (b. 1804)

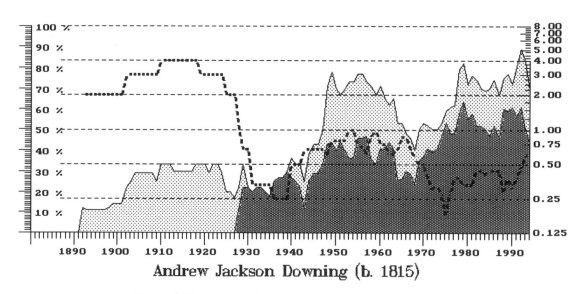

Andrew Jackson Downing (b. 1815)

Figure 10.10   (continued)

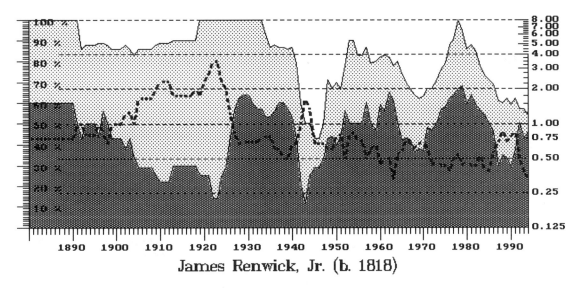

James Renwick, Jr. (b. 1818)

Figure 10.10 (continued)

especially after the completion of his Richards Medical Research Building at the University of Pennsylvania (1964). The rise was steeper in the international than in the domestic literature. Overall, his international index grew slowly but steadily.

Few American architects of superstar status in the twentieth century achieved fame directly from the international literature; most of them made their initial marks in texts of a national scope. This finding must not be confused with the well-known but completely unrelated fact of successful persons achieving notoriety in increasingly wider circles, locally, regionally, and nationally, and only as a final step internationally. The international texts of the corpus are not necessarily wider in scope than the national ones. A book devoted to a segment of the twentieth century may well have a "smaller" subject matter than one coping with the totality of American architecture; as a result, it may command finer levels of detail and cite local architects who would not normally be expected to appear in a general national survey.

Besides, there was a period in the architectural history of this country when major architects entered the literature directly from the international scene. With few exceptions, every notable American architect born between 1743 and 1818 left his mark in the international literature before being noticed in the one devoted to America only (figure 10.10). The exceptions ares L'Enfant, McIntire, and Parris. The curves for Strickland, Bogardus, and John A. Roebling are inconclusive. The pattern becomes less stable for persons born after 1818.

Architects sharing a stylistic or historical unit often display a similar evolution in their international indexes, suggesting that the curves reflect not only

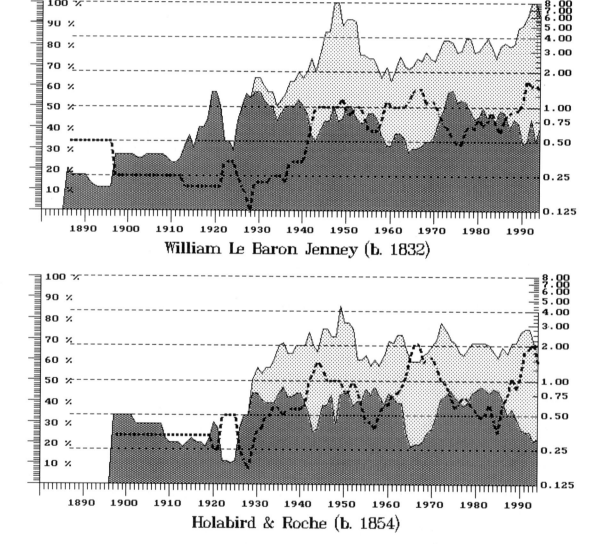

Figure 10.11 The Chicago School

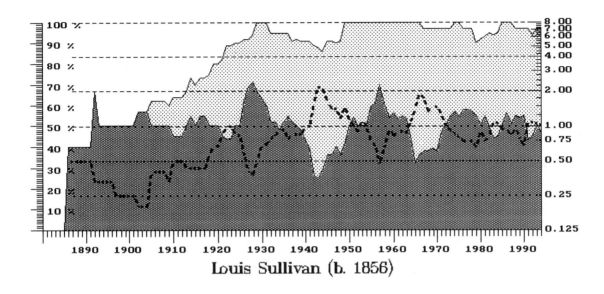

Louis Sullivan (b. 1856)

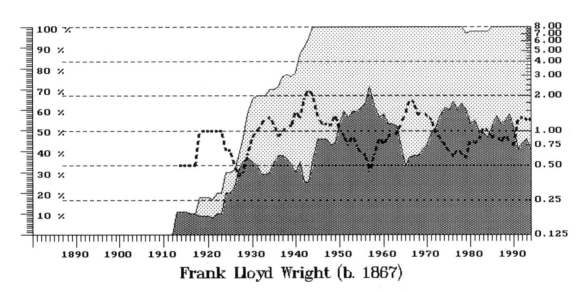

Frank Lloyd Wright (b. 1867)

Figure 10.11   (continued)

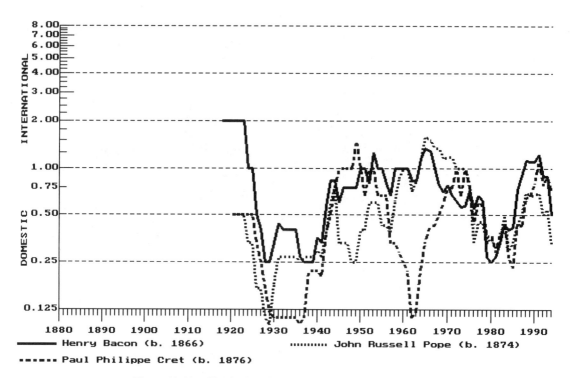

Figure 10.12 Classical architects

individual but groupal development. Jenney, Holabird & Roche, and Sullivan, linked in their careers and their historiographies by their participation in the Chicago School, made their presence felt in the domestic literature first (figure 10.11). Jenney and Holabird & Roche never leaned toward the international scene, unlike Sullivan; their curves remain around or below the middle ground. Still, an overall dynamic is common to all three architects, reflected by the parallelism in the evolution of their international coefficients.

Wright shows a slightly stronger international presence, at least in the second stretch of his ascent, during the 1930s and 1940s. Once his supremacy is established, the curve necessarily remains in the middle area of the diagram, because with his gigantic stature he becomes an inevitable point of reference in both types of discourses.

For the sake cf simplicity and economy of space, only the evolution of the coefficients is given in the ensuing figures. The coefficients are more revealing than the breakdown of citations. The international and domestic frames of reference in the literary careers of Bacon, Pope, and Crct also evolved in parallel (figure 10.12), like their histograms (figures 5.10 and 5.11). Not only were they cited approximately with the same frequency, but their citations were split between the national and international frames of reference in similar ways. This suggests the existence of groups of related architects and texts, discussed in the preceding chapter.

The emergence of the leading architects of the International Style during the 1940s was very different (figure 10.13). Although they generally started form the middle area, they unequivocally evolved toward the international pole. With their gigantic role, however, they dominated both types of literature. This precluded significant departures from the center or wide oscillations in the curves, in contrast to the ones of figure 10.12.

Figure 10.14 shows still another pattern, visible in the curves of California regionalists Maybeck, the Greene brothers, and Gill. Starting from the neutral central zone, they became increasingly stronger in the domestic literature until the last decade, when a tilt toward the other side took place.

Schindler and Neutra initiated their careers in this country as European emigres, under the spell of the International Movement. Their international presence was stronger at first; but they gradually become disengaged from the East Coast and Midwestern power centers dominated by Gropius and Mies, and established their own regional identity in California. As this happened, their indexes sloped toward the domestic pole (figure 10.15). Regionalism plays a larger role in the domestic frame of reference than in the international one, as evidenced by the leanings in the curves of William Wurster and Harwell Hamilton Harris (figure 10.16).

Although they were not regionalists, the literary careers of Edward Larrabee Barnes and Romualdo Giurgola also evolved almost entirely within a domestic frame of reference (figure 10.16). Buckminster Fuller, Paul Rudolph, John Portman, and Cesar Pelli, on the other hand, came to literary existence almost entirely within the wider outlook of the architecture of the world (figure 10.17), in consonance with, or in contradistinction to, other worldwide personalities and from the perspective of worldwide issues.

Architects of the younger generation are also associated with one type of discourse or the other. Donlyn Lyndon, Thom Mayne, and Susana Torre have all been featured more prominently in the domestic than the international literature (figure 10.18), and the reverse is true of James Wines, Christopher Alexander, Batey & Mack, and Rem Koolhaas (figure 10.19). Wines's and Alexander's strong showing in international discourse may perhaps relate to their embrace of issues of universal appeal, such as witticism or user participation, as opposed to the more indigenous nature of the concerns raised by critics in relation to the work of, say, Lyndon.

Agrest & Gandelsonas, Rodolfo Machado, Jorge Silvetti, and Emilio Ambasz are sometimes thought of as a group—the Argentineans—because of their ancestry, personal connections, similar theoretical stances, and frequent common presence in certain journals, professional circles, and universities. They share, too, in a discursive space: their literary careers evolved in an international frame of reference (figure 10.20). Susana Torre is also a member of this loosely defined group, yet in terms of discourse she belongs elsewhere (figure 10.18). Index analytical classifications may or may not coincide with more conventional groupings.

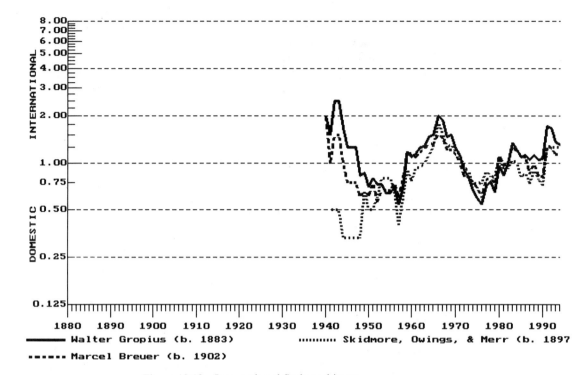

Figure 10.13   International Style architects

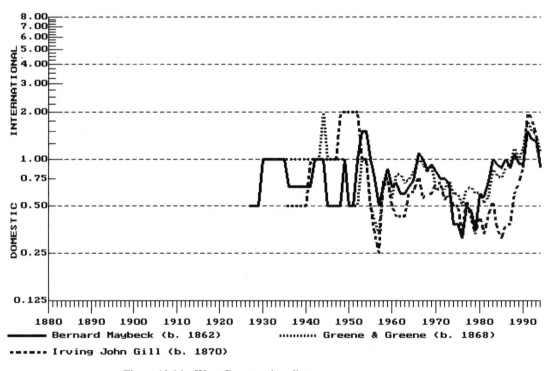

Figure 10.14   West Coast regionalists

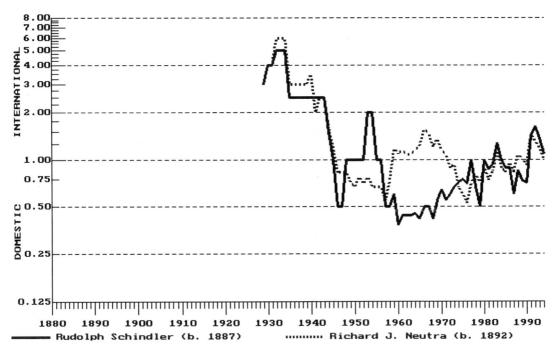

Figure 10.15   Modern regionalists

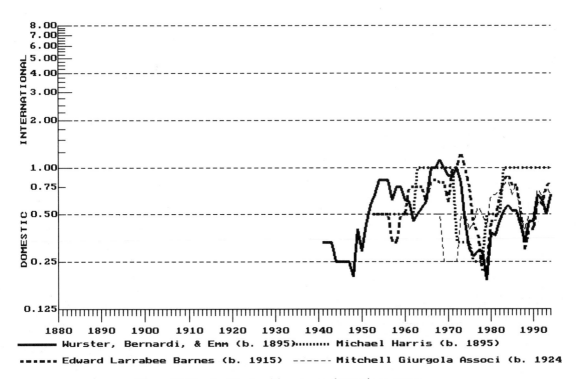

Figure 10.16   Architects with a strong domestic presence

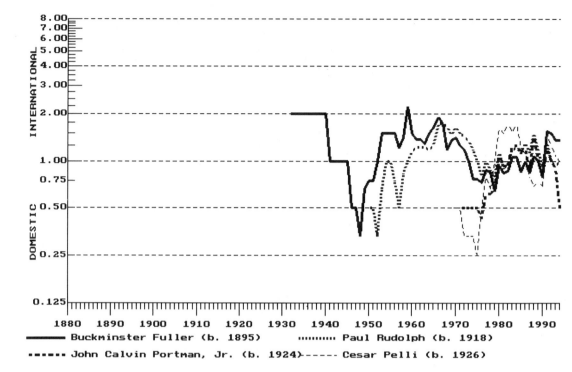

Figure 10.17   Architects with a strong international presence

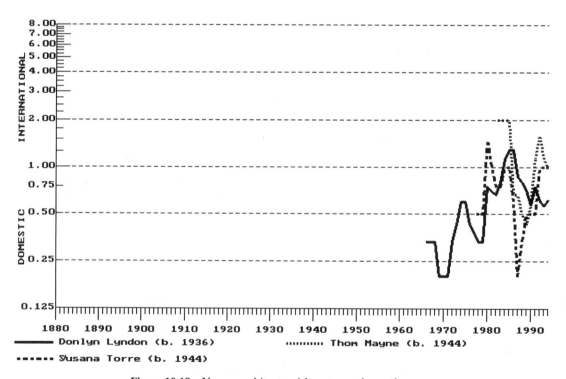

Figure 10.18   Young architects with a strong domestic presence

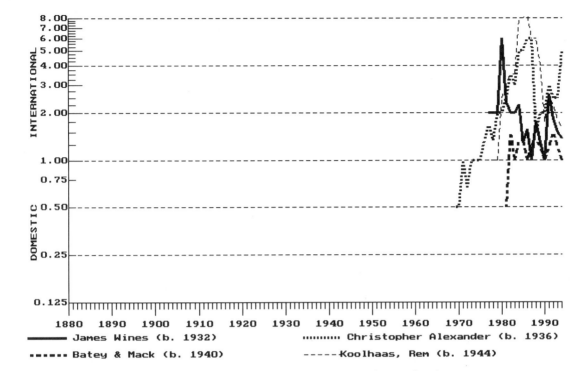

Figure 10.19   Young architects with a strong international presence

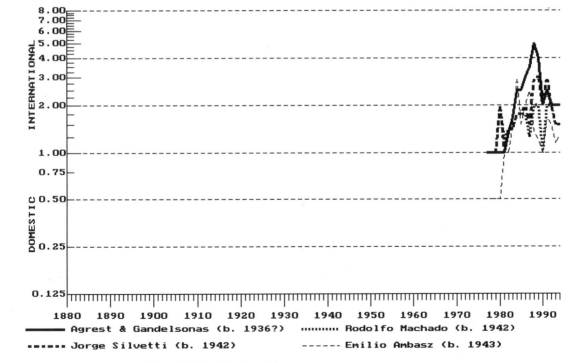

Figure 10.20   The Argentineans

As shown in figure 10.10, it was common for architects of the early Republican times to start their literary careers in the international arena and to become established in the national frame of reference only as a second step. The reverse is true for many contemporary American architects, such as Philip Johnson, Minoru Yamasaki, I. M. Pei, Charles Moore, Robert Venturi, Peter Eisenman, and Robert A. M. Stern (figures 10.21 and 10.22).

The question about the divergent international coefficients of Hejduk, Gwathmey, and Graves, left unanswered at the beginning of this section, can now be answered. The three architects did, indeed, arise jointly on the literary horizon around the late 1960s, as recognized and for a time consolidated by the publication of *Five Architects*; but their paths in the literature separated at the mid-1970s (figure 10.23). The process parallels their architectural evolution:

The Five Architects started from a common beginning—a modernist view of art and architecture—and have each truck out in new directions. Buried in the work of the Five Architects, considered a nearly seamless whole in the early 1970s, were their individual tendencies and diverse valuations of the intellectual and historical resources at their disposal. These architects' work, of great influence, both nationally and internationally, now scarcely bears a family resemblance.[4]

Anomalous Texts

Looking at the indexes it was possible to foretell the frame of reference of almost 80 percent of the texts of the corpus. From the perspective to be explored in this section, these are the least interesting texts: with reality following expectations, there is nothing to report about them. By looking into the texts with failed predictions, on the other hand, we may be able to learn something that was previously unknown.

The failures are marked with asterisks in column [4] of figure 10.5. The most glaring cases are those at the beginning and end of the series. For convenience, they are listed again in figure 10.24 separated in two groups—those devoted to the domestic scene featuring architects most often associated with an international frame of reference, and those dealing with the architecture of the world referencing architects typically found in the context of domestic discourse. These categories of texts are hereby designated A and B, respectively. The A texts are generally published more recently than the B texts, and they deal with a less distant past. This is visualized by plotting their coverage span and publication dates along a time scale (figures 10.25 and 10.26, texts arranged by publication date).

Each of the groups can be regarded as a subdiscourse, and it can be subjected to the same analytic technique used earlier for the entire corpus. Figure 10.27 lists by order of birth all architects cited in at least one-half of the A texts, and figure 10.28 does the same with the architects in B texts. The listings, comparable to those of figures 10.1 and 10.2, characterize each subdiscourse. Names

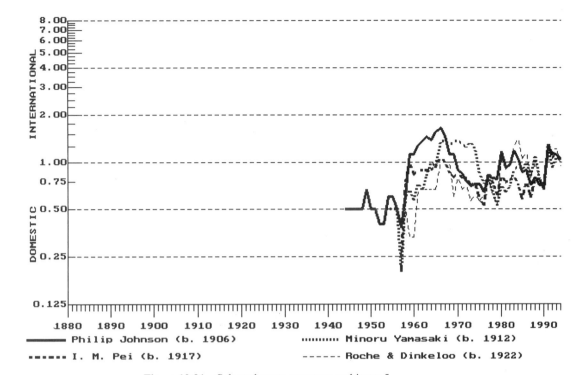

Figure 10.21   Selected contemporary architects I

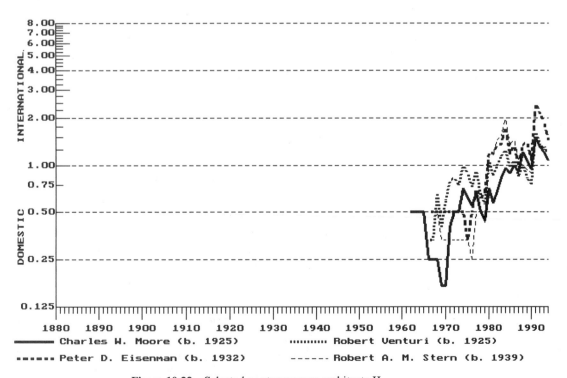

Figure 10.22   Selected contemporary architects II

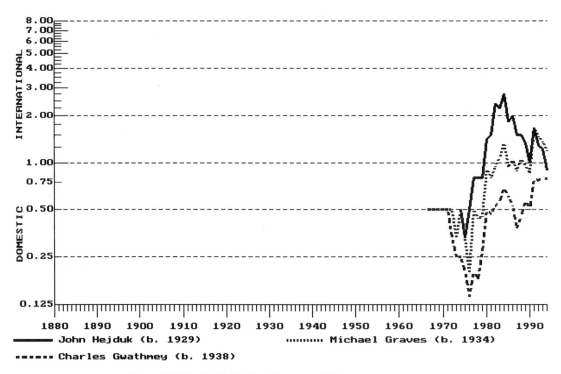

Figure 10.23   Hejduk, Gwathmey, and Graves

specific to each list are flagged with an asterisk; all of them are so marked, indicating that the listings are completely divergent. Moreover, the architects in each list belong to very different periods: those of figure 10.27 are relatively recent, the ones of figure 10.28 being born much earlier. This is consistent with text coverage as plotted in figures 10.25 and 10.26.

Far from constituting isolated irregularities, the anomalous texts fit a pattern. The B texts were published prior to World War II and some predate World War I, or even the turn of the century. At the time they were written, the modern luminaries and their disciples had not yet reached dominance, and the earlier masters now recognized as their precursors had not yet faded away as unworthy of the brave new world. Although global in their outlook, the B texts featured Colonial and nineteenth-century architects later to be found only in the domestic literature. This is consistent with the fact that Federal American architects reached the literature through international discourse (figure 10.10). At the time most of the B texts were written, still no fracture had occurred in discourse between the national and international frames of reference. No anomaly is present in those texts, after all.

The B text with the latest date of publication is Hitchcock's *Architecture. Nineteenth and Twentieth Centuries*, of 1958. The work is remarkable because it features early American architects in worldwide discourse at a time when the architects of the younger generation in America had already monopolized inter-

Figure 10.24   Texts with the most atypical choices of architects

Column headings:
[1]   International predictor
[2]   Date
[3]   Title

[1]	[2]	[3]

(a) Domestic texts with international architects:

[1]	[2]	[3]
1.15	1981	Searing: *Speaking a New Classicism. American Architecture Now*
1.14	1981	Wolfe: *From Bauhaus to Our House*
1.11	1950	Egbert: *Organic Expression and American Architecture*
1.11	1983	Colquhoun et al: *Promising Directions in American Architecture*
1.11	1985	*Cross Currents of American Architecture* (AD Profile)
1.11	1981	Stern: *American Architecture: After Modernism*
1.10	1990	Hays & Burns (eds.): *Thinking the Past: Recent American Architecture*
1.05	1989	Russell: *Architecture and Design 1970–1990*
1.05	1975	Blake & Quint: *Modern Architecture America*
1.04	1993	Heyer: *American Architecture in the Late 20th Century*
1.03	1965	Ulanov: *The Two Worlds of American Art*
1.03	1990	AIA: *American Architecture of the 1980s.*
1.03	1941	Johnson: "Architecture" (in *The American Year Book*)
1.02	1972	Fitch: *American Building: The Environmental Forces that Shaped It*
1.02	1989	*AIA Encyclopedia of Architecture, Design, Engineering ...* (main entries only)
1.02	1973	Boorstin: *The Americans: The Democratic Experience*
1.02	1993	Sarfatti Larson: *Behind the Postmodern Facade*
1.02	1985	Diamondstein: *American Architecture Now II*
1.01	1988	Pulos: *The American Design Adventure: 1940–1975*
1.01	1965	Drexler: *Modern Architecture USA*
1.00	1985	Marder: *The Critical Edge: Controversy in American Architecture*
1.00	1952	Hitchcock & Drexler: *Built in USA. Post-war Architecture*

(b) International texts with domestic architects:

[1]	[2]	[3]
0.67	1897	Statham: *Modern Architecture*
0.67	1888	Arnold: *Studies in Architecture at Home and Abroad* ·
0.68	1856	Heck: *The Art of Building in Ancient and Modern Times*
0.70	1909	Hamlin, A.D.F.: *A Text-Book of the History of Architecture*, 8th ed.
0.70	1848	Tuthill: *History of Architecture from the Earliest Times*
0.71	1918	Kimball & Edgell: *A History of Architecture*
0.72	1940	Hamlin, T.: *Architecture Through the Ages*
0.72	1891	Fergusson: *History of Modern Styles of Architecture*
0.73	1934	Whitaker: *The Story of Architecture*
0.73	1931	Fletcher: *A History of Architecture*, 9th ed.
0.73	1928	Hamlin, A.D.F.: *A Text-Book of the History of Architecture*, 18th pr.
0.73	1862	Fergusson: *History of the Modern Styles of Architecture*
0.74	1896	Hamlin, A.D.F.: *A Text-Book of the History of Architecture*
0.75	1902	Sturgis: *A Dictionary of Architecture and Building*
0.76	1958	Gloag: *Guide to Western Architecture*
0.76	1892	*The Dictionary of Architecture*
0.76	1950	Watterson: *Five Thousand Years of Building*
0.76	1930	Conant (ed.): *Modern Architecture*
0.77	1948	Pevsner: *An Outline of European Architecture*

Figure 10.24   (continued)

[1]	[2]	[3]
0.78	1921	Fletcher: *A History of Architecture*, 6th ed.
0.78	1958	Hitchcock: *Architecture: Nineteenth and Twentieth Centuries*
0.79	1938	Richardson & Corfiato: *The Art of Architecture*
0.80	1888	Gwilt: *An Encyclopedia of Architecture*
0.81	1905	Fletcher: *A History of Architecture*, 5th ed.
0.81	1953	Hamlin, T.: *Architecture Through the Ages*, rev ed.

national attention. An anomaly among the anomalies, Hitchcock's work is unusual. Others may have written with as much care about the architectural past of this country, but only he did it within the framework of an oeuvre devoted to the architecture of the world.

The A texts are diametrically opposite. They tend to be recent, are devoted to American architecture only, deal with the recent past, and feature architects most often discussed in the international context. Treatment is generally laudatory, except for Wolfe. Collectively, they constitute an effort to appropriate nationally an image originally developed within an international frame of reference. Philip Johnson's presence in this group with his early article of 1941 is noteworthy; he anticipated future developments in more ways than one.

The domestic text with the strongest tilt toward international architects is *Speaking a New Classicism: American Architecture Now*, the companion to the 1981 exhibit at Smith College Museum of Art. Curator Helen Searing acknowledges in the introductory essay that Classicism is an international movement, and that confining the survey to the Unites States was only an essential first step (p. 9). The system erred in its appraisal, but not because of a flaw in the underlying logic: the architects represented flourish in international discourse, and focusing on them as an American phenomenon was, and remains, atypical.

The next A text is *From Bauhaus to Our House*, by Wolfe (1981). This is the only book among the hundreds reviewed that I could not easily classify at the outset as domestic or international. Nowhere except on the cover flap is it stated that the book deals with American architecture. The first chapter is devoted to European events seen through the eyes of "[y]oung American architects … [who] are roaming through Europe." The remaining chapters are clearly, if not explicitly, devoted to America. In a narrow sense, the book is about this country, and the system's prediction to the contrary is in error. But the book is indeed atypical, and that is what the failed prediction ultimately means.

Donald Drew Egbert's 1950 essay on organic expression and American architecture is the next case of mistaken guess. The author declares at the outset that "recent American architecture will be studied with special reference to only three great architects" that is , Sullivan, Wright, and Gropius. This choice, most infrequent in studies devoted to this country, made the system flag the text as unusual.

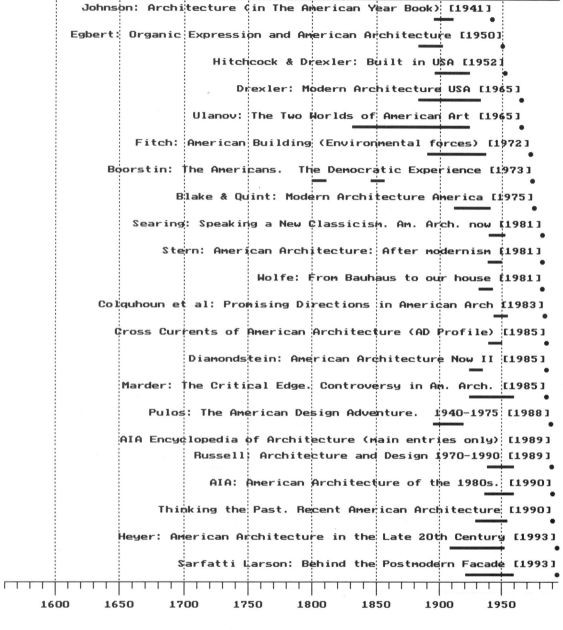

Figure 10.25 Coverage and publication dates of the texts of figure 10.24a

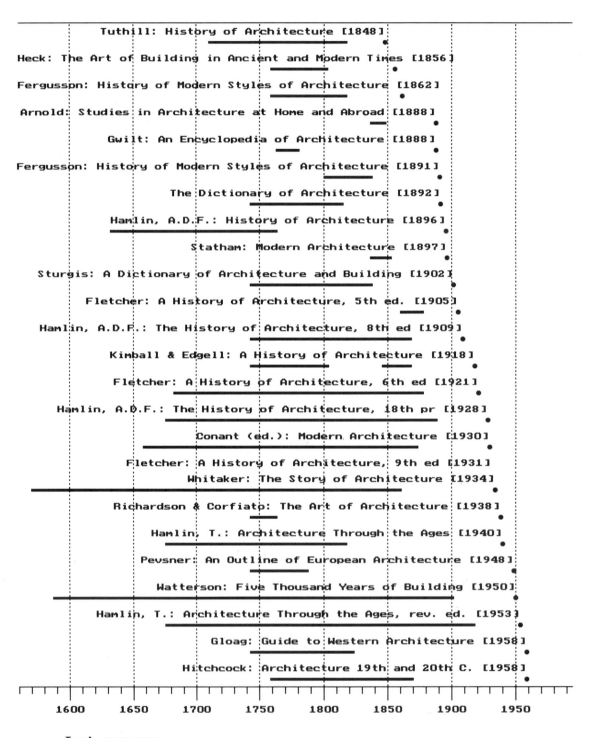

Tuthill: History of Architecture [1848]

Heck: The Art of Building in Ancient and Modern Times [1856]

Fergusson: History of Modern Styles of Architecture [1862]

Arnold: Studies in Architecture at Home and Abroad [1888]

Gwilt: An Encyclopedia of Architecture [1888]

Fergusson: History of Modern Styles of Architecture [1891]

The Dictionary of Architecture [1892]

Hamlin, A.D.F.: History of Architecture [1896]

Statham: Modern Architecture [1897]

Sturgis: A Dictionary of Architecture and Building [1902]

Fletcher: A History of Architecture, 5th ed. [1905]

Hamlin, A.D.F.: The History of Architecture, 8th ed [1909]

Kimball & Edgell: A History of Architecture [1918]

Fletcher: A History of Architecture, 6th ed [1921]

Hamlin, A.D.F.: The History of Architecture, 18th pr [1928]

Conant (ed.): Modern Architecture [1930]

Fletcher: A History of Architecture, 9th ed [1931]

Whitaker: The Story of Architecture [1934]

Richardson & Corfiato: The Art of Architecture [1938]

Hamlin, T.: Architecture Through the Ages [1940]

Pevsner: An Outline of European Architecture [1948]

Watterson: Five Thousand Years of Building [1950]

Hamlin, T.: Architecture Through the Ages, rev. ed. [1953]

Gloag: Guide to Western Architecture [1958]

Hitchcock: Architecture 19th and 20th C. [1958]

1600   1650   1700   1750   1800   1850   1900   1950

━━━━ Text coverage

•   Text publication date

Figure 10.26 Coverage and publication dates of the texts of figure 10.24b

Figure 10.27 Typical listing of architects in the texts of figure 10.24(a)

Column headings:
[1] Birth date
[2] Name

[1]	[2]
1867	*Frank Lloyd Wright
1883	*Walter Gropius
1886	*Ludwig Mies van der Rohe
1897	*Skidmore, Owings, & Merrill
1902	*Marcel Breuer
1906	*Philip Johnson
1910	*Eero Saarinen
1917	*I. M. Pei
1918	*Paul Rudolph
1925	*Charles W. Moore
1925	*Robert Venturi
1931	*Denise Scott Brown
1934	*Michael Graves
1934	*Richard Meier
1939	*Robert A. M. Stern

* not included in the listing of figure 10.28

Figure 10.28 Typical listing of architects in the texts of figure 10.24(b)

Column headings:
[1] Birth date
[2] Name

[1]	[2]
1743	*Thomas Jefferson
1759	*Dr. William Thornton
1762c	*James Hoban
1763	*Charles Bulfinch
1764	*Benjamin Henry Latrobe
1781	*Robert Mills
1802	*Richard Upjohn
1804	*Thomas Ustick Walter
1818	*James Renwick, Jr.
1827	*Richard Morris Hunt
1838	*Henry Hobson Richardson
1847	*McKim, Mead, & White
1856	*Louis Sullivan
1869	*Bertram Grosvenor Goodhue

* not included in the listing of figure 10.27

Multinuclear Texts Revisited

The corpus contains several instances of multinuclear texts with an international frame of reference: *A History of Architecture* by Kimball and Edgell (1918), *A Concise History of Western Architecture* by Jordan (1969), and Scully's recent *Architecture. The Natural and the Manmade* (1991) are conspicuous examples (see figures 4.30–4.35). These books are devoted to the architecture of the world, not to America. When expunging from the index all the non-American names, certain damage was inevitably done to the delicate balance that characterizes a good literary work. Discontinuities evidenced by their profiles are probably a result of this operation. Multinuclearity in the American contributions to worldwide texts suggests not that the texts, but America's architectural participation, was piecemeal or disjointed. Despite their widely different dates of publication, these three books agree to a surprising degree in placing America's engagement in worldwide architectural affairs around two periods, one starting with Jefferson and the other encompassing the writers' own lifetimes.

Key Monuments in the History of Architecture (H. Millon, ed., 1965, figure 4.32) displays not two but three peaks. The key to the puzzle is the same: the book addresses world architecture, not the architecture of this country, and the profile must therefore be interpreted with caution.

Notes

1. L'Enfant is cited in seventy-eight texts with an American frame of reference and forty-seven texts about the world; the figures for Clérisseau are thirty-five and thirteen.

2. Tallmadge, Thomas E.: *The Story of Architecture in America*. New York: Norton, 1927.

3. *Five Architects*, with essays by Kenneth Frampton and Colin Rowe. New York: Wittenborn, 1972.

4. Hurtt, Steven W.: Introduction. In *Five Architects Twenty Years Later*. College Park, MD: School of Architecture, University of Maryland, 1992 (pages not numbered).

11   Issues of Gender Equity among Writers and Architects

In his novel *Cat's Cradle*, Kurt Vonnegut portrays a scholar of dubious sanity who is capable of determining the sexual orientation of the indexer of a book merely from the organization of the index. I, too, profess to know how to gather information about gender-related issues from indexes. How many among the architects discussed in the literature are women? How many of the writers are? How do gender ratios in the two fields compare? Did gender distribution among writers and architects vary with time? How much, and how fast? How many women writers and architects excelled in their fields, and who are they? Are there any differences between texts authored by scholars of one gender or the other? Do male (or female) writers tend to favor architects of their own gender in their choice of examples? These questions may not be as titillating as those that preoccupied my fictional comrade, but they are intriguing in their own way.

Society takes considerable interest in issues of gender, race, and ethnicity. The first of these areas is ideally suited for index analytical inquiry. The gender of architects and writers, unlike their racial or ethnic background, in most cases can be ascertained on the basis their first names or the personal pronouns used when referring to them. (Admittedly, this entails certain risks: the author of a recent book on women architects cheerfully counted Jacquelin Robertson among her subjects.) No comparable linguistic markers exist for race or ethnicity; before dealing with these fields one would have to gather the pertinent information from external sources. This is no menial task, especially in the case of less prominent architects and writers.

Gender Distribution Among Writers

The texts of the corpus were classified into four categories, depending on whether their authors (or editors, or writing teams, whoever is given primary credit) are men, women, a combination of the two, or unknown. A team was counted as a combination when it includes at least one man and one woman.

When in doubt about the gender of a person I followed Hanks and Hodges's *Dictionary*.[1] The category "unknown" was used for names not found in the dictionary, for ambiguous names, and for persons whose first names are neither given nor known. The cases of unknown gender are ignored in this chapter; consequently, the totals do not match those given elsewhere. In the case of collaborative efforts, credit is split half-way between the genders to simplify the data entry and computation process. (The resulting error is likely to be a small inflation in female percentages.)

Two hundred eighty-eight of the 380 texts of the corpus were by men, 38 were by women, 20 are the product of collaboration between men and women, and the information was not provided in 32 cases. Men scholars are responsible for 86 percent of the items of the corpus and their female counterparts for the rest. The list of women writers includes two true pioneers, Louise C. Tuthill who published in 1848 the first history of architecture to be written in the United States by a writer of either gender, and Mariana Griswald van Rensselaer.[2]

The chronological distribution of texts written or edited by women is more revealing than their total numbers. It could be obtained from a count of items written by men and women in the corpus year by year, but short-term fluctuations would obscure more important long-term trends. Let us use again the concept of texts remaining in short-term memory for a few years, as developed in chapter 5. The number of years texts are alive and the number of active items in public consciousness year by year are graphed in figure 5.2.

Figure 11.1 shows the same curve (minus items by scholars of unknown gender) with texts discriminated according to the gender of the authors. Women's participation in the corpus started to increase in 1980 and almost reached parity a few years later.[3] Although extrapolations may be unwarranted because of the limited size of the sample, it seems to have taken an upward swing during the 1980s.

Quantitative issues are but one side of the gender gap. Numerical parity between men and women writers is likely to be achieved at some point. Will equality be followed by sexual blindness? Or do gender-specific differences, cultural more likely than natural, exist between men and women architectural writers? According to worn stereotypes, women are interested in interior design and domestic architecture, whereas men write about bridges and regional planning.

Perhaps there are other, more subtle differences. Index analysis is poorly equipped to deal with them, however, except for one aspect. The period addressed in each text—its coverage span—is available in the data base (chapter 4). An interesting distinction between men and women writers arises by comparing the coverage of the texts they wrote. Figure 11.2 shows (vertically) the number of texts by men and women covering the work of architects according to their birth year, which is displayed horizontally. It is organized like figure 4.4, except that texts are now broken down by gender of author instead of publication date. The discontinuity for year 1743, discussed in chap-

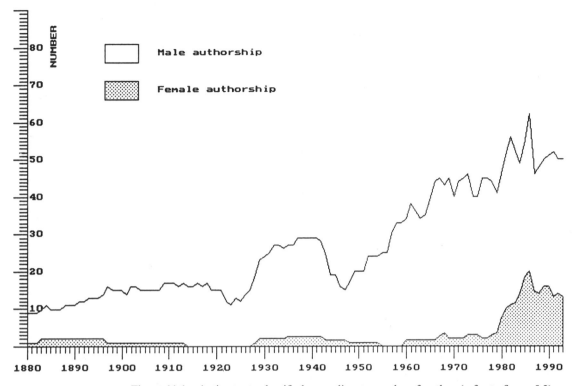

Figure 11.1   Active texts classified according to gender of author (refer to figure 5.2)

ter 4, is all but gone if one looks only at the female corpus. The breakage in the curve marks the appearance of Thomas Jefferson, widely seen during the heyday of the Modern Movement as the starting point of the historical narrative, to the detriment of the pre-Federal past. The phenomenon, it now turns out, was primarily a male affair. Women writers have always displayed a more comprehensive, less fragmented view of the architectural past of this country than men.

Out of curiosity, I plotted a graph similar to figure 7.4, to see if any perceptible distinction in foresight or predictability emerges between texts written by men and women (figure 11.3). There are too few by women to warrant conclusions, but tentatively, one may remark that they remain clear from the four corners of the diagram, which are characterized by combinations of extreme values on both scales.

Gender Distribution among Architects

Architects were assigned gender the same way as writers. Individuals, firms, and teams were classified four ways—as men, women, combinations, and

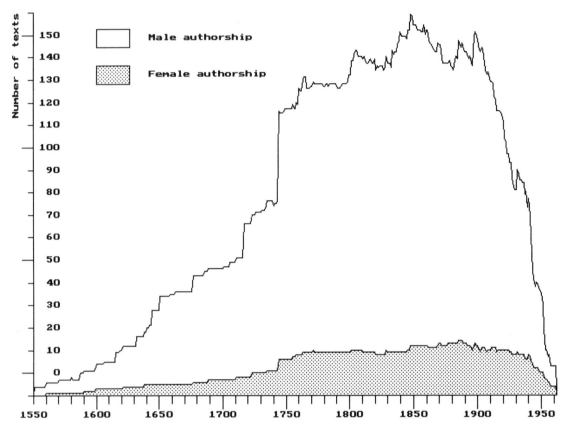

Figure 11.2 Number of texts covering the past discriminated by gender of the author (refer to figure 4.4)

unknowns. Entities of unknown gender were ignored, and teams with a combination were counted half-male and half-female.

The gender gap among the architects cited in the literature is more pronounced than among writers, which is not surprising in view of the fact that writing has been open for women for much longer than designing and building. Barely 2.5 percent of the architects in the literary universe are women. The ratio is commensurate with the number of practicing women architects, who in 1980 were estimated to account for 2 percent of the total.[4]

Only 282 female architects or firms are cited in at least one text in the corpus, 66 are cited in two or more texts, and only 33 are featured in five texts or more. Values for men also fall, but not in the same proportion. As the number of citations required to be counted is increased and the architects in the group become fewer and more famous, women's participation as a percentage of the total gradually shrinks: it is 3.5 percent among architects featured in one text, but only 1.2 percent of those cited in thirty-one texts or more (figure 11.4).

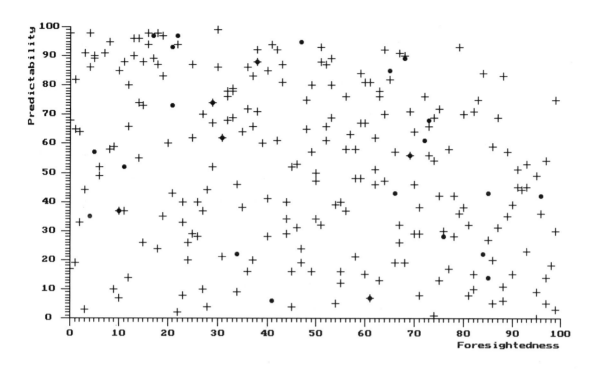

Figure 11.3 Text scattered according to foresight and predictability and classified by gender of author or editor

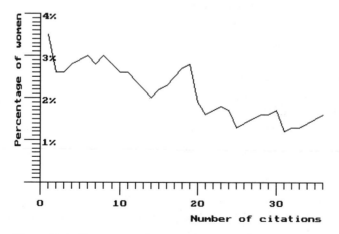

Figure 11.4 Percentage of women among architects who have achieved certain levels of citations

The limited presence of women within the most prestigious ranks in the literature is consistent with their participation at other levels of the profession, and the pyramidal structure of the profession itself. Women account for 30 to 40 percent of the student body in architectural schools; in 1987 they composed 7.1% of the AIA membership.[5] Because of the natural sequencing of stages in a professional career, redress of gender inequities must occur first in the student population and then in the profession, starting at the junior layers and reaching the senior positions only later. Access to the lower echelons of literary recognition comes even after that, and only as a final stage may parity be achieved among the luminaries.

Another way to quantify the imbalance is by the number of citations received by men and women. Men are cited, as an average, in thirteen texts of the corpus; women are mentioned in only eight.

There is only 1 woman among the 100 most prominent architects in the literature: Denise Scott-Brown. Mentioned in seventy-three texts of the corpus, she places eighty-seventh among all architects by raw rankings (see figure 3.4), or fifty-ninth according to adjusted rankings (figure 5.1). The Architects' Collaborative includes two women among their principals—Jean Fletcher and Sarah Pillsbury—and is counted therefore as a partially female firm. Cited in seventy-three texts like Scott-Brown, they slip to the one hundred twenty-fourth position among all architects when citations are adjusted.

Women architects and firms with women principals most often cited in the literature are listed in figures 11.5 and 11.6, ranked (within the female universe only) in terms of raw and adjusted citations, respectively. The list includes writers (Harriet Beecher Stowe, Edith Wharton) and designers (Anni Albers) when they are credited with architectural ideas.

Gender parity is likely to result from women's increased access to the profession rather than from changing attitudes in the literature. The written word, however, is also an important agent of reform. There is a specialized literature on women in architecture.[6] It would be interesting to know to what extent, if any, this sectional output has influenced the main body of the literature as represented in the corpus. Do women architects typically appear in the specialized literature first? How does citation in the subliterature affect their destiny in the main literature? Did any women architects make their way into the main literature directly? How many? When? Index analysis lends itself well to face these sort of issues, but not without first collecting and processing the indexes of the literature on women architects.

In a gender-neutral environment, the people listed in figures 11.5 and 11.6 are comparable with hundreds of others who have reached similar prominence in the literature. Yet in the context of the feminist movement's struggle for redress, these women became heroines in a subnarrative that is partly independent of the main plot. Each time a new concern sweeps through the body of society, the history of architecture is rewritten. A new type of comment is starting to appear in the texts. The twelve volumes of *The Smithsonian Guide to Historic America*,

Figure 11.5 The 35 women architects and firms with women principals most prominent in the literature (raw ranking; compare with figure 3.4)

Column headings:
[1] Rank
[2] Citations
[3] Birth date
[4] Name

[1]	[2]	[3]	[4]
1	73	1883	The Architects' Collaborative (Jean Fletcher, Sarah Pillsbury)
1	73	1931	Denise Scott Brown
3	38	1949	Arquitectonica (or DPZ) (Elizabeth Plater-Zyberk)
4	30	1872	Julia Morgan
5	24	1873	Marion Mahony Griffin
6	23	1944	OMA (Office for Metropolitan Architecture) (Zoe Zenghelis, Madelon Vriesendorp)
7	20	1959	Maya Ying Lin
8	19	1810?	Gervase Wheeler
8	19	1912	Ray Kaiser Eames
8	19	1917	Florence Knoll
11	13	1936?	Agrest & Gandelsonas (Diana Agrest)
11	13	1942	Margaret I. McCurry
13	12	1800	Catherine Esther Beecher
13	12	1926	Dion Neutra
15	11	1865	Elsie De Wolfe (Lady Mendl)
15	11	1944	Susana Torre
17	10	1862	Edith Wharton
17	10	1943	Halsband & Kliment (Frances Halsband)
19	9	1811	Harriet Beecher Stowe
19	9	1904	Russell Wright (Mary Wright)
19	9	1950	Zaha Hadid
22	8	1868	Theodate Pope Riddle
22	8	1889	Marion Sims Wyeth
22	8	1924	Sarah Pillsbury Harkness
22	8	1940?	ACE (Lucia Howard)
22	8	1940	Cynthia Weese
27	7	1899	Dorothy Liebes
28	6	1894	Aino Aalto
28	6	1899	Anni Albers
28	6	1905	Catherine Bauer
28	6	1914	Westermann & Miller (Helge Westermann)
28	6	1915	Jean Fletcher (cited alone)
28	6	1919	Landes Gores
28	6	1942	Chimacoff-Peterson (Barbara Littenberg)
35	5	1868c	Sophia Hayden
35	5	1872	Beatrix Farrand
35	5	1920	Ann Griswold Tyng
35	5	1950?	Mary Miss

Figure 11.6 The 35 women architects and firms with women principals most prominent in the literature (adjusted ranking; compare with figure 5.1)

Column headings:
[1] Rank
[2] Citations
[3] Birth date
[4] Name

[1]	[2]	[3]	[4]
1	0.37	1883	The Architects' Collaborative (Jean Fletcher, Sarah Pillsbury)
1	0.59	1931	Denise Scott Brown
1	0.69	1949	Arquitectonica (or DPZ) (Elizabeth Plater-Zyberk)
4	0.18	1872	Julia Morgan
5	0.14	1873	Marion Mahony Griffin
5	0.36	1944	OMA (Office for Metropolitan Architecture) (Zoe Zenghelis, Madelon Vriesendorp)
5	0.48	1959	Maya Ying Lin
8	0.11	1810?	Gervase Wheeler
8	0.13	1912	Ray Kaiser Eames
8	0.13	1917	Florence Knoll
8	0.12	1936?	Agrest & Gandelsonas (Diana Agrest)
8	0.20	1942	Margaret I. McCurry
13	0.07	1800	Catherine Esther Beecher
13	0.11	1926	Dion Neutra
15	0.06	1865	Elsie De Wolfe (Lady Mendl)
15	0.17	1944	Susana Torre
17	0.06	1862	Edith Wharton
17	0.16	1943	Halsband & Kliment (Frances Halsband)
19	0.05	1811	Harriet Beecher Stowe
20	0.05	1904	Russell Wright (Mary Wright)
20	0.24	1950	Zaha Hadid
22	0.04	1868	Theodate Pope Riddle
22	0.05	1889	Marion Sims Wyeth
22	0.07	1924	Sarah Pillsbury Harkness
22	0.09	1940?	ACE (Lucia Howard)
22	0.09	1940	Cynthia Weese
27	0.04	1899	Dorothy Liebes
28	0.04	1894	Aino Aalto
29	0.03	1899	Anni Albers
29	0.04	1905	Catherine Bauer
29	0.04	1914	Westermann & Miller (Helge Westermann)
29	0.04	1915	Jean Fletcher (cited alone)
29	0.05	1919	Landes Gores
29	0.09	1942	Chimacoff-Peterson (Barbara Littenberg)
35	0.03	1868c	Sophia Hayden
35	0.03	1872	Beatrix Farrand
35	0.04	1920	Ann Griswold Tyng
35	0.14	1950?	Mary Miss

for example, although written by a variety of scholars, follow a common pattern: a description of the manmade environment of an area or a state starts almost invariably with references to the first structures erected by Native Americans, then the first buildings by white men, then the first by Anglos, and now, occasionally, this is followed by the first dwellings in the region designed or conceived by women. This would hardly have happened without feminist scholarship and politics, which acted in a concerted fashion: the former made available the information, the latter created a climate conducive to its use.

Let us look at the historical record. Figure 11.7 shows the yearly evolution of the number of architects and firms cited in at least two texts of the corpus, classified by gender, since 1900. Not a single woman appears in the universe during the first half of the century. Then in 1950 they start to emerge. First comes Dorothy Liebes, a furniture and textile designer who qualifies as an architect only under the broad definitions used for this study. She is followed by The Architects' Collaborative (with partners Fletcher and Pillsbury), Marion Manley, and Florence Schuster Knoll in 1952, Lily Swann Saarinen in 1953, Landes Gores in 1954, and Gervase Wheeler and Elsie De Wolfe in 1955. Three women whose writing had an impact on architectural ideas—Catherine Esther Beecher, Harriet Beecher Stowe, and Edith Wharton—enter the literary universe between 1960 and 1961, with Ray Kaiser Eames and Dion Neutra. A short period of stagnation follows during the first half of the 1960s (see figure 11.8, showing the bottom of figure 11.7 enlarged). Growth resumes in 1965, with Marion Mahoney Griffin, Marion Sims Wyeth, and Julia Morgan, and Denise Scott-Brown from the younger generation, entering the universe by the end of the decade.

Many men also entered the universe during the same period; but women's gains were proportionally more significant. Figure 11.9 shows the female population in the literary universe as a percentage of the total. The ratio is still very low (2.5 percent of the total, as reported earlier) but it shows slow, steady progress. The universe is defined cumulatively; it changes by aggregation rather than substitution of names, which generates considerable inertia.

A more dynamic view is obtained by looking at the distribution of birth dates within the universe. Figure 11.10a gives the numbers of men and women architects in the literature born in twenty-year periods, like figure 5.3. Women's participation among the youngest generation (those born between 1941 and 1960) has reached a sweeping 19 percent (figure 11.10b).

Two factors seem to account for this course of events. Obviously, greater numbers of women are entering and succeeding in the profession. In addition to a new type of practitioner, a fresh type of writer is now sensitive to the work of women. Two distinct streams in the roster of female architects have entered the universe since the midcentury. On the one hand, are women who were between thirty-five and fifty years of age by the time of their second citation; namely, Liebes, Fletcher, Pillsbury, Manley, Knoll, Lily Saarinen, Landes Gores, Ray Eames, Dion Neutra, and Scott-Brown. Still in the early stages of their careers,

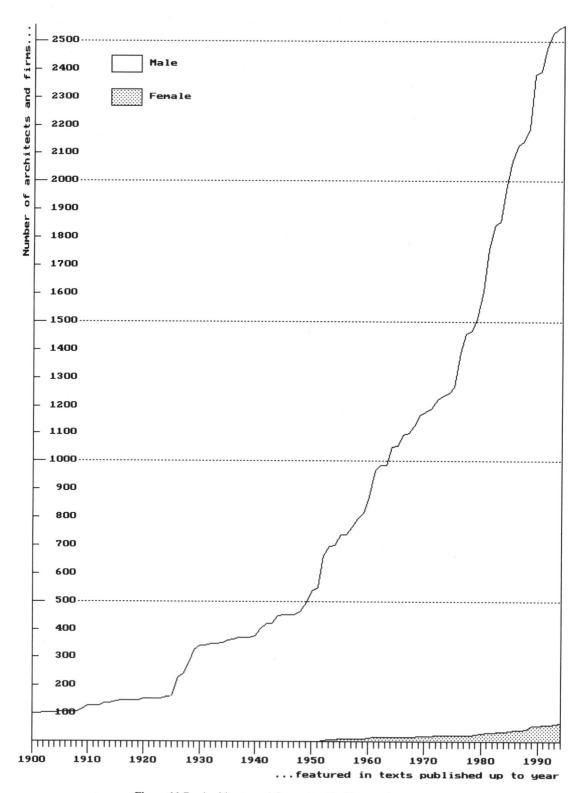

Figure 11.7 Architects and firms classified by gender

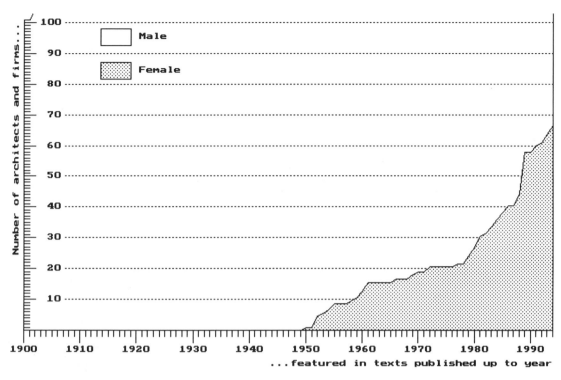

Figure 11.8 Architects and firms classified by gender (zooming into bottom area of figure 11.7)

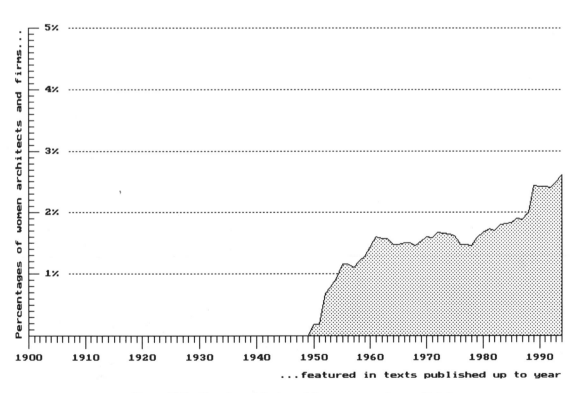

Figure 11.9 Female architects and firms as percentages of total

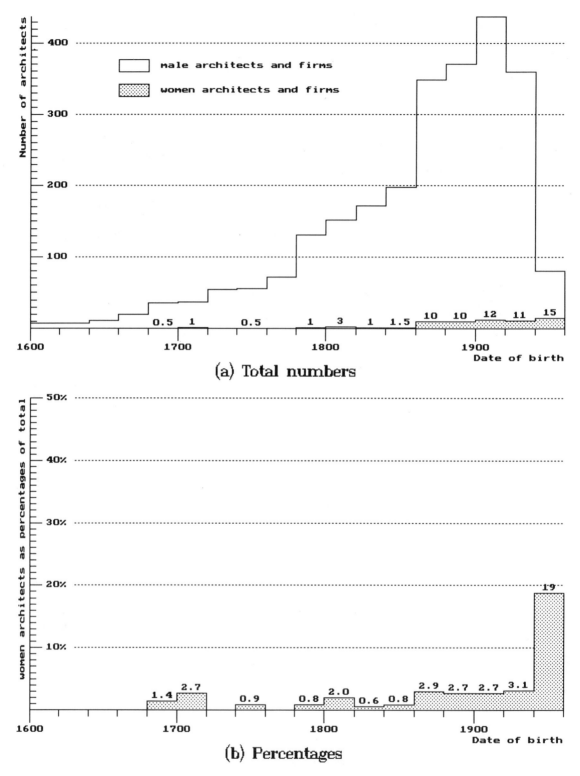

Figure 11.10   Architects and firms classified according to gender and date of birth

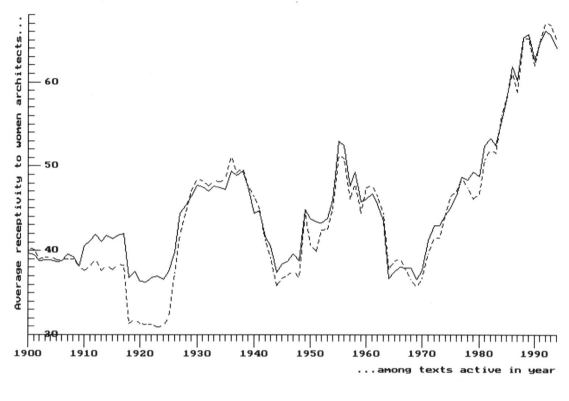

Figure 11.11   Receptivity to the work of female architects

they could hardly have been featured in the literature theretofore. The other group of women lived and worked much earlier. De Wolfe, Morgan, and novelist Wharton, the three born between 1862 and 1872, made their contributions during the 1920s and 1930s and were long gone by the time they were recognized. The same is true to an even larger extent of Gervase Wheeler, whose book on domestic architecture, which earned her a place in the population of architects, was published in 1855(?), and of Catherine Esther Beecher and Harriet Beecher Stowe, born one year apart in 1810 and 1811. Their arrival in the literature after 1950 signals emerging willingness to acknowledge the work of women once neglected.

But caution is in order. To proclaim an attitudinal change on the basis of the data reviewed so far, it would be necessary to show that the rate of entry of older women into the universe surpasses the rate of entry of older men. This, however, is not the case, nor could it be: first, because not enough women architects practiced before the midcentury; and second, because many newly recognized men in the seventeenth and eighteenth centuries entered the universe as a consequence of renewed interest in Colonial architecture. Receptivity to the work of women architects probably increased in the literature since 1970, but further analysis of the record is necessary to show it convincingly.

Receptivity to the Work of Female Architects

Do writers give preferential treatment to architects of their own gender, citing them more often than those of opposite sex? Is there rampant (or covert) chauvinism in the architectural literature? Judging from the works in the corpus, the response is mixed.

I computed the percentage of women architects within the population of each text. Next, I found the average percentage of citations for all texts written by women, which turned out to be 1.90 percent. This means that of every 100 architects cited in an average text by a woman, 1.9 are women. The percentage in texts written by men is substantially lower: 1.46. Comparable results are obtained by tallying citations from men and women writers received by men and women architects. As an average, 18.9 percent of citations of men come from women writers; but women architects can expect to receive 21.3 percent of their citations from other women. The numbers suggest a certain level of polarization, with members of each sex caring for their own.

Such a picture may be flawed because it fails to take into account that the average man and the average woman sat down to write at different historical times and in different contexts, and wrote about different subjects. As indicated in the preceding section, the distribution of women architects along the temporal continuum is rather uneven; few of them lived and worked before the middle of the last century. Historians dealing with Colonial architecture could hardly cite many women architects, no matter how genuinely they might try, whereas those writing about contemporary architecture have a better chance to do so. In addition, even the few women architects who lived and worked in the past are only now starting to be recognized, as a result of feminist critique, and to become available, so to speak, for additional citations. With their numbers and ratio in the universe steadily growing over the past two decades (figure 11.7), the date at which a text is being written affects the likelihood of encountering the work of women. In conclusion, the percentage of female citations in a text is governed by the period covered and by the time of its writing as decisively as by the inclinations of the writer.

For a subtler gauging of each text's (or writer's) receptivity to the work of women architects I developed an index based not on the number of citations, but on a relationship between that number and the one that might have been expected in function of the period covered in the work and its publication date. The index, defined and discussed in the appendix, runs from zero (lowest receptivity found in the corpus) to ninety-nine (highest value found). The average receptivity for all texts by men is forty-nine; the average for those written or edited by women is fifty-four. The difference is modest, but in any case, with female receptivity surpassing that of males, the numbers point in the direction of a sex war.

Two of the most receptive works to women designers are Kouwenhoven's *Made in America* (1948) and *The Tastemakers* by Lynes (1949), both heavily focused on domestic design. Also high on the receptivity ranking are the volumes of *The Smithsonian Guide to Historic America*; many of the women in this case are not architects in the conventional sense but are cited in connection with the design and construction of their own homes. More poignant, two of the three texts with the least sensitivity for women architects were written by women—Ada Louise Huxtable's 1960 article "Twentieth-Century Architecture" and *American Architecture Now* by Barbara Diamondstein. Because of the low number of names involved, however, the results for these texts are not significant (see appendix), and in any case, abstaining from the gender war may not be reprehensible after all.

A greater correlation exists between receptivity and publication date than between receptivity and gender. The evolution of the average receptivity for texts in short-term memory year by year is graphed in figure 11.11. Although one can see ups and downs, the long-term tendency is unmistakable: sensitivity to women architects has been growing consistently through the century. A curve drawn for books by men only (dashed line) runs almost coincident with the one representing all texts, indicating that the trend is not a consequence of the increasing participation of women in the pool of authors and editors.

The significance of this finding must be emphasized. It does not mean increasing participation of women in the profession and the literature, as evidenced in figures 11.1, 11.7, 11.8, and 11.9; this has already been factored into the equation. All other things being equal, the line of figure 11.11 should have been approximately horizontal, running near the middle of the diagram. But all other things were not equal. Sensitivity to the contributions of women, as different from the contributions themselves, has been on the rise. We have no reason, however, for complacency. Receptivity measurements are relative; texts are evaluated in comparison to other texts. Midlevel receptivity would be good in an environment of justice, but abhorrent in the midst of prejudice. The curve of figure 11.11 may be allowed to stabilize, and it will, when the curves of figures 11.6 and 11.8 have reached acceptable levels.

Notes

1. Hanks, Patrick, and Flavia Hodges: *A Dictionary of First Names*. Oxford, New York: Oxford University Press, 1990.

2. For a discussion of their contributions see Doumato, L. Louise Tuthill's Unique Achievement, and L. Koenigsberg: Mariana van Rensselaer: An Architecture Critic in Context, both in Berkeley, Ellen Perry (ed.): *Architecture: A Place for Women*. Washington, DC, London: Smithsonian Institution Press, 1989.

3. Five women authors in 1980 (Kloss Ball, Davern, Diamondstein, Emanuel, Rifkind) were followed by Searing and the editor of *The World Almanac* in 1981, McCoy and Hart Wright in 1982, McLoud in 1983, and Flon and Pokinsky in 1984.

4. Harmon, Robert B.: *The Feminine Influence in Architecture: A Selected Bibliography*. Monticello, IL: Vance Bibliographies A-243, 1980.

5. Berkeley, Ellen Perry (ed.): *Architecture. A Place for Women*. Washington, London: Smithsonian Institution Press, 1989.

6. Although some items go back to the past century, the area as a whole has experienced rapid growth since the 1970s. For a bibliography up to 1980, see Harmon, op. cit. For more recent items see the bibliography in *Women in American Architecture 1888– 1988 "That Exceptional One"*. Washington, DC: American Architectural Foundation, 1988.

Appendix: Procedures, Formulas, and Validity of Results

Chapter 3: The Universe

Validity of the Results

The results in the chapter are influenced by two factors: the selection of the corpus and the requirement of two citations minimum for an architect to be in the universe. The latter is clearly arbitrary. The universe could have been open to architects with only one citation, or limited to those cited more times. The more restrictive the definition, the smaller the universe. The rate of growth, however, is remarkably consistent regardless of the minimum number adopted. The data were processed for 1, 5, 10, 20, 50, 100, and 200 citations. In each case, the universe doubles approximately every twenty years. The names of the most frequently cited architects are independent of the minimum; and the age distribution also remains approximately the same. The minimum adopted results from a compromise between expediency and scope. A single citation would yield results with a finer grain, at the cost of a greater burden on the data-collection and -processing systems. More restrictive definitions would reduce the breadth of the study: significant young architects who have not yet accumulated many citations would be eliminated from the roster.

Had the corpus included more texts, fewer texts, or a different selection, the number of citations obtained by the various architects could have been somewhat different, but the numbers of architects and their names, and to a large extent their ranking as expressed in figure 3.4, would not have varied significantly. This is especially true in the case of a large corpus. The same extends to adjusted rankings and to the histograms of chapter 5. Inevitable omissions in the corpus will be corrected as circumstances allow; but the impact of the changes on this part of the outcome is likely to be limited. The list of famous architects and their histograms are less prone to revision than the list of texts.

The names of people in figure 3.4 would not be substantially different, but small variations in their rank order would obviously be expected if other texts had been used. The impact would be most noticeable in figures 3.5 through 3.8, which depend on arbitrary thresholds placed between the first and second rank orders, the third and fourth, the twelfth and thirteenth, and the fiftieth and fifty-first. Minor changes in the composition of the corpus could impel architects across those thresholds, altering the diagrams.

The problem is significant only at the higher-ranked, more restrictive classifications. If the fifty-first and fiftieth architects were to switch places, the bulk of the fifty highest-ranked names would still remain largely as it was. When one is looking at the highest rank, a switch between the first two positions leaves nothing in place. As new texts were entered into the data base over the years, I sometimes noticed significant changes in the length of the bars of the leading architects in figure 3.5, and even in the names listed over the bars. McKim, Mead, & White, for example, often emerged as leaders for the 1950s and early 1960s, only to disappear as still more texts were entered into the corpus.

The uncertainty about leading position is more acute for certain epochs than for others. The oddity is clarified in figure A.1 of this appendix. The architects with the highest cumulative numbers of citations are at the top, as portrayed in figure 3.5. The second band graphs the evolution of the number of citations they accumulated, taken from figure 3.3. The difference between the highest and the next highest number of citations year by year is displayed in the lower middle of figure A.1, using a different ordinate scale. Up to the late 1880s and then again briefly during several periods after the midcentury, the difference between the leading architect and the runner-up was only one text citation. Adding or eliminating one text from the corpus could result in a change in the name of the leading architect! The distance between the leader and the runner-up is expressed as a percentage of the number of texts in the corpus at the bottom of figure A.1. The critical years are marked by the lowest percentage differences from 1953 to 1975. With hundreds of items in the corpus, a minor text substitution could have changed the most frequently cited architect.

Chapter 4: Text Coverage

Computation of Coverage Spans and Profiles

A text's coverage for a given time interval is measured by a relationship between the number of architects featured in the text born within the period, and the pertinent architects in the universe. An architect is pertinent if he or she pertains to the subject matter of the work, and was presumably familiar to the author at the time of writing. Both conditions are readily tested by the system: pertinence to subject matter depends on whether the architect was born within the period covered in the text, and familiarity is presumed if the architect entered the universe no later than during the year of publication.

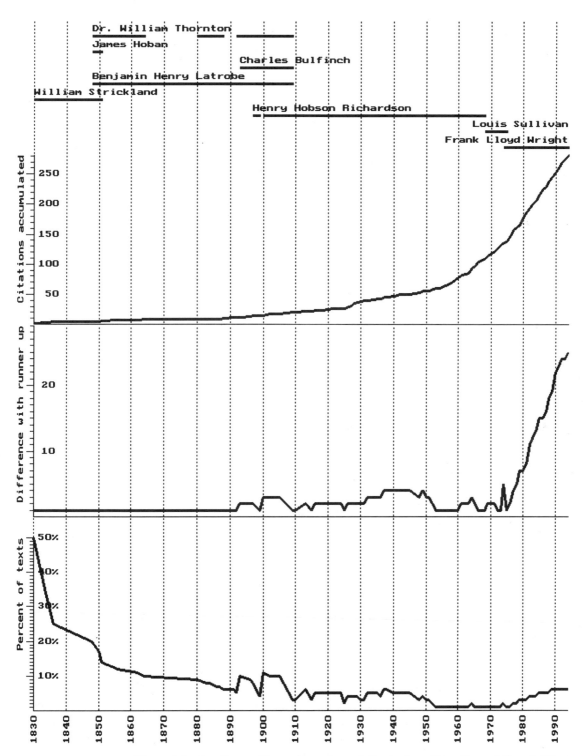

Figure A.1 Leading architects (from figure 3.5): citations (from figure 3.3) and difference with runner-up

Several intensity formulas can be devised; each returns a value for every relevant interval. An interval is defined by a beginning and an ending date. The coverage span is the interval that maximizes the value returned by the formula.

A segment of the universe or the text population is a list of names within an interval. Let n be the number of names in a segment of the text population, and N be the number of pertinent names in the corresponding segment of the universe. The goal is to find a formula for variable $F(n, N)$, such that F is maximized for an interval that an independent observer would judge to be a reasonable coverage span for the text.

The simplest possible formula is:

$$F_1 = n.$$

F_1 is maximized when n contains all architects cited in the text. Using this formula, coverage invariably extends from the earliest architect cited in the text to the latest. In most cases this is clearly excessive.

The next formula considered is:

$$F_2 = \frac{n}{N}.$$

F_2 is maximized for the interval that contains the highest concentration of names featured in the text. Segments with only one name (in other words, years with only one architect) must be barred, because they yield $F_2 = 1$ when the architect is cited, but the intervals returned, being only one year long, lack practical interest. In addition, imposing $F_2 < 1$ precludes obtaining segments of the universe that are coincident with segments of the population. The value is maximized when there is such a coincidence, but the intervals in such cases are almost invariably too short. Even with these stipulations the intervals derived from F_2 were consistently too small.

The formula finally adopted was the geometric mean of F_1 and F_2:

$$F = \frac{n \cdot \sqrt{N}}{N}$$

(i.e., $F^2 = F_1 \cdot F_2$).

Two additional rules were specified: spans must be at least ten years long, and must end no later than twenty-six years before publication date.

Coverage spans are governed by the birth dates of the architects cited; therefore, only dates in which architects in the text population were born are worth testing; the others lack practical interest. With densely populated texts, even this may burden the system excessively. In the current version of the software the maximum number of dates to be tested is forty; when there are more dates, the system selects forty as evenly spaced as possible. As each interval consists of a pair of dates, with 40 dates there are $(40 \times 39)/2 = 780$ intervals to test. Every interval tested determines a point in the coverage profile.

The interval that maximizes the value returned by the formula is what matters, not the value itself, which is meaningless. To discourage intertext coverage comparisons, the highest value returned by the formula is converted to 100, with the other values rescaled accordingly.

Conditions for Multinuclear Texts

When a coverage profile displays more than one peak, the text may be multinuclear. The following conditions must be met: the spans corresponding to the peaks must be disjoint; the height of the lowest peak must be at least one-third of the highest; and each span must be at least ten years long.

Chapter 5: Histograms

Further Citation Adjustments

I explored various ways to tally citation frequencies within a text and, indirectly, citation lengths. Only the index, however, could be used; looking at the text (let alone reading citation content) was excluded from the outset because of the implicit data-gathering burden. Index analysis is limited to the analysis of indexes. None of the procedures described below was adopted. The formulas for the various types of adjustments are given in the next section.

Weighing Pages

As indexes list every page on which a citation appears, prominently featured names are typically followed by scores of page numbers. These could be used as an indication of citation frequency, and indirectly of their length. I did not pursue this approach for several reasons.

One must stop somewhere. Should all texts count the same, one might ask? Some are brief articles, others are lengthy tracts. Texts, not only citations, could be weighted for length. Once on this slippery road, no end is in sight. A bestseller with hundreds of thousands of copies should count more than an obscure publication. Copies printed, copies sold, or number of times each copy was used (on the basis of library circulation data or secondary citation analysis) could all be factored into the researcher's equation. Common sense calls for limiting the number of variables to the extent compatible with meaningful results.

The first citation in a text is the most important. Citations are subject to a law of diminishing returns. This could be reflected in properly chosen coefficients. I gave the first citation 100 percent value and the ensuing ones zero, a somewhat brutal weighing scale but one that reflects, in principle, the law of diminishing returns. The watershed is between being in the discourse, no matter in what capacity, and being left out altogether.

I presented this idea in Uruguay not too long ago. As I sensed a certain skepticism among a section of the audience, I mentioned a conversation of the day before. I was visiting Eladio Dieste, one of the most respected Uruguayan architects. I had seen an advance copy of Udo Kulterman's *Architecture of the 20th Century*, which presumably was not yet known in Uruguay. Dieste's work, I told him, was featured in the book. Mr. Dieste did not ask me how many times was he cited or on how many pages, nor did I volunteer this information. It was irrelevant to my point, which was that Mr. Dieste, once recognized primarily within the context of South American regional brick architecture, had gained in stature to become a part of discourse about twentieth-century architecture of the world. His presence in Kulterman's book supported my claim, regardless of the number of citations.

Page sizes differ. The shortest possible page would contain only one word. In texts formatted this way, the number of pages in the index would reflect the number of occurrences of the name. Conversely, texts could be printed on only one gigantic page. In this case, every name would have only one page in the index, always the same regardless of how many times it was cited. Real pagination varies between these hypothetical extremes. Citation rankings based on page counts would be affected by this inessential aspect of the text, which may change from edition to edition or through translations. Ignoring the number of pages is consistent with considering all books reissued into volumes of only one page.

Consistency with other studies is important. In traditional citation analysis a distinction is made between reference studies and citation studies. If an article is cited five times in a text, this counts as five citations but only one reference. Virtually all so-called citation studies are reference studies.[4] The same is true for this project.

Weighing the Number of Architects Cited

An architect might be cited in *American Architecture* (ed. Hunt, 1984), and also in *American Architecture Now* (Diamondstein, 1980). The former is a field guide on noteworthy buildings in every state of the union, with a total of 785 architects mentioned; the latter is a series of interviews with only 14 personalities. Hunt could not possibly grant each architect as much space as Diamondstein; nevertheless, when tallying raw or adjusted rankings, citations in these two books count the same. This could be corrected by an appropriate weighing factor: a citation by Hunt would count for 1/785, and one by Diamondstein for 1/14. The quotients would reflect citation length if space were evenly divided among all architects featured in each text; this is not true in most cases, but it is a defensible hypothesis in the absence of information. Unlike the procedure just discussed, which requires going back to the indexes to count the number of pages reported, this one could be readily implemented with the data already on file.

Citation lengths are now expressed as a fraction of the total text size. But some texts are long, others are short. In the case of those devoted only to America, length can be measured in number of pages (easy to collect, but subject to variations in page size), or number of words (more accurate, but prohibitively laborious to gather). The operation becomes even more complex when the text deals with the world, and the sections devoted to America are not easily separated. A more elegant way of assessing the length of a text is by its coverage span (chapter 4), which can be measured in numbers of years or, preferably, in numbers of architects in the universe at the time of publication who were born within the coverage span.

Such rankings of American architects were used in an early version of this study. They were computed like the adjusted rankings, with two additional weighing operations. First, each citation was divided by the number of architects cited, to reflect citation length. Second, it was multiplied by the population of the universe at publication time who were born within the coverage span, to reflect text coverage length. The list of 100 most famous American architects did not change substantially: 91 names appeared in both lists, approximately in the same order.

The histograms presented in chapter 5 were also developed both ways. Although the values of the curves differed, their pattern did not: when one histogram rose, so did the other, and vice versa. For the sake of simplicity, I elected not to perform these weighing operations. The added programming and computational burden is trivial; but the hindrance of explaining more complex operations and the inevitable loss in clarity are not.

Weighing Probabilities

I explored still one more idea. I imagined a world in which architectural writers, before embarking on a project, choose the period they wanted to write about on the basis of their interests and expertise. Next, they set the number of architects they intend to write about, based, perhaps, on the availability of space, time, and other resources. Reluctant to take the responsibility of deciding which pertinent architects of the universe to feature, authors in this strange world resort to a lottery. The number of citations an architect could expect to receive if all the books were written under these conditions can be calculated by simple probabilities. Comparing actual citations with probable citations yields still another ratio to be used as a basis for ranking.

The outcome was, at first, startling: the leading places were occupied by twentieth-century superstars Venturi, Stern, Johnson, Eero Saarinen, Meier, Graves, Moore, Gwathmey, and Pei. The results were due to a computational oddity. With the rapid growth of the universe, the probabilities of random citation for contemporary architects are becoming exceedingly low; when used as divisors, the quotients are very high. The anomaly was corrected by setting a fixed size for the universe, say, 800 names. Only the 800 most prominent architects in the universe were entered into the drawing. The resulting ranking almost duplicated those obtained by the preceding methods.

Formulas for Citation Tallies

Raw citation tallies used in chapter 3 and several adjustment procedures described in chapter 5 are based on the values of the following expressions:

raw citations

$$\sum_{T=T1}^{T=T_{max}} Cit(A, T);$$

adjusted citations

$$\frac{\sum_{T=T1}^{T=T_{max}} Cit(A, T)}{\sum_{T=T1}^{T=T_{max}} (Univ(T, 2) + PeriphCit(A, T))};$$

text citation probability

$$P(T) = Nr(T)/Univ(T, 1);$$

weighted citations

$$\frac{\sum_{T=T1}^{T=T_{max}} Cit(A, T) * 1/P(T))}{\sum_{T=T1}^{T=T_{max}} ((Univ(T, 2) + PeriphCit(A, T)) * 1/P(T))},$$

where

$T1$, T_{max} are the first and last texts of the corpus;

$Cit(A, T)$ is a binary variable that equals 1 if architect A is cited in text T, or zero otherwise;

$Univ(T, 1)$ is the number of architects included in the universe of one citation at the time of publication of T, plus the number of architects cited in the text, included in the universe, and not included in the coverage span;

$Univ(T, 2)$ same as above, but the universe in this case is composed of all architects who accumulated two citations;

$PeriphCit(A, T)$ (Peripheral Citations) is a binary variable that equals 1 if A is cited in T and A was not born within the coverage span of T; it is zero otherwise. The value is introduced to avoid the possibility of quotients greater than 1; and

$Nr(T)$ is the number of architects cited in T.

The Duration of Short-Term Memory

The corpus contains too few texts to allow for meaningful histograms before the year 1880; consequently, the date is designated as the origin for all histograms. By setting the short-term memory for 1880 at eighty years, the earliest text in the corpus, published in 1815, is assured some incidence on the curves during the initial years of the histogram.

Not every text in memory is pertinent to every architect. A text is pertinent if the architect is cited in the text, or his birth date is included in the text coverage and he entered the universe no later than at text publication time. Only pertinent texts affect the histograms. With fewer than four or five, each text becomes excessively influential in the outcome, and the histogram is often jerky.

The number of pertinent texts affecting each point in the histogram depends on a number of factors. One of them, the architect's citation pattern in the corpus, is a given. Others can be influenced by an astute design of short-term memory. As shown in figure 4.4, comparatively few texts cover the work cf architects born before 1743 or after 1940; in most cases, no meaningful histograms can be drawn for them. This is not to imply, however, that histograms are always easy to produce for architects born between those dates. Consider, for example, someone born in 1870: there would be probably too few relevant texts during the first two or three decades of the twentieth century for a reliable histogram, because the members of the person's generation would still be too young to attract the attention of writers. In addition to citation pattern and memory duration, the number of relevant texts depends on the architect's birth date and age at each point of the histogram.

The shaded area in figure A.2 shows a range of possible numbers of pertinent texts influencing histograms, year by year. The upper limit is the total number of texts in short-term memory, from figure 5.2. If every text in memory were pertinent to the architect, this would be the number of texts to be reckoned with. The lower limit shows the number of pertinent texts guaranteed with memory duration chosen, year by year, for architects born since 1743, fifty years of age or older.[1] The real number of pertinent texts may be anywhere in the shaded area. According to the graph, the number will generally be adequate for most architects, especially after 1910; before that date there might be only one, two, or three relevant texts. The short-term memory duration parameters chosen are hereby justified. Histograms for architects born before 1743, or running before 1910, or while they are less than fifty years old, must be used with caution because they may be based on too few texts.

Another factor influencing the design of short-term memory is the computation of text histograms in chapter 8, which requires figuring out the distance from each text to the centroid of the system of active texts. As the number of such texts increases, the computation becomes more cumbersome. Sixty-five texts in active memory is the maximum the system can currently handle.

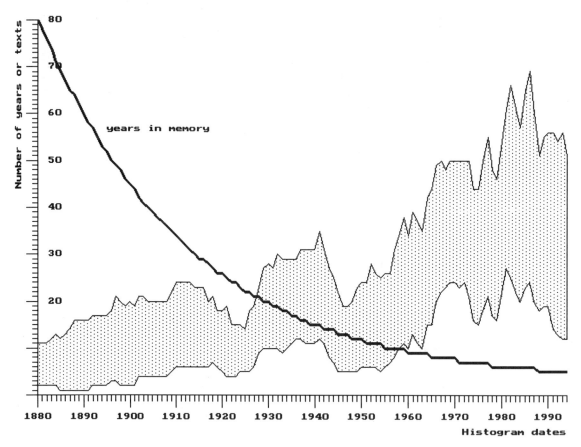

Figure A.2 Range of pertinent texts for architects born since 1748 fifty years of age or older with short-term memory as specified

Dummy Omissions

When architects enter the literature at a very young age, their histograms often reach 100 percent citations for the first few years. This is no indication of brilliance, but the result of a numerical oddity. As most texts covering the work of their generation are yet to be written, these architects tend to accumulate citations, but few or no hard absences. With no omissions, one citation may suffice to propel the adjusted citation count to 100 percent. To correct the problem, I relaxed the rule for a lack of citation to be counted as an omission: the content span of the text must include the birth date of the architect, but it is no longer necessary that it be published after the architect enters the universe. This increases the number of possible hard absences. If the number still remained too small, I assigned the architect a number of *dummy* omissions that do not correspond to any real text. The number of dummy omissions, D, is a function of T, the number of texts in short-term memory spanning the life of the architect:

T	*D*
0	1.5
1	1.0
2	0.5
3 or more	None

Dummy omissions and the relaxed definition of adjusted citations are used for histograms only.

Histograms

Histograms depend on the duration of short-term memory. Let us explore the effect of alternative definitions of short-term memory. If ninety years had been remembered in 1920 and only three years in 1994, the "years in memory" curve would be steeper and the total number of texts in memory would remain lower (figure A.3; compare with figure 5.2). Or, the memory duration curve could be flattened (forty-five years for 1880, eight years for 1994), with faster growth in the number of texts (figure A.4). Users of the electronic companion to this book may replace their own values for the default definition of the short-term memory, and obtain the histograms of all architects redrawn for the new parameters. The histograms for Frank Lloyd Wright (figures A.5 and A.6) would not be substantially different from the one adopted (figure 5.3). The date of his arrival at the 100 percent citation level would vary slightly, but so would the expectations of steady ascent against which the curves are assessed; to a certain extent, the parameters balance each other out.

The notch for the omission in the Brooklyn Museum catalogue is still there in the new histograms, although with somewhat altered proportions. With a shorter permanence of texts in memory, the impact of a single text is shorter but deeper (figure A.5); with longer permanence the notch becomes more elongated but shallower (figure A.6). Changes in the parameters affect all histograms the same way. A single histogram has limited informative value; it becomes useful when it is compared with other histograms. This can be done effectively even if the parameters are arbitrary and individual histograms are slanted.

Steady Histograms

Steady histograms are composed of two straight lines: one rising from the first citation to an ideal stabilization point, followed by a constant (horizontal) line. As short-term memory decreases with time, theoretically the rising segment of a steady histogram should be a curve of increasing gradient, not a straight line. As the impact of this factor is negligible, it is ignored.

The lines are calculated on the basis of two assumptions: the lapse between first citation and stabilization reflects the number of years texts remain in short-term memory at the time of the first citation; and the area enclosed

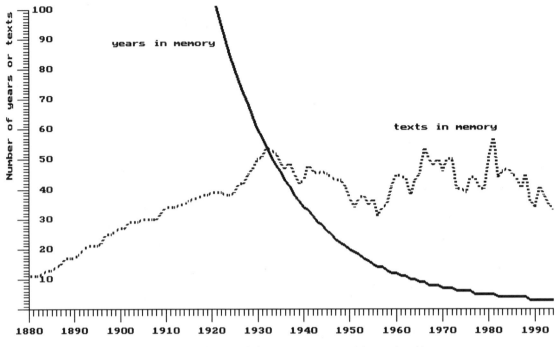

Figure A.3   Evolution of short-term memory (alternative A)

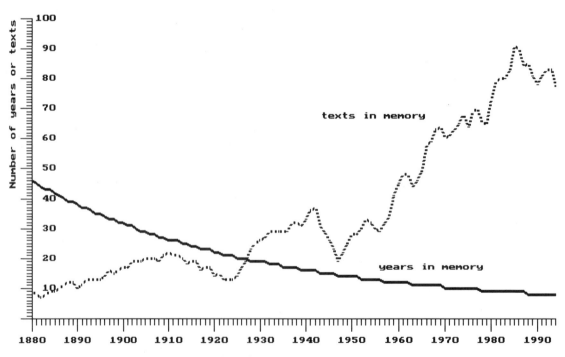

Figure A.4   Evolution of short-term memory (alternative B)

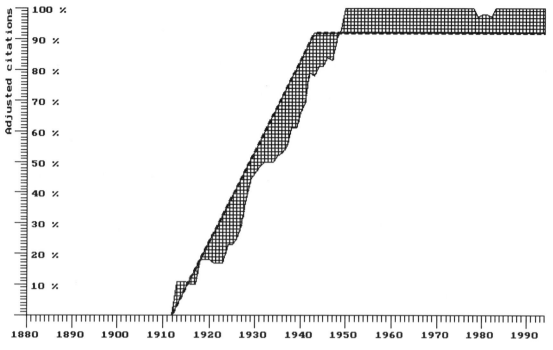

Figure A.5 Frank Lloyd Wright's histogram with short-term memory set to alternative A (from figure A.3)

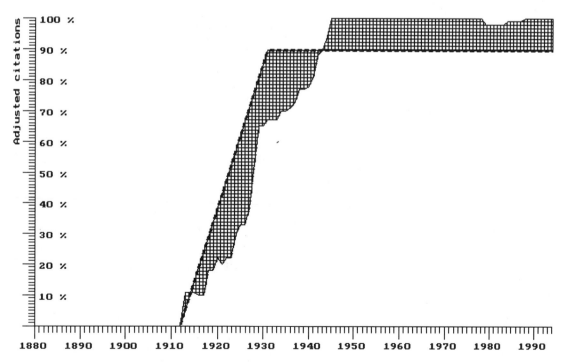

Figure A.6 Frank Lloyd Wright's histogram with short-term memory set to alternative B (from figure A.4)

between the steady histogram and the horizontal axis equals the area contained between the real histogram and the horizontal. The first condition is designed to reflect the time it takes fully to replace the texts in memory; the second condition ensures that the volume of citations as rearranged remains approximately the same as before the operation.[2]

Deviations from steadiness are marked with shading in the histograms. As a consequence of the second condition, the shaded areas below and above the straight lines are always equal.

To obtain the percentiles cited in the chapter, architects are ranked in terms of normalcy. The curves of older architects often display larger shaded areas merely because they are extended over a longer time span. To put all architects on a comparable standing before ranking, the shaded areas are divided by the duration of the histograms. The quotients obtained reflect standard yearly deviations.

Chapter 7: Predictable and Unpredictable Lists of Names

Predicting Names for a Text

Originally, the task presented in the chapter consisted of predicting the names to be granted main entries in the fifth volume if the *AIA Encyclopedia*. A generalized version of the procedure is described here—one used to predict the names in every text of the corpus, compare predictions with reality, assign a numerical value to the fit, and rank the texts accordingly.

Discharging the task requires identifying the available data, finding a prediction strategy, and defining a way to evaluate the results. The data for each text include the number of architects cited, publication date, coverage, the universe of architects at the time of publication, and the citations accumulated by each architect at publication time.

The strategy consists of generating a list of architects sorted according to their likelihood to be included in the volume. This can be achieved in a variety of ways, most of which follow a common pattern. The list should contain architects with appropriate dates of birth, in accordance with the work's coverage. All architects in the universe must be considered, not only those born within the coverage span. Outstanding personalities with birth dates slightly off the coverage may take precedence over lesser known figures born at the right time. The list must be sorted according to some priority rule, based on adjusted or raw citations, or both.

All architects in the universe of two citations at the time of text publication are ranked according to a number obtained as the product of two values: their adjusted citations at publication time, and a coefficient representing their centrality to the coverage span. In case of ties, ranking is by raw citations, and if ties persist, by birth date. (Later date of birth is given higher priority because the person had less time to gather citations.) Names are predicted according to the ranking.

Results were evaluated by the percentage of correct guesses. Several strategies differing primarily in the centrality coefficient were tested, and the one with the best overall performance was adopted.

Chapter 8: Isonomy and Text Histograms

Kappas and Adjusted Kappas

Each text of the corpus entails a partition of the universe into two classes—architects who are cited and those who are not. Two texts define a partition into four classes—architects cited in both texts, in one but not in the other, in the latter but not in the former, and in none. Let [1], [2], [3], and [4] be the number of architects in each of these groups:

		Text B	
		Architects cited	Architects not cited
Text A	Architects cited	[1]	[3]
	Architects not cited	[4]	[2]

The kappa is an association measurement defined by Cohen[3] as:

$$kappa = (Po - Pc)/(1 - Pc),$$

where

$$Total = [1] + [2] + [3] + [4],$$

$$Po = ([1] + [2])/Total, \text{ and}$$

$$Pc = (([1] + [3])/Total) * (([1] + [4])/Total) +$$
$$(([2] + [3])/Total) * (([2] + [4])/Total).$$

The kappa and other similar statistics based on a four-partite division of a population cannot be applied to our field directly because quadrant [2] is ill defined. Given any two texts, the list of architects not cited in neither one nor the other is time dependent; as more architects enter the universe, the category swells with more names.

This forced me to use a more sensitive classification. Architects are said to be *pertinent* to a text if they are cited in the text, or they were born within the text's coverage span and were in the universe at the time of publication of the text. Each text now entails a partition of the universe into three classes—the architects cited, the pertinent architects not cited, and the nonpertinent architects.

With two texts, the universe is divided into nine classes, six of which are relevant to the association measurement:

		Text B		
		Cited	Pertinent, not cited	Not pertinent
	Cited	[1]	[3]	[5]
Text A	Pertinent, not cited	[4]	[2]	
	Not pertinent	[6]		

The kappas are computed by adding the numbers in box [5] to those in box [3], and the numbers of box [6] to those in box [4], and then using Cohen's formula. Conceptually, this amounts to assuming that the numbers in boxes [7] to [9] (missing in the diagram) contain zeros, and that no distinction is made between pertinet and nonpertinent architects.

Adjusted kappas differ from kappas in two ways: first, architects not pertinent to either text (those in boxes [5] and [6]) are ignored; and second, a minimum overlap between texts is required for kappa to be computed. If the minimum overlap requirement is not met, adjusted kappa is set at zero.

The overlap between two texts is the lesser of values A and B:

$$A = ([1] + [3])/([1] + [3] + [5]),$$

$$B = ([1] + [4])/([1] + [4] + [6]).$$

A represents the pertinence to text B of the architects cited in A; B represents the pertinence to text A of the citations in B. To meet the overlap requirement both ratios must be equal to or greater than $1/3$.

The pairings of figure 8.1 and the text histograms of figures 8.6 and following are based on kappas. Adjusted kappas are used for the pairings of figures 8.2 and 8.3, and for the clusters of figure 8.4.

When using adjusted kappas, the population of architects affecting the statistics is composed of those pertinent to both texts. Without the adjustment, the population includes, in addition, the architects cited in one text or the other. Either way, the population varies for different pairings of texts; under those circumstances, capricious results may be generated. This must be kept in mind when evaluating the outcome of chapters 8 and 9.

Clouds and Distance to the Centroid

To represent configuration of texts as a multidimensional cloud of points, kappa values ranging between one and minus one are transformed into distance measurements ranging between 0 and 100 by using the simple rule

Distance $= 50 * (1 - \text{kappa})$.

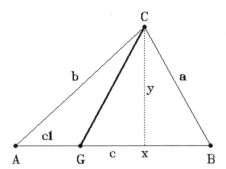

Figure A.7   Finding the distance to the centroid (diagram)

All texts in a cloud are assigned the same weight. To determine the distance of a point to the centroid one must gradually diminish the number of points in the cloud. This is done by repeatedly replacing two points (*A* and *B*, figure A.7) by their common center of gravity, which is a new point *G* with a mass equal to the sum of the masses, located on the segment defined by the original points at distances inversely proportional to the masses of those points. Let *c* be the distance between *A* and *B*, C_1 the distance between *A* and *G*, *K* the weight on *A*, and 1 the weight on *B*:

$$c_1 = c/(K + 1).$$

The distance of *G* to each to the remaining points in the clouds must now be calculated. Let *C* be one of the remaining points. No matter how many the dimensions of the cloud, the distance is determined by simple plane geometry. Let *y* be the height of triangle *ABC*, and *x* the distance from *A* to the projection of *C* on *AB*:

$$b^2 = x^2 + y^2 \therefore y^2 = b^2 - x^2$$

$$a^2 = (c - x)^2 + y^2$$

$$a^2 - b^2 = c^2 - 2cx$$

$$x = (b^2 + c^2 - a^2)/2c$$

$$Dist^2 = y^2 + (c_1 - x)^2$$

$$Dist = \sqrt{(b^2 + c_{12} - 2c_1 x)}.$$

Chapter 10: Cotextuality

International Coefficient of an Architect

Hypothesis: every architect has a measurable propensity to be cited in discourse of an international (or national) frame of reference. Some gravitate toward one end of the spectrum, some toward the other, and some remain in the middle. The goal is to assign a coefficient to each one that will reflect those tendencies. One coefficient (national or international) will suffice; the other is its complement. The values must lend themselves to empirical verification. If the hypothesis were erroneous, no such confirmation would be possible; verification will validate not only the coefficients but the also the hypothesis.

Coefficients are verified by using them in a game that consists of predicting whether each text of the corpus is devoted to the Unites States only or to the world. Predictions are based on a value—the text predictor—obtained from multiplying the coefficients of all architects featured in the text. For example, if the predictor is greater than one, the text is international. The effectiveness of a coefficient is given by the ratio of correct guesses when the coefficient is used to generate a predictor for every text in the corpus.

Every text is either domestic or worldwide in scope; accordingly, each citation of an architect is either a domestic or a world citation, depending on the kind of text in which it occurs. Let *DomA* and *WldA* be the number of an architect's citations in each of the types of texts.

The simplest coefficient would be the ratio of the two numbers—*WldA/DomA*. Architects could be ranked accordingly, from those most often cited in international publications to those most often found in the domestic literature. The ratios are easy to obtain and understand, but their effectiveness as predictors is limited. Guessing "international" when the product of the ratios is greater than one leads to correct results 60 percent of the times. That is better than a blind guess, which is successful only one time in two, but not as good as it could be.

Ratios have limited effectiveness because they ignore the actual size of *WldA* and *DomA*: little known, rarely mentioned architects are given the same importance as luminaries, which skews the results. Using the difference of citations *WldA-DomA* as a coefficient would take care of the problem, but at the cost of creating another: minor percentage differences in the citations of famous architects would carry inordinate weight in the outcome.

To find a function of *WldA* and *DomA* that is likely to be a good predictor, let us start from the guessing procedure itself and work our way backward. The information to be tapped includes the lists of citations of American architects in all texts, and the frame of reference of every text in the corpus except the one subject to the guess. Six variables define the problem:

WldC   Number of texts in the corpus with a worldwide frame of reference

DomC   Number of texts in the corpus with a domestic frame of reference

WldA   An architect's number of citations in worldwide texts

DomA   An architect's number of citations in domestic texts

I   An architect's international coefficient as a function of the preceding variables

P   Text predictor, equal to the product of coefficients of all architects cited in a text

WldC and *DomC* are constants for any composition of the corpus. *WldA*, *DomA*, and *I* are architect-dependent variables; *P* is a text-dependent variable. The goal is to devise an coefficient that will reflect the impact on *P* caused by the citation, or lack of citation, of an architect. "Impact" means the effect that an architect's presence or absence has on the likelihood of the text being national or international. A formula for the coefficient cannot be deduced from the given, but it can be constructed with the help of several loose assumptions, and it can be tested.

Let P_1 be the desired value of *P* if a certain architect is not cited in a text, and P_2 be the desired value of *P* if he is cited. The first assumption is that the architect's coefficient is proportional to the difference between P_2 and P_1. This is unlikely to be true in every case, but it is reasonable nevertheless. If it makes no difference whether the architect is cited or not, the coefficient should be zero. Or, the greater the effect of an architect's citation or lack thereof, the greater the coefficient.

The second assumption is that a text predictor *P* generally reflects the ratio between *WldC* and *DomC*—the number of worldwide and domestic texts in the corpus. Again, this is surely untrue in many cases, but it is the best assumption in the face of ignorance. Consequently, we may write:

$$P_1 = WldC/DomC.$$

Another way of thinking of the predictor is as the ratio between a numerator and a denominator. Let the numerator be the sum of all the worldwide citations (*WldA*) of all the architects cited in the text, and the denominator be the sum of all their domestic citations (*DomA*). Once again, we do not know how many there are, but it is reasonable to think that their numbers are proportional to *WldC* and *DomC*, the third assumption.

Let *K* be an appropriate constant. The expression can be rewritten to state:

$$P_1 = (WldC * K)/(DomC * K).$$

The numerator and denominator reflect the actual international and domestic citations of all architects in the text before a given architect is cited. If he happens to be cited, his international and domestic citations will be added to the numerator and denominator.

$$P_2 = ((WldC * K) + WldA)/((DomC * K) + DomA).$$

The greater the value of *K*, the lesser the impact of any given architect.

The coefficient *I* is intended to reflect the difference between P_2 and P_1:

$$I = ((WldC * K) + WldA)/((DomC * K) + DomA) - WldC/DomC.$$

The fourth assumption is that

$$K = 1/(WldA + DomA),$$

in other words, the "smaller" the architect (the fewer his total citations), the greater K and therefore the less the impact of his presence or absence. Conversely, the "greater" the architect, the weightier he is.

Substituting K for this value, I can be rewritten as:

$$I = \frac{WldC/(WldA + DomA) + WldA}{DomC/(WldA + DomA) + DomA} - \frac{WldC}{DomC}.$$

The coefficient may be multiplied by any constant, and constants may be added to it without affecting the resulting rankings. Multiplying it by $DomC/WldC$, and subtracting one from it, I may be rewritten as:

$$I = \frac{DomC}{WldA} * \frac{WldA(WldA + DomA) + WldC}{DomA(WldA + DomA) + DomC}.$$

This is the formula used for the computations of chapter 10. Note that the coefficient equals one when $WldA = DomA = $ zero; in other words, no prediction can be made one way or the other before an architect has been cited at least once.

When calculating coefficients for a given year, as in the histograms of chapter 10, the symbols $WldC$, $DomC$, $WldA$, and $DomA$ refer to currently active texts.

The procedure to play the guessing game is as follows:

1. Specify, for each texts of the corpus, whether it is national or international.

2. Figure out the number of national and international texts in which each architect is cited, and compute the coefficient with the formula given above. Do not count his citation in the text being guessed.

3. Figure out the predictor of each text as the product of the coefficients of all architects cited.

4. Rank all known texts in terms of decreasing predictors. The ranking is likely to start with international texts, end with domestic ones, and have the two intermingling in between.

5. Determine the cut-off predictor that best divides national and international texts in the ranking. The value is likely to be close to one, but it need not be exactly one.

6. Figure out the predictor for the unknown text (as in step 3).

7. If the predictor from step 6 is lower than the cut-off point found in step 5, guess that the unknown text is domestic; guess international otherwise.

The method yields a correct result for 291 of the 380 texts of the corpus (figure 10.5); the success rate is 77 percent. By using adjusted instead of raw citations the rate is raised to 78 percent.

How good are these results? A person guessing randomly between two frames of reference would face 50 percent chance of success. An astute gambler could raise the odds: 209 texts in the corpus (55 percent) are devoted exclusively to

American architecture. By betting "national' every time, he could secure a 55 percent rate of success by the end of the series.

Guessing on the basis of coefficients raises the success rate full 22 percentage points above clever gambling. This seems rather significant. To see how significant it really is, let us figure out the probabilities of duplicating the system's performance merely by chance.

Betting "national" consistently, as a clever gambler would do, the rate of success cannot be improved upon. If every text of the corpus is subject to a guess, 55 percent is both the lower and higher ceiling for the gambler's expectations. To improve the outcome at least once in a while, he must use another strategy.

The total number of guessing arrays available to the gambler equals the number of permutations of 380 objects (guesses) that can be of only two kinds, international and domestic. That number is $2^{380} = 2.5 \times 10^{114}$. Most of the arrays, however, would never be chosen by a clever gambler. He knows the proportion of domestic and world texts in the corpus, 55 and 45 percent, respectively. He would only choose guess arrays in which the two types mix in the right proportion. The expected rate of success with such a mix is $0.55 \times 0.55 + 0.45 \times 0.45 = 50.5$ percent, where the first term represents the number of expected correct "domestic" guesses and the second term the expected correct "world" guesses.

There are 1.5×10^{112} arrays of 380 guesses with the proper mix of "domestic" and "world." Only 1.7×10^{77} of them include 291 or more correct guesses. The gambler's chances of succeeding 291 times or more, and thus duplicating the rate of success of the procedure, are the ratio between the two figures. The odds of meeting or beating the performance of the system are on the order of 1 in 10^{35}.

The analysis validates the use of international coefficients to predict the frame of reference of texts, confirming the plausibility of associating certain architects with either one frame of reference or the other.

Chapter 11: Issues of Gender Equity

Ranking Texts by Gender Receptivity

Ranking texts by receptivity to the work of women architects is more involved than rankings by foresight or predictability, developed in chapters 6 and 7. Ultimately, however, it rests solely on simple divisions and comparisons between the resulting numbers, like those earlier rankings.

The data comprise the following items for each text in the corpus:

Tot Total size of the text population, which is composed of all the architects cited in the text

Fem Number of women architects in the text (including one-half of the firms and teams having at least one woman as a partner, principal, or team member)

Also used are text publication date, coverage, and number and gender of the architects in the pertinent universe. The last consists of the architects and firms born within the text's coverage and included in the universe by the year of publication.

The following quotients result directly from the data:

Per   Actual percentage of women's citations in the text, equal to *Fem/Tot*.

Exp   Expected percentage of citations of women, equal to the percentage of women within the pertinent universe. This is the percentage to be expected if writers were to pick their subjects randomly from the universe.

Rat   Ratio between actual and expected percentages of women, or *Per/Exp*. *Rat* is defined only when *Exp* is greater then zero.

The texts are classified into four groups, from 1 to 4. Texts in lower-number groups are considered more receptive. The definition of the groups and the ranking criteria within each group are as follows:

1. The highest positions in the ranking are for texts that cite women when no women are expected: *Exp* = 0 and *Per* > 0. Precedence within the group goes to texts with a higher *Per*, and in the case of ties, to those with a higher *Fem*. If a tie persists, the one published earlier goes first.

2. The next highest group in the ranking is composed of texts citing women when women are indeed expected: *Exp* > 0 and *Per* > 0. Sequencing within the section is by decreasing *Rat*s. In case of ties, greater *Per*s take precedence, then greater *Fem*s, and ultimately, if necessary, earlier publication date.

3. Texts with no actual or expected citations of women (*Exp* = 0 and *Per* = 0) come next. Ties are resolved placing first those with the lowest total numbers of citations (*Tot*s) and then those published earlier.

4. Finally, the ranking closes with texts in which women's citations are expected but not materialized: *Exp* > 0, *Per* = 0. Precedence is by increasing *Exp*s, then by publication date.

The resulting ranking of all texts in the corpus is reported in figure A.8. The critical data within each group (the one that primarily determines ranking) is printed in bold. The gender of the writers, editors, or persons otherwise responsible for the texts is marked in column [2].

Results for texts with small populations may be deceiving. In her 1960 article, Huxtable cited only fifteen architects; with women's participation in her universe at 4.2 percent, the expected number of women architects in her article was only 0.6. One isolated citation would have placed Huxtable comfortably above the expectations. This is true to an even larger extent for Diamondstein's *American Architecture Now*, were expectation is truly borderline, $14 \times 0.0354 = 0.5$! More significant from this perspective are the results for the 1957 edition of

Figure A.8 Texts ranked according to receptivity to female architects

Column headings:
[1] Percentile
[2] Author gender: + male, * female, ^combination
[3] FEM: Number of women architects in text
[4] TOT: Total number of architects in text
[5] PER: Percentage of women architects in text
[6] EXP: Expected percentage of women architects
[7] RAT: Ratio of [4] and [5]
[8] Publication date
[9] Author and title

[1]	[2]	[3] FEM	[4] TOT	[5] PER	[6] EXP	[7] RAT	[8]	[9]
Group I: PER > 0, EXP = 0 (women architects cited, not expected)								
99	+	3.0	41	**7.32**	0.00		1948	Kouwenhoven: *Made in America*
99	+	2.0	37	**5.41**	0.00		1974	Scully: *Modern Architecture*, 2nd ed. rev.
99	+	2.0	45	**4.44**	0.00		1949	Lynes: *The Tastemakers*
99		1.0	33	**3.03**	0.00		1941	*Pencil Points:* "Forty Under Forty"
99	+	1.0	36	**2.78**	0.00		1897	Van Brunt: *Architecture and Society*
98	+	1.0	40	**2.50**	0.00		1926	Jackson: *Development of American Architecture 1783–1830*
98	+	1.0	45	**2.22**	0.00		1929	Hitchcock: *Modern Architecture*
98	+	1.0	66	**1.52**	0.00		1955	Scully: *The Shingle Style and the Stick Style*
98		1.0	67	**1.49**	0.00		1910	*Men and Women of America: A Biographical Dictionary*
97		1.0	68	**1.47**	0.00		1926	*The Architectural Record* American Architect Golden Anniversary Number
97	+	3.0	218	**1.38**	0.00		1949	Larkin: *Art and Life in America*
97	+	1.0	76	**1.32**	0.00		1930	Cheney: *The New World Architecture*
97	+	0.5	41	**1.22**	0.00		1966	Stern: *40 Under 40: An Exhibition of Young Talent in Architecture*
96	+	1.0	105	**0.95**	0.00		1927	Tallmadge: *The Story of Architecture in America*
96	+	1.0	134	**0.75**	0.00		1936	Tallmadge: *The Story of Architecture in America*, rev. ed.
96	+	1.0	168	**0.60**	0.00		1928	Edgell: *The American Architecture of To-day*
Group II: PER > 0, EXP > 0 (women architects cited and expected)								
96	+	4.0	78	5.13	0.58	**8.81**	1987	Kostof: *America by Design*
95	+	2.0	39	5.13	0.84	**6.09**	1992	Reynolds: *Nineteenth Century Architecture*
95	+	0.5	26	1.92	0.39	**4.94**	1965	Millon (ed.): *Key Monuments in the History of Architecture*
95	*	6.0	184	3.26	0.76	**4.27**	1980	Ball: *Architecture and Interior Design*
94	+	5.0	167	2.99	0.70	**4.25**	1955	Tunnard & Reed: *American Skyline*
94	+	6.5	136	4.78	1.17	**4.10**	1983	Pulos: *American Design Ethic: A History of Industrial Design to 1940*
94	*	2.0	38	5.26	1.31	**4.01**	1984	Pokinski: *Development of the American Modern Style*
94	+	1.5	7	21.43	6.01	**3.56**	1988	Johnson & Wigley: *Deconstructivist Architecture*
93	+	5.5	147	3.74	1.09	**3.42**	1986	Stern: *Pride of Place: Building the American Dream*
93		4.5	97	4.64	1.39	**3.35**	1979	*The American Renaissance 1876–1917* (without Catalogue)
93	+	1.5	38	3.95	1.20	**3.29**	1983	Portoghesi: *Postmodern*
93	+	1.0	81	1.23	0.39	**3.20**	1972	Jordy: *American Buildings: Progressive and Academic Ideals*
92	+	1.5	171	0.88	0.28	**3.13**	1955	Andrews: *Architecture, Ambition, and Americans*
92	+	1.5	18	8.33	2.82	**2.96**	1991	Scully: *Architecture: The Natural and the Manmade*
92	+	1.0	23	4.35	1.47	**2.96**	1957	Maas: *The Gingerbread Age*
92	^	38.0	1297	2.93	1.00	**2.92**	1989	Kennedy (ed.): *Smithsonian Guide to Historic America*
91	+	3.5	49	7.14	2.46	**2.90**	1988	Klotz: *The History of Postmodern Architecture*
91	+	4.5	89	5.06	1.76	**2.87**	1986	Barford: *Understanding Modern Architecture*
91	*	4.0	101	3.96	1.42	**2.80**	1967	Ross: *Taste In America*
91	+	6.5	35	18.57	6.67	**2.79**	1981	Stern: *American Architecture: After Modernism*
90		8.5	182	4.67	1.69	**2.76**	1950	AIA: *Contemporary Architecture in the United States 1947–1949*

Figure A.8   (continued)

[1]	[2]	[3]	[4]	[5]	[6]	[7]	[8]	[9]
90	+	4.0	50	8.00	2.91	**2.74**	1991	*The Illustrated Dictionary of 20th Century Designers*
90	+	3.0	91	3.30	1.23	**2.68**	1985	Kostof: *A History of Architecture: Settings & Rituals*
89	+	2.5	54	4.63	1.74	**2.67**	1958	Peter: *Masters of Modern Architecture*
89	∧	10.0	212	4.72	1.80	**2.62**	1986	De Long, Searing, Stern: *American Architecture* (exhibition)
89	*	5.5	180	3.06	1.19	**2.57**	1985	Maddex: *Master Builders*
89	∧	3.5	98	3.57	1.40	**2.55**	1984	Poppeliers et al.: *What Style Is It?*
88	+	2.0	35	5.71	2.32	**2.46**	1994	Doremus: *Classical Styles in Modern Architecture*
88	*	1.0	35	2.86	1.17	**2.44**	1985	Crouch: *History of Architecture from Stonhenge to Skyscrapers*
88	+	1.0	24	4.17	1.71	**2.43**	1989	Devlin: *Portraits of American Architecture*
88	∧	5.0	111	4.50	1.88	**2.39**	1986	De Long, Searing, Stern: *American Architecture* (symposium)
87	+	34.0	612	5.56	2.35	**2.37**	1989	*AIA Encyclopedia of Architecture, Design, Engineering, and Construction*
87		1.0	25	4.00	1.70	**2.35**	1977	Milwaukee Art Center: *An American Architecture*
87	+	4.0	56	7.14	3.06	**2.34**	1984	Klotz: *Revision der Moderne*
87	+	13.0	302	4.30	1.89	**2.28**	1988	Pulos: *The American Design Adventure: 1940–1975*
86	∧	5.5	169	3.25	1.45	**2.25**	1986	Wilson et al.: *The Machine Age in America 1918–1941*
86	+	1.0	16	6.25	2.93	**2.13**	1971	Jencks: *Architecture 2000*
86	+	1.0	65	1.54	0.74	**2.09**	1971	Gillon: *Early Illustrations of American Architecture*
86	*	1.0	25	4.00	1.93	**2.07**	1985	Diamondstein: *American Architecture Now II*
85	+	11.5	369	3.12	1.55	**2.02**	1980	Hunt: *Encyclopedia of American Architecture*
85	+	12.0	441	2.72	1.47	**1.85**	1982	*Macmillan Encyclopedia of Architects* (Placzek, ed.)
85	+	4.5	104	4.33	2.38	**1.82**	1991	Sharp: *Illustrated Encyclopedia of Architects and Architecture*
84	+	3.5	63	5.56	3.08	**1.81**	1977	Stern (ed.): "Forty Under Forty"
84	+	5.5	119	4.62	2.57	**1.80**	1993	LeBlanc: *20th Century American Architecture*
84	+	2.5	20	12.50	6.98	**1.79**	1991	Papadakis: *A Decade of Architectural Design*
84	+	5.5	169	3.25	1.86	**1.75**	1988	Scully: *American Architecture and Urbanism*, new rev. ed.
83	+	2.5	61	4.10	2.38	**1.72**	1994	Striner: *Art Deco*
83	*	14.5	156	9.29	5.42	**1.72**	1993	Sarfatti Larson: *Behind the Postmodern Facade*
83	+	7.5	151	4.97	2.91	**1.70**	1993	Kulterman: *Architecture in the 20th Century*
83	+	3.5	104	3.37	1.98	**1.70**	1989	*AIA Encyclopedia of Architecture, Design, Engineering and Contruction* (main entries only)
82		2.5	140	1.79	1.06	**1.69**	1976	Panek: *American Architectural Styles 1600–1940*
82	+	1.0	51	1.96	1.17	**1.68**	1965	Early: *Romanticism in American Architecture*
82	+	16.5	415	3.98	2.39	**1.66**	1994	Packard (ed.): *Encyclopedia of American Architecture* (main entries only)
82	*	2.5	84	2.98	1.79	**1.66**	1988	Hollingworth: *Architecture of the 20th Century*
81	+	1.5	88	1.70	1.03	**1.65**	1990	Kennedy: *Rediscovering America*
81	+	1.0	46	2.17	1.32	**1.65**	1984	Jervis: *Design & Designers*
81	+	3.0	59	5.08	3.13	**1.63**	1981	Jencks: *The Language of Post-Modern Architecture*, 3rd ed.
81	∧	0.5	31	1.61	1.01	**1.60**	1988	Larkin et al.: *Colonial Design in the New World*
80	+	5.0	150	3.33	2.11	**1.58**	1986	Lampugnani: *Encyclopedia of 20th Century Architecture*
80	+	1.5	109	1.38	0.88	**1.56**	1970	Osborne: *The Oxford Companion to Art*
80	+	4.5	130	3.46	2.26	**1.53**	1961	Jones: *Architecture Today and Tomorrow*
79	∧	4.5	126	3.57	2.35	**1.52**	1989	Wodehouse & Moffett: *A History of Western Architecture*
79	*	1.5	48	3.13	2.09	**1.49**	1992	Weber: *American Art Deco*
79	+	2.5	189	1.32	0.89	**1.48**	1978	Andrews: *Architecture, Ambition and Americans*, rev. ed.
79	+	2.5	85	2.94	1.99	**1.48**	1973	Jacobus: *American Art of the 20th Century*
78	+	3.5	77	4.55	3.07	**1.48**	1984	Jencks: *The Language of Post-Modern Architecture*, 4th ed.
78	+	13.5	414	3.26	2.21	**1.48**	1992	Gowans: *Styles and Types of North American Architecture*
78	+	4.5	140	3.21	2.18	**1.47**	1959	McCallum: *Architecture USA*
78	+	2.0	85	2.35	1.60	**1.47**	1980	Frampton: *Modern Architecture*
77	+	3.0	85	3.53	2.48	**1.42**	1991	Copplestone: *Twentieth-Century World Architecture*
77	+	0.5	77	0.65	0.46	**1.41**	1992	Garrett: *Classical America*

Figure A.8   (continued)

[1]	[2]	[3]	[4]	[5]	[6]	[7]	[8]	[9]
77	+	3.0	147	2.04	1.48	**1.38**	1981	Thorndike: *Three Centuries of Notable American Architects*
77	+	1.0	47	2.13	1.56	**1.37**	1988	Norberg-Schulz: *New World Architecture*
76	+	1.5	43	3.49	2.56	**1.37**	1973	Jencks: *Modern Movements in Architecture*
76	+	2.0	138	1.45	1.07	**1.36**	1976	Platt: *America's Gilded Age*
76	+	2.5	79	3.16	2.43	**1.30**	1972	Sharp: *Visual History of 20th C Architecture*
76	+	1.5	38	3.95	3.05	**1.29**	1954	Giedion: *A Decade of Contemporary Architecture*, 2nd ed.
75	+	2.5	62	4.03	3.19	**1.26**	1980	Portoghesi: *Architecture 1980*
75	*	1.5	39	3.85	3.13	**1.23**	1990	Cottom-Winslow: *Environmental Design*
75		2.0	49	4.08	3.38	**1.21**	1985	AIA J.: 7th to 9th Annual Reviews of New American Architecture
74	+	3.5	264	1.33	1.10	**1.21**	1969	Whiffen: *American Architecture Since 1780*
74	+	1.5	65	2.31	1.92	**1.20**	1952	Hitchcock & Drexler: *Built in USA. Post-war Architecture*
74	*	2.0	22	9.09	7.69	**1.18**	1981	Searing: *Speaking a New Classicism: American Architecture now*
74	+	4.5	90	5.00	4.27	**1.17**	1991	Jencks: *The Language of Post-Modern Architecture*, 6th ed.
73		0.5	35	1.43	1.24	**1.15**	1979	*The American Renaissance 1876–1917* (Catalogue only)
73	+	1.5	60	2.50	2.20	**1.14**	1964	Pehnt: *Encyclopedia of Modern Architecture*
73	+	2.5	143	1.75	1.54	**1.13**	1969	Scully: *American Architecture and Urbanism*
73	∧	1.0	8	12.50	11.11	**1.13**	1991	Noever (ed.): *Architecture in Transition*
72	+	1.5	52	2.88	2.60	**1.11**	1981	Wolfe: *From Bauhaus to Our House*
72	∧	1.0	61	1.64	1.50	**1.10**	1985	Klein & Fogle: *Clues to American Architecture*
72	+	2.0	135	1.48	1.37	**1.08**	1966	Fitch: *American Building: The Historical Forces that Shaped It*
72	+	1.5	192	0.78	0.74	**1.06**	1958	Hitchcock: *Architecture: Nineteenth and Twentieth Centuries*
71	+	1.5	158	0.95	0.91	**1.05**	1975	Loth & Trousdale: *The Only Proper Style*
71	∧	8.5	139	6.12	5.94	**1.03**	1989	Peel, Powell & Garrett: *20th-Century Architecture*
71	*	15.5	840	1.85	1.81	**1.02**	1991	Williamson: *American Architects and the Mechanics of Fame*
71		2.5	162	1.54	1.52	**1.01**	1981	*The New Encyclopaedia Britannica*, 15th ed.
70	+	4.5	202	2.23	2.21	**1.01**	1991	Wodehouse: *Roots of International Style Architecture*
70	+	19.0	346	5.49	5.51	**1.00**	1989	Krantz: *American Architects*
70	+	3.0	45	6.67	6.73	**0.99**	1987	Jencks: *Post-Modernism: The New Classicism in Art and Architecture*
69	∧	2.0	78	2.56	2.59	**0.99**	1991	Gossel & Lenhauser: *Architecture in the 20th Century*
69	+	2.0	170	1.18	1.19	**0.98**	1985	Handlin: *American Architecture*
69	+	1.0	194	0.52	0.54	**0.96**	1977	Brown: *American Art to 1900*
69	∧	3.5	67	5.22	5.61	**0.93**	1990	Hays & Burns (eds.): *Thinking the Past: Recent American Architecture*
68	+	2.5	188	1.33	1.43	**0.93**	1953	Ferriss: *Power in Buildings*
68	+	3.5	297	1.18	1.30	**0.91**	1992	Whiffen: *American Architecture Since 1780*
68	+	4.0	295	1.36	1.50	**0.91**	1979	Roth: *A Concise History of American Architecture*
68	+	1.5	89	1.69	1.87	**0.90**	1982	Curtis: *Modern Architecture Since 1900*
67	+	1.0	57	1.75	2.02	**0.87**	1992	Thomas & Lewis: *American Architectural Masterpieces*
67		1.0	34	2.94	3.40	**0.87**	1982	AIA J.: 4th to 6th Annual Reviews of New American Architecture
67		2.5	55	4.55	5.37	**0.85**	1988	AIA J.: 10th to 12th Annual Reviews of New American Architecture
67	+	2.0	67	2.99	3.53	**0.84**	1985	Marder: *The Critical Edge: Controversy in American Architecture*
66	+	5.0	43	11.63	13.89	**0.84**	1986	Allen: *Emerging Voices: New Generation of Architects in America*
66	+	2.5	68	3.68	4.41	**0.83**	1980	Kulterman: *Architecture in the Seventies*
66	*	4.0	203	1.97	2.42	**0.81**	1982	McCoy & Goldstein: *Guide to U.S. Architecture 1940–1980*
66	*	2.0	117	1.71	2.10	**0.81**	1987	Oppenheimer Dean: "75 Turbulent Years of American Architecture"
65	+	1.0	121	0.83	1.02	**0.81**	1977	Richards: *Who's Who in Architecture*
65	+	2.5	204	1.23	1.52	**0.80**	1976	White: *The Architecture Book*
65	+	5.0	409	1.22	1.53	**0.80**	1961	Burchard & Bush-Brown: *The Architecture of America*
64	+	2.0	51	3.92	5.00	**0.78**	1977	Jencks: *The Language of Post-Modern Architecture*, rev. ed.
64	+	1.5	73	2.05	2.63	**0.78**	1994	Peter: *The Oral History of Modern Architecture*

Figure A.8   (continued)

[1]	[2]	[3]	[4]	[5]	[6]	[7]	[8]	[9]
64	+	3.5	112	3.13	4.02	**0.78**	1993	Heyer: *American Architecture in the Late 20th Century*
64	+	1.5	86	1.74	2.26	**0.77**	1991	Sharp: *Twentieth Century Architecture: A Visual History*
63	+	9.5	304	3.13	4.07	**0.77**	1977	Smith, C. R.: *Supermannerism*
63	∧	1.5	19	7.89	10.42	**0.76**	1990	Papadakis & Watson (eds.): *New Classicism: Omnibus Volume*
63	+	0.5	57	0.88	1.18	**0.74**	1967	Giedion: *Space, Time, and Architecture*, rev. ed.
63	+	2.0	144	1.39	1.96	**0.71**	1986	Duncan: *American Art Deco*
62	+	1.0	29	3.45	4.88	**0.71**	1977	Jencks: *The Language of Post-Modern Architecture*
62		2.5	249	1.00	1.43	**0.70**	1972	*Encyclopaedia Britannica*, 14th ed. (1972)
62	+	2.5	215	1.16	1.66	**0.70**	1976	Tafuri & Dal Co.: *Modern Architecture*
62	+	0.5	47	1.06	1.55	**0.68**	1980	Raeburn: *Architecture of the Western World*
61	+	3.5	337	1.04	1.52	**0.68**	1976	Wodehouse: *American Architects from the Civil War to the Present*
61	∧	5.0	36	13.89	20.59	**0.67**	1983	Colquhoun et al.: *Promising Directions in American Architecture*
61	*	1.5	181	0.83	1.23	**0.67**	1985	Maddex: *Built in the USA: American Buildings from A to Z*
61	+	1.0	130	0.77	1.15	**0.67**	1974	Kidney: *The Architecture of Choice: Eclecticism in America 1880–1930*
60	∧	1.5	120	1.25	1.87	**0.67**	1993	Van Vynckt (ed.): *International Dictionary of Architects & Architecture*
60	+	0.5	107	0.47	0.72	**0.65**	1959	Reed: *The Golden City*
60	+	2.5	63	3.97	6.12	**0.65**	1975	Blake & Quint: *Modern Architecture America*
59	+	6.0	564	1.06	1.69	**0.63**	1952	Hamlin, T.: *Forms and Functions of 20th Century Architecture*
59	*	9.5	129	7.36	11.90	**0.62**	1989	Russell: *Architecture and Design 1970–1990*
59	+	2.0	83	2.41	3.92	**0.62**	1981	Sanderson: *International Handbook of Contemporary Developments in Architecture*
59	+	3.0	324	0.93	1.51	**0.61**	1981	Whiffen & Koepper: *American Architecture 1607–1976*
58	+	0.5	46	1.09	1.82	**0.60**	1966	Jacobus: *Twentieth Century Architecture: The Middle Years 1940–66*
58	+	1.0	64	1.56	2.62	**0.60**	1973	Cook & Klotz: *Conversations with Architects*
58	+	3.0	478	0.63	1.07	**0.59**	1960	Condit: *American Building Art: The 19th & the 20th Centuries*
58	∧	4.5	72	6.25	10.91	**0.57**	1990	AIA: *American Architecture of the 1980s.*
57	+	1.0	104	0.96	1.68	**0.57**	1972	Jordy: *American Buildings: Impact of European Modernism*
57	+	1.0	43	2.33	4.30	**0.54**	1990	Jencks: *The New Moderns from Late to Neo-Modernism*
57	+	3.0	406	0.74	1.41	**0.52**	1976	Smith, K.: *A Pictorial History of Architecture in America*
57	*	1.0	132	0.76	1.49	**0.51**	1978	Williamson: "An Architectural Family Tree"
56	+	1.0	130	0.77	1.52	**0.51**	1968	Portoghesi: *Dizionario enciclopedico di architettura e urbanistica*
56		0.5	40	1.25	2.47	**0.51**	1961	*Contemporary Architecture of the World 1961*
56	∧	1.0	142	0.70	1.41	**0.50**	1981	Rugoff: *Encyclopedia of American Art*
56	+	0.5	30	1.67	3.41	**0.49**	1982	Portoghesi: *After Modern Architecture*
55	+	0.5	70	0.71	1.48	**0.48**	1970	Hamilton: *19th & 20th Century Art: Painting, Sculpture, Architecture*
55	+	2.0	126	1.59	3.31	**0.48**	1982	Jencks: *Architecture Today*
55	+	0.5	51	0.98	2.08	**0.47**	1959	Joedicke: *A History of Modern Architecture*
54	*	4.0	239	1.67	3.60	**0.47**	1989	Wright: *Sourcebook of Contemporary North American Architecture*
54	+	0.5	80	0.63	1.36	**0.46**	1970	Mendelowitz: *A History of American Art*
54	*	1.5	161	0.93	2.06	**0.45**	1980	Emanuel (ed.): *Contemporary Architects*
54	+	1.0	53	1.89	4.17	**0.45**	1974	Scully: *The Shingle Style Today*
53	+	4.0	284	1.41	3.14	**0.45**	1961	Von Eckardt (ed.): *Mid-Century Architecture in America*
53	+	1.0	149	0.67	1.54	**0.44**	1980	Reid: *The Book of Buildings*
53	∧	1.5	256	0.59	1.35	**0.43**	1960	Pierson & Davidson: *Arts in the United States*
53	+	5.5	826	0.67	1.54	**0.43**	1981	Smith, K.: *The Architecture of the United States*
52	*	0.5	99	0.51	1.24	**0.41**	1968	Norman: *Traveler's Guide to American Art*
52		1.5	272	0.55	1.40	**0.39**	1964	*Encyclopaedia Britannica*, 14th ed. (1964)
52	+	5.5	967	0.57	1.55	**0.37**	1984	Hunt: *American Architecture: A Field Guide*
52	+	0.5	72	0.69	1.92	**0.36**	1994	Packard (ed.): *Encyclopedia of American Architecture*
51	+	1.0	182	0.55	1.54	**0.36**	1976	Pevsner: *A History of Building Types*
51	+	0.5	92	0.54	1.55	**0.35**	1966	Benevolo: *History of Modern Architecture*

Figure A.8   (continued)

[1]	[2]	[3]	[4]	[5]	[6]	[7]	[8]	[9]
51	*	7.5	612	1.23	3.51	**0.35**	1985	Stimpson: *Fieldguide to Landmarks of Modern Architecture in United States*
51		0.5	43	1.16	3.33	**0.35**	1979	*AIA J.:* 1st to 3rd Annual Reviews of New American Architecture
50	+	0.5	54	0.93	2.81	**0.33**	1959	Kulterman: *Architecture of Today*
50	∧	1.0	15	6.67	21.28	**0.31**	1991	Cook & Llewellyn-Jones: *New Spirit in Architecture*
50		0.5	47	1.06	3.88	**0.27**	1980	*GA Document Special Issue 1970–1980*
49	+	1.0	106	0.94	3.67	**0.26**	1977	Stern: *New Directions in American Architecture*, rev. ed.
49		0.5	26	1.92	8.06	**0.24**	1985	*Cross Currents of American Architecture* (AD Profile)
49	∧	0.5	174	0.29	1.22	**0.24**	1979	Brown et al.: *American Art*
49	+	0.5	177	0.28	1.33	**0.21**	1966	Myers: *McGraw-Hill Dictionary of Art*
48	+	37.5	268	13.99	70.00	**0.20**	1994	Byars: *The Design Encyclopedia*
48	+	0.5	65	0.77	4.65	**0.17**	1971	Kulski: *Architecture in a Revolutionary Era*
48	+	0.5	76	0.66	4.12	**0.16**	1966	Heyer: *Architects on Architecture*
48	+	0.5	312	0.16	1.05	**0.15**	1964	Gowans: *Images of American Living*
47	+	2.5	131	1.91	13.04	**0.15**	1962	Dixon: *Architectural Design Preview, USA*
47	+	0.5	48	1.04	7.14	**0.15**	1972	Chermayeff: *Observations on American Architecture*
47	*	0.5	177	0.28	2.00	**0.14**	1982	Wright: *Highlights to Recent American Architecture 1945–1978*
47	+	0.5	262	0.19	1.45	**0.13**	1966	Green: *American Art: A Historical Survey*
46	*	0.5	163	0.31	2.75	**0.11**	1980	Davern: *Architecture 1970–1980*
46	+	1.0	85	1.18	11.11	**0.11**	1969	Stern: *New Directions in American Architecture*
46	+	0.5	313	0.16	1.53	**0.10**	1976	Hammett: *Architecture in the United States*
46	*	0.5	239	0.21	2.17	**0.10**	1992	Bayer: *Art Deco Architecture*
45	+	3.0	34	8.82	100.00	**0.09**	1993	Economakis (ed.): *Building Classical: A Vision of Europe and America*
45	+	1.5	116	1.29	25.00	**0.05**	1957	McCallum: "Genetrix: Personal Contributions to American Architecture"
45	+	8.0	159	5.03	100.00	**0.05**	1988	Stern: *Modern Classicism*

Group III: PER = 0, EXP = 0 (women architects neither cited nor expected)

[1]	[2]	[3]	[4]	[5]	[6]	[7]	[8]	[9]
44		0.0	**2**	0.00	0.00		1830	*American Journal of Science & Arts:* "Architecture in the United States"
44		0.0	**2**	0.00	0.00		1887	Longfellow: "The Course of American Architecture"
44		0.0	**4**	0.00	0.00		1888	Arnold: *Studies in Architecture at Home and Abroad*
44	+	0.0	**5**	0.00	0.00		1888	Gwilt: *An Encyclopedia of Architecture*
43	+	0.0	**7**	0.00	0.00		1856	Heck: *The Art of Building in Ancient and Modern Times*
43	+	0.0	**7**	0.00	0.00		1925	Kimball: *Three Centuries of American Architecture*
43	+	0.0	**8**	0.00	0.00		1929	Taut: *Modern Architecture*
43	+	0.0	**8**	0.00	0.00		1949	Conder: *An Introduction to Modern Architecture*
42	+	0.0	**8**	0.00	0.00		1952	Jones: *O Strange New World*
42	+	0.0	**9**	0.00	0.00		1815	Latrobe(?): "State of the Fine Arts in the United States"
42	+	0.0	**9**	0.00	0.00		1862	Fergusson: *History of the Modern Styles of Architecture*
42	+	0.0	**10**	0.00	0.00		1851	Greenough: "American Architecture" and "Aesthetics at Washington"
41	+	0.0	**10**	0.00	0.00		1932	Hitchcock & Johnson: *The International Style*
41	+	0.0	**10**	0.00	0.00		1973	Rowland: *A History of the Modern Movement*
41		0.0	**11**	0.00	0.00		1900	Mackson: *American Architecture Interiors & Furniture*
41	+	0.0	**11**	0.00	0.00		1937	Behrendt: *Modern Building*
40	+	0.0	**12**	0.00	0.00		1932	*The World Almanac and Book of Facts 1932*
40	+	0.0	**12**	0.00	0.00		1962	Pevsner: "Architecture and Applied Arts"
40	+	0.0	**13**	0.00	0.00		1897	Statham: *Modern Architecture*
39	+	0.0	**13**	0.00	0.00		1945	Reilly: *Some Contemporary American Buildings*
39	*	0.0	**13**	0.00	0.00		1973	Glubok: *Composite of books 1970–1973*
39	+	0.0	**14**	0.00	0.00		1896	Hamlin, A.D.F.: *A Text-Book of the History of Architecture*
39	+	0.0	**14**	0.00	0.00		1940	Roth: *The New Architecture*

Figure A.8   (continued)

[1]	[2]	[3]	[4]	[5]	[6]	[7]	[8]	[9]
38	+	0.0	15	0.00	0.00		1880	Benjamin: *Art in America*
38	*	0.0	16	0.00	0.00		1883	van Rensselaer: "Recent Architecture in America"
38	+	0.0	16	0.00	0.00		1927	Reagan: *American Architecture of the Twentieth Century*
38	+	0.0	16	0.00	0.00		1938	Richardson & Corfiato: *The Art of Architecture*
37		0.0	17	0.00	0.00		1836	Cleveland: *Review of American Builder's General Price Book*
37	+	0.0	17	0.00	0.00		1884	Levy: *Modern American Architecture*
37	+	0.0	17	0.00	0.00		1930	Hoak & Church: *Masterpieces of Architecture in the United States*
37	+	0.0	18	0.00	0.00		1937	*The World Almanac and Book of Facts 1937*
36	+	0.0	19	0.00	0.00		1864	Jarves: *The Art-idea*
36		0.0	19	0.00	0.00		1892	*The Dictionary of Architecture*
36	*	0.0	20	0.00	0.00		1848	Tuthill: *History of Architecture from the Earliest Times*
36	+	0.0	20	0.00	0.00		1952	*The World Almanac and Book of Facts 1952*
35	+	0.0	21	0.00	0.00		1834	Dunlap: *History of the Arts of Design in the United States*
35	+	0.0	22	0.00	0.00		1902	Schuyler: "United States Architecture"
35	+	0.0	22	0.00	0.00		1924	Jackson: *American Colonial Architecture*
34	+	0.0	24	0.00	0.00		1916	Hamlin, A.D.F.: "25 Years of American Architecture"
34	+	0.0	24	0.00	0.00		1948	Pevsner: *An Outline of European Architecture*
34	+	0.0	25	0.00	0.00		1905	Fletcher: *A History of Architecture*, 5th ed.
34	+	0.0	25	0.00	0.00		1921	Fletcher: *A History of Architecture*, 6th ed.
33	+	0.0	26	0.00	0.00		1915	Eberlein: *The Architecture of Colonial America*
33	+	0.0	27	0.00	0.00		1909	Hamlin, A.D.F.: *A Text-Book of the History of Architecture*, 8th ed.
33	+	0.0	28	0.00	0.00		1941	Johnson: "Architecture" (in *The American Year Book*)
33	+	0.0	29	0.00	0.00		1941	Saint-Gaudens: *The American Artist and His Times*
32	+	0.0	30	0.00	0.00		1909	Bragdon: "Architecture in The United States"
32	+	0.0	30	0.00	0.00		1937	Newcomb: *Spanish-Colonial Architecture in the United States*
32	+	0.0	32	0.00	0.00		1891	Fergusson: *History of Modern Styles of Architecture*
32	+	0.0	32	0.00	0.00		1949	Bannister: *From Colony to Nation*
31	+	0.0	33	0.00	0.00		1893	Baedecker: *The United States*
31	+	0.0	33	0.00	0.00		1902	Sturgis: *A Dictionary of Architecture and Building*
31	+	0.0	33	0.00	0.00		1934	Whitaker: *The Story of Architecture*
31		0.0	33	0.00	0.00		1942	Museum of Modern Art: *What is Modern Architecture?*
30	+	0.0	36	0.00	0.00		1918	Kimball & Edgell: *A History of Architecture*
30	+	0.0	40	0.00	0.00		1966	Tatum: *The Arts in America: The Colonial Period*
30	+	0.0	42	0.00	0.00		1924	Mumford: *Sticks and Stones*
29	+	0.0	44	0.00	0.00		1941	Giedion: *Space, Time, and Architecture*
29	+	0.0	48	0.00	0.00		1952	Eberlein & Hubbard: *American Georgian Architecture*
29	+	0.0	50	0.00	0.00		1892	Schuyler: *American Architecture—Studies*
29		0.0	53	0.00	0.00		1941	*Architectural Record:* "American Architecture 1891–1941"
28	+	0.0	53	0.00	0.00		1968	Millar: *The Architects of the American Colonies*
28	*	0.0	55	0.00	0.00		1929	LaFollette: *Art in America*
28	+	0.0	56	0.00	0.00		1928	Hamlin, A.D.F.: *A Text-Book of the History of Architecture*, 18th pr.
28	+	0.0	57	0.00	0.00		1897	*The Architectural Record Great American Architects Series*
27	+	0.0	57	0.00	0.00		1932	Barr, Hitchcock, Johnson, & Mumford: Modern Architects
27	+	0.0	59	0.00	0.00		1899	Ware: *The Georgian Period*
27	+	0.0	59	0.00	0.00		1920	Greber: *L'Architecture aux Etats-Unies*
27	+	0.0	59	0.00	0.00		1940	Hamlin, T.: *Architecture Through the Ages*
26	*	0.0	64	0.00	0.00		1928	Jackman: *American Arts*
26	*	0.0	64	0.00	0.00		1944	Mock: *Built in America 1932–1944*
26		0.0	67	0.00	0.00		1886	*L'Architecture Americaine*
26		0.0	68	0.00	0.00		1910	*The Encyclopaedia Britannica*, 11th ed.
25	+	0.0	68	0.00	0.00		1931	Fletcher: *A History of Architecture*, 9th ed.
25	+	0.0	74	0.00	0.00		1930	Conant (ed.): *Modern Architecture*
25	+	0.0	78	0.00	0.00		1948	Fitch: *American Building: The Forces that Shape It*

Figure A.8   (continued)

[1]	[2]	[3]	[4]	[5]	[6]	[7]	[8]	[9]
24		0.0	**81**	0.00	0.00		1926	Berlin: *Ausstellung Neuer Amerikanischer Baukunst*
24	∧	0.0	**81**	0.00	0.00		1935	Cahill & Barr: *Art in America*
24	+	0.0	**84**	0.00	0.00		1928	Kimball: *American Architecture*
24	+	0.0	**85**	0.00	0.00		1942	Newcomb: *History of Modern Architecture*
23	+	0.0	**98**	0.00	0.00		1850	Sears: *A New and Popular Pictorial Description of the United States*
23	+	0.0	**108**	0.00	0.00		1952	Morrison: *Early American Architecture*
23	+	0.0	**111**	0.00	0.00		1913	Schuyler: *American Architecture and Other Writings*
23	+	0.0	**218**	0.00	0.00		1944	Hamlin, T.: *Greek Revival Architecture in America*
22	+	0.0	**226**	0.00	0.00		1926	Hamlin, T.: *The American Spirit in Architecture*
22	+	0.0	**296**	0.00	0.00		1929	Sexton: Composite of books published in 1928–31

Group IV: PER = 0, EXP > 0 (women architects expected but not cited)

[1]	[2]	[3]	[4]	[5]	[6]	[7]	[8]	[9]
22	+	0.0	91	0.00	**0.19**	0.00	1950	Watterson: *Five Thousand Years of Building*
22	+	0.0	67	0.00	**0.21**	0.00	1953	Tunnard: *The City of Man*
21	+	0.0	81	0.00	**0.31**	0.00	1959	Francastel: *Les Architects Cele + bres*
21	+	0.0	120	0.00	**0.34**	0.00	1950	P/A: "United States Architecture 1900–1950"
21	+	0.0	42	0.00	**0.58**	0.00	1972	Bacon: *Architecture and Townscape*
21	+	0.0	24	0.00	**0.66**	0.00	1958	Gloag: *Guide to Western Architecture*
20		0.0	56	0.00	**0.67**	0.00	1972	*Encyclopaedia Britannica*, 14th ed. (main entries only)
20	+	0.0	67	0.00	**0.75**	0.00	1970	Pierson: *American Building: Colonial and Neo-classical styles*
20	+	0.0	107	0.00	**0.76**	0.00	1953	Hamlin, T.: *Architecture Through the Ages*, rev ed.
19	+	0.0	18	0.00	**0.76**	0.00	1962	Banham: *Guide to Modern Architecture*
19	+	0.0	124	0.00	**0.77**	0.00	1989	Kennedy: *Greek Revival America*
19		0.0	68	0.00	**0.77**	0.00	1964	*Encyclopaedia Britannica*, 14th ed. (main entries only)
19	+	0.0	8	0.00	**0.85**	0.00	1959	Bode: *The Anatomy of American Popular Culture 1840–61*
18	+	0.0	15	0.00	**0.87**	0.00	1964	Hilberseimer: *Contemporary Architecture*
18	+	0.0	75	0.00	**0.88**	0.00	1968	McLanathan: *The American Tradition in the Arts*
18	+	0.0	20	0.00	**0.89**	0.00	1969	Norton: *The Arts in America: The 19th Century*
18	+	0.0	67	0.00	**0.94**	0.00	1961	Fletcher: *A History of Architecture (ed. Cordingley)*
17	+	0.0	31	0.00	**0.98**	0.00	1957	Morris: *A Century of AIA*
17	+	0.0	77	0.00	**0.98**	0.00	1977	Richards: *Who's Who in Architecture* (main entries only)
17	+	0.0	71	0.00	**0.98**	0.00	1978	Pierson: *American Buildings: Technology & the Picturesque*
17	+	0.0	32	0.00	**0.98**	0.00	1985	Macrae-Gibson: *The Secret Life of Buildings*
16	+	0.0	33	0.00	**1.05**	0.00	1970	Osborne: *The Oxford Companion to Art* (main entries only)
16	*	0.0	59	0.00	**1.08**	0.00	1980	Rifkind: *A Field Guide to American Architecture*
16	+	0.0	48	0.00	**1.11**	0.00	1978	Burton: *A Choice Over Our Heads*
16	+	0.0	68	0.00	**1.12**	0.00	1971	Cohen: *History of American Art*
15	+	0.0	95	0.00	**1.16**	0.00	1957	Gutheim: *1857–1957: One Hundred Years of Architecture in America*
15	+	0.0	21	0.00	**1.20**	0.00	1974	Norberg-Schulz: *Meaning in Western Architecture*
15	+	0.0	91	0.00	**1.20**	0.00	1986	Watkin: *A History of Western Architecture*
14	+	0.0	29	0.00	**1.20**	0.00	1964	Muschenheim: *Elements of the Art of Architecture*
14	+	0.0	7	0.00	**1.22**	0.00	1950	Egbert: *Organic Expression and American Architecture*
14	+	0.0	66	0.00	**1.26**	0.00	1960	Andrews: *Architecture in America*
14	+	0.0	12	0.00	**1.26**	0.00	1965	Collins: *Changing Ideals in Modern Architecture: 1750–1950*
13	+	0.0	13	0.00	**1.27**	0.00	1959	Jones: *Form Givers at Mid-century*
13	+	0.0	7	0.00	**1.28**	0.00	1967	Rosenblum: *Transformations in Late 18th Century Art*
13	+	0.0	44	0.00	**1.30**	0.00	1956	*Architectural Record:* "100 Years of Significant Building"
13	+	0.0	46	0.00	**1.31**	0.00	1965	Ulanov: *The Two Worlds of American Art*
12	+	0.0	30	0.00	**1.32**	0.00	1951	Giedion: *A Decade of Contemporary Architecture*
12	+	0.0	25	0.00	**1.33**	0.00	1961	Scully: *Modern Architecture*
12	+	0.0	55	0.00	**1.33**	0.00	1965	Rogers: *What's Up in Architecture*
12	+	0.0	37	0.00	**1.34**	0.00	1969	Jordan: *A Concise History of Western Architecture*
11	+	0.0	56	0.00	**1.34**	0.00	1976	*The World Almanac and Book of Facts 1977*

Figure A.8   (continued)

[1]	[2]	[3]	[4]	[5]	[6]	[7]	[8]	[9]
11	+	0.0	54	0.00	**1.36**	0.00	1967	Hillier: *From Tepees to Towers*
11	+	0.0	9	0.00	**1.36**	0.00	1977	Stierlin: *Encyclopaedia of World Architecture*
11	+	0.0	287	0.00	**1.37**	0.00	1982	Condit: *American Building: Materials and techniques*
10	+	0.0	22	0.00	**1.38**	0.00	1994	Peter: *The Oral History of Modern Architecture* (interviewees only)
10	*	0.0	37	0.00	**1.39**	0.00	1987	Yarwood: *A Chronology of Western Architecture*
10	+	0.0	80	0.00	**1.39**	0.00	1975	Fletcher: *A History of Architecture* (ed. Palmes)
9	+	0.0	40	0.00	**1.40**	0.00	1966	Read: *Encyclopedia of the Arts*
9		0.0	40	0.00	**1.40**	0.00	1964	Tschacbasov: *Teachers Manual for the Study of Art History*
9	+	0.0	33	0.00	**1.45**	0.00	1963	Jacobus: *Modern Architecture*
9	+	0.0	285	0.00	**1.46**	0.00	1968	Condit: *American Building . . . from beginning to the Present*
8	*	0.0	58	0.00	**1.48**	0.00	1975	Varian: *American Art Deco Architecture*
8	+	0.0	69	0.00	**1.50**	0.00	1980	Hunt: *Encyclopedia of American Architecture* (main entries only)
8	+	0.0	41	0.00	**1.50**	0.00	1980	Nuttgens: *Pocket Guide to Architecture*
8	∧	0.0	67	0.00	**1.50**	0.00	1986	Trachtenberg & Hyman: *Architecture from Prehistory to PostModernism*
8	+	0.0	100	0.00	**1.50**	0.00	1987	Musgrove (ed.): *Fletcher's History of Architecture*, 19th ed.
7	+	0.0	23	0.00	**1.50**	0.00	1962	*The World Almanac and Book of Facts 1962*
7	+	0.0	36	0.00	**1.51**	0.00	1983	Frampton (w. Futagawa): *Modern Architecture 1851–1945*
7	*	0.0	52	0.00	**1.52**	0.00	1981	*The World Almanac and Book of Facts 1982*
7	+	0.0	54	0.00	**1.55**	0.00	1971	*The World Almanac and Book of Facts 1972*
6	+	0.0	14	0.00	**1.56**	0.00	1970	Hofmann & Kultermann: *Modern Architecture in Color*
6	+	0.0	38	0.00	**1.57**	0.00	1983	Nuttgens: *The Story of Architecture*
6	+	0.0	100	0.00	**1.58**	0.00	1983	Risebero: *Modern Architecture and Design*
6	+	0.0	29	0.00	**1.58**	0.00	1966	*The World Almanac and Book of Facts 1967*
5	+	0.0	7	0.00	**1.63**	0.00	1982	Pothorn: *Architectural Styles*
5	+	0.0	4	0.00	**1.65**	0.00	1976	Brolin: *The Failure of Modern Architecture*
5	+	0.0	35	0.00	**1.69**	0.00	1988	Nuttgens: *Understanding Modern Architecture*
4	+	0.0	32	0.00	**1.76**	0.00	1969	Joedicke: *Architecture Since 1945*
4	+	0.0	56	0.00	**1.79**	0.00	1990	*The World Almanac and Book of Facts 1991*
4	*	0.0	40	0.00	**1.79**	0.00	1992	Newhouse: *The Builders: Marvels of Engineering*
4	+	0.0	59	0.00	**1.82**	0.00	1993	Roth: *Understanding Architecture*
3	+	0.0	14	0.00	**2.10**	0.00	1973	Boorstin: *The Americans: The Democratic Experience*
3	+	0.0	49	0.00	**2.11**	0.00	1990	Saunders: *Modern Architecture* (Photographs by Stoller)
3	*	0.0	36	0.00	**2.11**	0.00	1984	Flon (ed.): *The World Atlas of Architecture*
3	+	0.0	45	0.00	**2.12**	0.00	1988	Gibberd: *Architecture Source Book*
2	+	0.0	52	0.00	**2.27**	0.00	1965	Drexler: *Modern Architecture USA*
2	+	0.0	46	0.00	**2.60**	0.00	1972	Fitch: *American Building: The Environmental Forces that Shaped It*
2	+	0.0	123	0.00	**2.77**	0.00	1979	Drexler: *Transformations in Modern Architecture*
2	+	0.0	101	0.00	**2.88**	0.00	1964	Creighton: *American Architecture*
1	+	0.0	11	0.00	**3.08**	0.00	1976	Kulterman: *New Architecture in the World*
1	+	0.0	80	0.00	**3.26**	0.00	1957	USIA: *Architecture USA* (ed: Blake?)
1	+	0.0	44	0.00	**3.45**	0.00	1977	Blake: *Form Follows Fiasco*
1	*	0.0	18	0.00	**3.45**	0.00	1980	Diamondstein: *American Architecture Now*
0	*	0.0	15	0.00	**4.17**	0.00	1960	Huxtable: *Twentieth-Century Architecture*

Architecture USA, by the U. S. Information Agency, the second least-receptive text to women in the corpus according to the ranking. With 80 architects featured and 3.8 percent in the universe being women, three women architects would have been necessary for women to be granted equal presence as men, but not one was cited.

Validity

The ranking of texts in figure A.8 differs from earlier rankings by discovery (figure 6.3) or predictability (figure 7.3). In those cases the rankings were made on the basis of numerical indexes defined and computed before the ranking. Figure A.8 has numerical criteria within each group, but no consistent receptivity measurement runs through the entire ranking. The percentiles of column [1] were used as a receptivity index to generate figure 11.11. Averaging percentiles implies assuming that the receptivity increment between any two consecutive items of the list is a constant, which is not generally true in ranked lists. Finding no other way to measure receptivity, I hypothesized that such increments are constant. This is in line with comparable assumptions made elsewhere in the project, such as granting the same weight to all texts and making no allowances for different lengths or numbers of citations in each text.

The conclusions about receptivity must be applied guardedly. The results of the chapter have varying degrees of validity, depending on how many and how sweeping generalizations went into their formulation. The curves of figures 11.1 and 11.7 through 11.9 are quite reliable, as they are affected only by the assumption about the useful life of texts. Everything else results directly from text and names counts and gender attributions, all of which are unambiguous and reasonably error free.

The results of figure 11.2 are somewhat weaker epistemologically, because they depend on the measurement of text coverage, which in turn rests on a number of especially developed formulas. Errors in text coverage seep into column [5] of figure A.8, because the expected percentage of female architects in a text is contingent on the period covered. The second test for the absence of gender discrimination (based on equal average receptivity among men and women writers) and the findings about gradual improvements in attitude toward the work of women (figure 11.11) also hinge on the premise that the loss of receptivity among successive positions in the ranking is a constant. How credible are these conclusions in the final analysis? More plausible than impressionistic appreciations based merely on whim. They result from empirical data and explicit criteria, and as such, they can be tested and verified. The data base can be enlarged, the criteria perfected, and the package reprocessed as often as necessary for increasingly more convincing approximations to the truth.

Notes

1. No upper limit to their date of birth is necessary because the fifty-year minimum age requirement eliminates architects born after 1943. (Cut-off date for the project at the time of my writing is 1994.)

2. The qualifier "approximately" is necessary because the Y axis measures adjusted (percentage) citations rather than raw citation numbers. As the basis for the percentages changes from year to year, the areas enclosed under the curves represent citations only in an approximate way. Again, a more precise computation was deemed unnecessary.

3. Cohen, J. A.: A coefficient of agreement for nominal scales. *Educational and Psychological Measurement*, 1960, vol. 20, pp. 36–46.

Chronological Listing of Texts in the Corpus

1815

1. Anonymous (possible author Benjamin Latrobe): Remarks on the Progress and Present State of the Fine Arts in the United States. *Analectic Magazine*, November 1815, vol. 6, p. 363.

1830

2. Anonymous: Architecture in the United States. *American Journal of Sciences and Arts*, January-June 1830, vol. 17, pp. 99, 249; July-December 1830, vol. 18, pp. 11, 212.

1834

3. Dunlap, William: *History of the Rise and Progress of the Arts of Design in the United States*. Introduction by William P. Campbell. New York: Benjamin Bloom, 1965. (First published: 1834).

1836

4. Cleveland, H. R., Jr.: Review of American Builder's General Price Book, by James Gallier, Boston, 1834. *North American Review*, October 1836, vol. 43, p. 356.

1848

5. Tuthill, Louise Caroline: *History of Architecture from the Earliest Times; Its Present Condition in Europe and the United States*. Philadelphia: Lindsay & Blakiston, 1848.

1850

6. Sears, Robert (ed.): *A New and Popular Pictorial Description of the United States: Containing an Account of the Topography, Settlement, History, Revolutionary and Other Interesting Events, Statistics, Progress in Agriculture, Manufactures, and Population, &c., of each State in the Union*. New York: Robert Sears, 1950.

1851

7. Greenough, Horatio: American Architecture. *Democratic Review*, August 1843, and *Aesthetics at Washington*. Washington: Jno. T. Powers, 1851. (both reissued in *Memorial of Horatio Greenough*, (Henry T. Tuckerman, ed.) New York: G. P.

Putnam, 1853, and *Form and Function. Remarks on Art, Design, and Architecture* (Harold A. Small, ed.). Berkeley, Los Angeles: University of California Press, 1947).

1856

8. Heck, Johann Georg: *The Art of Building in Ancient and Modern Times, or Architecture Illustrated.* New York: Appleton, 1856.

1862

9. Fergusson, James: *History of the Modern Styles of Architecture. Being a Sequel to the Handbook of Architecture.* London: John Murray, 1862.

1864

10. Jarves, James Jackson: *The Art-Idea: Sculpture, Painting, and Architecture in America.* New York: Hurd & Houghton, 1864. Reprinted: Benjamin Rowland, Jr. (ed.): Cambridge: Belknap Press of Harvard University Press, 1960.

1880

11. Benjamin, Samuel Green Wheeler: *Art in America: A Critical and Historical Sketch.* New York: Harper, 1880.

1883

12. van Rensselaer, Mariana: Recent Architecture in America. City Dwellings. *Century Magazine,* 1883, vol. XXXI, pp. 548–558, 677–687.

1884

13. Levy, Albert: *Albert Levy's Architectural Photographic Series. Thirty-First Series: Modern American Architecture. Street Fronts, Stores, Office Buildings, etc.* New York: Albert Levy, 1884.

1886

14. *L'Architecture Americaine.* Paris: André, Daly Fils, 1886. Reprinted as *American Victorian Architecture. A Survey of the 70's and 80's in Contemporary Photographs.* With a New Introduction by Arnold Lewis and Notes on the Plates by Keith Morgan. New York: Dover, 1975.

1887

15. Longfellow, W. P. P.: The Course of American Architecture. *New Princeton Review,* January-March-May 1887, vol. 3, pp. 200–211.

1888

16. Arnold, C. D.: *Studies in Architecture at Home and Abroad.* Photo-Gravure, 1888.

17. Gwilt, Joseph: *An Encyclopaedia of Architecture. Historical, Theoretical, and Practical.* Revised, portions re-written, and with additions (in 1899) by Wyatt Papworth. New impression. London, New York, Bombay: Longmans, Green, 1899.

1891

18. Fergusson, James: *History of the Modern Styles of Architecture*, 3rd ed. Revised by Robert Kerr. London: John Murray, 1891.

1892

19. Schuyler, Montgomery: *American Architecture—Studies*. New York: Harper & Brothers, 1892.

1893

20. Architectural Publication Society: *The Dictionary of Architecture*. Vols. I–IV. London: Thomas Richards, 1892.

21. Baedecker, Karl (ed.): *The United States, with an Excursion into Mexico. A Handbook for Travellers*. Leipzig, New York: 1893. Reprinted: New York: Da Capo Press, 1971.

1896

22. Hamlin, A. D. F.: *A Text-Book of the History of Architecture. College Histories of Art* (J. C. Van Dyke, ed.). New York, London, Bombay: Longmans, Green, 1896.

1897

23. *The Architecture Record Great American Architects Series*. No 1: "The Work of McKim, Mead & White," by Russell Sturgis (May 1895); No 2: "A Critique of the Works of Adler & Sullivan, D. H. Burnham & Co., Henry Ives Cobb," by Montgomery Schuyler (December 1895); No 3: "A Critique of the Works of Shepley, Rutan & Coolidge and Peabody & Stearns," by Russell Sturgis (July 1896); No 4: "A Review of the Work of George B. Post," by Russell Sturgis (1898); No 5: "A Review of the Works of Bruce Price," by Russell Sturgis (1899), and No 6: "The Works of Charles C. Haight," by Montgomery Schuyler (1899) (Reprinted as *Great American Architects Series*. New York: Da Capo Press, 1977.

24. Statham, Henry Heathcote: *Modern Architecture. A Book for Architects and the Public*. London: Chapman & Hall, 1897.

25. Van Brunt, Henry: *Architecture and Society. Selected Essays of Henry Van Brunt* (essays referenced originally published between 1879 and 1897.) Cambridge: Belknap Press of Harvard University, 1969.

1899

26. Ware, William Rotch: *The Georgian Period. A Collection of Papers Dealing with "Colonial" or XVIII-Century Architecture in the United States*, Boston: American Architect and Building News Company, 1899 (vol. 1); 1901 (vol. II); 1902 (vol. III).

27. Mackson, I.: *American Architecture Interiors and Furniture During the Latter Part of the Nineteenth Century*. Boston: Geo. H. Polley, 1900.

1902

28. Schuyler, Montgomery: United States, Architecture of. In *A Dictionary of Architecture and Building, Biographical, Historical and Descriptive*. Sturgis, Russell (ed.). London, New York: Macmillan, 1902.

29. Sturgis, Russell (ed.): *A Dictionary of Architecture and Building, Biographical, Historical and Descriptive*. London, New York: Macmillan, 1902. Reprinted: Detroit: Gale Research, 1966.

1905

30. Fletcher, Banister: *A History of Architecture on the Comparative Method*, 5th ed. New York: Charles Scribner's Sons, 1921.

1909

31. Bragdon, Claude: Architecture in the United States. I, II, and III. *Architectural Record*, June 1909, vol. 25, no. 6, pp. 426–443; July 1909, vol. 26, no. 1, pp. 38–45; August 1909, vol. 26, no. 2, pp. 86–96.

32. Hamlin, A. D. F.: *A Text-Book of the History of Architecture*, 8th ed. New York: Longmans, Green, 1909.

1910

33. *Men and Women of America: A Biographical Dictionary of Contemporaries*. New York: L. R. Hamersly, 1910.

34. *Encyclopaedia Britannica* (Hugh Chisholm, ed.), 11th ed. Cambridge: Cambridge University Press, 1910–1911.

1913

35. Schuyler, Montgomery: *American Architecture and Other Writings*. Cambridge: Belknap Press of Harvard University, 1961 (William H. Jordy and Ralph Coe, eds.) (Writings referenced originally published during 1891–1913).

1915

36. Eberlein, Harold Donaldson: *The Architecture of Colonial America*. Boston: Little, Brown, 1915.

1916

37. Hamlin, A. D. F.: Twenty-Five Years of American Architecture. *Architectural Record*, July 1916, vol. XL, no. 1, pp. 1–14.

1918

38. Kimball, Fiske, and George Harold Edgell: *A History of Architecture*. New York: Harper & Row, 1918.

1920

39. Greber, Jacques: *L'Architecture aux Etats-Unies. Preuve de la Force d'Expansion du Génie Francais. Hereuse Association de Qualités admirablement complementaires*. Paris: Payot, 1920.

1921

40. Fletcher, Banister: *A History of Architecture on the Comparative Method*, 6th ed. New York: Charles Scribner's Sons, 1921.

1924

41. Jackson, Joseph Francis Ambrose: *American Colonial Architecture*. Philadelphia: David McKay, 1924.

42. Mumford, Lewis: *Sticks and Stones. A Study of American Architecture and Civilization*. New York: Norton, 1924.

1925

43. Kimball, Fiske: Three Centuries of American Architecture. *Architectural Record*, June 1925, vol. 32, pp. 560–564.

1926

44. Akademie der Kunste zu Berlin: *Ausstellung Neuer Amerikanischer Baukunst*. Berlin: Akademie der Kunste zu Berlin, 1926. (Almost identical publication released as *Osterreichisches Museum fur Kunst und Industrie: Ausstellung Neuer Amerikanischer Baukunst*. Vienna: 1926.)

45. Hamlin, Talbot Faulkner: *The American Spirit in Architecture*. Vol. XIII, *The Pageant of America. A Pictorial History of the United States* (R. H. Gabriel, ed.). New Haven, CT: Yale University Press, 1926.

46. Jackson, Joseph Francis Ambrose: *Development of American Architecture 1783–1830*. Philadelphia: David McKay, 1926.

47. American Architect Golden Aniversary Number: *Architectural Record*, January 5, 1926, vol. 129, no. 2488. (includes "Fifty Years of American Architecture," by Royal Cortissoz; "Fifty Years Ago," by C. H. Blackall; "Types, Past and Present," by Thomas E. Tallmadge; "Industrial Buildings," by George C. Nimmons; "Fifty Years Progress Toward an American Architecture," by Alfred C. Bossom; "City and Regional Planning Since 1876," by Flavel Shurtleff; "A Half Century of Landscape Architecture," by Charles Wellford Leavitt; "Fifty Years of Architecture in the United States," and "Great American Architects of the Last Half Century," by William H. Crocker).

1927

48. Reagan, Oliver (ed.): *American Architecture of the Twentieth Century. A Series of Photographs and Measured Drawings of Modern Civic, Commercial and Industrial Buildings*. New York: Architectural Book Publishing Co., 1927.

49. Tallmadge, Thomas E.: *The Story of Architecture in America*. New York: Norton, 1927.

1928

50. Edgell, George Harold: *The American Architecture of Today*. New York: AMS Press, 1970 (reprint of the 1928 ed.)

51. Hamlin, A. D. F.: *A Text-Book of the History of Architecture* (with a chapter on Contemporary Architecture by Talbot Faulkner Hamlin), rev. New York: Longmans, Green, 1928.

52. Jackman, Rilla Evelyn: *American Arts*. Chicago: Rand McNally, 1928.

53. Kimball, Fiske: *American Architecture*. Indianapolis, New York: Bobbs-Merrill, 1928.

1929

54. Hitchcock, Henry-Russell: *Modern Architecture. Romanticism and Reintegration*. New York: Payson & Clarke, 1929.

55. LaFollette, Suzanne: *Art in America*. New York, London: Harper & Brothers, 1929. Reprinted: New York, Evanston: J. & J. Harper Editions, 1968.

56. Sexton, Random Williams: *American Commercial Buildings of Today*; *American Apartment Houses, Hotels, and Apartment Hotels of Today*; *The Logic of Modern Architecture*; *Exteriors and Interiors of Modern American Buildings*; *American Country Houses of Today*; *American Theatres of Today*; *American Public Buildings of Today*. New York: Architectural Book Publishing Co., 1928–31.

57. Taut, Bruno: *Modern Architecture*. London: The Studio, 1929.

1930

58. Cheney, Sheldon: *The New World Architecture*. New York: Tudor, 1930.

59. Conant, Kenneth L. (ed.): *Modern Architecture*. Boston: University Prints, 1930.

60. Hoak, Edward Warren, and Willis Humphrey Church (eds.): *Masterpieces of Architecture in the United States. Memorials, Museums, Libraries, Churches, Public Buildings and Office Buildings*. New York: Charles Scribner's Sons, 1930.

1931

61. Fletcher, Banister: *A History of Architecture on the Comparative Method*, 9th ed. London: B. T. Bratsford, 1931.

1932

62. Barr, Alfred H., Jr., Henry-Russell Hitchcock, Jr., Philip Johnson, and Lewis Mumford: *Modern Architects*. New York: Museum of Modern Art and Norton, 1932.

63. Hitchcock, Henry-Russell, and Philip Johnson: *The International Style: Architecture since 1922*. New York: Norton, 1932. Reprinted: New York: Norton, 1966.

64. American Architects. In *The World Almanac and Book of Facts for 1932* (Robert Hunt Lyman, ed.). New York: New York World-Telegram, 1932 (p. 731).

1934

65. Whitaker, Charles Harris: *The Story of Architecture from Rameses to Rockefeller*. New York: Halcyon House, 1934.

1935

66. Cahill, Holger, and Alfred H. Barr, Jr. (eds.): *Art in America. A Complete Survey*. New York: Reynal & Hitchcock, 1935(?).

1936

67. Tallmadge, Thomas E.: *The Story of Architecture in America*, rev. New York: Norton, 1936.

1937

68. Behrendt, Walter Curt: *Modern Building. Its Nature, Problems, and Forms.* New York: Harcourt, Brace, 1937.

69. Newcomb, Rexford: *Spanish-Colonial Architecture in the United States.* New York: J. J. Augustin, 1937.

70. American Architects. In *The World Almanac and Book of Facts for 1937* (Robert Hunt Lyman, ed.). New York: New York World-Telegram, 1937 (p. 734).

1938

71. Richardson, Albert Edward, and Hector O. Corfiato: *The Art of Architecture.* London: English University Press, 1938.

1940

72. Hamlin, Talbot Faulkner: *Architecture Through the Ages.* New York: Putnam's Sons, 1940.

73. Roth, Alfred: *The New Architecture.* Zurich: Les Editions d'Architecture, 1940.

1941

74. American Architecture: 1891–1941. *Architectural Record*, January 1941, vol. 89, pp. 41–136.

75. Forty Under Forty. *Pencil Points*, March 1941, vol. 22, p. 74.

76. Giedion, Sigfried: *Space, Time, and Architecture. The Growth of a New Tradition.* Cambridge: Harvard University Press, 1941.

77. Johnson, Philip: Architecture. In *The American Year Book. A Record of Events and Progress. Year 1941* (William M. Schuyler, ed.). New York: Thomas Nelson & Sons, 1942.

78. Saint-Gaudens, Homer: *The American Artist and His Times.* New York: Dodd, Mead, 1941.

1942

79. Museum of Modern Art: *What Is Modern Architecture?* New York: Museum of Modern Art, 1942.

80. Newcomb, Rexford: *History of Modern Architecture.* Scranton, PA: International Textbook, 1942.

1944

81. Hamlin, Talbot: *Greek Revival Architecture in America.* New York: Oxford University Press, 1944.

82. Elizabeth Mock (ed.): Built in USA 1932–1944. New York: Museum of Modern Art, 1944. Reprinted: 1968.

1945

83. Reilly, Charles: Some Contemporary American Buildings. *Architects' Year Book*, 1945 vol. 1, pp. 120–131.

1948

84. Fitch, James Marston: *American Building. The Forces that Shape It.* Boston: Houghton Mifflin, 1948.

85. Kouwenhoven, John Atlee: *Made in America: The Arts in Modern Civilization.* New York: Norton, 1967.

86. Pevsner, Nikolaus: *An Outline of European Architecture.* New York: Charles Scribner's Sons, 1948 (first American ed.).

1949

87. Art Institute of Chicago: *From Colony to Nation; An Exhibition of American Painting, Silver, and Architecture from 1650 to the War of 1812.* Chicago: Art Institute of Chicago, 1949. (The architecture section of the exhibition was arranged by Turpin C. Bannister.)

88. Conder, Neville: *An Introduction to Modern Architecture.* New York: Pellegrini & Cudahy; London: Shenval Press, 1949(?).

89. Larkin, Oliver W.: *Art and Life in America.* New York: Rinehart, 1949.

90. Lynes, Russell: *The Tastemakers.* New York: Harper & Brothers, 1949.

1950

91. American Institute of Architects: *Contemporary Architecture in the United States 1947–1949.* Washington, DC: American Institute of Architects, 1950.

92. Egbert, Donald Drew: The Idea of Organic Expression and American Architecture. In *Evolutionary Thought in America* (Stow Parsons, ed.). New York: Braziller, 1956. (Original copyright: 1950).

93. Progressive Architecture Editors (consultants: Henry S. Churchill, James Marston Fitch, Talbot F. Hamlin, Carroll L. V. Meeks, and Fred N. Severud): "U.S. Architecture 1900–1950. *Progressive Architecture*, January 1950, vol. 31, pp. 49–103.

94. Watterson, Joseph: *Architecture. Five Thousand Years of Building.* New York: Norton, 1950.

1951

95. Giedion, Sigfried: *A Decade of Contemporary Architecture.* Zurich: Girsberger, 1951; New York: George Wittenborn, 1954.

1952

96. Eberlein, Harold Donaldson, and Cortland Van Dyke Hubbard: *American Georgian Architecture.* Bloomington, IN: Indiana University Press, 1952. Reprinted: New York: Da Capo Press, 1976.

97. Hamlin, Talbot (ed.): *Forms and Functions of Twentieth Century Architecture*. New York: Columbia University Press, 1952.

98. Hitchcock, Henry-Russell, and Arthur Drexler (eds.): *Built in USA; Post-War Architecture*. New York: Museum of Modern Art, 1952.

99. Jones, Howard Mumford: *O Strange New World. American Culture: The Formative Years*. New York: Viking Press, 1964 (original copyright 1952).

100. American Architects. In *The World Almanac and Book of Facts for 1932* (Harry Hansen, ed.). New York: New York World-Telegram and Sun, 1952 (p. 382).

101. Morrison, Hugh Sinclair: *Early American Architecture from the First Colonial Settlement to the National Period*. New York: Oxford University Press, 1952.

1953

102. Ferris, Hugh: *Power in Buildings; an Artist's View of Contemporary Architecture*. New York: Columbia University Press, 1953.

103. Hamlin, Talbot Faulkner: *Architecture Through the Ages*, rev. New York: Putnam's Sons, 1953.

104. Tunnard, Christopher: *The City of Man*. New York: Charles Scribner's Sons, 1953.

1954

105. Giedion, Sigfried: *A Decade of Contemporary Architecture*, 2nd ed. New York: George Wittenborn, 1954.

1955

106. Andrews, Wayne: *Architecture, Ambition, and Americans. A Social History of American Architecture*. New York: Harper & Brothers, 1955.

107. Scully, Vincent: *The Shingle Style and the Stick Style. Architectural Theory and Design from Richardson to the Origins of Wright*. New Haven, CT: Yale University Press, 1955.

108. Tunnard, Christopher, and Henry Hope Reed, Jr.: *American Skyline*. Boston: Houghton Mifflin, 1955.

1956

109. One Hundred Years of Significant Building. *Architectural Record*, June 1956, vol. 119, no. 7, pp. 147–154; July 1956, vol. 120, no. 1, pp. 203–206; August 1956, vol. 120, no. 2, pp. 171–174; September 1956, vol. 120, no. 1, pp. 237–240; October 1965, vol. 120, no. 4, pp. 191–194; November 1956, vol. 120, no. 5, pp. 197–200; December 1956, vol. 120, no. 6, pp. 177–180; January 1957, vol. 121, no. 1, pp. 169–172; February 1957, vol. 121, no. 2, pp. 199–206; March 1957, vol. 121, no. 3, pp. 223–226; April 1957, vol. 121, no. 4, pp. 201–204; Summary (by E. Kaufman) May 1957, vol. 121, no. 5, pp. 203–208.

1957

110. Gutheim, Frederick Albert: *1851–1957. One Hundred Years of Architecture in America*. New York: Reinhold, 1957.

111. Maas, John: *The Gingerbread Age. A View of Victorian America.* New York, Toronto: Rinehart, 1957.

112. McCallum, Ian R. M.: Genetrix, Personal Contributions to American Architecture. *Architectural Review*, May 1957, vol. 121, pp. 336–386.

113. Morris, Edwin Bateman: *A Century of AIA.* Ceramic Tile Industry, 1957(?).

114. U.S. Information Agency: *Architecture USA.* Washington, DC: U.S. Information Service, 1957(?) (editor: Peter Blake?).

1958

115. Gloag, John: *Guide to Western Architecture.* New York: Macmillan, 1958.

116. Hitchcock, Henry-Russell: *Architecture. Nineteenth and Twentieth Centuries. The Pelican History of Art.* Harmondsworth: Penguin, 1958.

117. Peter, John: *Masters of Modern Architecture.* New York: Braziller, 1958.

1959

118. Bode, Carl: *The Anatomy of American Popular Culture 1840–1861.* Berkeley, Los Angeles: University of California Press, 1959.

119. Francastel, Pierre (ed.): *Les Architects Celèbres.* Vol. II, *Editions D'Art.* Paris: Lucien Mazenod, 1959.

120. Joedicke, Jurgen: *A History of Modern Architecture.* New York: Praeger, 1959.

121. Jones, Cranston: Form Givers at Midcentury. *American Federation of Arts, and Times Magazine*, 1959.

122. Kulterman, Udo: *Architecture of Today. A Survey of New Building Throughout the World.* New York: Universe Books, 1959.

123. McCallum, Ian R. M.: *Architecture USA.* New York: Reinhold, 1959.

124. Reed, Henry Hope, Jr.: *The Golden City.* Garden City, NY: Doubleday, 1959. Reprinted: New York: Norton, 1970.

1960

125. Andrews, Wayne: *Architecture in America. A Photographic History from the Colonial Period to the Present.* New York: Atheneum Publishers, 1960.

126. Condit, Carl W.: *American Building Art. The Nineteenth Century.* New York: Oxford University Press, 1960. *American Building Art—The Twentieth Century.* New York: Oxford University Press, 1961.

127. Huxtable, Ada Louise: Twentieth-Century Architecture. *Art in America*, 1960, vol. 4, pp. 46–55.

128. Pierson, William H., and Martha Davidson (eds.): *Arts of the United States. A pictorial survey.* (Chapters on architecture: Morrison, Hugh: "Architecture of the Seventeenth and Eighteenth Centuries;" Jordy, William H.: "Architecture of the Federal Period and Nineteenth Century;" and Scully, Vincent: "Architecture of the Twentieth Century.") New York: McGraw-Hill, 1960.

1961

129. Burchard, John, and Albert Bush-Brown: *The Architecture of America: A Social and Cultural History.* Boston: Little, Brown, 1961.

130. Editorial Committee of Contemporary Architecture of the World: *Contemporary Architecture of the World 1961.* Tokyo: Shokokusha, 1961(?).

131. Fletcher, Banister: *A History of Architecture on the Comparative Method,* 17th ed. revised by R. A. Cordingley. London: Athlone Press; New York: Charles Scribner's Sons, 1961.

132. Jones, Cranston: *Architecture Today and Tomorrow.* New York: McGraw-Hill, 1961.

133. Scully, Vincent: *Modern Architecture, the Architecture of Democracy.* New York: Braziller, 1961.

134. Von Eckardt, Wolf (ed.): *Mid-Century Architecture in America. Honor Awards of the American Institute of Architects, 1949–1961.* Foreword by Philip Will, Jr., FAIA. Baltimore: The Johns Hopkins University Press, 1961.

1962

135. American Architects and Some of Their Achievements. In *The World Almanac and Book of Facts for 1962* (Harry Hansen, ed.). New York: New York World-Telegram and Sun, 1962 (p. 402).

136. Banham, Reyner: *Guide to Modern Architecture.* Princeton, NJ: Van Nostrand, 1962.

137. Dixon, John: *Architectural Design Preview, U.S.A.* New York: Reinhold, 1962.

138. Pevsner, Nikolaus: Architecture and the Applied Arts. In J. Cassou, E. Langui, and N. Pevsner (eds.), *Gateway to the Twentieth Century. Art and Culture in a Changing World.* New York: McGraw-Hill, 1962.

1963

139. Jacobus, John, Jr.: Modern Architecture. In *World Architecture. An Illustrated History.* Introduction by H. R. Hitchcock. New York: McGraw-Hill, 1963(?).

1964

140. Creighton, Thomas Hawk: *American Architecture.* Washington, DC: R. B. Luce, 1964.

141. *Encyclopaedia Britannica,* 14th ed. Chicago: William Benton, 1964. (All names cited.)

142. *Encyclopaedia Britannica,* Chicago: William Benton, 1964. 14th ed. (Only names given individual entries).

143. Gowans, Alan: *Images of American Living: Four Centuries of Architecture and Furniture as Cultural Expression.* New York: J. B. Lippincott, 1964.

144. Hilberseimer, Ludwig: *Contemporary Architecture. Its Roots and Trends.* Chicago: Paul Theobald, 1964.

145. Muschenheim, William: *Elements of the Art of Architecture.* New York: Viking Press, 1964.

146. Pehnt, Wolfgang (ed.): *Encyclopedia of Modern Architecture.* New York: Harry N. Abrams, 1964.

147. Tschacbasov, Nahum (comp.): *Teachers' Manual for the Study of Art History and Related Courses.* New York: American Library Color Slide Co., 1964.

1965

148. Collins, Peter: *Changing Ideals in Modern Architecture: 1750–1950.* Montreal: McGill University Press, 1965.

149. Drexler, Arthur: *Modern Architecture USA.* New York: Museum of Modern Art, 1965.

150. Early, James: *Romanticism and American Architecture.* New York: A. S. Barnes, 1965.

151. Millon, Henry H. (ed.) with essays by Alfred Frazer: *Key Monuments of the History of Architecture.* New York: Harry N. Abrams, 1965.

152. Rogers, W. G.: *What's Up in Architecture. A Look at Modern Building.* New York: Harcourt, Brace & World, 1965.

153. Ulanov, Barry: *The Two Worlds of American Art. The Private and the Popular.* New York: Macmillan; London: Collier-Macmillan, 1965.

1966

154. Benevolo, Leonardo: *History of Modern Architecture.* Cambridge: MIT Press, 1966. Original Italian: 1961.

155. Fitch, James Marston: *American Building. 1. The Historical Forces that Shaped It.* Boston: Houghton Mifflin, 1966.

156. Green, Samuel M.: *American Art. A Historical Survey.* New York: Ronald Press, 1966.

157. Heyer, Paul: *Architects on Architecture. New Directions in America.* New York: Walker, 1966.

158. Jacobus, John M.: *Twentieth Century Architecture: The Middle Years 1940–1966.* New York: Praeger, 1966.

159. Myers, Bernard S. (ed.): *McGraw-Hill Dictionary of Art.* New York: McGraw-Hill, 1966.

160. Read, Herbert (ed.): *Encyclopedia of the Arts.* New York: Meredith Press, 1966.

161. Stern, Robert A. M.: *Forty Under Forty: An Exhibition of Young Talent in Architecture.* New York: American Federation of Arts, 1966.

162. American Architects and Some of Their Achievements. In *The World Almanac and Book of Facts for 1967* (Luman H. Long, ed.). New York: Newspaper Enterprise Association, 1966 (p. 481).

163. Tatum, George B.: Architecture. In *The Arts in America: The Colonial Period* (Louis B. Wright, George B. Tatum, John W. McCoubrey, and Robert C. Smith, eds.). New York: Charles Scribner's Sons, 1966.

1967

164. Giedion, Sigfried: *Space, Time and Architecture. The Growth of a New Tradition*, rev. Cambridge: Harvard University Press, 1967.

165. Hiller, Carl E.: *From Tepees to Towers. A Photographic History of American Architecture*. Boston, Toronto: Little, Brown, 1967.

166. Ross, Ishbel: *Taste in America. An Illustrated History of the Evolution of Architecture, Furnishings, Fashions, and Customs of the American People*. New York: Thomas Y. Crowell, 1967.

167. Rosenblum, Robert: *Transformations in Late Eighteenth Century Art*. Princeton, NJ: Princeton University Press, 1967.

1968

168. Condit, Carl W.: *American Building. Materials and Techniques from the Beginning of the Colonial Settlements to the Present*. Chicago: University of Chicago-Press, 1968.

169. McLanathan, Richard: *The American Tradition in the Arts*. New York: Harcourt Brace Jovanovich, 1968.

170. Millar, John Fitzhugh: *The Architects of the American Colonies; or, Vitruvius Americanus*. Barre, MA.: Barre Publishers, 1968.

171. Norman, Jane: *Traveler's Guide to America's Art*. New York: Meredith Press, 1968.

172. Portoghesi, Paolo (ed.): *Dizionario enciclopedico di architettura e urbanistica*. Roma: Istituto Editoriale Romano, 1968–9 (6 vols).

1969

173. Joedicke, Jurgen: *Architecture Since 1945: Sources and Directions*. New York: Praeger, 1969.

174. Jordan, R. Furneaux: *A Concise History of Western Architecture*. London: Thames & Hudson, 1969. First American edition: New York: Harcourt, Brace & World, 1970.

175. Norton, Paul F.: Architecture. In *The Arts in America: The 19th Century* (Wendell D. Garrett, Paul F. Norton, Alan Gowans, and Joseph T. Butler, eds.). New York: Charles Scribner's Sons, 1969.

176. Scully, Vincent: *American Architecture and Urbanism*. New York: Praeger, 1969.

177. Stern, Robert A. M.: *New Directions in American Architecture*. New York: Braziller, 1969.

178. Whiffen, Marcus: *American Architecture Since 1780: A Guide to the Styles*. Cambridge: MIT Press, 1969.

1970

179. Hamilton, George Heard: *19th and 20th Century Art: Painting, Sculpture, Architecture*. New York: Harry N. Abrams, 1970.

180. Hofmann, Werner, and Udo Kulterman: *Modern Architecture in Color*. London: Thames & Hudson, 1970. Original German: 1969.

181. Mendelowitz, Daniel M.: *A History of American Art*, 2nd ed. New York: Holt Rinehart & Winston, 1970.

182. Osborne, Harold (ed.): *The Oxford Companion to Art*. Oxford: Clarendon Press, 1970.

183. Osborne, Harold (ed.): *The Oxford Companion to Art*. Oxford: Clarendon Press, 1970. (Main entries only.)

184. Pierson, William H., Jr.: *American Buildings and Their Architects. The Colonial and Neo-Classical Styles*. Garden City, NY: Doubleday, 1970.

1971

185. Cohen, George M.: *A History of American Art*. New York: Dell, 1971.

186. Gillon, Edmund V., Jr.: *Early Illustrations and Views of American Architecture*. New York: Dover, 1971.

187. American Architects and Some of Their Achievements. In *The World Almanac and Book of Facts for 1972* (Luman H. Long, ed.). New York: Newspaper Enterprise Association, 1971 (pp. 358–359).

188. Jencks, Charles: *Architecture 2000. Predictions and Methods*. London: Studio Vista, 1971.

189. Kulski, Julian Eugene: *Architecture in a Revolutionary Era*. Nashville, TN, London: Aurora Publishers, 1971.

1972

190. Bacon, Edmund N.: Architecture and Townscape. In *A Portrait from the Twentieth Century American Civilization* (Daniel J. Boorstin, ed.). New York: McGraw-Hill, 1972.

191. Encyclopaedia Britannica, ed. Chicago: William Benton, 1972. (All names cited.)

192. *Encyclopaedia Britannica*, 14th ed. Chicago: William Benton, 1972. (Only names given individual entries.)

193. Chermayeff, Ivan: *Observations on American Architecture* (with photographs by Elliott Erwitt). New York: Viking Press, 1972.

194. Fitch, James Marston: *American Building. 2. The environmental forces that shaped it*, 2nd ed. Boston: Houghton Mifflin, 1972.

195. Jordy, William H.: *American Buildings and Their Architects. Progressive and Academic Ideals at the Turn of the Century*. Garden City, NY: Doubleday, 1972.

196. Jordy, William H.: *American Buildings and Their Architects. The Impact of European Modernism in the Mid-Twentieth Century*. Garden City, NY: Doubleday, 1972.

197. Sharp, Dennis: *A Visual History of Twentieth-Century Architecture*. Greenwich, CT: New York Graphic Society, 1972.

1973

198. Cook, John V., and Heinrich Klotz: *Conversations with Architects*. New York: Praeger, 1973.

199. Boorstin, Daniel J.: *The Americans: The Democratic Experience*. New York: Random House, 1973.

200. Glubok, Shirley: *The Art of Colonial America* (1970); *The Art of the Old West* (1971); *The Art of the New American Nation* (1972); *The Art of the Spanish in the US and Puerto Rico* (1972); *The art of America from Jackson to Lincoln* (1973); *The Art of the Southwest Indians* (1973?). New York: Macmillan, dates as listed.

201. Jacobus, John: Sections on Architecture. In *American Art of the 20th Century. Painting, Sculpture, Architecture* (Sam Hunter and John Jacobus, eds.). New York: Harry N. Abrams, 1973.

202. Jencks, Charles: *Modern Movements in Architecture*. Garden City, NY: Anchor Press/Doubleday, 1973.

203. Rowland, Kurt: *A History of the Modern Movement: Art Architecture Design*. New York: Van Nostrand Reinhold, 1973.

1974

204. Kidney, Walter C.: *The Architecture of Choice: Eclecticism in America 1880–1930*. New York: Braziller, 1974.

205. Norberg-Schulz, Christian: *Meaning in Western Architecture*. New York: Praeger, 1974.

206. Scully, Vincent: *Modern Architecture, the Architecture of Democracy*, 2nd ed. New York: Braziller, 1974.

207. Scully, Vincent: *The Shingle Style Today, or the Historian's Revenge*. New York: Braziller, 1974.

1975

208. Blake, Peter, and Bernard Quint, for U.S. Information Agency: *Modern Architecture America*. Washington, DC: U.S. Information Service, 1975(?).

209. Loth, Calder, and Julius Trousdale Sadler, Jr.: *The Only Proper Style*. Boston: New York Graphic Society, 1975.

210. Palmes, J. C. (ed.): *Sir Banister Fletcher's a History of Architecture*, 18th ed. New York: Charles Scribner's Sons, 1975.

211. Varian, Elayne H.: *American Art Deco Architecture*. New York: Finch College Museum of Art 1975(?).

1976

212. Brolin, Brent C.: *The Failure of Modern Architecture*. New York: Van Nostrand Reinhold, 1976.

213. Hammett, Ralph W.: *Architecture in the United States. A Survey of Architectural Styles Since 1776*. New York: Wiley, 1976.

214. Kulterman, Udo: *New Architecture in the World*, rev. Boulder, CO: Westview Press, 1976.

215. Panek, R. T.: *American Architectural Styles 1600–1940*. Dover, MA: Architectural Styles, 1976.

216. Platt, Frederick: *America's Gilded Age: Its Architecture and Decoration*. South Brunswick: A. S. Barnes, 1976.

217. Pevsner, Nikolaus: *A History of Building Types*. Bollingen Series 19. Princeton, NJ: Princeton University Press, 1976.

218. Smith, George Everard Kidder: *A Pictorial History of Architecture in America*. New York: American Heritage, 1976.

219. American Architects and Some of Their Achievements. In *The World Almanac and Book of Facts for 1977* (George E. Delury, ed.). New York: Newspaper Enterprise Association, 1976 (p. 368).

220. Tafuri, Manfredo, and Francesco Dal Co: *Modern Architecture*. New York: Harry N. Abrams, 1979. Orignal Italian: 1976.

221. White, Norwal: *The Architecture Book*. New York: Alfred A. Knopf, 1976. (Main entries only.)

222. Wodehouse, Lawrence: *American Architects from the Civil War to the First World War*. Detroit: Gale Research, 1976; and *American Architects from the First World War to the Present*. Detroit: Gale Research, 1977.

1977

223. Blake, Peter: *Form Follows Fiasco: Why Modern Architecture Hasn't Worked*. Boston: Little, Brown, 1977.

224. Brown, Milton W.: *American Art to 1900. Painting-Sculture-Architecture*. New York: Harry N. Abrams, 1977.

225. Jencks, Charles: *The Language of Post-Modern Architecture*. New York: Rizzoli, 1977.

226. Jencks, Charles: *The Language of Post-Modern Architecture*, rev. New York: Rizzoli, 1977.

227. Milwaukee Art Center: *An American Architecture. Its Roots, Growth & Horizons*. Milwaukee, WI: Milwaukee Art Center, 1978.

228. Richards, J. M. (ed.): *Who's Who in Architecture from 1400 to the Present*. American consultant: Adolf K. Placzek. New York: Holt Rinehart & Winston, 1977. (Main entries only.)

229. Richards, J. M. (ed.): *Who's Who in Architecture from 1400 to the Present*. American consultant: Adolf K. Placzek. New York: Holt Rinehart & Winston, 1977.

230. Smith, C. Ray: *Supermannerism. New Attitudes in Post-Modern Architecture*. New York: Dutton, 1977.

231. Stern, Robert A. M.: *New Directions in American Architecture*, rev. New York: Braziller, 1977.

232. Stern, Robert A. M. (ed.): Forty Under Forty. *Architecture and Urbanism*, January 1977, vol. 73.

233. Stierlin, Henri: *Encyclopaedia of World Architecture*. New York: Facts on File, 1977. (2 vols.).

1978

234. Andrews, Wayne: *Architecture, Ambition and Americans. A Social History of American Architecture*, rev. New York: Free Press, 1978.

235. Burton, Lawrence: *A Choice Over Our Heads. A Guide to Architecture and Design Since 1830*. London: Talisman Books, 1978.

236. Pierson, William H., Jr.: *American Buildings and Their Architects. Technology and the Picturesque, the Corporate and the Early Gothic Styles*. Garden City, NY: Doubleday, 1978.

237. Williamson, Roxanne: An Architectural Family Tree that Traces the Paths to Fame. *AIA Journal*, January 1978, vol. 67, no. 1, pp. 46–48, 54.

1979

238. The First Annual Review of New American Architecture. *AIA Journal*, Mid-May 1978, pp. 79–117; The Second Annual Review of New American Architecture, and Kaleidoscope of Current Work. Mid-May 1979, pp. 104–159; The Third Annual Review of New American Architecture. Mid-May 1980, pp. 125–189.

239. *The American Renaissance 1876–1917*. Brooklyn, NY: Brooklyn Museum, 1979.

240. *The American Renaissance 1876–1917. Guide to the Exhibition and Illustrated Catalogue*. Brooklyn, NY: Brooklyn Museum, 1979.

241. Brown, Milton W., Sam Hunter, John Jacobus, Naomi Rosenblum, and David M. Sokol: *American Art. Painting, Sculpture, Architecture, Decorative Arts, Photography*. Englewood Cliffs, NJ: Prentice Hall; New York: Harry N. Abrams, 1979.

242. Drexler, Arthur: *Transformations in Modern Architecture*. New York: Museum of Modern Art, 1979.

243. Roth, Leland M.: *A Concise History of American Architecture*. New York: Harper & Row, 1979.

1980

244. Ball, Victoria Kloss: *Architecture and Interior Design. Europe and America from the Colonial Era to Today*. New York: Wiley, 1980.

245. Davern, Jeanne M. (ed.): *Architecture 1970–1980. A Decade of Change*. New York: McGraw-Hill, 1980.

246. Diamondstein, Barbaralee: *American Architecture Now*. New York: Rizzoli, 1980.

247. Emanuel, Muriel (ed.): *Contemporary Architects*. New York: St. Martin's Press, 1980.

248. Frampton, Kenneth: *Modern Architecture: A Critical History*. New York, Toronto: Oxford University Press, 1980.

249. *Global Architecture*, Document Special Issue 1970–1980.

250. Hunt, William Dudley, Jr. (ed.): *Encyclopedia of American Architecture*. New York: McGraw-Hill, 1980.

251. Hunt, William Dudley, Jr. (ed.): *Encyclopedia of American Architecture*. New York: McGraw-Hill, 1980. (Main entries only.)

252. Kulterman, Udo: *Architecture in the Seventies*. New York: Architectural Book Publishing Company, 1980.

253. Nuttgens, Patrick: *Simon and Schuster's Pocket Guide to Architecture*. New York: Simon & Schuster, 1980.

254. Portoghesi, Paolo (ed.): *Architecture 1980: The Presence of the Past. The Venice Biennal*. New York: Rizzoli, 1980.

255. Raeburn, Michael (ed.): *Architecture of the Western World*. New York: Rizzoli, 1980.

256. Reid, Richard: *The Book of Buildings. A Panorama of Ancient, Medieval, Renaissance and Modern Structures*. Chicago: Rand McNally, 1980.

257. Rifkind, Carole: *A Field Guide to American Architecture*. New York: New American Library, 1980.

1981

258. *New Encyclopaedia Britannica*. Chicago: Encyclopaedia Britannica, 1981.

259. Jencks, Charles: *The Language of Post-Modern Architecture*, 3rd ed. New York: Rizzoli, 1981.

260. Rugoff, Milton (ed.): *Encyclopedia of American Art*. New York: Dutton, 1981. (Sections on architecture by Paul F. Norton, Alan Burnham, David Gebhard and C. Ray Smith; on landscape by Henry Hope Reed; on furniture by Charles F. Hummel, Marilyn Johnson Bordes and Dianne H. Pilgrim).

261. Sanderson, Warren (ed.): *International Handbook of Contemporary Developments in Architecture*. Westport, CT, London: Greenwood Press, 1981. (Includes chapters 1. Warren Sanderson: "Trends in Contemporary Architecture," (pp. 3–29), 3. Robert W. White: "Technology and Architectural Design," 4. Robert Bruegman: "Preservation, Restoration, and Conservation," and 37. Eugene J. Johnson: "United States of America," (pp. 501–524).

262. Smith, George Everard Kidder: *The Architecture of the United States*. Garden City, NY: Anchor Press/Doubleday, 1981 (3 vols.).

263. Searing, Helen (ed.): *Speaking a New Classicism: American Architecture Now*. With essays by Helen Searing and Henry Hope Read. Northampton, MA: Smith College Museum of Art, 1981. (Architects included in exhibit only.)

264. American Architects and Some of Their Achievements. In *The World Almanac and Book of Facts for 1982*. (Hanna Umlauf Lane, ed.). New York: Newspaper Enterprise Association, 1981 (p. 367).

265. Stern, Robert A. M. (ed.): American Architecture: After Modernism. *Architecture and Urbanism*, March 1981.

266. Thorndike, Joseph J., Jr. (ed.): *Three Centuries of Notable American Architects.* New York: American Heritage, 1981.

267. Whiffen, Marcus, and Frederick Koeper: *American Architecture 1607–1976.* Cambridge: MIT Press, 1981.

268. Wolfe, Tom: *From Bauhaus to Our House.* New York: Farrar Strauss Giroux, 1981.

1982

269. The Fourth Annual Review of New American Architecture. *AIA Journal*, Mid-May 1981, pp. 137–219; The Fifth Annual Review of New American Architecture. Mid-May 1982, pp. 123–203; The Sixth Annual Review of New American Architecture. May 1982, pp. 149–237.

270. Condit, Carl W.: *American Building. Materials and Techniques from the First Colonial Settlements to the Present*, 2nd ed. Chicago, London: Chicago University Press, 1982.

271. Curtis, William J. R.: *Modern Architecture Since 1900.* Englewood Cliffs, NJ: Prentice-Hall, 1982.

272. Jencks, Charles: *Architecture Today.* New York: Rizzoli, 1982.

273. Placzek, Adolf K. (ed.): *Macmillan Encyclopedia of Architects.* London: Free Press, 1982.

274. McCoy, Esther, and Barbara Goldstein: *Guide to U.S. Architecture, 1940–1980.* Santa Monica, CA: Arts + Architecture Press, 1982.

275. Portoghesi, Paolo: *After Modern Architecture.* New York: Rizzoli, 1982. Original Italian: 1980.

276. Pothorn, Herbert: *Architectural Styles. An Historical Guide to World Design.* New York: Facts on File, 1991. Original German: 1979.

277. Wright, Sylvia Hart: *Highlights of Recent American Architecture. A Guide to Contemporary Architects and Their Leading Works Completed 1945–1978.* Metuchen, NJ, London: Scarecrow Press.

1983

278. Colquhoun, Alan, Kenneth Frampton, Mary McLeod, Robert A. M. Stern, and Edward Mendelson: Forum: Promising Directions in American Architecture. Precis IV American Architecture in Search of Traditions. *Journal of the Graduate School of Architecture and Planning*, 1983, pp. 6–17.

279. Frampton, Kenneth (photographs by Yukio Futagawa): *Modern Architecture 1851–1945.* New York: Rizzoli, 1983.

280. Nuttgens, Patrick: *The Story of Architecture.* Englewood Cliffs, NJ: Prentice-Hall, 1983.

281. Portoghesi, Paolo: *Postmodern. The Architecture of the Postindustrial Society.* New York: Rizzoli, 1983. Original Italian: 1982.

282. Pulos, Arthur J.: *American Design Ethic. A History of Industrial Design to 1940.* Cambridge: MIT Press, 1983.

283. Risebero, Bill: *Modern Architecture and Design: An Alternative History.* Cambridge: MIT Press, 1983.

1984

284. Flon, Christine (ed.): *The World Atlas of Architecture.* London: Mitchell Beazley; Boston: G. K. Hall, 1984.

285. Hunt, William Dudley, Jr.: *American Architecture. A Field Guide to the Most Important Examples.* New York: Harper & Row, 1984.

286. Jencks, Charles: *The Language of Post-Modern Architecture*, 4th ed. New York: Rizzoli, 1984.

287. Jervis, Simon: *The Facts on File Dictionary of Design and Designers.* New York: Facts on File, 1984.

288. Klotz, Heinrich (ed.): *Die Revision der Moderne. Postmoderne Architektur 1960–1980.* Munich: Prestel Verlag, 1984.

289. Pokinski, Deborah Frances: *The Development of the American Modern Style.* Ann Arbor, MI: UMI Research Press, 1984.

290. Poppeliers, John C., Allen Chambers, Jr., and Nancy B. Schwartz: *What Style Is It? A Guide to American Architecture.* Washington, DC: Preservation Press, 1984.

1985

291. The Seventh Annual Review of New American Architecture. *Architecture*, May 1984, pp. 165–313; The Eighth Annual Review of New American Architecture. May 1985, pp. 173–320. The Ninth Annual Review of New American Architecture. May 1986, pp. 172–229.

292. *Cross Currents of American Architecture.* London: AD Architectural Design Profile, 1985.

293. Crouch, Dora P.: *History of Architecture. From Stonehenge to Skyscrapers.* New York: McGraw-Hill, 1985.

294. Diamondstein, Barbaralee: *American Architecture Now. II.* New York: Rizzoli, 1985.

295. Handlin, David P.: *American Architecture.* London, New York: Thames & Hudson, 1985.

296. Klein, Marilyn W., and David P. Fogle: *Clues to American Architecture.* Washington, DC: Starrhill Press, 1985.

297. Kostof, Spiro: *A History of Architecture. Settings and Rituals.* New York, Oxford: Oxford University Press, 1985.

298. Macrae-Gibson, Gavin: *The Secret Life of Buildings. An American Mythology of Architecture.* Cambridge: MIT Press, 1985.

299. Maddex, Diane (ed.): *Built in the U.S.A. American Buildings from Airports to Zoos.* Washington, DC: Preservation Press, 1985.

300. Maddex, Diane (ed.): *Master Builders. A Guide to Famous American Architects.* Washington, DC: Preservation Press, 1985.

301. Marder, Tod A. (ed.): *The Critical Edge. Controversy in Recent American Architecture.* Cambridge, London, MIT Press, 1985.

302. Stimpson, Miriam F.: *A Field Guide to Landmarks of Modern Architecture in the United States.* Englewood Cliffs, NJ: Prentice-Hall, 1985.

1986

303. Allen, Gerald (ed.): *Emerging Voices.* New York: Architectural League of New York, 1986.

304. Barford, George: *Understanding Modern Architecture.* Worcester, MA: Davis Publications, 1986.

305. De Long, David D., Helen Searing, and Robert A. M. Stern (eds.): *American Architecture: Innovation and Tradition.* New York: Rizzoli, 1986 (Symposium proceedings only).

306. De Long, David D., Helen Searing, and Robert A. M. Stern (eds.): *American Architecture: Innovation and Tradition.* New York: Rizzoli, 1986 (Exhibition only).

307. Duncan, Alastair: *American Art Deco.* London: Thames & Hudson, 1986.

308. Lampugnani, Vittorio Magnago (ed.): *Encyclopedia of 20th-Century Architecture.* New York: Harry N. Abrams, 1986. Also published as *The Thames and Hudson Encyclopaedia of 20th-Century Architecture.* London: Thames & Hudson, 1986.

309. Stern, Robert A. M.: *Pride of Place. Building the American Dream.* Boston: Houghton Mifflin; New York: American Heritage, 1986.

310. Trachtenberg, Martin, and Isabelle Hyman: *Architecture from Prehistory to Post-Modernism. The Western Tradition.* New York: Harry N. Abrams, 1986.

311. Watkin, Donald: *A History of Western Architecture.* New York: Thames & Hudson, 1986.

312. Wilson, Richard Guy, Dianne H. Pilgrim, and Dickran Tashjian: *The Machine Age in America 1918–1941.* New York: Brooklyn Museum, 1986.

1987

313. Jencks, Charles: *Post-Modernism. The New Classicism in Art and Architecture.* New York: Rizzoli, 1987.

314. Kostof, Spiro: *America by Design.* New York, Oxford: Oxford University Press, 1987.

315. Musgrove, John (ed.): *Fletcher's History of Architecture*, 19th ed. London: Butterworths.

316. Oppenheimer Dean, Andrea: Seventy-Five Turbulent Years of American Architecture. *Architecture*, December 1987, vol. 76, issue 12, pp. 72–103.

317. Yarwood, Doreen: *A Chronology of Western Architecture.* New York and Oxford, England: Facts on File, 1987.

1988

318. The Tenth Annual Review of New American Architecture. *Architecture*, May 1987, pp. 83–187; The Eleventh Annual Review of New American Architecture. May 1988, pp. 117–195; The Twelfth Annual Review of New American Architecture. May 1989, pp. 91–167.

319. Gibberd, Vernon: *Architecture Source Book*. Secaucus, NJ: Wellfleet Press, 1988.

320. Hollingworth, Mary: *Architecture of the 20th Century*. Greenwich, CT: Brompton, 1988.

321. Johnson, Philip, and Mark Wigley: *Deconstructivist Architecture*. New York: Museum of Modern Art, 1988.

322. Klotz, Heinrich: *The History of Postmodern Architecture* (with a postscript written for this edition). Cambridge, London: MIT Press, 1988. Original German: 1984.

323. Larkin, David, June Sprigg, and James Johnson: *Colonial Design in the New World*. New York: Stewart, Tabori & Chang, 1988.

324. Norberg-Shulz, Christian: *New World Architecture*. New York: Princeton Architectural Press, 1988.

325. Nuttgens, Patrick: *Understanding Modern Architecture*. London, Sydney, Wellington: Unwin Hyman, 1988.

326. Pulos, Arthur J.: *The American Design Adventure 1940–1975*. Cambridge, London: MIT Press, 1988.

327. Scully, Vincent: *American Architecture and Urbanism*, rev. New York: Henry Holt, 1988.

328. Stern, Robert A. M., and Raymond W. Gastil: *Modern Classicism*. New York: Rizzoli, 1988.

1989

329. Wilkes, Joseph A. (ed.): *Encyclopedia of Architecture, Design, Engineering, & Construction*. Washington, DC: American Institute of Architects; New York: Wiley, 1988 (vols. 1 & 2); 1989 (vols. 3 & 4); 1990 (vol. 5).

330. Wilkes, Joseph A. (ed.): *Encyclopedia of Architecture, Design, Engineering, & Construction*. Washington, DC: American Institute of Architects; New York: Wiley, 1988 (vols. 1 & 2); 1989 (vols. 3 & 4); 1990 (vol. 5). (Main entries only.)

331. Devlin, Harry: *Portraits of American Architecture. Monuments to a Romantic Mood, 1830–1900*. Boston: David R. Godine, 1989.

332. Kennedy, Roger G.: *Greek Revival America*. Photographs by John M. Hall, Jack Kotz, Robert Lautman, Mark Zeek. New York: Stewart, Tabori & Chang, 1989.

333. Kennedy, Roger (ed.): *The Smithsonian Guide to Historic America*. I. Henry Wiencek: *Virginia and the Capital Region* (1989); II. Henry Wiencek: *Southern New England* (1989); III. Michael S. Durham: *The Mid-Atlantic States* (1989); IV. Vance Muse: *Northern New England* (1989); V. William Bryant Logan: *The Deep South* (1989); VI. Suzanne Wincker: *The Great Lakes* (1989); VII. William Bryant Logan

and Susan Ochshorn: *The Pacific States* (1989); VIII. Jerry Caramillo Dunn: *The Rocky Mountain States* (1989); IX. Patricia L. Hudson: *The Carolinas and the Appalachian States* (1989); X. Michael S. Durham: *The Desert States* (1990); XI. Alice Gordon: *Texas and the Arkansas River Valley* (1990); XII. Suzanne Wincker: *The Plains States* (1990). New York: Stewart, Tabori & Chang (dates as noted).

334. Krantz, Les (ed.): *American Architects. A Survey of Award-Winning Contemporaries and Their Notable Works.* New York, Oxford: Facts on File, 1989.

335. Russell, Beverly: *Architecture and Design 1970–1990. New Ideas in America.* New York: Harry N. Abrams, 1989.

336. Peel, Lucy, Polly Powell, and Alexander Garrett: *An Introduction to 20th-Century Architecture.* Secaucus, NJ: Chartwell Books, 1989.

337. Wodehouse, Lawrence, and Marian Moffett: *A History of Western Architecture.* Mountain View, CA: Mayfield, 1989.

338. Wright, Sylvia Hart: *Sourcebook of Contemporary North American Architecture from Postwar to Postmodern.* New York: Van Nostrand Reinhold, 1989.

1990

339. *American Architecture of the 1980s.* Foreword by Donald Canty. Introduction by Andrea Oppenheimer Dean. Washington, DC: American Institute of Architects, 1990.

340. Cottom-Winslow, Margaret: *Environmental Design. The Best of Architecture and Technology.* Glen Cove, NY: Library of Applied Design, 1990.

341. Jencks, Charles: *The New Moderns from Late to Neo-Modernism.* New York: Rizzoli, 1990.

342. American Architects and Some of Their Achievements. In *The World Almanac and Book of Facts for 1991* (Mark H. Hoffman, ed.). New York: Pharos Books, 1991 (p. 340).

343. Kennedy, Roger G.: *Rediscovering America.* Boston: Houghton Mifflin, 1990.

344. Papadakis, Andreas, and Harriet Watson (eds.): *New Classicism. Omnibus Volume.* Foreword by Leon Krier. New York: Rizzoli, 1990.

345. Saunders, William S.: *Modern Architecture.* Photographs by Ezra Stoller. New York: Harry N. Abrams, 1990.

346. Hays, K. Michael, and Carol Burns (eds.): *Thinking the Present. Recent American Architecture.* New York: Princeton Architectural Press, 1990.

1991

347. Cook, Peter, and Rosie Llewellyn-Jones: *New Spirit in Architecture.* New York: Rizzoli, 1991.

348. Copplestone, Trevin: *Twentieth-Century World Architecture.* London: Brian Todd, 1991.

349. Gossel, Peter, and Gabriele Lenthauser: *Architecture in the Twentieth Century*. Koln: Benedikt Taschen Verlag, 1991.

350. Jencks, Charles: *The Language of Post-Modern Architecture*, 6th ed. New York: Rizzoli, 1991.

351. Noever, Peter (ed.): *Architecture in Transition. Between Deconstruction and New Modernism*. Introduction by Alois Martin Muller. Munich: Prestel, 1991.

352. Papadakis, Andreas, and James Steele: *A Decade of Architectural Design*. London: Academy Editions, 1991.

353. Scully, Vincent: *Architecture. The Natural and the Manmade*. New York: St. Martin's Press, 1991.

354. Sharp, Dennis (ed.): *The Illustrated Encyclopedia of Architects and Architecture*. New York: Whitney Library of Design, 1991.

355. Sharp, Dennis: *Twentieth Century Architecture. A Visual History*. New York, Oxford: Facts on File, 1991.

356. *The Illustrated Dictionary of Twentieth Century Design*. Introduction by Peter Dormer. New York: Mallard Press, 1991.

357. Williamson, Roxanne Kuter: *American Architects and the Mechanics of Fame*. Austin, TX: University of Texas Press, 1991.

358. Wodehouse, Lawrence: *Roots of International Style Architecture*. West Cornwall, CT: Locust Hill, 1991.

1992

359. Bayer, Patricia: *Art Deco Architecture. Design Decoration and Detail from the Twenties and Thirties*. New York: Harry N. Abrams, 1992.

360. Garrett, Wendell: *Classical America. The Federal Style and Beyond*. Photography by Paul Ruchelan. New York: Rizzoli, 1992.

361. Gowans, Alan: *Styles and Types of North American Architecture. Social Function and Cultural Expression*. New York: Icon Editions, 1992.

362. Newhouse, Elizabeth L. (ed.): *The Builders. Marvels of Engineering*. Washington, DC: National Geographic Society, 1992.

363. Reynolds, Donald Martin: *Nineteenth Century Architecture*. Cambridge: Cambridge University Press, 1992.

364. Reagan, Oliver (ed.): *American Architectural Masterpieces*. An anthology comprising *Masterpieces of Architecture in the United States*, measured and drawn by Edward Warren Hoak and Willis Humphrey Church, and *American Architecture of the Twentieth Century*, with a preface by Lewis Mumford. In a new edition with essays by George E. Thomas and Michael E. Lewis. New York: Princeton Architectural Press, 1992.

365. Weber, Eva: *American Art Deco*. New York: Crescent Books, 1992.

366. Whiffen, Marcus: *American Architecture Since 1780. A Guide to the Styles*, rev. Cambridge, London: MIT Press, 1992.

1993

367. Economakis, Richard (ed.): *Building Classical: A Vision of Europe and America*, with an introduction by Demetri Porphyrios. London: Academy Editions, 1993. (Only architects with work illustrated.)

368. Heyer, Paul: *American Architecture. Ideas and Ideologies in the Late Twentieth Century*. New York: Van Nostrand Reinhold, 1993.

369. Kulterman, Udo: *Architecture in the 20th Century*. New York: Van Nostrand Reinhold, 1993.

370. LeBlanc, Sydney: *Whitney Guide [to] 20th Century American Architecture. 200 Key Buildings*. Foreword by Ralph Lerner. New York: Whitney Library of Design, 1993.

371. Roth, Leland M.: *Understanding Architecture. Its Elements, History, and Meaning*. New York: Icon Editions, 1993.

372. Sarfatti Larson, Magali: *Behind the Postmodern Facade. Architectural Change in Late Twentieth-Century America*. Berkeley, Los Angeles, London: University of California Press, 1993.

373. Van Vynckt, Randall J. (ed.), Doreen Yarwood (European consultant), and Suhail Butt (photo and graphic researcher): *International Dictionary of Architects and Architecture*. Detroit, London, Washington, DC: St. James Press, 1993.

1994

374. Byars, Mel: *The Design Encyclopedia*. New York: Wiley, 1994. (Main entries only.)

375. Doremus, Thomas L.: *Classical Styles in Modern Architecture: From the Colonnade to Disjunctured Space*. New York: Van Nostrand Reinhold, 1994.

376. Peter, John: *The Oral History of Modern Architecture: Interviews with the Greatest Architects of the Twentieth Century*. New York: Harry N. Abrams, 1994.

377. Peter, John: *The Oral History of Modern Architecture: Interviews with the Greatest Architects of the Twentieth Century*. New York: Harry N. Abrams, 1994 (Interviewees only.)

378. Striner, Richard: *Art Deco*. New York: Abbeville Press, 1994.

379. Packard, Robert (Balthazar Korab, illustration editor): *Encyclopedia of American Architecture*, 2nd ed. New York: 1995.

380. Packard, Robert (Balthazar Korab, illustration editor): *Encyclopedia of American Architecture*, 2nd ed. New York: 1995. (Main entries only.)

Listing of Authors, Editors, and Photographers in the Corpus

Note: Numbers refer to text ID numbers.

Name Index

Title Index

Subject Index